THE PSYCHOLOGY OF MEANINGFUL VERBAL LEARNING

By the Same Author

Ego Development and the Personality Disorders
Theory and Problems of Adolescent Development
Theory and Problems of Child Development
Maori Youth

THE PSYCHOLOGY OF
MEANINGFUL
VERBAL LEARNING

An Introduction to School Learning

By   **DAVID P. AUSUBEL**

Bureau of Educational Research
University of Illinois

GRUNE & STRATTON   New York and London

Library of Congress Catalog Card No. 63-13252
Printed in U.S.A.

(PC-B)

TO
PEARL AND LAURA

CONTENTS

Preface

THIS BOOK IS CONCERNED with the psychology of how individuals
comprehend, learn, organize, and remember the large volume of meaningful verbal materials which are presented to them by an educational
agency such as the school. It does not purport to embrace other types
of school learning as, for example, rote learning, motor skills and perceptual learning, concept formation, thinking, and problem-solving; or
systematically to consider motivational, emotional, attitudinal, personality, interpersonal, and social variables impinging on school learning. Any
attempt to include such diverse aspects of learning under a single body
of cohesive principles would not only court theoretical disunity, but
would also, of necessity, require superficial coverage, disjointed treatment, and platitudinous, unincisive analysis of the phenomena involved
and of their underlying mechanisms. Nevertheless, despite the self-
imposed, limited scope of this book, it is evident that it covers the major
cognitive learning activities that take place in the school environment,
the kind of learning that constitutes the primary objective of the school
as a social institution, namely, the efficient and meaningful transmission
of the important subject-matter disciplines.

The aim of this book is to organize and interpret the relatively sparse
research data in this central area of school learning around a unified
theory of meaningful, verbal "reception." learning and retention. Important gaps obviously exist at the present time in the empirical underpinning of such a theory, but the filling of these gaps is considered more
likely once the theory itself is explicitly formulated. This theory includes
the following component elements: a distinction between the rote-
meaningful and the "reception"-"discovery" dimensions of learning; a
concept of "meaning" in terms of nonarbitrary, substantive relatability to
cognitive structure; a distinction between logical and psychological
meaning and between rote and meaningful learning processes; a two-
stage subsumption process whereby new material is meaningfully incorporated into and retained within cognitive structure; the concept of
dissociability strength as a criterion of meaningful retention; the threshold
of availability; the centrality of cognitive structure, and of its properties
of relevance, stability, clarity, and discriminability, for the efficient learning and retention of new material; a cognitive structure concept of
transfer; derivative versus correlative subsumption; the principles of
progressive differentiation and integrative reconciliation, both with respect to the organization of cognitive structure, and as ways of pro-

graming new material; the cognitive "organizer" technique of didactic exposition; the psychological and educational significance of the concrete-abstract dimension of cognitive development; and the psychological and educational limitations of learning by discovery. Task variables (practice and instructional materials) are reinterpreted in terms of their influence on cognitive structure, and in terms of the mediational effects of cognitive structure on their actions. Rote learning and motivational-attitudinal variables are not basically discussed in the text as ends in themselves, but largely for purposes of contrasting their effects and/or underlying mechanisms with those of the cognitive variables involved in meaningful learning.

This volume is primarily intended as a textbook for advanced courses in educational psychology and the psychology of school learning, and as a reference work for specialists and research workers in educational psychology. Its use by undergraduate students with some psychological sophistication is certainly not contraindicated.

I am indebted to my wife, Pearl Ausubel, and to Dr. Donald Fitzgerald of the University of Alberta for critical reading of portions of the manuscript, and also to Mrs. Mary Lou Stahlke and Mrs. Martha L. Jones for help in preparing the manuscript for publication.

DAVID P. AUSUBEL

Urbana, Illinois
January 1963

ACKNOWLEDGMENTS

The Author wishes to acknowledge the courtesy of the following publishers in permitting the use of excerpts from some of my previously published articles and books:

Grune and Stratton, Inc., for *Theory and Problems of Adolescent Development* (1954), and *Theory and Problems of Child Development* (1958).

The John Dewey Society and the Philosophy of Education Society, for "The Nature of Educational Research," *Educational Theory* (1953), and "In Defense of Verbal Learning," *Educational Theory* (1961).

The American Psychological Association, Inc., for "The Influence of Intention on the Retention of School Materials," *Journal of Educational Psychology* (1957); "Retroactive Inhibition and Facilitation in the Learning of School Materials," *Journal of Educational Psychology* (1957); "The Use of Advance Organizers in the Learning and Retention of Meaningful Verbal Material," *Journal of Educational Psychology* (1960); and "The Role of Discriminability in Meaningful Verbal Learning and Retention," *Journal of Educational Psychology* (1961).

Dembar Publications, Inc., for "Proactive Inhibition in the Forgetting of Meaningful School Material," *Journal of Educational Research* (1958).

Bureau of Publications, Teachers College, Columbia University. "Viewpoints from Related Disciplines: Human Growth and Development," *Teachers College Record* (1959).

American Educational Research Association, for "Meaningful Learning and Retention: Intrapersonal Cognitive Variables," *Review of Educational Research* (1961).

National Association of Secondary School Principals, for "Learning by Discovery: Rationale and Mystique," *The Bulletin* (1961).

The Journal Press, for "A Subsumption Theory of Meaningful Verbal Learning and Retention," *Journal of General Psychology* (1962).

The University of Chicago Press, for "Can Children Learn Anything That Adults Can—And More Efficiently?" *Elementary School Journal* (1962).

University of North Carolina Press, for "Implications of Preadolescent and Early Adolescent Cognitive Development for Secondary School Teaching," *High School Journal* (1962).

The Association of American Medical Colleges, for "A Transfer of the Training Approach to Improving the Functional Retention of Medical Knowledge," *Journal of Medical Education* (1962).

National Association for Research in Science Education, for "Some Psychological Considerations in the Objectives and Design of an Elementary-School Science Program," *Science Education* (1963).

Child Development Center for Preschool Children and *Orientamenti Pedogogici*, for "Stages of Intellectual Development and Their Implications for Early Childhood Education," *Orientamenti Pedagogici* (1963).

Grateful acknowledgment is also due to the following for permitting brief quotations from their publications:

American Association of Colleges for Teacher Education for excerpts from E. P. Torrance, "Gifted Children," in *Recent Research and Developments and their Implications for Teacher Education* (1960).

American Association of Physics Teachers, for excerpts from G. C. Finlay, "Secondary School Physics: The Physical Science Study Committee," *American Journal of Physics* (1960).

American Council on Education for excerpts from R. W. Tyler, "The Education of Teachers: A Major Responsibility of Colleges and Universities," *Educational Record* (1958).

American Psychological Association, Inc., for excerpts from A. Newell, J. C. Shaw, and A. H. Simon, "Elements of a Theory of Human Problem Solving," *Psychological Review* (1958); and from C. I. Hovland, Computer Simulation of Thinking," *American Psychologist* (1960).

Basic Books, Inc., for excerpts from Bärbel Inhelder and J. Piaget, *The Growth of Logical Thinking from Childhood to Adolescence* (1958).

Bureau of Educational Research and Service, Ohio State University, for excerpts from S. L. Pressey, "Basic Unresolved Teaching-Machine Problems," *Theory into Practice* (1962).

Cambridge University Press, for excerpts from F. C. Bartlett, *Remembering* (1932).

The Harvard Educational Review, for excerpts from J. S. Bruner, "The Act of Discovery," *Harvard Educational Review* (1961).

Harvard University Press, for excerpts from J. S. Bruner, *The Process of Education* (1960).

International Universities Press, Inc., for excerpts from I. H. Paul, "Studies in Remembering," *Psychological Issues* (1959).

Saturday Review, for excerpts from J. S. Bruner, "After Dewey What?" *Saturday Review* Education Supplement, June 17, 1961.

Training Research Laboratory, University of Illinois, for excerpts from D. G. Beane, "A Comparison of Linear and Branching Techniques of Programed Instruction in Plane Geometry," Technical Report No. 1 (July 1962).

University of Chicago Press, for excerpts from J. C. Stanley, "The Role of Instruction, Discovery, and Revision in Early Learning," *Elementary School Journal* (1949).

University of Toronto Press, for excerpts from A. Porter, "The Mechanical Representation of Processes of Thought," In *Memory, Learning and Language* (1959).

John Wiley and Sons, Inc., for excerpts from J. W. Getzels and P. W. Jackson, *Creativity and Intelligence* (1962).

THE PSYCHOLOGY OF MEANINGFUL
VERBAL LEARNING

CHAPTER 1.

Introduction: Scope and Strategy

THE AIM OF THIS BOOK is to present a comprehensive theory of how human beings learn and retain large bodies of subject matter in classroom and similar learning environments. Its scope is limited to the "reception" learning and retention of meaningful material. "Reception" learning refers to the situation where the content of the learning task (what is to be learned) is presented to rather than independently discovered by the learner. That is, the learner is merely required to comprehend the material meaningfully, and to incorporate it or make it available or functionally reproducible for future use. In the absence of such a theory, inappropriate explanatory principles have been uncritically extrapolated from experimental findings on nonverbal or on short-term, fragmentary, and rote verbal learning. As a result, not only have advances in the efficient programing of verbal classroom learning been impeded, but teachers have also been encouraged to perceive meaningful verbal materials as rote in character. The upshot of this situation has been that many teachers have either persisted in using rote teaching methods, or have rejected didactic verbal exposition as unsuitable for classroom instruction.

It is true, of course, that the school is also concerned with developing the student's ability to use acquired knowledge in solving particular problems, that is, his ability to think systematically, independently, and critically in particular fields of inquiry. This latter function of the school, although inseparable in practice from its transmission-of-knowledge function, is less central in terms of the amount of time that can be reasonably allotted to it, the objectives of education in a democratic society, and what can be realistically expected from most students.* Furthermore, as is also true in the case of rote learning, discovery learning (*e.g.*, thinking, problem-solving, inductive concept formation) requires an entirely different set of explanatory principles that cannot be conveniently considered in a treatise on reception learning.

It should also be evident that meaningful verbal** learning constitutes the principal means of augmenting the learner's store of knowledge both within and outside the classroom. The rote learning of lists of nonsense syllables or

---

*These points will be elaborated in greater detail in Chapter 7. It may be noted here, however, that problem-solving activity may also eventuate in knowledge. But except in early childhood it is not a conspicuous feature in the acquisition of new concepts. For the most part in the formal education of the individual, the educational agency merely transmits ready-made concepts, categorical schemata, and relational propositions. It will be argued later that the development of problem-solving ability is a legitimate objective of education in its own right, but that a problem-solving or discovery approach is not a practical means of transmitting subject-matter content.

**Verbal learning is used here in the more general sense of the term, and is inclusive of subverbal intuitive understanding and of other types of symbolic learning.

1

of arbitrarily paired adjectives is representative of few defensible tasks in modern classrooms. It is difficult to find supportive evidence for Underwood's assertion that "much of our educational effort is devoted to making relatively meaningless verbal units meaningful" (6, p. 111). Some classroom learning, such as the letter symbols, foreign language vocabulary, and the symbols used to represent the chemical elements, does approach the rote level. Such rote-like learning, however, tends to form a very small part of the curriculum, especially beyond the elementary-school years once children have mastered the basic letter and number symbols. Furthermore, unlike the learning of paired associates, the associations formed under these circumstances are not wholly arbitrary but involve the learning of representational equivalence, *i.e.*, learning that particular symbols are equivalent in meaning to already meaningful concepts in cognitive structure (*i.e.*, an individual's prevailing organization, clarity, and stability of knowledge in a given subject-matter area).

From a process standpoint, the scope of the theory of learning elaborated in this book is limited to various principles of cognitive organization and inter-action and to various mechanisms of cognitive accretion and decrement. It deals (a) with systematic changes in the emergence, identifiability, and availability of valid meanings as *presented* ideational materials interact initially and repeatedly with (and are incorporated into) cognitive structure; (b) with factors increasing and decreasing the incorporability of these materials, as well as their subsequent long-term stability or availability; and (c) with the most efficacious ways of manipulating existing cognitive structure so as to enhance the incorporability and longevity of presented materials.

Excluded from consideration in this book, in addition to rote and discovery learning as topics in their own right, are such noncognitive kinds of learning as classical and instrumental conditioning and motor skills learning, and such less complex kinds of cognitive learning as perceptual and simple discrimination learning. These latter types of learning not only require different explanatory principles, but their relevance for classroom learning is, at best, only indirect and tangential. Hence their consideration would so broaden the scope of the field that coverage would necessarily become superficial, fragmentary, unsystematic, and disjointed. The psychology of specific school subjects is not considered since this book is concerned with general principles applicable to all kinds and grade levels of subject matter.

Also, although their importance for classroom learning is in no sense discounted, no systematic attention is paid to motivational, emotional, and attitudinal factors in learning; to incentive, reinforcement, and interpersonal conditions; or to ego-involvement and personality variables. These latter factors are considered only insofar as they influence the mechanisms underlying meaningful reception learning and retention; it is believed that they can be studied much more fruitfully and economically within the framework of another body of learning theory concerned with subjective rather than objective aspects of the learning process.

Cognitive and motivational-interpersonal factors undoubtedly influence the learning process concomitantly, and probably interact in various ways. Classroom learning does not take place in a social vacuum but only in relation to other individuals who themselves—despite the existence of personal emotional ties—act largely as impersonal representatives of the culture. During the course of personality development the individual also acquires a characteristic motivational orientation to learning. This not only affects his mode of acquiring new value judgments, but also influences the scope, the depth, and the efficiency of the learning process. Nevertheless, for purposes of logical analysis or empirical investigation, either set of factors can be systematically varied while the other is held constant.

Because relatively few well-controlled studies of meaningful reception learning have been conducted, it is obvious that the theory presented in this work must of necessity be highly tentative and exploratory in nature, and more in the nature of a series of hypotheses than reflective of a definitive body of research data. Yet a beginning must be made somewhere. Relevant theory stimulates and gives direction to relevant research effort which, in turn, sharpens, modifies and expands the original theory.

The practical implications of such theory and research for actual teaching practices in the classroom are self-evident. Before we could ever hope effectively to manipulate the classroom learning environment for the optimal acquisition of meaningful subject matter, we would first have to know a great deal more about the organizational and developmental principles whereby human beings acquire and retain stable bodies of knowledge. Such principles, however, will forever elude us unless we abandon the untenable assumptions that there is no real distinction either between the logic of a proposition and how the mind apprehends it, or between the logical structure of subject-matter organization and the actual series of cognitive processes through which an immature and developing individual incorporates information and propositions into a stable body of knowledge. It is perfectly logical from the standpoint of a mature scholar, for example, to write a textbook in which topically homogeneous materials are segregated into discrete chapters and treated throughout at a uniform level of conceptualization. But how congruent is this approach with highly suggestive findings that one of the major cognitive processes involved in the learning of any new subject is progressive differentiation of an originally undifferentiated field? Once we learn more about cognitive organization and development than the crude generalizations that educational and developmental psychology can currently offer, it will be possible to employ organizational and sequential principles in the presentation of subject matter that actually parallel both the existing structure and developmental changes in the organization of the intellect.

To avoid the cardinal sin of violating in my presentation the very pedagogic principles I espouse, a genuine attempt will be made to organize this book in accordance with the above-stated generalization about the acquisition of knowledge in a new, uncharted field. An overview of basic principles will be presented in Chapter 2 before separate components of the theory are elaborated in individual chapters.

RESEARCH STRATEGY IN CLASSROOM LEARNING

Three principal reasons account for the dearth of knowledge about classroom learning. First, the vast majority of studies in the field of school learning have been conducted by teachers and other non-professional research workers in education. These studies have been typically characterized by serious inadequacies in conceptualization and rigorousness of research design, and have been too narrowly oriented toward improving particular academic skills or technics of instruction, rather than toward the discovery of more general principles affecting the improvement of classroom learning and instruction.

Second, the more rigorously conducted research in learning theory has been largely undertaken by psychologists unconnected with the educational enterprise who have investigated problems quite remote from the type of learning that goes on in the classroom. The focus has been on animal learning or on short-term, fragmentary, rote and non-verbal human learning, rather than on the learning and retention of organized bodies of meaningful material. Even those psychologists who were engaged in military and industrial training programs during and after World War II were, by and large, more concerned with developing efficacious technics of learning and teaching highly specific skills, often of a motor or technical nature, rather than with analysis and investigation of more general problems of cognitive learning and instruction. Hence, despite the huge sums of money spent for such research, and its over-all success relative to the limited and specific objectives envisaged, it has not had wide applicability to other learning situations, and has had relatively little theoretical impact on the psychology of human learning.

Experimental psychologists can hardly be criticized, however, if laboratory studies of short-term, fragmentary and rote learning have had little applicability to the classroom. Like all pure research efforts in the basic sciences, these studies were only designed to yield general laws of behavior as ends in themselves, quite apart from any practical utility. The blame, if any is to be assigned, must certainly lie with educational psychologists who, in general, have failed to conduct the necessary applied research, and have been content with extrapolating the findings of their experimental colleagues.

Finally, for the past generation educational psychologists per se have been preoccupied with measurement and evaluation, personality development, mental hygiene, and social psychology. Despite the self-evident centrality of classroom learning and cognitive development for the psychological aspects of education, these areas were largely ignored, both theoretically and research-wise.

"Basic Science" versus Applied Approach

The tendency among educational psychologists to extrapolate uncritically research findings from laboratory studies of simplified learning situations to the classroom learning environment, accounts in large measure for our lack of knowledge about school learning processes. It reflects the fascination which many research workers feel for the "basic science" approach to research in the applied sciences, as well as their concomitant failure to appreciate its inherent limitations. Gage,[3] for example, argues that progress in educational psychology is made more rapidly by focusing indirectly on "basic science" problems in general psychology than by trying to come to grips directly with the applied problems that are more indigenous to the field. Spence[5] perceives classroom learning as much too complex to permit the discovery of general laws of learning, and advocates a straightforward application to the classroom situation of the laws of learning discovered in the laboratory. Melton's[4] position is more eclectic. He would search for "basic science" laws of learning in both laboratory and classroom contexts, and would leave to the educational technologist the task of conducting the research necessary for implementing these laws in actual classroom practice.

The position adopted in this book is that the principles governing the nature and conditions of meaningful, verbal reception learning can be discovered only through an applied or engineering type of research that actually takes into account the distinctive attributes of this phenomenon as it occurs in the classroom.[1] We cannot merely extrapolate general "basic science" laws derived from the laboratory study of qualitatively different and vastly more simple instances of learning. Laws of classroom learning* at an applied level are needed by the educational technologist before he can hope to conduct the research preparatory to effecting scientific changes in teaching practices. Contrary to Spence's[5] contention, the greater complexity and number of determining variables involved in meaningful verbal learning does not preclude the possibility of discovering precise laws with wide generality from one educational situation to another. It simply means that such research demands experimental ingenuity and sophisticated use of modern technics of research design.

The "basic science" research approach is predicated on the very defensible notion that applied sciences are ultimately related to knowledge in the underlying sciences on which they are based. It can be convincingly demonstrated, for example, that progress in clinical medicine is intimately related to progress in biochemistry and bacteriology; that progress in engineering is intimately related to progress in physics and chemistry; and that progress in education is similarly dependent upon advances in psychology, statistics, sociology and philosophy. However, two important kinds of qualifications have to be placed on the value of basic science research for the applied sciences: qualifications of purpose or orientation, and qualifications of level of applicability.

By definition, basic science research is concerned with the discovery of general laws of physical, biological, psychological and sociological phenomenology as an end in itself. Researchers in these fields have no objection, of course, if their findings are applied to practical problems which have social value; in fact there is reason to believe that they are motivated to some extent by this consideration. But the design of basic science research bears no *intended* relation whatsoever to problems in the applied disciplines, the aim being solely to advance knowledge. Ultimately, of course, such knowledge is applicable in a very broad sense to practical problems; but since the research design is not oriented to the solution of these problems, this applicability is apt to be quite indirect and unsystematic, and relevant only over a time period which is too long to be meaningful in terms of the short-range needs of the applied disciplines.

The second qualification has to do with the level at which findings in the basic sciences can be applied once their relevancy has been established. It

---

*These laws are just as "basic" as "basic science" laws. The term "basic" refers to the distinction between "pure" and applied sciences. It does not mean "fundamental." In the latter sense, applied research is just as "basic" as research in the pure sciences.

should be self-evident that such findings enjoy a much higher level of generality than the problems to which they can be applied. At the applied level, specific ends and conditions are added which demand additional research to make manifest the precise way in which the general law operates in the specific case. That is, the applicability of general principles to specific problems is *not given* in the statement of the general principle, but must be specifically worked out for each individual problem. Knowledge about nuclear fission, for example, does not tell us how to make an atomic bomb or an atomic-powered airplane.

In fields such as education, the problem of generality is further complicated by the fact that the practical problems often exist at higher levels of complexity with respect to the order of phenomenology involved than the basic science findings requiring application. That is, new variables are added which may qualitatively alter the general principles from the basic science to such an extent that, at the applied level, they only have substrate validity but no explanatory or predictive value. For example, antibiotic reactions that take place in test tubes do not necessarily take place in living systems, methods of learning employed by animals in mazes do not necessarily correspond to methods of learning children use in grappling with verbal materials in classrooms.

The basic science approach in educational research, therefore, is subject to many serious disadvantages. Its relevancy is too remote and indirect because it is not oriented toward solving educational problems, and its findings, if relevant, are applicable only if much additional research is performed to translate general principles into the more specific form they have to assume in the task-specialized and more complex contexts of pedagogy.[1]

Many of the better known generalizations in educational psychology—the principle of readiness, the importance of maturation in learning, the concrete to abstract trend in conceptualizing the environment—fit these analogies perfectly. They are interesting and potentially useful ideas to curriculum specialists, but have little practical utility in designing a curriculum until they are particularized at an applied level of operations. The need for particularization is well illustrated by the principle of readiness. At the present time we can only speculate what curriculum sequences might conceivably look like if they took into account precise and detailed (but currently unavailable) research findings on the emergence of readiness for different subject-matter areas, for different subareas and levels of difficulty within an area, and for different technics of teaching the same material. Because of the unpredictable specificity of readiness as shown, for example, by the fact that four- and five-year-olds can profit from training in pitch but not in rhythm, valid answers to such questions cannot be derived from logical extrapolation but require meticulous empirical research in a school setting. The next step would involve the development of appropriate teaching methods and materials to take optimal advantage of existing degrees of readiness and to increase readiness wherever necessary and desirable. But since we generally do not have this type of research data available, except perhaps in the field of reading, we can only pay lip service to the principle of readiness in curriculum planning.

The "basic science"-extrapolation approach, of course, offers several very attractive methodological advantages in verbal learning experiments. First, by using nonsense syllables of equal meaningfulness, it is possible to work with additive units of equal difficulty. Second, by using relatively meaningless learning tasks (*i.e.*, equated nonsense syllables), it is possible to eliminate, for the most part, the indeterminable influence of meaningful antecedent experience, which naturally varies from one individual to another. But it is precisely this interaction of new learning tasks with existing cognitive structure that is the distinctive feature of meaningful learning.

Thus, although the use of nonsense syllables adds undoubted methodological rigor to the study of learning, the very nature of the material limits the applicability of findings on such experiments to a type of short-term learning that is rare both in everyday situations and in the classroom. Nevertheless, even though there are no *a priori* grounds for supposing that learning and retention occur in the same way for meaningful and for relatively meaningless materials, the findings from rote-learning experiments have been commonly extrapolated to meaningful learning situations. One cannot have one's cake and eat it too. If one chooses the particular kind of methodological rigor associated with the use of rote materials, one must also be satisfied with applying the findings from such experiments only to rote learning situations.

Much of the psychology of learning that teachers in training study today is based on findings from rote learning experiments which have been borrowed wholesale without any attempt to test their applicability to the kind of learning situations that exist in classrooms. It would be a shocking situation indeed if a comparable procedure were followed in medicine, *i.e.*, if physicians employed therapeutic technics validated only *in vitro* or by animal experimentation.

Unfortunately, the influence of theories of rote learning is not restricted to theoretical conceptions of or experimental approaches to school learning. The willingness of educational psychologists to extrapolate the findings of rote studies naturally led them to neglect the nature and conditions of meaningful verbal learning and retention. This delayed the discovery of more effective technics of verbal exposition, as well as helped perpetuate the use of traditional rote technics of teaching. These latter technics dominate much of actual educational practice, particularly in the secondary school and university. Meaningful materials are frequently taught and learned as if they were rote in character, and hence are retained, if at all, both inefficiently and with unnecessary difficulty. In still other educational quarters *all* verbal exposition is perceived as *necessarily* encouraging rote learning and is accordingly proscribed. Only within the last few years have curriculum specialists and educational psychologists concerned themselves with substantive and programmatic aspects of the problem of facilitating the meaningful acquisition and retention of viable bodies of knowledge.

Psychology versus Educational Psychology

Since both psychology and educational psychology deal with the problem of learning, how can we distinguish between the special research interests of each discipline in this area? As an applied science, education is not concerned with the general laws of learning *per se*, but only with those properties of learning that can be related to efficacious ways of deliberately effecting stable changes in individuals which have social value. Education, therefore, refers to guided or manipulated learning deliberately directed toward specific practical ends. These ends may be defined as the long-term acquisition of a stable body of knowledge (ideas, concepts, facts), values, habits, skills, ways of perceiving, adjusting, and aspiring, and of the capacities needed for acquiring them.

The psychologist's interest in learning, on the other hand, is much more general. Many other aspects of learning apart from the efficient achievement of designated competencies and capacities for growth in a directed context concern him. More typically, he investigates the nature of current, fragmentary, or short-term learning experiences rather than the kinds of long-term learning involved in assimilating extensive and organized bodies of knowledge, values, habits and skills.

The following kinds of learning problems, therefore, are particularly indigenous to educational research: (a) discovery of the nature of those aspects of the learning process affecting the long-range stability and meaningfulness of organized bodies of knowledge, skills, etc. in the learner; (b) long-range modification (improvement) of learning capacities; (c) discovery of those personality and cognitive aspects of the learner and of the interpersonal and social aspects of the learning environment that affect motivation for learning and characteristic ways of assimilating material; and (d) discovery of appropriate and maximally efficient practices and ways of organizing and presenting learning materials, of deliberately motivating and directing learning toward specified goals.[1]

RELEVANT CURRENT TRENDS IN EDUCATIONAL THOUGHT

The focus of attention in this book on the process of meaningful reception learning and on ways of enhancing it is in accord with three recent trends of thought and opinion in education—increased emphasis on the importance and quality of intellectual training in the schools, greater stress on knowledge as an end in itself, and increased willingness on the part of the school to take more responsibility for the direction of learning. Concern over these issues has greatly reduced national preoccupation with and heated public controversy about such pseudo-issues as whether students today learn as much in school as did prior generations of students, whether the curriculum has become "softer," whether Johnny can read, whether training in pedagogy is a necessary part of teacher education, and whether intellectual training should be the *exclusive* function of the school.

Greater Concern with Intellectual Training

Increased concern with the intellectual content and quality of the curriculum is being manifested in many different ways. First, scientists, scholars, curriculum experts and psychologists are collaborating in a host of curriculum reform movements placing greater emphasis on the basic, unifying principles of the various disciplines, on more efficient programming of subject matter, on consonance with recent advances in knowledge, and on adequate depth of coverage. Second, the subject-matter preparation of teachers is receiving greater attention in the form of teachers institutes in mathematics and science, fifth-year teachers education programs, and higher subject-matter requirements for high school certification. Third, numerous experiments are being conducted in classroom organization and administration, all of which are directed toward the more efficient teaching of subject matter, namely, team teaching, ungraded schools, the use of specialist teachers in elementary-school science and mathematics, the differentiated grouping of pupils by subject, the organization of special programs for gifted students, the use of teacher's aides, and the flexible scheduling of classes in terms of the number of pupils and the amount of time allotted to each. Fourth, the subject-matter content of the curriculum is being increased through such measures as a longer school year and day, the requirement of both more units and of more mandatory and fewer elective subjects for high-school graduation, the introduction into the elementary schools of foreign language and of more advanced mathematics and science instruction, the offering of college-level courses for capable senior high-school students, and greater emphasis on homework. Finally, there is much frenzied activity in the area of teaching aids, e.g., films, educational television, teaching machines, Cuisenaire rods and Stern blocks, and the use of tapes, records, and laboratory methods in foreign-language teaching.

These recent developments do not imply that the American school had previously repudiated intellectual training as its primary and distinctive function. It is true, of course, that this has often appeared to be the case because of the strident pronouncements of certain extreme proponents of the child-centered point of view who adopted a *laissez-faire* attitude toward the goal of intellectual competence. These latter individuals frequently derogated knowledge of subject matter, advocated the use of children's existing interests as the main criterion in constructing the curriculum, and placed major emphasis on the attainment of optimal personality development and social adjustment in a maximally permissive school environment. But although this position had many adherents among professors of education, it never prevailed, either in belief or practice, in more than a bare handful of public schools. Present concern with intellectual competence and with the quality of the curriculum, therefore, is more a matter of increased emphasis than a radical shift in the objectives of American education.

Actually the child-centered and subject-matter approaches constitute a pseudo-dichotomy that causes serious disagreement only among extremists at either end of the continuum. No realistic advocate of the subject-matter approach suggests that the school should disregard the personality development and social adjustment of pupils, or that subject matter should be taught without due regard for such relevant factors as readiness, individual differences in intellectual ability, and social-class motivations (or lack of motivation) for learning; and similarly, constructive proponents of the child-centered approach largely emphasize noncognitive determinants and outcomes of learning because of their importance in learning subject matter. The difference again is more one of emphasis than of basic goals. The fact that noncognitive determinants and outcomes of learning are not considered in this book does not mean that their significance is minimized or that an extreme subject matter approach is adopted (see p. 2). Furthermore, much explicit emphasis is placed on the importance of readiness and individual differences in cognitive capacity as factors influencing meaningful reception learning.

This greater emphasis upon quality of intellectual training is not without its dangers since it can be easily perverted to serve undesirable purposes. In the first place, higher standards, harder subjects and longer assignments are not ends in themselves. They are valueless and even pernicious unless the content of the subject matter involved is worthwhile, leads to meaningful knowledge, and is consonant with contemporary scholarship; unless the standards themselves are differentially adjusted so as to demand from each child what he can actually do and the best of which he is capable. Raised standards must not be used as a lever to eliminate from school those pupils in the lower range of intellectual ability. Rather, new ways must be found to motivate such pupils adequately and to teach them academic subject matter more effectively. Second, excellence is not synonymous with high examination scores irrespective of how they are achieved, the underlying motivation, the kind of knowledge they reflect, and each individual's distinctive pattern of abilities. In our present climate of frenzied competition for college entrance, there is a real danger that examination scores are becoming ends in themselves rather than symbols of genuine accomplishment and actual mastery of worthwhile knowledge.

More important than what pupils know at the end of the sixth, eighth, and twelfth grades is the extent of their knowledge at the ages of twenty-five, forty, and sixty, as well as their ability and desire both to learn more and to apply their knowledge fruitfully in adult life. In the light of these latter criteria, as, for example, in comparing the quantity and quality of our national research output in the pure and applied sciences with that of European countries, the American educational system stands up relatively well even though our school children are required to learn much less academic material. Higher academic standards therefore seem to have relatively little impact on real learning if they are merely formalistic rituals. Hence in setting our academic goals we must be more concerned with the *ultimate* intellectual objectives of schooling, namely, with the long-term acquisition of stable and usable bodies of knowledge and intellectual skills, and with the development of ability to think systematically, independently, and critically in particular fields of inquiry. The quality of. instruction obviously influences the outcome of these objectives—not only in the substantive content of subject matter but also in the organization, sequence, and manner of presenting learning experiences, their degree of meaningfulness, and the relative balance between the ideational and factual materials.

Responsibility for Organizing the Curriculum and Presenting Subject Matter

One extreme point of view associated with the child-centered approach to education is the notion that children are innately equipped in some mysterious fashion for knowing precisely what is best for them. This idea is obviously an outgrowth of the predeterministic theories of Rousseau, Gesell, and others that conceive of development as a series of internally regulated sequential steps that unfold in accordance with a prearranged design. According to these theorists, the environment facilitates development best by providing a maximally permissive field that does not interfere with the predetermined process of spontaneous maturation. From these assumptions it is but a short step to the claim that the child himself must be in the most strategic position to *know* and *select* those components of the environment that are most congruent with his current developmental needs, and hence most conducive to optimal growth. Empirical "proof" of this proposition is adduced from the fact that nutrition is adequately maintained and existing deficiency conditions are spontaneously corrected when infants are permitted to self-select their own diets. If the child can successfully choose his own diet he must certainly know what is best for him in all areas of growth, and should therefore be permitted to self-select everything including his curriculum.

In the first place, however, even if development were primarily a matter of internal ripening, there would still be no good reason for supposing that the child is therefore implicitly conversant with the current direction and facilitating conditions of development, and hence axiomatically equipped to make the most appropriate choices. Because the individual is sensitive in early childhood to internal cues of physiological need, we cannot conclude that he is similarly sensitive to cues reflective of psychological and other developmental needs; even in the area of nutrition, self-selection is a reliable criterion of need only during early infancy.

Second, unless one assigns a sacrosanct status to "endogenous motivations," there is little warrant for believing either that they alone are truly reflective of the child's *genuine* developmental requirements, or that environmentally derived needs are "imposed," authoritarian in spirit and inevitably fated to thwart the actualization of his developmental potentialities. Actually, most needs originate from without and are internalized in the course of the child's interaction and identification with significant persons in his family and cultural environments.

Third, one can never assume that the child's *spontaneously* expressed interests and activities are completely reflective of *all* of his important needs and capacities. Just because capacities can potentially provide their own motivation does not mean that they always or necessarily do so. It is not the possession of capacities that is motivating but the anticipation of future satisfactions once they have been successfully exercised; but because of such factors as inertia, lack of opportunity or appreciation of their existence, preoccupation with other activities, many capacities may never be exercised in the first place. Thus, children typically develop only *some* of their potential capacities, and their expressed interests cannot be considered coextensive with the potential range of interests they are capable of developing with appropriate stimulation.

In conclusion, therefore, the current interests and spontaneous desires of immature pupils can hardly be considered reliable guideposts and adequate substitutes for specialized knowledge and seasoned judgment in designing a curriculum. Recognition of the role of pupil needs in school learning does not mean that the scope of the syllabus should be restricted to the existing concerns and spontaneously expressed interests that happen to be present in a group of children growing up under particular conditions of intellectual and social class stimulation. In fact, one of the primary functions of education should be to stimulate the development of motivations that are currently nonexistent. It is true that academic achievement is greatest when pupils manifest felt needs to acquire knowledge as an end in itself. Such needs, however, are not endogenous but acquired—and largely through exposure to provocative, meaningful and developmentally appropriate instruction. Hence, while it is reasonable to consider the views of pupils and even, under certain circumstances, to solicit their participation in the planning of the curriculum, it makes little developmental or administrative sense to entrust them with responsibility for significant policy or operational decisions.

Two related propositions, stemming from the activity program movement, are that factual information and intellectual skills should always be acquired in the real-life, functional contexts in which they are customarily encountered (rather than through the medium of artificially contrived drills and exercises), and that a pupil's progress should be evaluated only in terms of his own potentialities. Many teachers, however, learned from their own experience that drills and exercises need not necessarily be rote in character and that they are essential, moreover, for acquiring many skills and concepts that do not occur frequently and repetitively enough in more natural settings. Similarly, they found it necessary to ignore much of the nonsense disseminated about incidental learning. They discovered that although it was possible for children to learn some things incidentally, deliberate and guided effort was required for the efficient learning of most types of academic material. Finally, they had to discount much of the exaggerated condemnation of school marks and group norms as unqualified evils. They found that stripped of their abuses marks were both indispensable tools for evaluating the acquisition of valid, worthwhile knowledge, and a quite necessary and unavoidable incentive for academic achievement in our competitive culture; and that while it was certainly useful to know how well a pupil was performing in terms of his own capabilities, this knowledge was no substitute for evaluation of his ability relative to the norm of his age group.

Some representatives of the progressive education movement speak with disdain about the school's role of imparting knowledge, contrasting it with the allegedly more desirable role of helping children learn by themselves. They assert that the former role is a paltry one and that it invariably results in the learning of glib and meaningless verbalisms. This, of course, is not necessarily true provided that the obvious abuses of verbal instruction are avoided. Meaningful verbal exposition is actually the most efficient way of teaching subject matter and leads to sounder and less trivial knowledge than when pupils serve as their own pedagogues. Neither is didactic exposition necessarily more passive and mechanical than independent data gathering. The unmotivated student who assembles his own learning material manifests no greater intellectual activity than the unmotivated student who receives expository instruction. The motivated student, on the other hand, reflectively considers, reworks, and integrates new material into his cognitive structure irrespective of how he obtains it.

The battle cry of the progressives that the student must assume responsibility for his own learning has been distorted into a doctrine of pedagogic irresponsibility. It has been interpreted to mean that the student's responsibility is to self-discover everything he has to learn, that is, to locate and organize his own materials from primary sources, to interpret them independently, to design his own experiments, and merely to use the teacher as a consultant and critic. But education is not a process of self-instruction. Its very essence inheres in the knowledgeable selection, organization, interpretation, and sequential arrangement of learning materials by pedagogically sophisticated persons. The school cannot in good conscience abdicate these responsibilities by turning them over to students in the name of democracy and progressivism. The student takes appropriate responsibility for his own learning when he accepts the task of learning actively and seeking to understand the material which he is taught; when he genuinely attempts to integrate it with what he already knows; when he does not avoid the effort and struggle of difficult new learning or demand spoon-feeding from his teacher; and when he takes it upon himself to ask the necessary questions about what he does not understand.

Another way in which educators have evaded responsibility for programing the content of instruction has been by hiding behind the slogan that the function of the school is to "teach children how to think—not what to think." This slogan also states a false dichotomy since the two functions are by no means mutually exclusive. Actually, as will be argued later, the transmission of subject matter can be considered the more primary function of the school. Most of the thinking that goes on in school is and should be supplementary to the process of reception learning, that is, concerned with having students assimilate subject-matter content in a more active, integrative, and critical fashion. Development of thinking or problem-solving ability can also be considered an objective of schooling in its own right, although it is a lesser objective than the learning of subject matter and is only partly teachable; but under no circumstances is it a proper substitute for reception learning or a feasible primary means of imparting subject-matter knowledge.

Fortunately, as evidenced by the phenomenal growth of the curriculum reform movements and of various forms of programed instruction, leading educators are currently returning to the more traditional educational view that the content of the curriculum is the teacher's and not the student's responsibility.

Knowledge as an End in Itself

Another encouraging trend on the current educational scene is a growing emphasis on the value of knowledge as an end in itself. The "life adjustment" movement has performed a valuable service by pointing out that the school cannot afford totally to disregard the expressed interests, current concerns and future vocational, family, and civic problems of high school students, particularly those who have no intention of attending the university. If young people perceive the school as uninterested in these problems, they react either by losing interest in academic studies or by feeling guilty for being preoccupied with supposedly trivial matters. If current concerns are not relieved they inevitably serve as distractions from other constituted responsibilities. Some extremists, however, carried this approach too far by adopting an anti-intellectual attitude toward secondary-school education. Any branch of knowledge that had no immediate applicability to practical problems of everyday living was summarily dismissed as a waste of time, and in some instances the curriculum was diluted by the addition of various frills and leisure-time activities. It was held that only intellectually superior or college-bound students should be exposed to academic subjects, and that these subjects are either valueless or too difficult for other students.

To be related to present needs and purposes, learning tasks need not necessarily deal with problems of adolescent adjustment. Academic knowledge can have relatedness to current motivations if its acquisition becomes, at least in part, a goal in its own right. It is unrealistic to expect that all school subjects can have, even remotely, utilitarian value or practical implications. The value of much of school learning can be defended only because it improves an individual's understanding of important ideas in his culture; and if adolescents could be motivated to perceive academic knowledge in this light, it would constitute an important part of their current psychological field.

Furthermore, even if youths not bound for college do require some prevocational and life-adjustment education, this does not mean that they could not benefit from academic subject matter. Appropriately taught and suitably modified in content to account for their intellectual ability, academic training is not only valuable as an end in itself but, in a more general way, is just as important a preparation for adult living as education that is more explicitly related to immediate developmental tasks.

REFERENCES

1. Ausubel, D. P. The nature of educational research. *Educ. Theory,* 1953, 3:314–320.
2. Ausubel, D. P. Viewpoints from other disciplines: Human growth and development. *Teachers Coll. Record,* 1959, 60:245–254.
3. Gage, N. L. Metatechnique in educational research. Urbana, Illinois: Bureau of Educational Research, University of Illinois, 1961.
4. Melton, A. W. The science of learning and the technology of educational methods. *Harvard Educ. Rev.,* 1959, 29:96–106.
5. Spence, K. W. The relation of learning theory to the technology of education. *Harvard Educ. Rev.,* 1959, 29:84–95.
6. Underwood, B. J. Verbal learning in the educative process. *Harvard Educ. Rev.,* 1959, 29:107–117.
7. Watson, R. I. The present status of educational psychology and of educational psychologists. Evanston, Illinois: Department of Psychology, Northwestern University, 1960.

CHAPTER 2.

Overview of Basic Concepts

IN THIS CHAPTER I propose to offer a brief overview of the major principles of the learning theory elaborated in this book. These principles will be presented with little accompanying detail, logical explication, or supportive evidence. The aim is to provide some general ideational scaffolding for the more detailed and documented consideration of the separate components of the theory that will follow in later individual chapters. Although this mode of organization inevitably makes for some redundancy, it more than compensates for this disadvantage by enhancing comprehensibility and meaningfulness.

THE NATURE OF RECEPTION LEARNING

Few pedagogic devices in our time have been repudiated more unequivocally by educational theorists than the method of expository verbal instruction. It is fashionable in many quarters to characterize verbal learning as parrot-like recitation and rote memorization of isolated facts, and to dismiss it disdainfully as an archaic remnant of discredited educational tradition. In fact, quite apart from whatever intrinsic value they may possess, many educational innovations and movements of the past three decades—activity programs, project and discussion methods, various ways of maximizing nonverbal and manipulative experience in the classroom, emphasis on "self-discovery," and on learning for and by *problem-solving*—owe their origins and popularity to widespread dissatisfaction with the technics of verbal instruction. It is commonly accepted today, for example, (at least in the realm of educational theory) (a) that meaningful generalizations cannot be presented or "given" to the learner, but can only be acquired as a product of problem-solving activity;[9] and (b) that all attempts to master verbal concepts and propositions are forms of empty verbalism unless the learner has recent prior experience with the realities to which these verbal constructs refer.[9,10]

Excellent reasons, of course, exist for the general disrepute into which expository teaching and verbal learning have fallen. The most obvious of these is that notwithstanding repeated policy declarations of educational organizations to the contrary, meaningful subject matter is still presented to pupils in preponderantly rote fashion. Another less obvious but equally important reason why meaningfulness is perceived as an exclusive product of problem-solving and discovery technics of learning, stems from two serious shortcomings of modern learning theory. First, psychologists have tended to subsume many *qualitatively* different kinds of learning processes under a single explanatory model. As a result, widespread confusion exists regarding basic distinctions between reception and discovery learning, and between rote and meaningful learning. It has not always been sufficiently clear, for example, that such categorically different types of learning as problem-solving and the under-

15

to confuse the reception-discovery dimension of the learning process with the rote-meaningful dimension; and (c) unwarranted generalization of the distinctive developmental conditions of learning and thinking in childhood to adolescence and adult life.

The use of the straw-man technic was, of course, the simplest and most effective way of discrediting the method of verbal exposition. Instead of describing this procedure in terms of its essential characteristics, it became fashionable to picture it in terms of its worst abuses. Examples of such abuses were naturally not very difficult to find, since an appreciable number of teachers still rely on rote verbal learning in teaching meaningful subject matter. Some of the more flagrantly inept practices include premature use of verbal technics with cognitively immature pupils; arbitrary presentation of unrelated facts without any organizing or explanatory principles; failure to integrate new learning tasks with previously presented materials; and the use of evaluation procedures that merely measure ability to recognize discrete facts or to reproduce ideas in the same words or in the identical context as originally encountered.[2]

Although it is entirely proper to caution teachers against these frequent misuses of verbal learning, it is not legitimate to represent them as inherent in the method itself. An approach to instruction which on logical and psychological grounds appears appropriate and efficient should not be discarded as unworkable simply because, like all pedagogic technics in the hands of incompetent or unintelligent teachers, it is subject to misuse. It would seem more reasonable to guard against the more common misapplications, and to relate the method to relevant theoretical principles and research findings that actually deal with the long-term learning and retention of large bodies of meaningful, verbally-presented materials.

The distinction between rote and meaningful learning is frequently confused with the reception-discovery distinction discussed above. This confusion is partly responsible for the widespread but unwarranted twin beliefs that reception learning is invariably rote and that discovery learning is inherently and necessarily meaningful. Both assumptions, of course, are related to the long-standing doctrine that the only knowledge one *really* possesses and understands is knowledge that one discovers by oneself. Actually, each distinction constitutes an entirely independent dimension of learning. Hence a much more defensible proposition is that *both* expository *and* problem-solving technics can be either rote *or* meaningful depending on the conditions under which learning occurs. In both instances meaningful learning takes place if the learning task can be related in nonarbitrary, substantive fashion to what the learner already knows, and if the learner adopts a corresponding learning set to do so.

It is true that by these criteria much potentially meaningful knowledge taught by verbal exposition results in rotely learned verbalisms. This rote outcome, however, is not inherent in the expository method *per se*, but rather in such abuses of this method as fail to satisfy the criteria of meaningfulness. There is much greater reluctance, on the other hand, to acknowledge that the aforementioned preconditions for meaningfulness also apply to problem-solving and laboratory methods. It should seem rather self-evident that performing laboratory experiments in cookbook fashion, without understanding

to confuse the reception-discovery dimension of the learning process with the rote-meaningful dimension; and (c) unwarranted generalization of the distinctive developmental conditions of learning and thinking in childhood to adolescence and adult life.

The use of the straw-man technic was, of course, the simplest and most effective way of discrediting the method of verbal exposition. Instead of describing this procedure in terms of its essential characteristics, it became fashionable to picture it in terms of its worst abuses. Examples of such abuses were naturally not very difficult to find, since an appreciable number of teachers still rely on rote verbal learning in teaching meaningful subject matter. Some of the more flagrantly inept practices include premature use of verbal technics with cognitively immature pupils; arbitrary presentation of unrelated facts without any organizing or explanatory principles; failure to integrate new learning tasks with previously presented materials; and the use of evaluation procedures that merely measure ability to recognize discrete facts or to reproduce ideas in the same words or in the identical context as originally encountered.[2]

Although it is entirely proper to caution teachers against these frequent misuses of verbal learning, it is not legitimate to represent them as inherent in the method itself. An approach to instruction which on logical and psychological grounds appears appropriate and efficient should not be discarded as unworkable simply because, like all pedagogic technics in the hands of incompetent or unintelligent teachers, it is subject to misuse. It would seem more reasonable to guard against the more common misapplications, and to relate the method to relevant theoretical principles and research findings that actually deal with the long-term learning and retention of large bodies of meaningful, verbally-presented materials.

The distinction between rote and meaningful learning is frequently confused with the reception-discovery distinction discussed above. This confusion is partly responsible for the widespread but unwarranted twin beliefs that reception learning is invariably rote and that discovery learning is inherently and necessarily meaningful. Both assumptions, of course, are related to the long-standing doctrine that the only knowledge one *really* possesses and understands is knowledge that one discovers by oneself. Actually, each distinction constitutes an entirely independent dimension of learning. Hence a much more defensible proposition is that *both* expository *and* problem-solving technics can be either rote *or* meaningful depending on the conditions under which learning occurs. In both instances meaningful learning takes place if the learning task can be related in nonarbitrary, substantive fashion to what the learner already knows, and if the learner adopts a corresponding learning set to do so.

It is true that by these criteria much potentially meaningful knowledge taught by verbal exposition results in rotely learned verbalisms. This rote outcome, however, is not inherent in the expository method *per se*, but rather in such abuses of this method as fail to satisfy the criteria of meaningfulness. There is much greater reluctance, on the other hand, to acknowledge that the aforementioned preconditions for meaningfulness also apply to problem-solving and laboratory methods. It should seem rather self-evident that performing laboratory experiments in cookbook fashion, without understanding

CHAPTER 2.

Overview of Basic Concepts

In this chapter I propose to offer a brief overview of the major principles of the learning theory elaborated in this book. These principles will be presented with little accompanying detail, logical explication, or supportive evidence. The aim is to provide some general ideational scaffolding for the more detailed and documented consideration of the separate components of the theory that will follow in later individual chapters. Although this mode of organization inevitably makes for some redundancy, it more than compensates for this disadvantage by enhancing comprehensibility and meaningfulness.

THE NATURE OF RECEPTION LEARNING

Few pedagogic devices in our time have been repudiated more unequivocally by educational theorists than the method of expository verbal instruction. It is fashionable in many quarters to characterize verbal learning as parrot-like recitation and rote memorization of isolated facts, and to dismiss it disdainfully as an archaic remnant of discredited educational tradition. In fact, quite apart from whatever intrinsic value they may possess, many educational innovations and movements of the past three decades—activity programs, project and discussion methods, various ways of maximizing nonverbal and manipulative experience in the classroom, emphasis on "self-discovery," and on learning for and by *problem-solving*—owe their origins and popularity to widespread dissatisfaction with the technics of verbal instruction. It is commonly accepted today, for example, (at least in the realm of educational theory) (a) that meaningful generalizations cannot be presented or "given" to the learner, but can only be acquired as a product of problem-solving activity;[9] and (b) that all attempts to master verbal concepts and propositions are forms of empty verbalism unless the learner has recent prior experience with the realities to which these verbal constructs refer.[9,10]

Excellent reasons, of course, exist for the general disrepute into which expository teaching and verbal learning have fallen. The most obvious of these is that notwithstanding repeated policy declarations of educational organizations to the contrary, meaningful subject matter is still presented to pupils in preponderantly rote fashion. Another less obvious but equally important reason why meaningfulness is perceived as an exclusive product of problem-solving and discovery technics of learning, stems from two serious shortcomings of modern learning theory. First, psychologists have tended to subsume many *qualitatively* different kinds of learning processes under a single explanatory model. As a result, widespread confusion exists regarding basic distinctions between reception and discovery learning, and between rote and meaningful learning. It has not always been sufficiently clear, for example, that such categorically different types of learning as problem-solving and the under-

CHAPTER 2.

Overview of Basic Concepts

IN THIS CHAPTER I propose to offer a brief overview of the major principles of the learning theory elaborated in this book. These principles will be presented with little accompanying detail, logical explication, or supportive evidence. The aim is to provide some general ideational scaffolding for the more detailed and documented consideration of the separate components of the theory that will follow in later individual chapters. Although this mode of organization inevitably makes for some redundancy, it more than compensates for this disadvantage by enhancing comprehensibility and meaningfulness.

THE NATURE OF RECEPTION LEARNING

Few pedagogic devices in our time have been repudiated more unequivocally by educational theorists than the method of expository verbal instruction. It is fashionable in many quarters to characterize verbal learning as parrot-like recitation and rote memorization of isolated facts, and to dismiss it disdainfully as an archaic remnant of discredited educational tradition. In fact, quite apart from whatever intrinsic value they may possess, many educational innovations and movements of the past three decades—activity programs, project and discussion methods, various ways of maximizing nonverbal and manipulative experience in the classroom, emphasis on "self-discovery," and on learning for and by *problem-solving*—owe their origins and popularity to widespread dissatisfaction with the technics of verbal instruction. It is commonly accepted today, for example, (at least in the realm of educational theory) (a) that meaningful generalizations cannot be presented or "given" to the learner, but can only be acquired as a product of problem-solving activity;[9] and (b) that all attempts to master verbal concepts and propositions are forms of empty verbalism unless the learner has recent prior experience with the realities to which these verbal constructs refer.[9,10]

Excellent reasons, of course, exist for the general disrepute into which expository teaching and verbal learning have fallen. The most obvious of these is that notwithstanding repeated policy declarations of educational organizations to the contrary, meaningful subject matter is still presented to pupils in preponderantly rote fashion. Another less obvious but equally important reason why meaningfulness is perceived as an exclusive product of problem-solving and discovery technics of learning, stems from two serious shortcomings of modern learning theory. First, psychologists have tended to subsume many *qualitatively* different kinds of learning processes under a single explanatory model. As a result, widespread confusion exists regarding basic distinctions between reception and discovery learning, and between rote and meaningful learning. It has not always been sufficiently clear, for example, that such categorically different types of learning as problem-solving and the under-

15

standing of presented verbal material have different objectives, and that conditions and instructional technics facilitating one of these learning processes are not necessarily relevant or maximally efficient for the other. Second, in the absence of an appropriate theory of meaningful verbal learning, many educational psychologists have tended to interpret long-term subject-matter learning in terms of the same concepts (*e.g.*, retroactive inhibition, stimulus generalization, response competition) used to explain instrumental conditioning, paired-associate learning, rote serial learning, maze learning, and simple discrimination learning.

An attempt will therefore be made in this chapter to distinguish between reception and discovery learning, to sharpen the existing distinction between rote and meaningful learning, and to consider the distinctive role of each of these types of learning in the total educational enterprise. It should then be clear that verbal reception learning can be genuinely meaningful without prior discovery experience or problem-solving activity, and that the weaknesses attributed to the method of expository verbal instruction do not inhere in the method itself but are derived from various misapplications.

Reception versus Discovery Learning

From the standpoint of enhancing intellectual development, no theoretical concern is more relevant or pressing in the present state of our knowledge than the need for distinguishing clearly among the principal kinds of cognitive learning (*i.e.*, rote and meaningful verbal learning, concept formation, and verbal and nonverbal problem-solving) that take place in the classroom. One significant way of differentiating among the latter types of classroom learning is to make two crucial process distinctions that cut across all of them— distinctions between reception and discovery learning and between rote and meaningful learning. The first distinction is especially important because most of the understandings that learners acquire both in and out of school are presented rather than discovered. And since most learning material is presented verbally, it is equally important to appreciate that verbal reception learning is not necessarily rote in character and can be meaningful without prior nonverbal and problem-solving experience.

In reception learning (rote or meaningful) the entire content of what is to be learned is presented to the learner in final form. The learning task does not involve any independent discovery on his part. He is only required to internalize the material (*e.g.*, a list of nonsense syllables or paired associates; a poem or geometrical theorem) that is presented to him so that it is available and reproducible at some future date. The essential feature of discovery learning (*e.g.*, concept formation, rote or meaningful problem-solving), on the other hand, is that the principal content of what is to be learned is not given but must be independently discovered by the learner before he can internalize it. The distinctive and prior learning task, in other words, is to discover something—which of two maze alleys leads to the goal, the precise nature of a relationship between two variables, the common attributes of a number of diverse instances, etc. The first phase of discovery learning, therefore, involves a process quite different from that of reception learning. The learner must rearrange a given array of information, integrate it with existing cognitive structure, and reorganize or transform the integrated combination in such a way as to create a desired end-product or discover a missing means-end relationship. After this phase is completed, the discovered content is internalized just as in reception learning.

It should be clear up to this point, therefore, that reception and discovery learning are two quite different kinds of processes, and that most classroom instruction is organized along the lines of reception learning. In the next section it will be shown that verbal reception learning is not necessarily rote in character, that much ideational material (e.g., concepts, generalizations) can be meaningfully internalized and made available without prior discovery experience, and that at no stage does the learner have to discover principles independently in order to be able to understand and use them meaningfully.

Reception and discovery learning are not only basically different in essential nature and process, but also differ with respect to their principal roles in intellectual development and cognitive functioning. Essentially, large bodies of subject matter are acquired through reception learning, and the everyday problems of living are solved through discovery learning. Some overlap of function, however, does exist: the knowledge acquired through reception learning is also used in everyday problem-solving, and discovery learning is commonly used in the classroom to apply, extend, integrate, and evaluate subject-matter knowledge and to test its comprehension. In laboratory situations discovery learning also leads to the contrived rediscovery of known propositions and, when employed by gifted persons, to significant new knowledge. Typically, however, the propositions discovered through problem-solving methods are rarely significant and worth incorporating into the learner's subject-matter knowledge. In any case, discovery technics hardly constitute an efficient primary means of transmitting the content of an academic discipline (see pp. 151–153).

Discovery learning is a psychologically more involved process than reception learning because it presupposes a problem-solving stage that precedes the emergence of meaning and the interiorization of information. But reception learning, on the whole, appears later developmentally and, in most instances, implies a greater degree of cognitive maturity. The young child learns most new concepts and propositions inductively through autonomous discovery, although self-discovery is not essential if concrete-empirical props are available. Reception learning, however, although occurring earlier, is not really prominent until the child is both capable of internal mental operations and can comprehend verbally presented propositions in the absence of current concrete-empirical experience (see pp. 116–119). The typical contrast here is between inductive concept formation with the aid of concrete-empirical props, on the one hand, and direct concept acquisition through verbal exposition, on the other.

Is Reception Learning Meaningful?

It is frequently maintained, as already pointed out, that abstract concepts and generalizations are forms of empty, meaningless verbalism unless the learner discovers them autonomously out of his own concrete, empirical, problem-solving experience. Careful analysis of this proposition reveals, in my opinion, that it rests on three serious logical fallacies: (a) a straw-man representation of the method of verbal learning; (b) the prevailing tendency

to confuse the reception-discovery dimension of the learning process with the rote-meaningful dimension; and (c) unwarranted generalization of the distinctive developmental conditions of learning and thinking in childhood to adolescence and adult life.

The use of the straw-man technic was, of course, the simplest and most effective way of discrediting the method of verbal exposition. Instead of describing this procedure in terms of its essential characteristics, it became fashionable to picture it in terms of its worst abuses. Examples of such abuses were naturally not very difficult to find, since an appreciable number of teachers still rely on rote verbal learning in teaching meaningful subject matter. Some of the more flagrantly inept practices include premature use of verbal technics with cognitively immature pupils; arbitrary presentation of unrelated facts without any organizing or explanatory principles; failure to integrate new learning tasks with previously presented materials; and the use of evaluation procedures that merely measure ability to recognize discrete facts or to reproduce ideas in the same words or in the identical context as originally encountered.[2]

Although it is entirely proper to caution teachers against these frequent misuses of verbal learning, it is not legitimate to represent them as inherent in the method itself. An approach to instruction which on logical and psychological grounds appears appropriate and efficient should not be discarded as unworkable simply because, like all pedagogic technics in the hands of incompetent or unintelligent teachers, it is subject to misuse. It would seem more reasonable to guard against the more common misapplications, and to relate the method to relevant theoretical principles and research findings that actually deal with the long-term learning and retention of large bodies of meaningful, verbally-presented materials.

The distinction between rote and meaningful learning is frequently confused with the reception-discovery distinction discussed above. This confusion is partly responsible for the widespread but unwarranted twin beliefs that reception learning is invariably rote and that discovery learning is inherently and necessarily meaningful. Both assumptions, of course, are related to the long-standing doctrine that the only knowledge one *really* possesses and understands is knowledge that one discovers by oneself. Actually, each distinction constitutes an entirely independent dimension of learning. Hence a much more defensible proposition is that *both* expository *and* problem-solving technics can be either rote *or* meaningful depending on the conditions under which learning occurs. In both instances meaningful learning takes place if the learning task can be related in nonarbitrary, substantive fashion to what the learner already knows, and if the learner adopts a corresponding learning set to do so.

It is true that by these criteria much potentially meaningful knowledge taught by verbal exposition results in rotely learned verbalisms. This rote outcome, however, is not inherent in the expository method *per se,* but rather in such abuses of this method as fail to satisfy the criteria of meaningfulness. There is much greater reluctance, on the other hand, to acknowledge that the aforementioned preconditions for meaningfulness also apply to problem-solving and laboratory methods. It should seem rather self-evident that performing laboratory experiments in cookbook fashion, without understanding the underlying substantive and methodological principles involved, confers precious little meaningful understanding, and that many students studying mathematics and science find it relatively simple to discover correct answers to problems without really understanding what they are doing. They accomplish the latter feat merely by rotely memorizing "type problems" and procedures for manipulating symbols. Nevertheless it is still not generally appreciated that laboratory work and problem-solving are not genuinely meaningful experiences unless they are built on a foundation of clearly understood concepts and principles, and unless the constituent operations are themselves meaningful.

The art and science of presenting ideas and information meaningfully and effectively—so that clear, stable, and unambiguous meanings emerge and are retained over a long period of time as an organized body of knowledge—is really the principal function of pedagogy. This is a demanding and creative rather than a routine or mechanical task. The job of selecting, organizing, presenting, and translating subject-matter content in a developmentally appropriate manner requires more than a rote listing of facts. If it is done properly it is the work of a master teacher and is hardly a task to be disdained.

Finally, it is important to appreciate the relationship between reception learning and various developmental considerations that affect its meaningfulness. Learners who have not yet developed beyond the concrete stage of cognitive development are unable meaningfully to incorporate within their cognitive structures a relationship between two or more abstractions unless they have the benefit of current or recently prior concrete-empirical experience.[12] During the concrete stage, roughly covering the elementary-school period, children are restricted by their dependence on concrete-empirical experience to a semi-abstract, intuitive understanding of abstract propositions. Such learners therefore cannot meaningfully comprehend verbally or symbolically expressed propositions without the aid of these concrete-empirical props, although they by no means have to discover these propositions autonomously in order to understand them meaningfully. Even during the elementary-school years the act of discovery is not indispensable for intuitive understanding and need not constitute a routine part of pedagogic technic. As every elementary-school teacher knows, meaningful verbal reception learning—without any problem solving or discovery experience whatsoever—is perhaps the commonest form of classroom learning, provided that the necessary props are available.

During the abstract stage of cognitive development, however, beginning in the junior-high-school period, students acquire most new concepts and learn most new propositions by *directly* grasping higher-order relationships between abstractions.[12] To do so meaningfully, they need no longer depend on current or recently prior concrete-empirical experience, and hence are able to by-pass completely the intuitive type of understanding reflective of such dependence. Through proper expository teaching they can proceed directly to a level of abstract understanding that is qualitatively superior to the intuitive level in terms of generality, clarity, precision, and explicitness. At this stage of development, therefore, it seems pointless to enhance intuitive understanding by using discovery technics.

This is the point at which some of the more zealous proponents of Progressive Education took a disastrously false turn. John Dewey had correctly recognized that meaningful understanding of abstract concepts and principles in childhood must be built on a foundation of direct, empirical experience, and for this reason advocated the use of project and activity methods in the elementary school. But he also appreciated that once a firmly grounded first-story of abstract understandings was established, it was possible to organize secondary and higher education along more abstract and verbal lines. Unfortunately, however, although Dewey himself never elaborated or implemented this latter conception, some of his disciples blindly generalized childhood limiting conditions, with respect to meaningful verbal reception learning, broadly enough to encompass learning over the entire life span. And this unwarranted extrapolation, frequently but erroneously attributed to Dewey himself, provided a pseudonaturalistic rationale for, and thus helped perpetuate, the seemingly indestructable myth that, under any and all circumstances, abstractions cannot possibly be meaningful unless preceded by direct, empirical experience.

Is Reception Learning Passive?

The emergence of meaning, as new concepts and ideas are incorporated into cognitive structure, is far from being a passive phenomenon. In view of the complex and variable nature of learners' intellectual backgrounds, much activity is obviously involved, but not the kind of activity characterizing discovery. Activity and discovery are not synonymous in the realm of cognitive functioning. Merely because potential meanings are presented, we cannot assume that they are necessarily acquired and that all subsequent loss is reflective of forgetting. Before meanings can be retained they must be acquired, and the process of acquisition is exceedingly active.

Meaningful reception learning involves more than the simple cataloguing of ready-made concepts within existing cognitive structure. In the first place, an implicit judgment of relevance is usually required in deciding under which proposition to catalog new knowledge. Second, some degree of reconciliation with existing knowledge is necessary, particularly if there are discrepancies or conflicts. Third, new propositions are customarily translated into a personal frame of reference consonant with the learner's experiential background, vocabulary, and structure of ideas. Lastly, some degree of reorganization under different, more inclusive concepts is sometimes required if a basis for reconciliation cannot be found.

All of this activity, however, stops short of actual discovery or problem-solving. Since the substance of the learning task is presented rather than discovered, the activity involved is limited to that required in understanding new meanings and integrating them into existing cognitive structure. This is naturally of a qualitatively different order than that involved in independently discovering solutions to new problems, i.e., the task of integrating and reorganizing new information and existing knowledge to satisfy the requirements of a given problem situation.

The extent of activity involved in meaningful reception learning obviously depends on the learner's general readiness and level of cognitive sophistication and on the availability within his cognitive structure of relevant subsuming concepts. Hence the degree of activity necessary would be substantially reduced if the presented material were appropriately programed to fit his experiential background and level of readiness. The extent to which meaningful reception learning is active is also a function of the learner's drive for integrative meaning and of his self-critical faculty. He may either attempt to integrate a new proposition with all of his existing relevant knowledge or remain content with establishing its relatedness to a single concept. Similarly, he may endeavor to translate the new proposition into terminology consistent with his own vocabulary and ideational background, or remain satisfied with incorporating it as presented. Finally, he may strive for the acquisition of precise, unambiguous meanings or be completely satisfied with vague, diffuse notions.

The main danger in meaningful reception learning is not so much that the learner will frankly adopt a rote approach, but that he will delude himself into believing that he has really grasped precise intended meanings when he has only grasped a vague and confused set of generalities and no real meaning whatsoever. It is not so much that he does not want to understand but that he lacks the necessary self-critical ability and is unwilling to put forth the necessary active effort involved in struggling with the material, looking at it from different angles, reconciling. it with related and contradictory knowledge, and translating it into his own frame of reference. He finds it easy enough to manipulate words so as to create an appearance of knowledge and thereby to delude himself and others that he really understands.

A central task of pedagogy, therefore, is to develop ways of facilitating an active variety of reception learning supplemented by an independent and critical approach to the understanding of subject matter. This involves, in part, the encouragement of motivations for and of self-critical attitudes toward acquiring precise and integrated meanings, as well as the use of other technics directed toward the same end. Precise and integrated understandings are, presumably, more likely to develop if the central, unifying ideas of a discipline are learned before more peripheral concepts and information are introduced; if the limiting conditions of general developmental readiness are observed; if precise and accurate definition is stressed, and emphasis is placed on delineating similarities and differences between related concepts; and if learners are required to reformulate new propositions in their own words. All of these latter devices come under the heading of pedagogic technics that promote an active type of meaningful reception learning. Teachers can help foster the related objective of critical thinking with regard to subject-matter content by encouraging students to recognize and challenge the assumptions underlying new propositions and to distinguish between facts and hypotheses and between warranted and unwarranted inferences. Much good use can also be made of Socratic questioning in exposing pseudo-understanding, in transmitting precise meanings, in reconciling contradictions, and in encouraging a critical attitude toward knowledge.

MEANINGFUL VERSUS ROTE LEARNING

By "meaningful learning" we also refer primarily to a distinctive kind of learning process, and only secondarily to a meaningful learning outcome—attainment of meaning—that necessarily reflects the completion of such a process. Meaningful learning as a process presupposes, in turn, *both* that the learner employs a meaningful learning set and that the material he learns is potentially meaningful to him. Thus, regardless of how much potential meaning may inhere in a given proposition, if the learner's intention is to memorize it verbatim, *i.e.*, as a series of arbitrarily related words, both the learning process and the learning outcome must necessarily be rote and meaningless. And conversely, no matter how meaningful the learner's set may be, neither the process nor outcome of learning can possibly be meaningful if the learning task itself consists of purely arbitrary associations as in paired-associate or rote serial learning.

Meaningful Learning Set

In meaningful learning the learner has a set to relate substantive (as opposed to verbatim) aspects of new concepts, information, or situations to relevant components of existing cognitive structure in various ways that make possible the incorporation of derivative, elaborative, correlative, supportive, qualifying or representational relationships. Depending on the nature of the learning task (*i.e.*, reception or discovery) the set may be either to discover or merely to apprehend and incorporate such relationships. In rote learning, on the other hand, the learner's set is to discover a solution to a problem, or to internalize material verbatim, as a discrete and isolated end in itself. Such learning obviously does not occur in a cognitive vacuum. The material *is* related to cognitive structure, but not in a substantive, nonarbitrary fashion permitting incorporation of one of the relationships specified above. Where discovery learning is involved, the distinction between rote and meaningful learning corresponds to that between "trial and error" and insightful problem solving.

Potentially Meaningful Material

A meaningful set or approach to learning, as already pointed out, only eventuates in a meaningful learning process and outcome provided that the learning material (task) itself is *potentially* meaningful. Insistence on the qualifying adjective "potential" in this instance is more than mere academic hair-splitting. If the learning material were simply considered meaningful, the learning process (apprehending the meaning and making it functionally more available) would be completely superfluous; the object of learning would obviously be already accomplished, by definition, before any learning was ever attempted and irrespective of the type of learning set employed. It is true that certain component elements of a current learning task as, for example, the individual words of a new geometrical theorem, may already be meaningful to the learner; but it is the meaning of the relational proposition as a whole which is the object of learning in this situation—not the individual meanings of its component elements. Thus, although the term "meaningful learning" necessarily implies the use of potentially meaningful learning tasks, it does not imply that the learning of meaningful as opposed to rote material is the distinctive feature of meaningful learning. Meaningful material may be perceived and reacted to meaningfully, but cannot possibly constitute a learning task in as much as the very term "meaningful" connotes that the object of learning was previously consummated.

Two important criteria determine whether new learning is potentially meaningful. The first criterion—nonarbitrary relatability to relevant concepts in cognitive structure, in the various ways specified above—is a property of the material itself. New material is *not* potentially meaningful if either the total learning task (*e.g.*, a particular order of nonsense syllables, a list of paired adjectives, a scrambled sentence) or the basic unit of the learning task (a particular pair of adjectives) is only relatable to such concepts on a purely arbitrary basis. This criterion of potential meaningfulness applies solely to the current learning task itself—not to any of its structural elements which may already be meaningful, such as the component letters of a nonsense syllable, each member of an adjective pair, or the component words of a scrambled sentence. The presence of meaningful component words, for example, no more detracts from the lack of potential meaningfulness in the task of learning the correct sequence of jumbled words in a scrambled sentence, than it adds to potential meaningfulness in the task of learning the meaning of a geometrical theorem. In both instances the meaningful components, although structurally part of the learning material, do not constitute part of the learning task in a functional sense.

The second important criterion determining whether learning material is potentially meaningful—its relatability to the *particular* cognitive structure of a particular learner—is more properly a characteristic of the learner than of the material *per se*. Phenomenologically, meaningfulness is an individual matter. Hence for meaningful learning to occur in fact, it is not sufficient that the new material simply be relatable to relevant ideas in the abstract sense of the term. The cognitive structure of the particular learner must include the requisite intellectual capacities, ideational content, and experiential background. It is on this basis that the potential meaningfulness of learning material varies with such factors as age, intelligence, occupation, cultural membership, etc. In other words, it is subsumability within or incorporability by a particular cognitive structure which converts potential into actual meaning, and which (given nonarbitrarily relatable material and a meaningful learning set) differentiates meaningful from rote learnng.

As long as the set and content conditions of meaningful learning are satisfied, the outcome should be meaningful and the advantages of meaningful learning (economy of learning effort, more stable retention and greater transferability) should accrue irrespective of whether the content to be internalized is presented or discovered, verbal or nonverbal.

Process Differences between Rote and Meaningful Reception Learning

In view of the foregoing, plausible reasons exist for believing that rotely and meaningfully learned materials are organized quite differently in cognitive structure and hence conform to quite different principles of learning and forgetting. First, meaningfully learned materials are related to existing concepts in cognitive structure in ways making possible the understanding of various kinds of significant (*e.g.*, derivative, qualifying, correlative) relationships. Most new ideational materials that pupils encounter in a school setting are nonarbitrarily and substantively relatable to a previously learned background of meaningful ideas and information. In fact, the curriculum is deliberately organized in this fashion to provide for the untraumatic introduction of new facts and concepts. Rotely learned materials, on the other hand, are discrete and relatively isolated entities which are only relatable to cognitive structure in an arbitrary, verbatim fashion, not permitting the establishment of the above-mentioned relationships. Second, because they are not anchored to existing ideational systems, rotely learned materials (unless greatly overlearned or endowed with unusual vividness) are much more vulnerable to forgetting, i.e., have a much shorter retention span.

These differences between rote and meaningful learning categories have important implications for the underlying kinds of learning and retention processes involved in each category. Rotely learned materials are essentially isolated from existing conceptual systems within cognitive structure, and hence are primarily influenced by the interfering effects of *similar* rote materials learned *immediately* before or after the learning task. Thus it is not unreasonable to explain the learning and retention of discrete rote units in such stimulus-response terms as intra-task and inter-task similarity, response competition, and stimulus or response generalization. With regard to meaningful learning and retention, however, it seems reasonable to suppose that learning materials are primarily influenced by the attributes of relevant and cumulatively established ideational systems in cognitive structure with which they interact. Compared to this type of extended interaction, concurrent interfering effects have relatively little influence and explanatory value.

THE SUBSUMPTION PROCESS IN LEARNING AND FORGETTING[5,6]

This brings us to a consideration of the mechanisms of accretion and long-term retention of large bodies of ideational material. Why do high-school and university students, for example, tend to forget so readily previous day-to-day learnings as they are exposed to new lessons? Extrapolating from studies of short-term rote learning in animal and human subjects, the traditional answer of educational psychology has usually been that subsequent learning experiences, which are similar to but not identical with previously learned materials, exert a retroactively inhibitory effect on the retention of the latter. But would it not be more credible to postulate that all of the existing, cumulatively established ideational systems, which an individual brings with him to any learning situation, has more of an interfering effect on the retention of new learning material (proactive inhibition) than brief exposure to subsequently introduced materials of a similar nature (retroactive inhibition)?

The model of cognitive organization proposed for the learning and retention of meaningful materials assumes the existence of a cognitive structure that is hierarchically organized in terms of highly inclusive conceptual traces* under which are subsumed traces of less inclusive subconcepts as well as traces of specific informational data. The major organizational principle, in other words,

---

*The term "trace" is used here simply as a hypothetical construct to account for the continuing representation of past experience in the nervous system and in present cognitive structure. No assumptions are made regarding the neurophysiological basis of the trace or regarding psychophysiological correlations.

is that of progressive differentiation of trace systems of a given sphere of knowledge from regions of greater to lesser inclusiveness, each linked to the next higher step in the hierarchy through a process of subsumption. It is incorrect, however, to conceive of this mode of organization as deductive in nature. The inductive-deductive issue is only relevant in considering the method of acquiring or presenting generalizations and supportive data, and the sequential procedure adopted in problem-solving. Irrespective of how they are acquired in the first place (inductively or deductively), new materials are incorporated into total cognitive organization in accordance with the same principle of progressive differentiation.

Meaningful reception learning occurs as potentially meaningful material enters the cognitive field and interacts with and is appropriately subsumed under a relevant and more inclusive conceptual system. The very fact that such material is subsumable in nonarbitrary, nonverbatim fashion (i.e., relatable to stable elements in cognitive structure) accounts for its potential meaningfulness and makes possible the establishment of meaningful relationships or the emergence of actual meaning. If it were not subsumable it would constitute rote material and form discrete and relatively isolated traces. Hence, it is postulated that both the learning and retention of potentially meaningful material are primarily influenced by the attributes of the particular concepts in cognitive structure with which they interact and by the nature of the interactional process. Existing congnitive structure, in other words, is the major factor affecting meaningful learning and retention.

The initial effects of subsumption, therefore, may be described as facilitation of both learning and retention. Only orienting, relational, and cataloguing operations are involved at first. These preliminary operations are obviously essential for meaningful learning and retention, since the hierarchical incorporation of new material into existing cognitive structure is both the basis for the emergence of all meaning, and must also necessarily conform to the prevailing principle of cognitive organization. Furthermore, subsumption of the traces of the learning task by an established ideational system provides anchorage for the new material, and thus constitutes the most orderly, efficient and stable way of retaining it for future availability. Hence, for a variable period of time, the recently catalogued subconcepts and informational data can be dissociated from their subsuming concepts and are reproducible as individually identifiable entities.

Although the stability of meaningful material is initially enhanced by anchorage to relevant conceptual foci in the learner's cognitive structure, such material is gradually subjected to the erosive influence of the conceptualizing trend in cognitive organization. Because it is more economical and less burdensome to retain a single inclusive concept than to remember a large number of more specific items, the import of the latter tends to be incorporated by the generalized meaning of the former. When this second or obliterative stage of subsumption begins, the specific items become progressively less dissociable as entities in their own right until they are no longer available and are said to be forgotten. Forgetting is thus a continuation or later temporal phase of the same interactional process underlying the availability established during learning; and the same subsumability that is necessary for meaningful reception learning somewhat paradoxically provides the basis for later forgetting.

This process of memorial reduction to the least common denominator capable of representing cumulative prior experience is very similar to the reduction process characterizing concept formation. A single abstract concept is more manipulable for cognitive purposes than the dozen diverse instances from which its commonality is abstracted; and similarly, the memorial residue of ideational experience is also more functional for future learning and problem-solving occasions when stripped of its tangential modifiers, particularized connotations, and less clear and discriminable implications. Hence, barring repetition or some other special reason (*e.g.*, primacy, uniqueness, enhanced discriminability, or the availability of a specially relevant and stable subsumer) for the perpetuation of dissociability, specific items of meaningful experience that are supportive of or correlative to an established conceptual entity tend gradually to undergo obliterative subsumption. In contrast to the behavioristic theory of memory (which only accounts satisfactorily for rote forgetting), it is held that the forgetting of meaningful material is attributable to obliterative subsumption under more inclusive and established concepts rather than to response competition or to stimulus or response generalization.

Unfortunately, however, the advantages of obliterative subsumption are gained at the price of losing the differentiated body of detailed propositions and specific information that constitute the flesh if not the skeleton of any body of knowledge. The main problem of acquiring a firm grasp of any academic discipline, therefore, is counteracting this inevitable process of obliterative subsumption that characterizes all meaningful learning. The traditional pedagogic approach used in attempting to realize this objective has been repetition or overlearning. The approach advocated in this volume, on the other hand, relies more on efficacious manipulation of existing cognitive structure in ways that maximize the learning and retention of new, potentially meaningful verbal material.

COGNITIVE STRUCTURE VARIABLES

Existing cognitive structure—an individual's organization, stability, and clarity of knowledge in a particular subject-matter field at any given time—is regarded as the major factor influencing the learning and retention of meaningful new material in this same field. The properties of cognitive structure determine both the validity and clarity of the meanings that emerge as new material enters the cognitive field, as well as the nature of the interactional process that takes place. If cognitive structure is stable, clear, and suitably organized, valid and unambiguous meanings emerge and tend to retain their individuality or dissociability. If, on the other hand, cognitive structure is unstable, ambiguous, disorganized or chaotically organized, it tends to inhibit learning and retention; but even under the best of circumstances—through the process of obliterative subsumption—it contributes to and helps account for the ordinary forgetting of knowledge. Hence it is only by strengthening relevant aspects of cognitive structure in ways that retard the rate of this obliterative process that new learning and retention can be facilitated. When we deliberately attempt to influence cognitive structure so as to maximize meaningful learning and retention we come to the heart of the educative process.

In my opinion, the most significant advances that have occurred in recent years in the teaching of such subjects as mathematics, chemistry, physics, and biology have been predicated on the assumption that efficient learning and functional retention of ideas and information are largely dependent upon the adequacy of cognitive structure, *i.e.*, upon the adequacy of an individual's existing organization, stability and clarity of knowledge in a particular subject-matter field. The acquisition of adequate cognitive structure, in turn, has been shown to depend upon both substantive and programmatic factors: (a) using for organizational and integrative purposes those substantive concepts and principles in a given discipline that have the widest explanatory power, inclusiveness, generalizability, and relatability to the subject-matter content of that discipline; and (b) employing those programmatic methods of presenting and ordering the sequence of subject matter that best enhance the clarity, stability, and, integratedness of cognitive structure for purposes of new learning and problem-solving.

Cognitive Structure and Transfer

In meaningful learning, cognitive structure is always a relevant and crucial variable, even if it is not deliberately influenced or manipulated so as to ascertain its effect on new learning. It is always at least a "silent partner" when other variables (*e.g.*, practice, materials, methods) act—as, for example, in those short-term learning situations where just a single unit of material is learned and transfer to new learning units is not measured. In these circumstances, however, its influence is indeterminable; we can only ascertain the effect of those variables that are manipulated or are otherwise measurable.

In the more general and long-term sense, cognitive structure variables refer to significant organizational properties of the learner's *total* knowledge in a given subject matter field and their influence on his future academic performance in the same area of knowledge. In the more specific and short-term sense, cognitive structure variables refer to the organizational properties of just the *immediately* (or proximately) relevant concepts within a particular subject matter field and their effects on the learning and retention of *small units* of related subject matter. In either sense, however, the learner's acquisition of a clear, stable, and organized body of knowledge constitutes *more* than just the major long-term objective of classroom learning activity, or the principal *dependent* variable (or criterion) to be used in evaluating the impact of all factors and conditions impinging on learning and retention. Cognitive structure is *also*, in its own right, the most significant *independent variable* influencing (facilitating, inhibiting, limiting) the learner's capacity for acquiring more *new* knowledge in the same field.

The importance of cognitive structure variables has been generally underestimated in the past because preoccupation with noncognitive, rote, and motor types of learning has tended to focus attention on such current situational and intrapersonal factors as practice, drive, incentive, and reinforcement variables. It is true that the influence of prior experience on current learning tasks is conventionally considered under the heading of positive and negative transfer (or proactive facilitation and inhibition); but such transfer is generally interpreted in terms of the *direct* interaction between the stimulus and response attributes of the two overlapping but essentially discrete learning tasks (*i.e.*, the recently experienced and the current).

Much more saliently than in laboratory types of learning situations, school learning requires the incorporation of new concepts and information into an existing and established cognitive framework with particular organizational properties. The transfer paradigm still applies here, and transfer still refers to the impact of prior experience upon current learning. But prior experience in this case is conceptualized as a cumulatively acquired, hierarchically organized, and established body of knowledge which is organically relatable to the new learning task, rather than as a recently experienced constellation of stimulus-response connections influencing the learning of another discrete set of such connections. Furthermore, the relevant aspects of past experience in this type of transfer paradigm are such organizational properties of the learner's subject-matter knowledge as clarity, stability, generalizability, inclusiveness, cohesiveness, and discriminability (*i.e.*, cognitive structure variables)— *not* degree of similarity between stimuli and responses in the two learning tasks; and recent prior experience is not regarded as influencing current learning by interacting *directly* with the stimulus-response components of the new learning task, but only insofar as it modifies significant relevant attributes of cognitive structure. Cognitive structure variables, in other words, are the principal factors involved in meaningful transfer, and transfer itself is largely a reflection of the influence of these variables.

Because training and criterion tasks in laboratory studies of transfer have usually been separate and discrete, we have tended to think in terms of how prior task A influences performance on criterion task B. If performance has been facilitated, in comparison with that of a control group which had not been exposed to task A, we say that positive transfer has occurred. Actually, however, in typical classroom learning situations, A and B are not discrete but continuous. A is a preparatory stage of B and a precursive aspect of the same learning process; B is not learned discretely but in relation to A. Hence in school learning we deal not so much with transfer in the literal sense of the term, as with the influence of prior knowledge on new learning in a continuous, sequential context.

Another confusing residue from laboratory studies is the fact that transfer of training has been traditionally tested by problem-solving rather than by new reception learning and retention. Actually, the principal effect of existing cognitive structure on new cognitive performance is on the learning and retention of new presented materials where potential meanings are given— not on the solution of problems requiring the application and reorganization of cognitive structure to new ends. Thus a transfer situation exists whenever existing cognitive structure influences new cognitive functioning, irrespective of whether it is in regard to reception learning or problem-solving.

Principal Variables Influencing Meaningful Reception Learning

One important variable affecting the incorporability of new meaningful material is the *availability in cognitive organization of relevant subsuming concepts at an appropriate level of inclusiveness* to provide optimal anchorage. The appropriate level of inclusiveness may be defined as that level which is as proximate as possible to the degree of conceptualization of the learning task— considered, of course, in relation to the existing degree of differentiation of the subject as a whole in the learner's cognitive background. Thus, the more unfamiliar the learning task, *i.e.*, the more undifferentiated the learner's background of relevant concepts, the more inclusive or highly generalized the subsuming concepts must be in order to be proximate. If appropriately relevant and proximate subsumers are not present, the learner tends to utilize the most relevant and proximate ones that are available.

Since it is highly unlikely that at any given stage in the learner's differentiation of a particular sphere of knowledge we can depend on the spontaneous availability of the most relevant and proximate subsuming concepts, the most efficient way of facilitating retention is to introduce appropriate subsumers and make them part of cognitive structure prior to the actual presentation of the learning task. The introduced subsumers thus become advance "organizers" or anchoring foci for the reception of new material. In effect they provide an introductory overview at the appropriate level of conceptualization.

A second important factor presumably affecting the retention of a potentially meaningful learning task is the extent to which it is *discriminable* from the established conceptual systems that subsume it. A reasonable assumption here, borne out by preliminary investigation,[6] would be that if the distinguishing features of the new learning material were not originally salient and clearly discriminable from stable subsuming foci, they could be adequately represented by the latter for memorial purposes, and would not persist as dissociable entities identifiable in their own right. In other words, only discriminable categorical variants of more inclusive concepts would have long-term retention value. The discriminability of new materials could be enhanced by repetition or by explicitly pointing out similarities and differences between them and their presumed subsumers in cognitive structure.

Lastly, the longevity of new meaningful material in memory has been shown to be a function of the stability and clarity of its subsumers.[6] Ambiguous and unstable subsumers not only provide weak anchorage for related new materials, but also cannot easily be discriminated from them. Factors probably influencing the clarity and stability of subsuming concepts include repetition, their relative age, the use of exemplars, and multi-contextual exposure.

The strategy advocated in this treatise for deliberately manipulating cognitive structure so as to enhance proactive facilitation or minimize proactive inhibition involves the use of introductory materials (*i.e.*, organizers) prior to the presentation of the actual learning task. These advance organizers consist of introductory material at a higher level of abstraction, generality, and inclusiveness than the learning task itself. The function of the organizer is to provide ideational scaffolding for the stable incorporation and retention of the more detailed and differentiated material that follows in the learning passage, as well as to increase discriminability between the latter and related, interfering concepts in cognitive structure.

READINESS

By readiness is meant the adequacy of existing cognitive equipment or capacity at a given age level for coping with the demands of a specified cognitive task. It can therefore be considered the developmental aspect of cognitive structure. Empirically, readiness is indicated by ability to profit from practice or learning experience. An individual manifests readiness when the outcomes of his learning activity, in terms of increased knowledge or academic achievement, are reasonably commensurate with the amount of effort and practice employed.

Readiness is a function of both general cognitive maturity and of more particularized learning experience. General cognitive maturity largely reflects age-level differences in intellectual status or stage of intellectual development. It also reflects, of course, individual differences in genic potentiality, incidental experience, and intellectual stimulation. The readiness attributable to particularized learning experience, on the other hand, reflects the learner's specific educational history, i.e., his particular cognitive background.

Thus, under general developmental readiness we would consider age-level changes in ability to cope with different kinds and levels of subject-matter that are reflective of progressive developmental changes in cognitive sophistication. Relevant aspects of cognitive sophistication that influence learning, retention, and thinking processes, and hence influence developmental readiness for different kinds and levels of subject matter, include, for example, the following: increased widening and complexity of the cognitive field; increased familiarity of the psychological world; greater differentiation of cognitive structure; greater precision and specificity of meanings; greater ability to comprehend and manipulate abstractions and relationships between abstractions— without recent or current reference to concrete, empirical experience; greater ability to deal with general propositions apart from particularized contexts; decreased subjectivity in approach to experience; increased attention span; increased differentiation of intellectual ability. Some of these changes in cognitive sophistication (e.g., increased differentiation of cognitive content, structure, and intellectual ability; greater precision and specificity of meanings) have self-evident implications for general developmental readiness insofar as it bears on the breadth-depth issue in curriculum.

Under particularized readiness we would consider the extent to which knowledge of one type or component of subject matter influences readiness for another type or component of subject matter.

Pedagogic Applications

By virtue of his distinctive degree of cognitive sophistication at every age level, the child has a characteristic way of approaching learning material and "viewing the world."[11] The pedagogic problem in readiness is to manipulate the learning situation in such a way that one takes account and optimal advantage of existing cognitive capacities and modes of assimilating ideas and information, as for example, the learner's objectivity-subjectivity, his level of generality or particularity, and the abstractness and precision of his conceptualization. "The task of teaching a subject to a child at any particular age is one of representing the structure of that subject in terms of the child's way of viewing things. The task can be thought of as one of translation."[11]

The objection has been offered that we can have no *direct* knowledge of an individual's cognitive structure and state of readiness, and that we would therefore be better advised to ignore these factors and manipulate other learning variables about which we have more direct knowledge and over which we have more direct control, e.g., situational and interpersonal variables, reinforcement, attributes and organization of the learning task, and the conditions of practice. All of these factors can be manipulated independently of any reference to the existing cognitive structure and capacities of the learner. But although it is true that we can have no direct knowledge of and control over these latter factors, we should not be unduly discouraged. We can make some fairly shrewd and accurate inferences about existing cognitive structure and readiness from detailed knowledge of the learner's educational background and from the use of diagnostic testing procedures. Furthermore, we can exercise some control over the readiness factor by providing special preparatory learning experiences at the desired level of sophistication.

Much more pertinent in terms of pedagogic applications is the serious dearth of research in the cognitive aspects of readiness. We desperately need studies indicating that certain kinds, components, and levels of subject matter which cannot be learned efficiently at one age level can be learned efficiently at another age level; studies showing that learning in a given subject-matter area is more efficient if preceded by a particular kind of other subject matter; studies which by taking general or particularized readiness factors into account achieve thereby superior learning and achievement; and studies showing that more difficult kinds and levels of subject matter—ordinarily not learnable at younger ages—can be learned successfully if appropriate changes in teaching method are made. Until the principle of readiness is particularized in each academic discipline with respect to the various subareas, levels of difficulty, and methods of teaching that can be most advantageously employed at each level of development, the principle will have little pedagogic utility.

The Nature of Readiness

There is little disagreement about the fact that readiness always crucially influences the efficiency of the learning process and often determines whether a given intellectual skill or type of school material is learnable at all at a particular stage of development. Most educators also implicitly accept the proposition that an age of readiness exists for every kind of learning. Postponement of learning experience beyond this age of readiness wastes valuable and often unsuspected learning opportunities, thereby unnecessarily reducing the amount and complexity of subject-matter content that can be mastered in a designated period of schooling. On the other hand, when a pupil is prematurely exposed to a learning task before he is ready for it, he not only fails to learn the task in question but also learns from the experience of failure, to fear, dislike and avoid it.

Up to this point, the principle of readiness—the idea that attained capacity limits and influences an individual's ability to profit from current experience or practice—is empirically demonstrable and conceptually unambiguous. Difficulty first arises when it is confused with the concept of *maturation*, and when the latter concept in turn is equated with a process of "internal ripening." The concept of readiness simply refers to the adequacy of existing capacity in relation to the demands of a given learning task. No specification is made to *how* this capacity is achieved—whether through prior practice of a specific nature (learning), through incidental experience, through genically regulated structural and functional changes occurring independently of enviromental influences, or through various combinations of these factors. Maturation, on the other hand, has a different and much more restricted meaning. It encompasses those increments in capacity that take place in the demonstrable absence of specific practice experience, *i.e.*, that are attributable to genic influences and/or incidental experience. Maturation, therefore, is not the same as readiness but is merely one of the two principal factors (the other being learning) that contributes to or determines the organism's readiness to cope with new experience. Whether or not readiness exists, in other words, does not necessarily depend on maturation alone but in many instances is solely a function of prior learning experience and most typically depends on varying proportions of maturation and learning.

To equate the principles of readiness and maturation not only muddies the conceptual waters, but also makes it difficult for the school to appreciate that insufficient readiness may reflect inadequate prior learning on the part of pupils because of inappropriate or inefficient instructional methods. Lack of maturation can thus become a conveniently available scapegoat whenever children manifest insufficient readiness to learn; and the school, which is thereby automatically absolved of all responsibility in the matter, consequently fails to subject its instructional practices to the degree of self-critical scrutiny necessary for continued educational progress. In short, while it is important to appreciate that the current readiness of pupils determines the school's current choice of instructional methods and materials, it is equally important to bear in mind that this readiness itself is partly determined by the appropriateness and efficiency of the previous instructional practices to which they have been subjected.

The conceptual confusion is further compounded when maturation is interpreted as a process of "internal ripening" essentially independent of *all* environmental influences, that is, of both specific practice and incidental experience. Readiness then becomes a matter of simple genic regulation unfolding in accordance with a predetermined and immutable time-table; and the school, by definition, becomes powerless to influence readiness either through its particular way of arranging specific learning experiences or through a more general program of providing incidental or nonspecific background experience preparatory to the introduction of more formal academic activities.

Actually, the embryological model of development implicit in the "internal ripening" thesis fits quite well when applied to human sensorimotor and neuromuscular sequences taking place during the prenatal period and early infancy. In the acquisition of simple behavioral functions (*e.g.*, locomotion, prehension) that more or less uniformly characterize all members of the human species irrespective of cultural or other environmental differences, it is reasonable to suppose that for all practical purposes genic factors alone determine the direction of development. Environmental factors only enter the picture if they are extremely deviant, and then serve more to disrupt or arrest the ongoing course of development than to generate distinctive developmental progressions of their own. Thus, the only truly objectionable aspect of this point of view is its unwarranted extrapolation to those more complex and variable components of later cognitive and behavioral development where unique factors of individual experience and cultural environment make important contributions to the direction, patterning, and sequential order of all developmental changes.

It is hardly surprising, therefore, in view of the tremendous influence on professional and lay opinion wielded by Gesell and his colleagues, that many people conceive of readiness in absolute and immutable terms, and thus fail to appreciate that except for such traits as walking and grasping, the mean age of readiness can never be specified apart from relevant environmental conditions. Although the modal child in contemporary America may first be ready to read at the age of six and one-half, the age of reading readiness is always influenced by cultural, subcultural, and individual differences in background experience, and in any case varies with the method of instruction employed and the child's IQ. Middle-class children, for example, are ready to read at an earlier age than lower-class children because of the greater availability of books in the home, and because they are "read to" and "taken places" more frequently.

REFERENCES

1. Ausubel, D. P. The use of advance organizers in the learning and retention of meaningful verbal material. *J. educ. Psychol.* 1960, *51*:267–72.

2. Ausubel, D. P. In defense of verbal learning. *Educ. Theory*, 1961, *11*:15–25.

3. Ausubel, D. P. A subsumption theory of meaningful learning and retention. *J. gen. Psychol.*, 1962, 66:213–24.

4. Ausubel, D. P. A transfer of the training approach to improving the functional retention of medical knowledge. *J. med. Educ.*, 1962, 37:647–55.

5. Ausubel, D. P., Robbins, Lillian C., and Blake, E. Retroactive inhibition and facilitation in the learning of school materials. *J. educ. Psychol.*, 1957, *48*: 334–43.

6. Ausubel, D. P., and Blake, E. Proactive inhibition in the forgetting of meaningful school material. *J. educ. Res.*, 1958, 52:145–49.

7. Ausubel, D. P., and Fitzgerald, D. Meaningful learning and retention: interpersonal cognitive variables. *Rev. educ. Res.*, 1961, *31*:500–10.

8. Ausubel, D. P., and Fitzgerald, D. The role of discriminability in meaningful verbal learning and retention. *J. educ. Psychol.*, 1961, 52:266–74.

9. Brownell, W. A., and Hendrickson, G. How children learn information, concepts, and generalizations. In *Learning and Instruction. Yearb. Nat. Soc. Stud. Educ.*, 1950, 49:Part I. pp. 92–128.

10. Brownell, W. A., and Sims, V. M. The nature of understanding. In *The Measurement of Understanding. Yearb. Nat. Soc. Stud. Educ.*, 1946, 45:Part I. pp. 27–43.

11. Bruner, J. S. *The Process of Education.* Cambridge, Mass.: Harvard University Press, 1960.

12. Inhelder, Bärbel, and Piaget, J. *The Growth of Logical Thinking from Childhood to Adolescence.* New York: Basic Books, 1958.

CHAPTER 3.

Meaningful Learning and Meaning

THE ESSENTIAL FEATURE OF meaningful learning is that it embodies a distinctive kind of learning process in which the learner employs a "set" to incorporate within his cognitive structure, in nonarbitrary, nonverbatim fashion, potentially meaningful materials which are subsumable by established entities within that structure. The outcome of this process, *i.e.*, the attainment of meaning, is a purely idiosyncratic psychological phenomenon in a particular person; it depends upon the subsumability of potentially meaningful material within his particular cognitive structure. Discovery is never a precondition for the emergence of meaning, but the availability of concrete-empirical props is often a limiting condition in the case of young or unsophisticated learners. Individuals also differ in their need for meaning generally and in their need for precise and integrated meanings. They differ, furthermore, with respect to their tendencies to be more or less self-critical in judging the adequacy of the meanings they acquire.

It is important to appreciate that meaningful learning is not synonymous with the learning of meaningful material. Meaningful material, in fact, cannot be meaningfullly *learned* because the accomplishment of the object of learning, namely, the attainment of meaning is already implied in the statement that the material is meaningful. Individual components of the learning task (*e.g.*, the separate words of a new proposition) can be meaningful in meaningful learning, but the learning task itself (in this case, the proposition per se) can never be more than *potentially* meaningful.* One can refer more legitimately to the *rote* learning of meaningful material because under these circumstances the attainment of new meaning is not the object of learning. The learning task in this instance is simply to learn arbitrary, verbatim associations between the meaningful components or to learn them in serial order.

It is not always easy to demonstrate that meaningful learning has occurred. Independent problem-solving is sometimes the only feasible way of testing whether students *really* comprehend meaningfully the ideas they are able to

---

*The fact that meaningful components do not constitute the object of learning or a criterion of potential meaningfulness does not mean that they have no influence whatsoever on the current learning task. It is much easier, for example, to learn arbitrary (rote) sequential associations between a series of meaningful words or relatively "meaningful" nonsense syllables than between a series of relatively "meaningless" nonsense syllables.[20] It is also obvious that before one can learn the meaning of a geometrical theorem, one must first know the meanings of its component words. The only point that is being made here is that nonarbitrary relatability of the *actual learning task* to cognitive structure rather than the presence of meaningful components is the determining factor in deciding whether learning material is or is not potentially meaningful.

verbalize. But here we have to be careful not to fall into a trap. To say that problem-solving is a valid, practical method of measuring the meaningful understanding of ideas, is *not* the same as saying that the learner who is unable to solve a representative set of problems, *necessarily* does not understand, but has merely memorized the principles exemplified by these problems. Successful problem-solving demands many *other* abilities and qualities, such as reasoning power, perseverance, flexibility, improvisation, sensitivity, and tactical astuteness, *in addition to* meaningful comprehension of the underlying principles. Hence, failure to solve the problems in question may reflect deficiencies in these latter factors rather than lack of genuine understanding. Another feasible method of testing the occurrence of meaningful learning that does not involve this latter difficulty of interpretation is to present the learner with a new learning passage that presupposes understanding of the prior learning task.

CONCEPTS OF MEANING

"Meaning," as used in this volume, is a relational concept, a phenomenological outcome of a meaningful learning process in which the potential meaning inherent in the external world becomes converted into an individualized psychological state or content of consciousness. From a behavioristic standpoint the basic assumption of such a view, *i.e.*, that meaning is always referable to a mental content (rather then to a "behavioral disposition" or to some mediational "replica of behavior"), is mentalistic and therefore objectionable;[34] but we feel that a psychological theory has no need to be apologetic about assuming the existence of differentiated states of consciousness. Meaning, therefore, in our view, always implies some form of representational equivalence between language (or symbols) and mental content. At the simplest level a symbol acquires meaning when it is able to evoke the same concrete image as the object which it signifies, or when it can evoke the same abstract or ideational content as another symbol with which it is synonymous. Categorical or conceptual symbols are similarly equivalent in a representational sense to the abstracted mental content of the particular images or ideas which their generality encompasses. At the level of relationships between ideas, stated propositions with potential meaning manifest actual meaning because they correspond to the ideational state of affairs that exists when their substantive import is subsumed in a relational sense by established and more inclusive ideas in cognitive structure.

Thus the essence of a representational symbol (or of symbolical meaning) implies more than the ability of a symbol to evoke the same response from an individual that the signified object does. Simply by virtue of contiguity, a symbol (conditioned stimulus) that is frequently and concomitantly presented with the adequate (unconditioned) stimulus acquires the same power to evoke the response as the original unconditioned stimulus. Similarly, by making use of the principles of contiguity, frequency and reinforcement, it is possible to train an animal or an infant to emit a verbal symbol in response to an appropriate stimulus or situation. In neither case, however, do we have an example of true representational symbolism: no reference or equivalence to actual ideational content exists. In the first instance, also, the symbol does not really represent something which it itself is not. It itself has simply become an adequate stimulus in its own right; it is reacted to as if it itself *were* the original stimulus rather than a sign designating the latter, and produces a reasonable or approximate facsimile of the original response. In the second instance, the verbal response also does not represent the stimulus or situation to which it refers; it is merely evoked by the stimulus.

A symbol therefore acquires representational properties only when it evokes an image or other ideational content in the reacting subject that is *cognitively equivalent* to that evoked by the designated object or situation itself. Mere adequacy as a stimulus or appropriateness as a response does not guarantee that a verbal cue or utterance has meaning as a symbol to the *reacting* individual, even though, in a strictly logical or mathematical sense, it *functions* effectively as a symbol, *i.e.*, as a sign that from the standpoint of the *observer* has the same behavioral effect as the stimulus it designates.

"Meaningfulness" in Studies of Rote Learning

The concept of meaning presented above differs markedly from the classical concept of meaningfulness evolved by investigators of rote learning. This latter concept is typically defined in terms of the percentage of subjects who are able to produce an association to a given nonsense syllable° within a limited period of time,[14] or in terms of the total number of different associations evoked by a particular verbal stimulus.[28] Actually these definitions of meaningfulness are derived from explanations of why materials characterized by this property are learned with greater facility than are materials not so characterized.°°

Thus Underwood[43,44] marshalls evidence to show that the meaningfulness of verbal units, and hence the facility with which they are learned, is a function of the relative frequency of their occurrence in the English language, and presumably in the learner's past experience. Increased frequency, he states, accounts for the greater availability of verbal responses; and availability, in turn, is a precondition for or the first stage of verbal associative learning. Noble[29] similarly demonstrated that frequency of presentation of verbal items varies directly with their familiarity and rate of learning;°°° he also found a high correlation between the familiarity of these syllables, as rated by subjects, and their meaningfulness as previously determined by the criterion of associative productivity. Other empirically supported explanations of the facilitating influence of meaningfulness on rote associative learning include the availability of other existing associations with stimulus and response members of a paired associate, which can mediate the learning of the new associa-

---

°A particular nonsense syllable as a whole may be more or less meaningful apart from its component letters in so far as it resembles and hence evokes associations with actual words. This is a type of derived meaning based on linguistic similarity.

°°A definition of meaningfulness in terms of the same factors that facilitate the learning of verbal units is obviously open to the charge of circularity: material is meaningful because it is learned more easily, and it is learned more easily because it is meaningful.

°°°Familiar items are already available and hence need not first be learned themselves before they can be associated with other items.

tion;[23] the transferability of existing verbal sequences[25] and grammatical habits;[33] and increased discriminability of meaningful stimuli by virtue of their prior association with implicit distinctive responses.[36]

Epstein, Rock, and Zuckerman[11] have shown that the effect of meaningfulness in learning is not reducible to familiarity, *i.e.*, that meaning is a significant independent factor. They found that lists of nouns were learned more readily than were lists of equally familiar conjunctions, and that lists of conjunctions were not learned more readily than were lists of prefamiliarized nonsense syllables. Meaningfulness, according to these investigators, only characterizes words "for which lexical meanings can be readily elicited when they are presented by themselves. . . . It enables the subject to go beyond what is learned," and thus enhances learning "because it makes possible organization or conceptual unit formation." Both this concept of meaning, and Newman's hypothesis that meaning inheres in the connectedness and structure of organization of the material to be learned,[26] are somewhat analogous to our view that potential meaning and subsumability in cognitive structure are necessary for phenomenological meaning.

All three latter views would regard such factors as the familiarity of a verbal unit, the frequency with which it is encountered, and the number of associations it evokes as correlates of the *degree* of meaningfulness rather than as the distinguishing characteristics of meaningfulness per se. The strength of the association between a representational symbol and the object or concept to which it refers, (and hence the availability of the symbol and its degree of meaningfulness), are functions of the frequency and variety of contexts in which the symbol is used or encountered. A highly meaningful symbol, therefore, tends both to be subjectively more familiar and to evoke more associations than a less meaningful symbol—but this is not the reason why it is meaningful in the first place.

Mediational Concepts of Meaning

One step removed from the simple contiguity or substitution concept of meaning discussed above is the mediational or modified behavioristic (S-R) concept of meaning developed by Osgood.[34] Osgood links "sign and significate° through partial identity of the [behavioral] disposition itself with the behavior produced by the significate. Thus, according to this view, words represent things because they produce in human organisms some replica of the actual behavior toward these things as a mediation process" (34, p. 7) A symbol associated with an object comes to mean (be a sign of) that object by virtue of giving rise to and becoming associated with a representational mediation process that is originally reflective of a fractional anticipatory response to the object itself. A sign's meaning, therefore, is essentially the representational mediation process it evokes, which is partially equivalent to the reactions evoked by the significate. Stated more formally, "a pattern of

---

°In Osgood's terminology a "significate" is roughly equivalent to an *object, i.e.,* "any pattern of stimulation which evokes reactions on the part of an organism"; and a "sign" is "any pattern of stimulation which is not [the significate] and yet evokes reactions relevant to [it]" (32, p. 691).

stimulation which is not the significate is a sign of that significate if it evokes in the organism a mediating process, this process (a) being some fractional part of the total behavior elicited by the significate and (b) producing responses which would not occur without the previous contiguity of non-significate and significate patterns of stimulation" (34, p. 7).

Basically, however, in terms of general theoretical orientation, this theory is not much different than the simple substitution theory. The meaning of a symbol still depends on the contiguity of sign and significate, and is still derived from the similarity between the mediating process and the response to the significate itself. In Osgood's system a sign has meaning (*i.e.*, represents its significate) only if it evokes a mediational process that is partially equivalent to the original significate-induced response. Osgood, however, expressly denies identity or equivalence between the sign-produced and the significate-produced reactions. In this latter sense the mediational hypothesis is obviously an advance over the simple substitution theory.

More important, however, is the fact that in the effort to avoid the supposed objectionability of a "mentalistic" approach, the mediational concept repudiates cognitive phenomenology and identifies meaning with an implicit behavioral response or disposition. But the evocation of relevant *implicit* responses is no more indicative of the existence of actual cognitive meaning than is the evocation of relevant explicit responses. Quite apart from the fact that simply by virtue of contiguity with the significate, signs may evoke behavioral dispositions without giving rise to any cognitive content° whatsoever, the kind of behavior instigated by a given sign is only *one* manifestation of what it means to the individual, and is not necessarily a criterion of its actual meaning. The behavior in question also has many other determinants in addition to the sign that apparently evokes it. Hence the same sign can elicit quite different responses or behavioral tendencies, and the same responses can be elicited by quite different signs.

Osgood attempts to measure meaning by means of a method called "semantic differentiation." This method requires the subject to rate a given concept along a limited number of bipolar adjectival scales which purport to be "representative of the major ways in which meanings vary." The meaning of the concept to the individual is thus mapped, so to speak, in semantic space with respect to three major dimensions—evaluation, potency, and activity.

A basic assumption, common both to the concept of meaning as a representational mediation process and to the method of measurement employed, is that "the meanings which different individuals have for the same signs will vary to the extent that their behaviors to the things signified have varied. This is because the composition of the representational process—which is the mean-

---

°This process of S-R conditioning should not be confused with the contiguity involved in forming a word-object association or establishing simple representational equivalence between a sign and the mental content evoked by its significate. In everyday situations this is illustrated by preschool children's acquisition of names for objects and by the learning of foreign-language vocabulary. Experimentally, a given nonsense syllable can be endowed with meaning by pairing it repetitively with a word or even with pairs of words possessing a common meaning.[37]

ing of the sign—is entirely dependent upon the nature of the total behavior occurring while the sign is being established" (34, p. 9). It is at this point that the theoretical disadvantages of the mediational concept of meaning become most evident, since a behavioristic theory is committed to including all of the behavioral, attitudinal, and affective reactions to a sign as part of its meaning while ignoring for the most part its phenomenological cognitive equivalent. Hence it can be argued that the semantic differential does not identify meaning in the cognitive sense but merely the attitudinal and affective connotations of this content. These connotations influence and are correlated with the cognitive meaning but are not really part of it. The actual meaning of "dog," for example, is the same for two persons who have the same cognitive concept of dog, even if the first individual cherishes dogs and the second despises them. Granted that these two attitudes reflect the respective past experiences of the two individuals and influence their respective behaviors toward the animal; but the actual *meaning* of "dog" only includes those cognitive representations of the distinctive attributes of dogs that distinguish them from cats, wolves, horses, and other animals.

This is not to deny the possibility that under certain circumstances attitudinal and affective elements may become part of conceptual content. For example, in three different cultures where dogs are respectively sacred, abhorrent, and regarded as vital to the economy, it is conceivable that the associated relevant attitudes and feelings may become incorporated into conceptual meaning. Under these circumstances, however, they actually constitute distinctive, defining attributes of the concept rather than correlated attitudes. But this somewhat extreme cross-cultural eventuality is hardly the typical situation in which the semantic differential is used.

LOGICAL AND PSYCHOLOGICAL MEANING

We have already distinguished between the potential meaning inherent in the statement of certain propositions, on the one hand, and actual, phenomenological meaning, which is the product of a meaningful learning process, on the other. Potential meaning becomes converted into actual meaning when a particular individual, employing a meaningful learning set, incorporates a potentially meaningful proposition within his cognitive structure. The distinction between logical and psychological meaning corresponds in essence to the distinction between potential and phenomenological meaning, but requires more explicit delineation.

The Concept of Logical Meaning

Logical meaning refers to the meaning inherent in potentially meaningful material. It implies that the learning material per se consists of possible and nonarbitrary relationships that *could* be nonarbitrarily incorporated on a nonverbatim basis by a hypothetical human cognitive structure that had the necessary ideational background and degree of readiness. This criterion of logical meaning applies primarily to the attributes of the material itself. If it (the material) possesses the characteristics of nonarbitrariness, lucidity and plausibility, then it is, by definition, also relatable to the aforementioned hypothetical cognitive structure. Obviously excluded, therefore, from the domain of logical meaning is the vast majority of the almost infinite number of possible relationships between concepts that can be formulated on the basis of purely random pairings. This does not mean that all propositions with logical meaning are necessarily valid or even logically correct. The questions of substantive and logical validity are issues that simply do not enter into a determination of logical meaning. Propositions based on unvalidated premises or on faulty logic may conceivably abound in logical or potential meaning.

Although nonmaterial, logical meaning is also part of the real world. It exists irrespective of whether or not it ever becomes transformed into psychological meaning—in the same sense that objects and events exist independently of whether they are perceived, or that the logical validity of a proposition is not dependent on the existence of a human mind to appreciate or test it.

Arbitrariness, of course, is a relative term. On the grounds of both the verbatim character of the learning task and the relative arbitrariness of the latter's relatability to cognitive structure, the learning of simple representational equivalents may be considered the least complex type of meaningful learning. It is intermediate in process between rote learning and the more complex types of meaningful learning.

Simple representational learning as, for example, the association of new words with concrete images, abstract concepts, or already meaningful symbols in cognitive structure, is relatively arbitrary in the sense that there is no plausible, logically cogent (nonarbitrary) reason why most verbal symbols are chosen to represent the particular objects or concepts to which they refer. Verbatim reproducibility is also essential if representational symbols are to function effectively as meaningful surrogates of the "real thing," in as much as only a very slight change (e.g., a single letter of a word) may drastically change or even reverse the meaning. On both counts, therefore, the learning of such symbols is the kind of meaningful learning most analogous to rote learning. Nevertheless, the incorporation of simple representational equivalents within cognitive structure is a much less arbitrary learning task than, for example, the incorporation of a randomly arranged sequence of nonsense syllables or paired adjectives and, in any case, meets the minimal criterion of meaningful learning. The type of cognitive process involved in simple representational learning is basic to the acquisition of language and accounts for the learning of all units of meaning in any system of symbols. In fact it is only by combining such unitary representational meanings in various ways that it is possible to produce less arbitrary relational propositions possessing greater potential meaningfulness.

Much school learning that is customarily referred to as rote learning (and which under certain circumstances could be purely rote) is really by design a form of simple representational learning, e.g., various aspects of the learning of multiplication and addition facts. Some rote learning may be involved as a means of maximizing speed of response and calculation, but in most modern schools the multiplication table, for example, is learned in relation to an existing background of meaningful number relationships. This type of learning is hardly comparable to the rote learning of paired associates since the learning task—the relation of number pairs to their product—has a meaningful referent in cognitive structure. In a sense the process is comparable to an actor's verbatim memorization of his lines after he acquires a meaningful grasp of their substance. Thus, in addition to purely rote and purely meaningful learning sets, learners may also have a set to learn both the substance of material in a meaningful way as well as its verbatim content.

In rote learning itself, the material involved may vary considerably in degree of arbitrariness—from material that under no circumstances is relatable to cognitive structure to material that is potentially meaningful, but cannot be meaningfully learned by the individual concerned, either because he lacks the necessary ideational background or because he does not employ a meaningful learning set. Between these two extremes are materials which have meaningful components, but are unrelatable to cognitive structure as learning tasks in their own right because of the inherent arbitrariness of the relationships between the components. In decreasing order of arbitrariness these include nonsense syllables of low association value, nonsense syllables of high association value, and paired adjectives.

Psychological Meaning

It is nonarbitrary subsumability of logically meaningful propositions within a *particular* cognitive structure that creates the possibility of transforming logical into psychological meaning. Hence, when an individual learns such propositions, he does not learn their logical meaning but the meaning they have for him, *i.e.,* what they signify to him. Psychological meaning is always an idiosyncratic phenomenon. The idiosyncratic nature of psychological meaning, however, does not rule out the possibility of social or shared meanings. The various individual meanings possessed by members of a given culture are ordinarily sufficiently similar to permit communication and interpersonal understanding. This intracultural homogeneity of shared meanings reflects both the same logical meaning inherent in potentially meaningful propositions and the interindividual commonality of ideational background.

It would be quite erroneous, however, to believe that an absolute or all-or-none difference in relatability to cognitive structure exists between rote and meaningful learning. Rote learning tasks are not mastered in a cognitive vacuum. They *are* related to and perceived against the learner's cognitive background. It is by virtue of this relatability, for example, that the meaningful structural components of nonsense syllables (letters) are perceived meaningfully, and that these syllables (considered as wholes) evoke meaningful associations (on the basis of linguistic similarity), and hence acquire some "secondary" or derived meaning. In both instances meaningfulness facilitates rote learning by enhancing the familiarity of the material, by obviating the need for prior learning of the component elements themselves, and by making possible the combination of these elements into larger meaningful units, thereby reducing the total number of discrete associations to be established. Relatability to cognitive structure also makes rote learning tasks vulnerable to concurrent interference from similar cognitive elements emanating from within the individual, as well as to comparable interference of environmental origin.

It would be more precise, therefore, to state that rote learning tasks *are* relatable to cognitive structure, but *only* in an arbitrary, verbatim fashion which does not permit the incorporation of derivative, elaborative, supportive, correlative or qualifying relationships within a relevant system of hierarchically organized ideas and information. It is primarily, with respect to these specific aspects of relatability to cognitive structure (arbitrary and verbatim versus nonarbitrary and substantive), rather than with respect to whether such relatability is or is not possible, that rote and meaningful learning differ; and it is these particular but fundamental differences in relatability which, in turn, necessitate the characteristic process differences underlying these two kinds of learning.

MEANINGFUL VERSUS ROTE LEARNING PROCESSES

Meaningfully and rotely learned materials are learned and retained in qualitatively different ways because meaningful learning tasks are, by definition, relatable and anchorable to relevant and more inclusive concepts in cognitive structure. Hence learning and retention outcomes in the case of meaningful learning are primarily influenced by those attributes of cognitive structure which influence the anchorage and dissociability of the new learning materials. Since rotely learned materials, on the other hand, do not interact with cognitive structure in a substantive, organic fashion, they are learned and retained in conformity with the laws of association, and are primarily influenced by the interfering effects of concurrently acting, similar rote materials.

Meaningful Learning Processes

Substantive and nonarbitrary incorporation of a learning task into relevant portions of cognitive structure, so that a meaningful relationship is established, implies that the learning material becomes an organic part of a particular, hierarchically organized conceptual system. It becomes imbedded within the latter system in a *relational* sense, that is, independently both of the verbatim integrity of the material and of specific, arbitrary connections within the material. This type of relatability to and incorporability by cognitive structure has two principal consequences for learning and retention processes. First, the newly learned material acquires anchorage to a stable conceptual system and is no longer dependent for its continued memorial existence on the rather frail human capacity for mantaining intact, arbitrary, and verbatim intra-material associations as discrete and isolated entities in their own right. As a result the temporal span of retention is greatly extended.

Second, the newly learned material becomes subject to the organizational principles governing the learning and retention of the system in which it is incorporated. To begin with, the very act of incorporation requires appropriate placement within a hierarchically organized system of knowledge, a system characterized by progressive differentiation of content on the basis of ideational inclusiveness, each part linked to the next higher (more inclusive) step in the organizational hierarchy through a process of subsumption. Later, after incorporation occurs, the new material initially retains its substantive identity, by virtue of being dissociable from its subsuming concept, and then gradually loses its identifiability as it becomes reduced to and undissociable from its subsumers.

In this type of learning-retention process, the formation and strengthening of arbitrary associative bonds between discrete, verbatim elements, isolated in an organizational sense from established conceptual systems, plays little if any role. The important mechanisms involved in this process are: (a) achievement of appropriate relational anchorage within a relevant and appropriately inclusive conceptual system; and (b) retention of the identifiability (dissociability) of the newly learned material. Such retention involves resistance to the progressively increasing inroads of obliterative subsumption or loss of dissociability characterizing the organization and long-term memorial integrity of cognitive systems (i.e., the tendency for the original interactional complex or organizational unit of subsuming concept and recently subsumed learning material to be reduced to a least common denominator, namely, to a slightly modified version of the subsumer itself). Significant variables influencing these mechanisms include the availability in cognitive structure of relevant and appropriate subsuming concepts, the stability of the latter concepts, and the extent to which they are discriminable from the learning material.

Rote Learning Processes

It has already been pointed out that rote learning tasks *are* relatable to cognitive structure, and that it is by virtue of this relatability (a) that already meaningful components of these tasks are perceived as such and thereby facilitate rote learning, and (b) that concurrent interference with rote learning arises from within cognitive structure. However, the extreme arbitrariness of the learning task's relatability to conceptual systems within cognitive structure, as well as the necessity for verbatim internalization and reproducibility, preclude the relational and substantive type of incorporation described above for meaningful learning, and make for a basically different kind of learning-retention process. Rote learning tasks can only be incorporated into cognitive structure in the form of arbitrary, intramaterial associations, that is, as discrete, self-contained entities organizationally isolated, for all practical purposes, from the learner's established conceptual systems. The requirement that arbitrary intramaterial associations be constituted on a verbatim rather than substantive basis (since anything less than complete verbatim accuracy is valueless in the case of purely arbitrary associations), further enhances the discreteness and isolated nature of rotely incorporated entities.

One important implication of the discrete and isolated incorporation of rote learning tasks within cognitive structure is that, quite unlike the situation in meaningful learning, anchorage to established conceptual systems is not achieved concomitantly. Hence, since the human brain is not efficiently designed for long-term, verbatim storage of arbitrary, intra-material associations, retention span for rote learnings is relatively brief. The much steeper gradient of forgetting in the case of rote as compared to meaningful learning, requires that we examine the rote retention process and the factors that influence it within a highly abbreviated time span. Delay beyond this brief time span leaves us with nothing to study.

A second important implication of arbitrary, verbatim incorporation of learning material within cognitive structure is that *association* necessarily constitutes the basic learning-retention mechanism, and the laws of association constitute, by definition, the basic explanatory principles governing these processes. The major goals of learning and retention, therefore, are to increase and maintain associative strength—not to achieve appropriate anchorage and preserve dissociability potential. Such variables as contiguity, frequency, and reinforcement are accordingly crucial for learning; and retention is primarily influenced by concurrent interferences (of both internal and external origin), on the basis of intra- and intertask similarity, response competition, and stimulus and response generalization. Superficially, this kind of interference may seem to resemble the interactions described for meaningful learning. It has been shown, for example, that the more stable (i.e., overlearned) original rote learning is,[21] and the more discriminable it is from interpolated material,[24] the less susceptible it is to retroactive inhibition. Actually however, these latter interactions take place between discrete systems of associations rather than between hierarchically organized conceptual systems and the new propositions they subsume; and underlying the retention process is the maintenance of associative strength rather than the preservation of dissociability.

To the extent that the learning task in simple representational learning is arbitrary and verbatim, the formation of associative bonds is the underlying learning process. In instances where various inherently unconnected items must be arbitrarily joined together, association is obviously the learning mechanism par excellence. It is also true, however, that in so far as a representational symbol is incorporated within a conceptual system on a relational basis, it is subjected to the particular organizational pressures (e.g., hierarchical placement, initial dissociability, memorial reduction) influencing the acquisition and long-term integrity of any component aspects of a conceptual system. The learning and retention of representational symbols, therefore, is partly a function of associative strength, and partly a function of anchorage and dissociability.

WHY MEANINGFUL LEARNING PROCESSES YIELD SUPERIOR LEARNING OUTCOMES

Several lines of evidence point to the conclusion that meaningful learning and retention are more effective than their rote counterparts. First, Jones and English[17] demonstrated that it is much easier to learn the substance of potentially meaningful material than it is to memorize the same connected material in rote, verbatim fashion. Second, material which can be learned meaningfully (e.g., poetry, prose, and observations of pictorial matter) is learned much more rapidly than arbitrary series of digits or nonsense syllables.[14,20,35] The same difference holds true for gradations of meaningful learning: simple narrative material is learned more quickly and remembered better than are more complex philosophical ideas that are difficult to understand.[35] An increase in the length of the material to be learned also adds relatively less learning time to meaningful than to rote learning tasks.[5,20] A third type of experimental evidence consists of studies demonstrating that various problem-solving tasks (e.g., card tricks, match stick problems) are retained longer and are more transferable[15,18] when subjects learn underlying principles rather than rotely memorize solutions.

A related line of experimental evidence showing that "substance" items are learned[5] and retained[8,9,26] more effectively than are "verbatim" items is more inferential than direct. Presumably, although verbatim items can be learned meaningfully, they are more likely to be rotely memorized than are concepts and generalizations. In this connection an ingeniously designed study by Newman,[26] comparing retention during periods of sleep and waking, throws light on the relative retention spans and respective forgetting processes of rotely and meaningfully learned materials. Unessential details of a narrative were remembered much better after a period of sleep than after a period of normal daily activity, whereas there was no corresponding difference in the case of substance items. A warranted inference here is that *immediate* retroactive interference, which is obviously greater during daily activity than during sleep, is an important factor in rote memory but does not significantly affect the retention of meaningfully learned materials.

Many classroom studies support the findings of this last-mentioned experimental approach. In general they show that principles, generalizations and applications of principles studied in such courses as biology, chemistry, geometry, and physics are remembered much better over periods of months and even years than are more factual items such as symbols, formulas, and terminology.[10,12,41,42,45] A second type of classroom evidence demonstrates that knowledge of number facts (*i.e.*, addition, subtraction, multiplication) learned with understanding is retained more effectively and is more transferable than when learned in mechanical, rote fashion.[1,3,22,39,40]

Many different kinds of explanations have been offered for this superiority of meaningful over rote learning and retention. One explanation identifies meaningful learning with the learning of meaningful material, and advances all of the arguments referred to above in the discussion of rote learning of meaningful versus nonmeaningful material. (see pp. 36–37) Our definition of meaningful learning, however, implies that it is a characteristic *process* in which meaning is a *product* or outcome of learning rather than an attribute of the content of what is to be learned. It is this process rather than the meaningfulness of the content that characterizes meaningful learning. Gestalt theorists,[18,19] on the other hand, identify insight and the understanding of relationships with the establishment of stable "structural" traces which are contrasted, in turn, with the relatively "rigid" and unstable discrete traces established by rotely memorized materials. This explanation, however, really begs the question because it accounts for the superiority of meaningful learning processes simply by endowing the neural representation of these processes with superior potency. In effect then, it is claimed that meaningful learning processes yield superior learning outcomes because they give rise to more stable traces. This obviously adds little to our understanding because the real problem is to explain why such processes are associated with more stable traces.

In accounting for Katona's research findings that meaningfully learned solutions to problems are retained more effectively than rotely learned solutions, Osgood offers a typical neobehavioristic explanation.[32] He states that the understanding of relationships reduces the sheer volume of what has to be remembered by rendering the details of the learning task reconstructable from memory of the principle itself. It is undeniable, of course, that the burden on memory is substantially less if one need only remember the substance of a connected and potentially meaningful proposition than if one must remember the verbatim content of a series of discrete, arbitrarily related verbal items. This *is* undoubtedly *one* of the factors accounting for the superiority of meaningful over rote learning. A more important reason for the greater stability of meaningful learning, however, inheres in the nonarbitrary and substantive incorporability (anchorability, subsumability) of meaningfully learned material within relevant and more inclusive propositions in cognitive structure. Hence, not only is meaningful learning easier, more economical, and less burdensome than rote learning in terms of time and effort, but it is also more available for later functional use in new learning and problem-solving.

It should be noted, however, that although rote learning is more difficult than meaningful learning in most circumstances, it may actually be easier for the individual who lacks the necessary ideational background for a particular learning task. It also often appears easier to the anxiety-ridden person who lacks confidence in his ability to understand difficult and unfamiliar new propositions.

Meaningful versus Rote Retention

An important methodological and theoretical issue comes to the fore when, as in the previous section, the relative efficacy of meaningful and rote retention is compared. Does the superiority of meaningful over rote retention reflect an actual difference in the efficacy of the respective *retention* processes, or does this superiority merely reflect the greater effectiveness of meaningful *learning?* Obviously if material were learned better to begin with, more incorporated meanings would be available at any subsequent time when retention was tested, even if the retention processes themselves were equally efficacious. That this is the case with respect to the *rote* learning of materials varying in degree of meaningfulness is shown by research which demonstrates that when more and less meaningful materials are learned to the same criterion of mastery (by allowing a greater number of learning trials for the less meaningful material) they do not differ in retention outcomes.*

If, however, our theory regarding the existence of fundamental differences between rote and meaningful retention processes is correct, we would *not* expect that if rotely and meaningfully learned materials were mastered equally well, they would also be remembered with equal effectiveness. According to subsumption theory, (see p. 51) the same variables influencing the outcome of meaningful learning, and the same factors accounting for the superiority of meaningful over rote learning processes, continue to operate during the retention interval and to affect retention outcomes. Hence, even if rotely and meaningfully learned materials were learned to the same criterion of mastery, the superiority of the meaningful retention process would be reflected in higher retention scores. In other words, one would be unable to compensate sufficiently for basic weaknesses in rote retention span and process (by ex-

---

*L. Postman and Lucy Rau, "Retention as a Function of the Method of Measurement." *Univer. Calif. Publ. Psychol.*, 1957, 8:217–70. Dowling and Braun,[7] however, found a positive relationship between retention and degree of meaningfulness when retention was measured by the methods of aided or unaided recall. This latter relationship did not prevail when retention was measured by the reconstruction and relearning methods. B. J. Underwood and J. Richardson ("The Influence of Meaningfulness, Intralist Similarity and Serial Position in Retention," *J. exp. Psychol.*, 1956, 52:119–26), on the other hand, found that meaningfulness did not significantly enhance recall but did facilitate relearning.

pending greater time and effort on learning) so as to equal the efficiency of meaningful learning. Unfortunately, however, research evidence is not presently available to test the validity of this proposition. Comparative studies of rote and meaningful learning are needed that are comparable to the research described above on the rote learning and retention of materials varying in meaningfulness.

REFERENCES

1. Anderson, G. L. Quantitative thinking as developed under connectionist and field theories of learning. In *Learning Theory in School Situations,* University of Minnesota Studies in Education. Minneapolis: University of Minnesota Press, 1949, pp. 40–73.
2. Ausubel, D. P. *Theory and Problems of Child Development.* New York: Grune & Stratton, 1958.
3. Brownell, W. A., and Moser, H. E. Meaningful versus mechanical learning: A study in Grade III subtraction. *Duke Univer. Res. Stud. Educ.,* 1949, No. 8.
4. Cieutat, V. J., Stockwell, F. E., and Noble, C. E. The interaction of ability and amount of practice with stimulus and response meaningfulness. *J. exp. Psychol.,* 1958, 56:193–202.
5. Cofer, C. N. A comparison of logical and verbatim learning of prose passages of different length. *Amer. J. Psychol.,* 1941, 54:1–20.
6. Davis, F. C. The relative reliability of words and nonsense syllables. *J. exp. Psychol.,* 1930, 13:221–34.
7. Dowling, R. M., and Braun, H. W. Retention and meaningfulness of material. *J. exp. Psychol.,* 1957, 54:213–17.
8. Edwards, A. L., and English, H. B. The effect of the immediate test on verbatim and summary retention. *Amer. J. Psychol.,* 1939, 52:372–75.
9. English, H. B., Welborn, E. L., and Kilian, C. D. Studies in substance memorization. *J. gen. Psychol.,* 1934, 11:233–60.
10. Eikenberry, D. H. Permanence of high school learning. *J. educ. Psychol.,* 1923, 14:463–82.
11. Epstein, W., Rock, I., and Zuckerman, C. B. Meaning and familiarity in associative learning. *Psychol. Monog.,* 1960, 74:(whole No. 491).
12. Frutchey, F. P. Retention in high school chemistry. *J. Higher Educ.,* 1937, 8: 217–18.
13. Gilliland, A. R. The rate of forgetting. *J. educ. Psychol.,* 1948, 39:19–26.
14. Glaze, J. A. The association value of nonsense syllables. *J. genet. Psychol.,* 1928, 35:255–69.
15. Hilgard, E. R., Irvine, R. P., and Whipple, J. E. Rote memorization, understanding, and transfer: an extension of Katona's card trick experiments. *J. exp. Psychol.,* 1953, 46:288–92.
16. Hunt, R. G. Meaningfulness and articulation of stimulus and response in paired-associate learning and stimulus recall. *J. exp. Psychol.,* 1957, 57:262–67.
17. Jones, M. G., and English, H. B. Notional *vs.* rote memory. *Amer. J. Psychol.,* 1926, 37:602–603.
18. Katona, G. *Organizing and Memorizing.* New York: Columbia University Press, 1940.
19. Koffka, K. *Principles of Gestalt Psychology.* New York: Harcourt, Brace, 1935.

CHAPTER 4.

The Subsumption Process in Learning and Retention

TEMPORALLY, THREE DISTINCT PHASES may be distinguished during meaningful reception learning and retention. First, potentially meaningful material must be *perceived* before it can be learned and retained. In fact, it would be more correct to say that individuals learn the information they perceive rather than that they learn information as such. During the perceptual phase, attitudes, motivations, expectations, and cultural frames of reference influence learning and retention through such mechanisms as selective emphasis, omission, and distortion (see p. 66). The second phase is concerned with the learning-retention process per se. The perceived, potentially meaningful information is subsumed by a relevant and appropriately inclusive conceptual system, becomes psychologically meaningful and available, and then gradually undergoes loss of dissociability and possible obliterative subsumption. This latter process is largely cognitive and, except for drives and self-critical attitudes relating to the adequacy and intergratedness of meanings, is not organically influenced by attitudinal and motivational variables (see p. 21). The third and final stage involves the reproduction of the retained information. It depends not only on the residual degree of availability (dissociability strength) in relation to the threshold of availability, but also on motivational and attitudinal factors influencing both this threshold and the actual process of reconstructing or reformulating the retained meanings into a verbal statement. In this volume, and particularly in this chapter, we are primarily concerned with the second phase in this sequence or with the learning-retention process.

It is important, nevertheless, to bear in mind these various temporal phases of meaningful reception learning and retention in seeking to account for the various sources of error in memory, *i.e.*, for the different factors causing discrepancies between learning material and reproduced memories of this material. In the first place, the discrepancies may be reflective of perceptual distortion or selective perception. Second, vague, diffuse, ambiguous, or erroneous meanings may emerge from the very beginning of the learning process because of the unavailability of relevant, inclusive subsumers in cognitive structure, because of the instability or unclarity of these subsumers, or because of the lack of discriminability between the learning material and the subsumers. This unfavorable outcome is particularly likely if the learner's need for and self-critical attitude about acquiring adequate meanings is deficient. Lastly, motivational or other factors raising the threshold of availability may inhibit the recall of available meanings, or available meanings may be altered in the very process of reconstructing remembered meanings in accordance with the requirements of the current situation.

50

CHAPTER 4.

The Subsumption Process in Learning and Retention

TEMPORALLY, THREE DISTINCT PHASES may be distinguished during meaningful reception learning and retention. First, potentially meaningful material must be *perceived* before it can be learned and retained. In fact, it would be more correct to say that individuals learn the information they perceive rather than that they learn information as such. During the perceptual phase, attitudes, motivations, expectations, and cultural frames of reference influence learning and retention through such mechanisms as selective emphasis, omission, and distortion (see p. 66). The second phase is concerned with the learning-retention process per se. The perceived, potentially meaningful information is subsumed by a relevant and appropriately inclusive conceptual system, becomes psychologically meaningful and available, and then gradually undergoes loss of dissociability and possible obliterative subsumption. This latter process is largely cognitive and, except for drives and self-critical attitudes relating to the adequacy and intergratedness of meanings, is not organically influenced by attitudinal and motivational variables (see p. 21). The third and final stage involves the reproduction of the retained information. It depends not only on the residual degree of availability (dissociability strength) in relation to the threshold of availability, but also on motivational and attitudinal factors influencing both this threshold and the actual process of reconstructing or reformulating the retained meanings into a verbal statement. In this volume, and particularly in this chapter, we are primarily concerned with the second phase in this sequence or with the learning-retention process.

It is important, nevertheless, to bear in mind these various temporal phases of meaningful reception learning and retention in seeking to account for the various sources of error in memory, *i.e.*, for the different factors causing discrepancies between learning material and reproduced memories of this material. In the first place, the discrepancies may be reflective of perceptual distortion or selective perception. Second, vague, diffuse, ambiguous, or erroneous meanings may emerge from the very beginning of the learning process because of the unavailability of relevant, inclusive subsumers in cognitive structure, because of the instability or unclarity of these subsumers, or because of the lack of discriminability between the learning material and the subsumers. This unfavorable outcome is particularly likely if the learner's need for and self-critical attitude about acquiring adequate meanings is deficient. Lastly, motivational or other factors raising the threshold of availability may inhibit the recall of available meanings, or available meanings may be altered in the very process of reconstructing remembered meanings in accordance with the requirements of the current situation.

pending greater time and effort on learning) so as to equal the efficiency of meaningful learning. Unfortunately, however, research evidence is not presently available to test the validity of this proposition. Comparative studies of rote and meaningful learning are needed that are comparable to the research described above on the rote learning and retention of materials varying in meaningfulness.

REFERENCES

1. Anderson, G. L. Quantitative thinking as developed under connectionist and field theories of learning. In *Learning Theory in School Situations*, University of Minnesota Studies in Education. Minneapolis: University of Minnesota Press, 1949, pp. 40–73.

2. Ausubel, D. P. *Theory and Problems of Child Development.* New York: Grune & Stratton, 1958.

3. Brownell, W. A., and Moser, H. E. Meaningful versus mechanical learning: A study in Grade III subtraction. *Duke Univer. Res. Stud. Educ.,* 1949, No. 8.

4. Cieutat, V. J., Stockwell, F. E., and Noble, C. E. The interaction of ability and amount of practice with stimulus and response meaningfulness. *J. exp. Psychol.,* 1958, 56:193–202.

5. Cofer, C. N. A comparison of logical and verbatim learning of prose passages of different length. *Amer. J. Psychol.,* 1941, 54:1–20.

6. Davis, F. C. The relative reliability of words and nonsense syllables. *J. exp. Psychol.,* 1930, 13:221–34.

7. Dowling, R. M., and Braun, H. W. Retention and meaningfulness of material. *J. exp. Psychol.,* 1957, 54:213–17.

8. Edwards, A. L., and English, H. B. The effect of the immediate test on verbatim and summary retention. *Amer. J. Psychol.,* 1939, 52:372–75.

9. English, H. B., Welborn, E. L., and Kilian, C. D. Studies in substance memorization. *J. gen. Psychol.,* 1934, 11:233–60.

10. Eikenberry, D. H. Permanence of high school learning. *J. educ. Psychol.,* 1923, 14:463–82.

11. Epstein, W., Rock, I., and Zuckerman, C. B. Meaning and familiarity in associative learning. *Psychol. Monog.,* 1960, 74:(whole No. 491).

12. Frutchey, F. P. Retention in high school chemistry. *J. Higher Educ.,* 1937, 8:217–18.

13. Gilliland, A. R. The rate of forgetting. *J. educ. Psychol.,* 1948, 39:19–26.

14. Glaze, J. A. The association value of nonsense syllables. *J. genet. Psychol.,* 1928, 35:255–69.

15. Hilgard, E. R., Irvine, R. P., and Whipple, J. E. Rote memorization, understanding, and transfer: an extension of Katona's card trick experiments. *J. exp. Psychol.,* 1953, 46:288–92.

16. Hunt, R. G. Meaningfulness and articulation of stimulus and response in paired-associate learning and stimulus recall. *J. exp. Psychol.,* 1957, 57:262–67.

17. Jones, M. G., and English, H. B. Notional *vs.* rote memory. *Amer. J. Psychol.,* 1926, 37:602–603.

18. Katona, G. *Organizing and Memorizing.* New York: Columbia University Press, 1940.

19. Koffka, K. *Principles of Gestalt Psychology.* New York: Harcourt, Brace, 1935.

pending greater time and effort on learning) so as to equal the efficiency of meaningful learning. Unfortunately, however, research evidence is not presently available to test the validity of this proposition. Comparative studies of rote and meaningful learning are needed that are comparable to the research described above on the rote learning and retention of materials varying in meaningfulness.

REFERENCES

1. Anderson, G. L. Quantitative thinking as developed under connectionist and field theories of learning. In *Learning Theory in School Situations,* University of Minnesota Studies in Education. Minneapolis: University of Minnesota Press, 1949, pp. 40–73.
2. Ausubel, D. P. *Theory and Problems of Child Development.* New York: Grune & Stratton, 1958.
3. Brownell, W. A., and Moser, H. E. Meaningful versus mechanical learning: A study in Grade III subtraction. *Duke Univer. Res. Stud. Educ.,* 1949, No. 8.
4. Cieutat, V. J., Stockwell, F. E., and Noble, C. E. The interaction of ability and amount of practice with stimulus and response meaningfulness. *J. exp. Psychol.,* 1958, 56:193–202.
5. Cofer, C. N. A comparison of logical and verbatim learning of prose passages of different length. *Amer. J. Psychol.,* 1941, 54:1–20.
6. Davis, F. C. The relative reliability of words and nonsense syllables. *J. exp. Psychol.,* 1930, 13:221–34.
7. Dowling, R. M., and Braun, H. W. Retention and meaningfulness of material. *J. exp. Psychol.,* 1957, 54:213–17.
8. Edwards, A. L., and English, H. B. The effect of the immediate test on verbatim and summary retention. *Amer. J. Psychol.,* 1939, 52:372–75.
9. English, H. B., Welborn, E. L., and Kilian, C. D. Studies in substance memorization. *J. gen. Psychol.,* 1934, 11:233–60.
10. Eikenberry, D. H. Permanence of high school learning. *J. educ. Psychol.,* 1923, 14:463–82.
11. Epstein, W., Rock, I., and Zuckerman, C. B. Meaning and familiarity in associative learning. *Psychol. Monog.,* 1960, 74:(whole No. 491).
12. Frutchey, F. P. Retention in high school chemistry. *J. Higher Educ.,* 1937, 8: 217–18.
13. Gilliland, A. R. The rate of forgetting. *J. educ. Psychol.,* 1948, 39:19–26.
14. Glaze, J. A. The association value of nonsense syllables. *J. genet. Psychol.,* 1928, 35:255–69.
15. Hilgard, E. R., Irvine, R. P., and Whipple, J. E. Rote memorization, understanding, and transfer: an extension of Katona's card trick experiments. *J. exp. Psychol.,* 1953, 46:288–92.
16. Hunt, R. G. Meaningfulness and articulation of stimulus and response in paired-associate learning and stimulus recall. *J. exp. Psychol.,* 1957, 57:262–67.
17. Jones, M. G., and English, H. B. Notional *vs.* rote memory. *Amer. J. Psychol.,* 1926, 37:602–603.
18. Katona, G. *Organizing and Memorizing.* New York: Columbia University Press, 1940.
19. Koffka, K. *Principles of Gestalt Psychology.* New York: Harcourt, Brace, 1935.

20. Lyon, D. O. The relation of length of material to time taken for learning and the optimum distribution of time. *J. educ. Psychol.*, 1914, 5:1–9, 85–91, 155–63.

21. McGeoch, J. A. The influence of degree of learning upon retroactive inhibition. *Amer. J. Psychol.*, 1929, 41:252–62.

22. McConnell, T. R. Discovery *vs.* authoritative identification in the learning of children. *Univer. Ia. Stud. Educ.*, 1934, 9:No. 5.

23. Mandler, G., and Huttenlocher, J. The relationship between associative frequency, associative ability, and paired-associate learning. *Amer. J. Psychol.*, 1956, 69:424–28.

24. Melton, A. W., and Irwin, J. McQ. The influence of degree of interpolated learning on retroactive inhibition and the overt transfer of specific responses. *Amer. J. Psychol.*, 1940, 53:175–203.

25. Miller, G. A., and Selfridge, J. A. Verbal context and the recall of meaningful material. *Amer. J. Psychol.*, 1950, 63:176–85.

26. Newman, E. B. Forgetting of meaningful material during sleep and waking. *Amer. J. Psychol.*, 1939, 52:65–71.

27. Noble, C. E. An analysis of meaning. *Psychol. Rev.*, 1952, 59:421–30.

28. Noble, C. E. The role of stimulus meaning (*m*) in serial verbal learning. *J. exp. Psychol.*, 1952, 43:437–46.

29. Noble, C. E. The meaning-familiarity relationship. *Psychol. Rev.*, 1953, 60:89–98.

30. Noble, C. E. The familiarity-frequency relationship. *J. exp. Psychol.*, 1954, 47:13–16.

31. Noble, C. E. The effect of familiarization upon serial verbal learning. *J. exp. Psychol.*, 1955, 49:333–38.

32. Osgood, C. E. *Method and Theory in Experimental Psychology*. New York: Oxford University Press, 1953.

33. Osgood, C. E. A behavioristic analysis of perception and language as cognitive phenomena. In *Contemporary Approaches to Cognition*. Cambridge, Mass.: Harvard University Press, 1957.

34. Osgood, C. E., Suci, G. J., and Tannenbaum, P. H. *The Measurement of Meaning*. Urbana, Ill.: University of Illinois Press, 1957.

35. Reed, H. B. Meaning as a factor in learning. *J. educ. Psychol.*, 1938, 29:419–30.

36. Sheffield, F. D. The role of meaningfulness of stimulus and response in verbal learning. Unpublished doctoral dissertation, Yale University, 1946.

37. Staats, C .K., and Staats, A. W. Meaning established by classical conditioning. *J. exp. Psychol.*, 1957, 54:74–80.

38. Stroud, J. B. Experiments on learning in school situations. *Psychol. Bull.*, 1940, 37:777–807.

39. Swenson, E. J. Organization and generalization as factors in learning, transfer, and retroactive inhibition. In *Learning Theory in School Situations*, University of Minnesota Studies in Education. Minneapolis: University of Minnesota Press, 1949, pp. 9–39.

40. Thiele, C. L. *The Contribution of Generalization to the Learning of the Addition Facts.* Contributions to Education, No. 763. New York: Bureau of Publications, Teachers College, Columbia University, 1938.

41. Tyler, R. W. What high school pupils forget. *Educ. Res. Bull.*, 1930, 9:490–97.

42. Tyler, R. W. Some findings from studies in the field of college biology. *Science Educ.*, 1934, *18*:133–42.
43. Underwood, B. J. Verbal learning in the educative processes. *Harvard educ. Rev.*, 1959, *29*:107–17.
44. Underwood, B. J., and Schulz, R. W. *Meaningfulness and Verbal Learning.* Chicago: Lippincott, 1960.
45. Ward, A. H., and Davis, R. A. Individual differences in retention of general science subject matter in the case of three measurable objectives. *J. exp. Educ.*, 1938, *7*:24–30.
46. Welborn, E. L., and English, H. Logical learning and retention: a general review of experiments with meaningful verbal material. *Psychol. Bull.*, 1937, *34*:1–20.

CHAPTER 4.

The Subsumption Process in Learning and Retention

TEMPORALLY, THREE DISTINCT PHASES may be distinguished during meaningful reception learning and retention. First, potentially meaningful material must be *perceived* before it can be learned and retained. In fact, it would be more correct to say that individuals learn the information they perceive rather than that they learn information as such. During the perceptual phase, attitudes, motivations, expectations, and cultural frames of reference influence learning and retention through such mechanisms as selective emphasis, omission, and distortion (see p. 66). The second phase is concerned with the learning-retention process per se. The perceived, potentially meaningful information is subsumed by a relevant and appropriately inclusive conceptual system, becomes psychologically meaningful and available, and then gradually undergoes loss of dissociability and possible obliterative subsumption. This latter process is largely cognitive and, except for drives and self-critical attitudes relating to the adequacy and intergratedness of meanings, is not organically influenced by attitudinal and motivational variables (see p. 21). The third and final stage involves the reproduction of the retained information. It depends not only on the residual degree of availability (dissociability strength) in relation to the threshold of availability, but also on motivational and attitudinal factors influencing both this threshold and the actual process of reconstructing or reformulating the retained meanings into a verbal statement. In this volume, and particularly in this chapter, we are primarily concerned with the second phase in this sequence or with the learning-retention process.

It is important, nevertheless, to bear in mind these various temporal phases of meaningful reception learning and retention in seeking to account for the various sources of error in memory, *i.e.*, for the different factors causing discrepancies between learning material and reproduced memories of this material. In the first place, the discrepancies may be reflective of perceptual distortion or selective perception. Second, vague, diffuse, ambiguous, or erroneous meanings may emerge from the very beginning of the learning process because of the unavailability of relevant, inclusive subsumers in cognitive structure, because of the instability or unclarity of these subsumers, or because of the lack of discriminability between the learning material and the subsumers. This unfavorable outcome is particularly likely if the learner's need for and self-critical attitude about acquiring adequate meanings is deficient. Lastly, motivational or other factors raising the threshold of availability may inhibit the recall of available meanings, or available meanings may be altered in the very process of reconstructing remembered meanings in accordance with the requirements of the current situation.

50

LEARNING VERSUS RETENTION

In reception (as contrasted to discovery) learning, the distinctive attribute of both learning and retention is a change in the availability or future reproducibility of the meanings derived from the perceived and subsumed learning material. Learning refers to the process of *acquiring meanings* from the potential meanings presented in the learning material, and of *making them more available*. It represents an increment in the availability of new meanings, *i.e.*, the situation that prevails when they emerge or are first established, or when their dissociability strength is increased by repetition or by conditions increasing discriminability. Retention, on the other hand, refers to the process of *maintaining the availability* of a replica of the acquired new meanings. Thus forgetting represents a decrement in availability, *i.e.*, the situation that prevails between the establishment of a meaning and its reproduction, or between two exposures to the learning material. Retention, therefore, is largely a later temporal phase and diminished aspect of the same phenomenon or functional capacity (the availability of internalized material) involved in learning itself. Later availability is always at least in part a function of initial availability. In the absence of intervening practice, therefore, delayed retention cannot possibly surpass immediate retention. The common phenomenon of reminiscence (the superiority of delayed over immediate retention) reflects the lowering of temporarily elevated thresholds of availability at a later testing of retention[3] *i.e.*, the subsequent release (disinhibition) of transitory inhibitory conditions (*e.g.*, repression; initial confusion after presentation of new material) operative immediately after learning.

·The relationship between *meaningful* learning and forgetting is even closer than that already indicated for reception learning generally. Meaningful retention is not only a later attenuated manifestation of the same availability function established during learning, but is also a later temporal phase of the *same interactional process* underlying this availability. During the learning phase, new ideational material forms an interactional product with a subsuming concept in cognitive structure, and depending on various factors (see below), has a given degree of dissociability therefrom. Continued interaction results in a gradual decrease in the dissociability of the new material (*i.e.*, in forgetting) until the interactional product is reduced to a least common denominator capable of representing the entire complex, namely, to the subsuming concept itself. The same cognitive factors* determining the original degree of dissociability at the time of learning (initial interaction) also determine the rate at which dissociability is subsequently lost during retention (later interaction). In rote learning, on the other hand, the same kind of cognitive interaction does *not* take place. Hence, rote learning represents an increment in availability (associative strength) involving one discrete cognitive process and set of variables, and rote forgetting represents a loss in this availability due to interference from *another* discrete process (and group of variables) set in motion shortly before or after learning.

---

*Some variables, however, (*e.g.*, such motivational variables as drive, reward and intention) may influence learning without influencing retention.[9]

Two reasons, therefore, probably account for the superiority of meaningful over rote retention outcomes. First, since meaningful learning is more effective because of the advantages inherent in substantive and nonarbitrary subsumability, a greater quantity of material is incorporated and made available for later retention. Second, over and above the retention difference attributable to superior learning, this same subsumability advantage further enhances the efficiency of the process whereby acquired meanings are retained. Similarly, within the domain of meaningful learning itself, we would expect these same two sources of retention superiority to be operative whenever a significant cognitive variable influences the learning-retention process. In other words, if experimental and control groups are used, the control group should not only learn less material than the experimental group, but should also forget what it learns at a more rapid rate. This state of affairs, however, can only be demonstrated if both immediate and delayed retention scores are available for both groups, and if the retention difference between the two groups increases from the first to the second testing.*

Depending on the method used to measure meaningful retention, one may obtain either quantitative or qualitative indices of the subsumption process operative during the retention interval. If one merely counts the number of concepts or propositions in a learning passage that the learner can recognize or identify correctly, one ascertains what portion of the learned material maintains sufficient dissociability strength to exceed the threshold of availability. If, on the other hand, one examines the *kind* of recognition errors that are committed, one also obtains a picture of the direction of memorial changes induced by the subsumption process. These changes include both the end-products of obliterative subsumption as well as various intermediate stages reflective of different degrees of dissociability strength. They must, of course, be differentiated from changes reflective of perceptual distortion and selective reconstruction.

The distinction between learning and forgetting is obviously much greater in discovery than in reception learning. In the former instance, repeated encounters with the learning task give rise to successive stages in an autonomous problem-solving process, whereas in the latter instance this same repetition (apart from some possible changes in degree and precision of meaning) primarily increases the future availability of the material. Thus the forgetting aspect of discovery learning hardly constitutes just a later continued phase of an original learning process that merely required the learner to internalize

---

*Immediate tests of meaningful retention may provide a misleading index of the actual availability of newly learned meanings. For a short time after initial learning, retention scores may be spuriously inflated by the availability of rotely learned elements with a brief retention span. This effect, however, may be counterbalanced by the temporary elevation of the threshold of availability immediately after learning, which would naturally tend to lower retention scores. But since both of these factors influence both experimental and control groups, they tend to have a leveling effect on any difference in immediate retention scores attributable to the influence of the experimental variable. Relatively small differences in immediate retention scores between experimental and control groups may therefore be spurious, and thus complicate the interpretation of findings in such studies.

and make presented material more available. It therefore has little in common with most of the first stage of learning in which meaning must first be discovered by problem-solving before it can be made available.

DERIVATIVE AND CORRELATIVE SUBSUMPTION

It is important to distinguish between two basically different kinds of subsumption that occur in the course of meaningful learning and retention. *Derivative* subsumption takes place when the learning material constitutes a specific example of an established concept in cognitive structure, or is supportive or illustrative of a previously learned general proposition. In either case the new material to be learned is directly and self-evidently derivable from or implicit in an already established and more inclusive concept or proposition in cognitive structure. Under these circumstances the meaning of the derivative material emerges quickly and effortlessly, and unless greatly overlearned tends to undergo obliterative subsumption very rapidly. The reason for the rapid obliterative subsumption is simply that the meaning of the new material can be very adequately represented by the more general and inclusive meaning of the established subsumer, and that this process of memorial representation is more efficient and less burdensome than the actual retention of supportive or illustrative data. If such data are needed they can be synthesized or reconstructed by appropriately manipulating specific elements of past and present experience so that they exemplify the desired concept or proposition. For example, in recounting a long past incident, one ordinarily retains only the substance of the experience and from this reconstructs or invents plausible details that are consistent with its general import and setting.

More typically, however, new subject matter is learned by a process of *correlative* subsumption. The new learning material in this case is an extension, elaboration, or qualification of previously learned propositions. It is incorporated by and interacts with relevant and more inclusive subsumers in cognitive structure, but its meaning is not implicit in and cannot be adequately represented by these latter subsumers. Nevertheless, in the interests of economy of cognitive organization and of reducing the burden of memory, the same trend toward obliterative subsumption occurs. This trend is particularly evident if the subsumers are unstable, unclear, or insufficiently relevant, and if the learning material is lacking in discriminability or is not overlearned. But in this instance the consequences of obliterative subsumption are not as innocuous as in the case of derivative subsumption. When correlative propositions lose their identifiability and can no longer be dissociated from their subsumers, a genuine loss of knowledge occurs. The subsumers cannot adequately represent the meaning of the propositions in question, and hence the availability of the subsumers in memory does not make possible a reconstruction of the substance of the forgotten material.

The problem of acquiring a body of knowledge, therefore, is largely concerned with counteracting the trend toward obliterative subsumption in retaining correlative materials. Bruner's exclusive emphasis on "generic learning" or acquiring "generic coding systems" as a means of facilitating school learning[16,17,18] is unrealistic because it focuses on derivative aspects of sub-

sumption which are atypical both of the subsumption process in general and
of most instances of assimilating new subject matter. It is true, as he asserts,
that most specific content aspects of subject matter can be forgotten with
impunity as long as they are derivable or can be reconstructed when needed
from those generic concepts or formulae which are worth remembering. But
the analogous forgetting of correlative content results in a loss of knowledge
that cannot be regenerated from residual generic concepts. The conceptualizing trend in memorial reduction (*i.e.*, obliterative subsumption), which is
functional or at the very worst innocuous in the case of derivative material,
constitutes the principal difficulty in acquiring a body of knowledge in the
more typical context of learning correlative propositions. Hence the problem
of meaningful learning and retention cannot ordinarily be solved by incorporating "a representation of the criterial characteristics of [a] situation, [or] a
contentless depiction of the ideal case,"[18] and then ignoring the loss of
specific content that occurs. The main purpose of learning generic concepts
and propositions is not so much to make possible the reconstruction of forgotten derivative instances as to provide stable anchorage for correlative
material; and it is the inhibition of the rate of obliterative subsumption in
relation to this material that is the major problem confronting teachers in
transmitting subject matter.

SUBSUMPTION OF ABSTRACT AND FACTUAL MATERIALS

The extent to which learning material is either abstract or factual in nature
has an important bearing on its longevity or on the rate at which obliterative
subsumption takes place. Comparison of the relative retention spans of substance and verbatim items (see p. 44) invariably shows that the longevity of
different components of the learning material, all other factors being equal,
varies directly with degree of abstractness. The principal distinction between
abstract and factual items, of course, is in terms of level of particularity or
proximity to concrete-empirical experience. Typically, however, abstract
material is also characterized by greater connectedness or less discreteness
than is factual material.

All factual material, furthermore, is not of one piece. Some factual material
can be learned meaningfully, whereas other factual data cannot be related to
cognitive structure in nonarbitrary, nonverbatim fashion, and hence must be
rotely learned; but even if factual matter is potentially meaningful, it is more
likely to be rotely learned than is abstract material because it is more difficult
to subsume under existing conceptual systems in cognitive structure. The
previously made distinction between derivative and correlative subsumption
is also important in accounting for the relative susceptibility to obliterative
subsumption of different kinds of potentially meaningful factual material.
Derivative facts undergo obliterative subsumption more rapidly, because, unlike correlative matter, their meaning can be adequately represented by the
conceptual systems that subsume them, thereby making possible a degree of
factual reconstruction that is satisfactory enough for most purposes of communication.

The greater longevity of abstract than of factual material can undoubtedly
be accounted for, in part, in terms of the superiority of meaningful over rote

learning and retention. Other credible explanations are that abstractions tend more often than factual material to be correlative rather than derivative in nature, and that they can often be incorporated in cognitive structure as suborganizers. Hence, because they are much less close than factual matter to the end-point of obliterative subsumption, they can be retained for longer periods of time.

SUBSUMPTION AND INDUCTIVE VERSUS DEDUCTIVE APPROACHES TO LEARNING

At first glance one might suppose that subsumption, in accordance with the principle of progressive differentiation, conforms to a deductive approach to cognitive organization and functioning. Actually, however, this supposition is only correct with respect to the relatively rare instances of derivative subsumption. Correlative materials quite obviously do not bear a deductive relationship to their subsumers in cognitive structure. Hence simply because subsumption is not an inductive process, we cannot consider it to be necessarily deductive in nature.

It is also true that irrespective of whether new propositions are acquired inductively or deductively, their incorporation in cognitive structure still follows the principle of progressive differentiation. At all age levels and at all levels of cognitive sophistication, new propositions—even when acquired inductively—are invariably subsumed under more inclusive, established conceptual systems in cognitive structure. Moreover, it is questionable whether a pure inductive approach ever exists as such in problem-solving. Human beings rarely start out *de novo* in approaching new problems. They either employ explicit explanatory principles (hypotheses) and try to fit the data to these hypotheses, or at the very least are implicitly guided from the outset by a set of general assumptions derived from past experience. In this sense, therefore, inductive problem-solving itself may be considered a subsidiary phase within a generally deductive approach.

COGNITIVE ORGANIZATION IN ELEMENTARY-SCHOOL CHILDREN

Does the same hierarchical organization of knowledge based on the principle of progressive differentiation hold true for elementary-school children as well as for adolescents and adults, despite the fact that such children are dependent on concrete-empirical experience in learning unfamiliar new abstractions and relationships between abstractions? It would appear that an affirmative answer to this question is warranted. Even though the initial emergence of abstract meanings must be preceded by an adequate background of concrete-empirical experience, once satisfactorily established, abstract concepts and propositions enjoy a very stable existence. They not only do not have to be reinforced by reference to concrete, particular experience in order to maintain their meaning, but they also serve as subsumers at or near the apex of hierarchical cognitive structure. Thus the cognitive organization of children differs mainly from that of adults in containing fewer abstract concepts, fewer higher-order abstractions, and more intuitive-nonverbal rather than abstract-verbal understandings of many propositions (see pp. 116–119). Children's learning of new verbal material can therefore proceed in much the same manner as in adults as long as proper allowance is made for the fewer number of higher-order abstract concepts and truly abstract propositions in cognitive structure, and for the need for concrete-empirical experience in acquiring abstract concepts and propositions.

DYNAMICS OF SUBSUMPTION AND DISSOCIABILITY

The essential feature of subsumption that makes dissociability and retention possible is the fact that a postulated state of equilibrium exists between the combined, undissociable interactional product of subsumer and subsumed element, on the one hand, and the component, dissociable individual entities comprising the interactional product, on the other. An analogous physical model for this state of affairs is the well-known principle of ionization or dissociation in chemistry which holds that a molecule in solution will dissociate into electrically charged equivalents of its component elements (ions) until some point of equilibrium between the dissociated and undissociated forms of the compound is achieved. This concept of a changing equilibrium between dissociable and undissociable forms of the interactional product created during the subsumption process, accounts for both the original maintenance and the gradual loss of dissociability of the newly learned material until it is no longer available in memory. As will be pointed out later, subsumption theory differs markedly from the Gestalt theory of retention in this respect. According to the latter theory, the assimilative process induced by interaction between traces is a matter of all-or-none replacement of a given trace by another stronger trace, on the basis of the similarity existing between them.

Consider, for example, the natural history of a potentially meaningful correlative concept or proposition (designated by the symbol a) which a learner relates to a relevant and more inclusive established proposition in his cognitive structure* (designated by the symbol A). As a result of the subsumptive process, an interactional product $A'a'$ is formed in which both original components are modified as a consequence of the interaction.** In this new product $A'a'$, a does not lose its identity completely since a dissociation equilibrium ($A'a' \rightleftharpoons A' + a'$) is set up in which a', depending on prevailing conditions, has a given dissociability strength as an identifiable entity.

---

*It is obviously an oversimplification to state that a new learning item a forms only a single interactional product with A. To a lesser extent it also forms interactional products with B, C, D, E, etc., the amount of assimilation in each case being roughly proportional to the latter's place along the gradient of relevance. The formation of these competing interactional products undoubtedly increases proactive inhibition.

**In the interaction, the subsumer is ordinarily modified much less than is the subsumed element because of its greater inclusiveness and stability. A recently learned abstract concept, however, may be modified considerably by particular new experience. The defining attributes, for example, may be broadened to include new features that were formerly excluded, or may be made less inclusive by excluding features that were originally included.

However, unless facilitating conditions, such as repeated exposure to a,[*] strengthens the dissociability of a', the dissociation equilibrium gradually shifts toward its ultimate end-point of zero dissociability. It is at this point that complete obliterative subsumption takes place: the interactional product $A'a'$ is no longer dissociable and is reduced to its least common denominator A'; and the subsumed, newly learned item a' becomes unavailable[**] or is forgotten. In the process of "leveling,"[2,74] for example, a, which is a specific derivative or illustration of A, or a slightly asymmetrical or incomplete variant of A, is simply reduced to A'; whereas in the process of "sharpening," a more striking aspect of a becomes its criterial feature and is remembered in accentuated form because it is subsumed under and eventually reduced to a pre-existing representation of this feature in cognitive structure.[***] Discontinuous and inverse principles, and principles with qualifying conditions, similarly tend to be remembered as continuous, direct, and unqualified in nature with the passage of time.[65]

The operation of obliterative subsumption is further illustrated by a study of rote learning and retention of a list of words, in which the subjects attempted to facilitate learning by organizing the task in a meaningful way.[12] An increase in the amount of clustering and in the number of "intrusion words'" occurred as the retention interval was lengthened. The increased clustering can be interpreted as a process of reduction to the categorical subsumers around which groups of words were organized; and the increased appearance of nonspecific intrusion words was presumably indicative of the reduction of specific words to their categorical equivalents.

The Threshold of Availability: Reminiscence

In order for subsumed materials to be available in memory, their dissociability strength must exceed the threshold of availability. The most important cause of the unavailability of meaningfully learned materials, therefore, is a fall in dissociability strength below the level required to reach this threshold.[****]

---

[*] The effects of overlearning on the dissociability equilibrium are considered in Chapter 8.

[**] Actually the item becomes unavailable long before the point of zero dissociability is reached, since subsumed materials are no longer available when their dissociability strength falls below the threshold of availability. Much residual dissociability strength, however, exists between this below-threshold level and the point of zero dissociability, but not enough to make the item available under ordinary conditions of recognition or recall. The existence of below-threshold dissociability strength may be demonstrated by the use of hypnosis[18,60] and the method of relearning.[19]

[***] This explanation of leveling and sharpening obviously differs from the traditional Gestalt account in terms of perceptually derived tensions within the trace.

[****] Whether or not dissociability strength is sufficient to reach threshold value is partly a function of the method used in measuring retention. Recognition and recall, for example, make quite different demands on the availability of a given item. In one case, the originally presented material is presented with other alternatives and the subject need only identify it; in the other, the subject must recreate the stimulus situation autonomously. Obviously, therefore, recognition can be successful at a much lower level of dissociability than can recall. The threshold of availability, in other words, is higher for recall than for recognition, holding dissociability strength constant.

Still another independent although secondary source of variability in the availability of subsumed materials inheres in fluctuations in the threshold of availability itself. Hence a particular item of knowledge may manifest more than sufficient dissociability strength to exceed the typically prevailing threshold value, but may still be unavailable because of some temporary elevation of the threshold of availability. The most common reasons for such an elevation of threshold value are (a) initial learning shock, (b) the competition of alternative memories, and (c) negative attitudinal bias or motivation not to remember (repression). Removal of these threshold-raising or memory-inhibiting factors (i.e., disinhibition) results in an apparent facilitation of memory. The most extreme example of disinhibition occurs during hypnosis when restriction of the learner's field of awareness reduces the competing effect of alternative memory systems to a bare minimum.[60]

Reminiscence (the Ballard-Williams phenomenon) refers to an apparent increment in the retention of meaningfully learned material over a period of two or more days without any intervening practice.* Since retention cannot possibly exceed original learning under these conditions, this phenomenon is probably reflective of spontaneous recovery from the threshold-elevating effects of initial learning shock. It is postulated, in other words, that a certain amount of confusion exists when new material is first subsumed within cognitive structure; that this confusion is gradually dissipated as relationships between the learning material and established concepts are clarified; and that the existence of the confusion and its gradual dissipation are paralleled by a corresponding initial elevation and a subsequent lowering of the threshold. This interpretation is strengthened by the fact that reminiscence occurs only when material is partially learned or not overlearned, and when practice trials are massed, that is, when opportunity for immediate confusion and later clarification exists.

The fact that reminiscence has only been convincingly demonstrated in elementary-school children,[61,62,73] and declines[61] or is not manifested at all[73] in older subjects, suggests that initial learning shock tends to decrease with increasing age as cognitive structure becomes more stable and better organized. Reminiscence also cannot be demonstrated for verbatim[21,22] and rotely-learned[72] materials unless measured within minutes after learning, inasmuch as the retention span of such materials is exceedingly brief. Increments in retention between earlier and later tests of availability (i.e., beyond the immediate test of retention) undoubtedly reflect the later removal of competing memories or of negative motivational factors temporarily raising the threshold of availability during the preceding retention test.

The genuineness of reminiscence was originally in doubt because early studies[10,21,22,73] used the same group of subjects in determining both initial and subsequent tests of retention. It was possible, therefore, to explain reminiscence in terms of the practice effect exerted by the immediate test of recall, or in terms of voluntary or involuntary rehearsal between immediate and later tests of retention. Since the reminiscence effect still shows up, how-

---

*Short-term reminiscence manifested two to six minutes after learning (i.e., the Ward-Hovland phenomenon) will not be considered here since it is concerned with rote memorization.

ever, when separate groups are used in determining immediate and later levels of availability,[61,62] it is in all probability more than a mere artifact of method of measurement.

ALTERNATIVE THEORIES OF RETENTION AND FORGETTING

Interference Theories

Interference theories of retention and forgetting were first advanced by the functionalist school of psychology as an alternative to the prevailing "law of disuse," and were later adopted in modified form by behaviorists and neobehaviorists. The law of disuse had been rendered suspect by the demonstration that unreinforced stimulus-response connections are weakened by continued use (extinction), and that unpracticed memories sometimes become more available days,[10,21][22,73] and even weeks[61] after original learning than they were at original testing (reminiscence). Furthermore, it was argued that time per se is not a cause or an explanation of change but simply a dimension in which change occurs.

Nevertheless, the validity of the proposition that the availability of memories declines spontaneously with time, was demolished neither by this latter consideration drawn from the general philosophy of science, nor by showing that memory in some instances decreases with use and increases with disuse. The dual explanations of spontaneous decay and active destruction are not mutually exclusive. Many events in nature are characterized by a distinctive time span determined in part by their own intrinsic properties and by the nature of the factors bringing them into being. Hence one does not necessarily have to account for the attenuation and termination of all phenomena solely in terms of the action of demonstrable or hypothetical opposing forces. When a particular memory comes into existence, in other words, it manifests a given degree of strength which, in the absence of facilitating conditions, gradually and spontaneously diminishes with time. Its longevity, therefore, is partly a function of this gradually and spontaneously declining strength irrespective of and in addition to the operation of other variables actively eroding its integrity. The spontaneous loss of memory strength may reflect both neurophysiological changes in the neural representation of memory and phenomenological changes of a psychological nature.

From a behavioristic standpoint, "a memory is nothing more than a response produced by a stimulus. [It] is merely the maintained association of a response with a stimulus over an interval of time. [Hence] the question of 'why we forget' comes down to this: What are the conditions under which stimuli lose their capacity to evoke previously associated responses? In other words the problem of forgetting is identical with the causes of response decrement. . . . Forgetting is a direct function of the degree to which substitute responses are associated with the original stimuli during the retention interval. This [is really] . . . a definition of retroactive interference. . . . Identity between responses in original and interpolated activities yields facilitation, whereas difference between responses yields interference (forgetting), and the magnitude of either facilitation or interference is a function of the stimulus similiarities between original and interpolated activities" (54, pp. 550-51).

The following kinds of behavioristic mechanisms have been proposed to account for retroactive interference: (a) *response competition:* the same stimulus associated with a given response during original learning becomes associated during the retention interval with a stronger competing response;[51] (b) *stimulus generalization:* a response associated with a given stimulus during original learning generalizes to other similar stimuli during the retention interval;[54] (c) *response generalization:* a stimulus associated with a given response during the original learning generalizes to similar responses during the retention interval;[54] (d) *unlearning:* the failure of the learner to make the initially learned responses when confronted by the relevant stimuli during the interval between learning and recall;[34] (e) *changed cues:* either some of stimuli present during original learning are absent during recall, or new stimuli evoking competing responses are present;[34] and (f) *changed set:* alteration during recall of the set established during learning.[34]

Evidence favoring the interference theory of forgetting comes from studies of rote learning showing that the degree of forgetting is directly related to the amount and similarity of activities interpolated during the interval between original learning and recall. When interpolated activity is reduced by such conditions as sleep,[37,70] hypnosis,[48,60] anesthesia,[63] and immobilization,[47] retroactive interference decreases; and when the amount and similarity of interpolated activity increases, retroactive interference correspondingly increases.[41,42,44,67,68] However Underwood's reinterpretation of the relevant data of many studies indicates that most forgetting of rotely learned material is "produced by interference—*not* from tasks learned *outside* the laboratory but from tasks learned *previously* in the laboratory; . . . . [and] that when interference from laboratory tasks is removed, the amount of forgetting is relatively quite small" (69, p. 51). But identifying the source of the interference with rote retention as being principally proactive rather than retroactive does not alter in any fundamental way either the basic premises or the validity of the interference theory.

The interference theory has little difficulty in explaining rote verbal learning and forgetting. The learning of discrete verbal units isolated from cognitive structure can be conceived of quite plausibly in terms of habit strength; and forgetting can be similarly conceptualized in stimulus-response terms as reflective of interference with established habit strength through such mechanisms as response competition and stimulus or response generalization. Specific responses purportedly become unavailable because they are superseded by competing associative tendencies with greater relative strength. Hence, the principal variable in rote forgetting is exposure to materials similar to but not identical with the learning task, shortly before (proactive interference) or after (retroactive interference) the learning session.

But when material is meaningfully learned (*i.e.*, interacts with subsuming concepts in cognitive structure instead of constituting a series of arbitrary and discrete associative tendencies), it seems more credible to define learning and forgetting in terms of the dissociability of the material from its subsumers at successive stages in the interactional process. In relation to this theoretical frame of reference, the major variables affecting retention are the availability of appropriate subsuming concepts in cognitive structure,[4,7] the stability and clarity of these concepts, and the discriminability of the learning material from its subsumers.[7] It is postulated, therefore, that the resistance of an ideational element to forgetting is not a simple function of the relative strength of the specific associative tendencies it embodies vis-a-vis other similar tendencies, but of its dissociability from other conceptual trace systems in which it is embedded. Instead of mechanical interference from a similar trace there is conceptual assimilation within a conceptual common denominator.

The inapplicability of behavioristic principles of proactive and retroactive interference to meaningfully learned verbal materials becomes evident when we use such materials in experimental studies of retention. For example, explicit study of a long passage about Christianity, immediately before or after the learning of a comparable passage about Buddhism, does not significantly impair the immediate or delayed Buddhism retention scores of college students in comparison with those of matched control subjects not exposed to the Christianity material.[*][6,8]

The short-term interference of similar elements, so crucial in rote forgetting, becomes relatively insignificant when meaningful materials are anchored to established subsuming concepts and progressively interact with them to the point of obliterative subsumption. Under these conditions the discriminability of the Buddhism material, and the clarity of the learner's knowledge of Christianity, are the significant determining variables.[6,7] The same studies also showed that retroactive exposure to material with the same ideational import as the learning passage, but differing in specific content, sequence, and mode of presentation, not only has no inhibitory effect on retention, but is just as facilitating as repetition of the learning passage.[8] Meaningfully (unlike rotely) learned materials obviously have a general substantive content that is transferable or independent of specific verbatim form and sequence.

To summarize, the subsumption theory of retention differs from the interference theory in defining retention in terms of the dissociability of an ideational element from its subsumers, rather than in terms of the freedom of discrete and arbitrary associations from the interfering effects of concurrently active rote elements. Subsumption theory takes into account the existing hierarchical organization of meaningfully learned materials in cognitive structure, the incorporation of new potentially meaningful materials within that structure, and the tendency for the new material to be reduced to a least common denominator of relevant established meanings. Unlike behavioristic concepts of interference which "postulate an association that is only modified at those points in time when members of the association are utilized," (54, p. 587) the subsumptive process, once initiated, occurs continuously until the point of zero dissociability is reached. In view of these differences and of the marked disparity between the respective retention spans of rotely and meaningfully learned materials, it hardly seems likely that the same type of retention process could underlie the two phenomena.

---

[*]Similar results were reported by J. F. Hall ("Retroactive Inhibition in Meaningful Material," J. educ. Psychol., 1955, 46:47–52) for meaningfully learned materials. Typical retroactive interference findings are obtained with meaningfully learned materials only when verbatim recall is also demanded (N. J. Slamecka, "Studies of Retention of Connected Discourse," Amer. J. Psychol., 1959, 72:409–16; J. G. Jenkins, and W. M. Sparks, "Retroactive Inhibition in Foreign Language Study," Psychol. Bull., 1940, 37:470).

Gestalt Theory

According to Gestalt theory,[40] forgetting is brought about by two principal mechanisms each of which has relatively little in common with the other. The first mechanism, *assimilation*, is conceptualized as a process whereby memory traces are obliterated, or replaced by similar traces in cognitive structure that are relatively more stable. Although this phenomenon is superficially similar to subsumption in that it implies fusion of or interaction between related elements,* rather than the substitution of new stimulus or response members in a previously learned stimulus-response association, it is theoretically more congruent with the interference concept of forgetting. The behavioristic mechanisms of response competition and stimulus or response generalization could quite adequately account for the occurrence of Gestalt assimilation.

The second, more distinctively Gestalt conception of forgetting is based on a notion of autonomous disintegration within traces. In the case of unstructured or poorly organized material (*e.g.*, where figure and ground are poorly differentiated), unstable chaotic traces are formed which rapidly undergo a type of spontaneous decay. In other instances, however, dynamic stresses derived from the original perception persist in the trace and are gradually resolved by such progressive changes in the direction of "closure," symmetry, and "good form" as leveling and sharpening.** Both assimilation and autonomous disintegration are also influenced by motivational factors such as intention and ego-involvement. These "quasi-needs" purportedly generate tensions which enhance the longevity of a trace by decreasing its susceptibility to the two mechanisms responsible for forgetting.***

---

*Both Gestalt and subsumption theories of forgetting differ from the interference theory in regarding the processes underlying retention as going on continuously rather than only during those times when the neural representations of the stimulus or response members of an association are exercised. While allowing that communication between trace systems and ongoing perceptual activity takes place, thereby making possible both recall and externally induced modification of traces, Gestalt theory holds that both autonomous disintegration within traces, and assimilative interaction between traces occur without actual activation of the traces themselves by ongoing excitatory activity. Both of these latter destructive processes are obviously not conscious. Memory traces and the processes they embrace only influence behavior and conscious activity when they communicate with ongoing excitation.

**Objective evidence of systematic changes in memory for visual forms bears on this issue but is equivocal in nature: The findings of Wulf,[74] Gibson,[24] Allport,[1] Perkins,[56] Brown[15] and Hall[27] tend to support, at least in part, the Gestalt prediction of progressive mnemonic changes in the direction of resolving intra-trace tensions. These studies, however, are open to the criticism that subjects are not always able to draw what they remember;[28] that when the *same* subjects are used in successive tests, their later memories are influenced by prior reproductions;[28] and that when the original figure rather than the subject's first reproduction is used as the criterion from which changes are measured, perceptual and memory changes are confounded.[54] Thus, when *different* groups of subjects are used at successive intervals,[30] and when memory is measured by successive comparisons of the same figure rather than by successive reproductions,[36] the resulting memory changes do not support the Gestalt thesis.

***The influence of motivational factors on retention is discussed in Chapter 9.

Subsumption and Gestalt theories, therefore, have two points in common which set them apart from connectionism. Both conceive of forgetting, in whole or part, as an assimilative rather than as an interference process, and both employ the concept of "trace" instead of such constructs as "habit strength" and "response tendency." These resemblances, however, are more terminological than substantive. The Gestalt concept of "replacement" merely describes assimilation as an end-result of cognitive activity without explaining how or why it occurs. Subsumption theory also only uses the term "trace" to refer to the continuing representation of past experience in the nervous system and in cognitive structure; the Gestalt assumptions regarding isomorphism and intra-trace dynamics are not accepted. Stripped of these latter connotations, it is felt that such terms as "trace" and "availability" describe more appropriately the memorial residue of ideas and information than such far-fetched behavioristic terms as "response tendency" and "habit strength."

Subsumption theory also differs from Gestalt theory in the following additional ways: (a) It attributes *all* forgetting, apart from spontaneous decay, to trace interaction, and (like interference theory) denies that autonomous disintegration of traces occurs as a result of the resolution of perceptually derived intra-trace tensions. Asymmetrical figures, for example, would sometimes be remembered as more symmetrical than originally perceived, not because of any autonomous changes within the traces, but because they were subsumed by and eventually reduced to a memorial residue of familiar geometrical concepts in cognitive structure. (b) It conceives of assimilation (loss of identifiability or decreased dissociability of newly learned materials) as a progressive phenomenon rather than as an all-or-none type of replacement in which reproducibility is lost completely and instantaneously. Assimilation is regarded as the final phase of a subsumptive process the initial effect of which is facilitative. An ideational element and its subsuming concept interact and set up an equilibrium process defining the dissociability of the former from the latter at any given point in time. The direction of this equilibrium then gradually shifts to the undissociable form of the interactional product which is its natural end-point. (c) Thus, assimilation is not conceived of as simple replacement of one trace by another, but as the outcome of a conceptualizing trend in memorial reduction. As a result of this trend, a highly inclusive and established trace system comes to represent the import of less generalized traces, the identifiability of which is correspondingly obliterated. (d) A meaningful ideational element is believed to be assimilated by a more inclusive trace system, not because of *similarity* between them per se, but because it is not sufficiently discriminable from the latter. Hence its import can be adequately represented by the generality of the more inclusive system. Similarity, of course, helps determine which potentially subsuming concepts in cognitive structure actually play principal and subsidiary subsuming roles, and is also one of the determinants of discriminability. A high degree of similarity can facilitate initial anchorage without necessarily leading rapidly to obliterative subsumption, provided that differences are also clearly and explicitly perceptible. (e) Forgetting is regarded as a continuation of the *same* interactional process established at the moment of learning. According to Gestalt assimilation theory, a given trace is first established at the time of learning, and then interacts with and is later replaced by *another* similar and separately established trace.

Bartlett's Theory of Memory

Subsumption theory also has elements in common with Bartlett's views[11] of cognitive functioning generally and of remembering in particular. His concept of *schema* as an organizing and orienting attitude or affect resulting from the abstraction and articulation of past experience—although somewhat vague with respect to both nature and mode of operation—is structurally and functionally comparable to that of a subsuming concept. In general, however, Bartlett's position on retention differs in two fundamental respects from subsumption theory. First, the schema itself is largely attitudinal and affective in nature rather than basically cognitive; in this sense it is similar to the connotative implications of a given concept as measured by Osgood's semantic differential (see p. 38). This difference probably reflects, in part, the fact that Bartlett's learning tasks consist of stories, pictures and figures instead of the impersonal substance of specific subject matter content. Second, Bartlett is primarily concerned with the perceptual and reproductive phases of meaningful learning and retention, and pays hardly any attention at all to the retention interval itself and its underlying processes. In accounting for the discrepancy between presented and remembered content, he emphasizes both the influence of idiosyncratic schemata on original perception of the material, and a process of "imaginative reconstruction" at the time of recall, as a result of which particular content is selected and invented in accordance with the nature and demands of the current situation (11, p. 213). Subsumption theory, on the other hand, begins with perceived rather than with presented content, and attributes most of the change between perception and recall to an intervening interactional process between subsumer and subsumed element. Thus, although the individual in remembering undoubtedly selects from what is available in memory, and also adds some new material suitable for the occasion, he is actually *reproducing,* for the most part, materials that have undergone memorial reduction rather than reconstructing the retained residue of original perception.

Bartlett[11] argues that laboratory experiments utilizing artificial methods of measurement and arbitrary, discrete learning tasks shed little light on the processes underlying perception and memory. His use of the *schema* concept represents, therefore, an attempt to interpret cognitive functioning in the light of the subject's emotions, attitudes, interests and drives as they actually influence cognition in real-life situations. He regards schemata as roughly analogous to generalized internal sets or dispositions which interact with sensory input in such a way as to render the product of the interaction meaningful and congruous with existing dispositions—as more or less coextensive with those "conditions within the organism that . . . determine which pictures, so to speak, the organism takes of a specific environment" (11, p. 209).

Thus schemata, according to Bartlett, tend to make the organism relatively independent of the environment, to combat the "overdetermination" of perception and behavior by "the last preceding member of a given series" of stimuli (11, p. 209). They account for "the fact that our percepts, thoughts, and behavior are on the whole consistent and orderly—reasonably appropriate though not necessarily logical—and that they are consistently related to previous acts of perceiving, thinking and behaving" (11, p. 181). In short they provide an enduring means which personality can use "quasi-permanently" to impose continuity and consistency on cognitive functioning without the necessity of improvising a controlling mechanism "*de novo*" each time the need arises (11, p. 157). Schemata are also "normally interconnected, organized together, and display, just as do the appetites, instinctive tendencies, interests and ideals which build them up, an order of predominance among themselves" (11, p. 212); and it is the relative persistence of this order for a given organism that gives memory "a peculiarly personal reference" (11, p. 308).

The impact of schemata on cognitive functioning is largely dependent, of course, on the use of stimulus content that is relatively unfamiliar, ambiguous, cryptic, and interpretable in several alternative ways. Schemata figure so prominently in Bartlett's work because this is precisely the type of learning materials he employed in his studies of memory. Using culturally unfamiliar narrative material similar to Bartlett's, Paul[55] found that distortion, forgetting, and importation occur particularly at those places in the text which contain gaps and ambiguities and are lacking in sufficient redundancy to be adequately coherent. A culturally familiar story on the other hand, is remembered relatively accurately and with few importations; it also retains much more of its content, coherence, and continuity. Explication of the gaps and ambiguities in the original versions of the unfamiliar stories significantly improves recall, but the quantity and quality of retention do not equal that of the familiar story.

Paul[55] suggests that the vagueness of the schema concept and its lack of explicit experimental underpinning account for the "surprisingly light impact . . . of Bartlett's work . . . on psychology:

"The major shortcoming is that, aside from his broad functionalistic formulations, he did not speculate about process, nor did he conduct definitive experiments (those that yield a yes-no answer) concerning the operation of schemas. He failed to delineate precisely the nature of schemas, and never suggested how we might picture the detailed workings of the processes governing schema formation and operation.

"This failure had at least two important consequences: (1) It prevented him from dealing adequately with the veridical and detailed recall that people are capable of—for example, memorization by rote. (2) It led him to overlook certain parameters of individual differences which, in the final analysis, must reflect the underlying processes of schema formation and operation. True, Bartlett recognized that people differ in interests and motives, in past experiences and expectations. But he did not concern himself with differences in ability to retain, and differences in the quality and character of remembering" (pp. 5–6).

The first opportunity for schemata to influence memory occurs when they interact with incoming stimulus content. The subject attempts to make the content meaningful in terms of a relevant schema as well as contextually consonant with it. Hence schemata significantly determine the initial interpretation of the stimulus, which, in turn, persistently influences the nature of what is retained. The importance of this initial interpretation (which is a perceptual product of the interaction between schema and stimulus input) for the later reproductive content of memory has been demonstrated for both verbal[38,39,43] and pictorial[20] material. Subjects are prone to perceive meanings that are compatible with their own attitudinal biases in reading ambiguous controversial materials,[43] and tend to interpret hypothetical behaviors of people in accordance with selective emphases embodied in experimentally manipulated advance sets.[38] Children are generally unable to remember a figure unless it reminds them of a familiar object,[25] and in reproducing unfamiliar and meaningless figures, they alter them in ways that increase their familiarity and meaningfulness.[33] The same tendency is also evident in problem-solving. Learners consistently tend to reduce problems to a level of difficulty which they can understand and make meaningful.[32] In studying qualitative changes in retention, therefore, it is important to use the immediate reproduction rather than the learning material itself as the baseline.

Bartlett[11] largely ignores the next phase in the learning-retention sequence during which time the perceptual version of the stimulus content is retained. He does note that condensation and simplification occur through the loss of inconsistent and irrelevant elements, and that some "dominant detail" persists; but he neither explicitly explains how these phenomena are effected nor considers them part of the retention interval or process per se. In fact he asserts that both the simplification process and the choice of the outstanding detail that serves as the focal point of mnemonic organization are part of the selective and rationalizing tendencies characteristic of the reconstructive phase of memory. Paul, however, found that contraction or skeletonization occurs gradually and progressively, and is a much more prominent feature of forgetting than is importation.[55] Often a given theme becomes secondary or subordinate to another theme before it is eventually lost or distorted. This loss opens further gaps, thereby isolating and making themes disconnected. The gaps, in turn, are closed either by importation or, more frequently by the "squeezing out" of old material. Skeletonization therefore seems to be analogous to the process of obliterative subsumption rather than a function of reconstruction.

The schema's principal impact on memory, according to Bartlett,[11] occurs during the reproductive phase:

"Remembering is not the re-excitation of innumerable fixed, lifeless and fragmentary traces. It is an imaginative reconstruction, or construction, built out of the relation of our attitude towards a whole active mass of organized past reactions or experience, and to a little outstanding detail which commonly appears in image or in language form. It is thus hardly ever really exact, even in the most rudimentary cases of rote recapitulation, and it is not at all important that it should be so. The attitude is literally an effect of the organism's capacity to turn round upon its own 'schemata', and is directly a function of consciousness" (p. 213).

Thus, in remembering, the subject differentially selects from what is available,* those elements that are both most consistent with his own attitudes, interests, and cultural milieu, and also most appropriate in terms of the

---

*Bartlett, as pointed out above, does not explain how availability is determined.

demands of the current situation. To this he adds some invented detail (to fill in gaps and enhance coherence, meaningfulness, and fit), and combines and reformulates both kinds of elements into a new, self-consistent whole. The reconstructed product, therefore, when compared to the original learning material, manifests such tendencies as simplification, condensation, rationalization, conventionalization, and importation.* Paul,[55] Northway,[50] Tresselt and Spragg,[66] McKillop,[43] and Taft[64] reported similar findings in the recall of value-laden narrative material. Hence it is not asserted that such tendencies do not exist, but rather that they reflect the operation of a subsumptive process during the retention interval *in addition* to some imaginative reconstruction in the course of reproduction.

Neurological Approaches

The psychologist interested in learning and retention is, by definition, concerned with psychological modification—accretion and decrement—occurring along a dimension of time. Since his interest in cognitive phenomena extends beyond simple perceptual activity, he is forced to recognize the existence of some continuing process in the nervous system that enables a replica of past experience to be represented in the present. Subsumption theory uses the concept of "trace" to designate this continuing neural activity. In this sense of the term, a trace is simply an unspecified neural correlate of presently available past experience. It bears a substrate relationship both to memory as a cognitive phenomenon and to the processes underlying memory, but explains neither phenomenon nor underlying processes. The position adopted here, in other words, is that cognitive phenomena can only be explained in terms of processes operative at a psychological level of phenomenology. Neurophysiological processes accompany and make certain cognitive events** possible but occur at a substrate level that has no explanatory value for these

---

*Most of the importations in Paul's study "seemed clearly to reveal and express the Ss' personal schemas in terms of their understanding of the results of the events in the story based upon their own conceptions and experiences" (55, p. 135). Although some were clearly decorative, the majority "enhanced continuity by closing gaps, forming transitions, and solving contradictions. They ameliorated ambiguity by transforming the unfamiliar into the familiar, the unlikely into the likely, and so forth. Frequently explications functioned by anticipating, preparing for, or merely repeating story material and thereby increased the redundancy and coherence of the reproduction." (p. 54)

**It is not implied that *all* cognitive phenomena have specific neurophysiological correlates. Such correlates undoubtedly exist for the raw material (*i.e.*, percepts and images) of cognitive operations, but the combination of and interactions between images and percepts involved in problem-solving, concept formation and thinking probably have no corresponding neural concomitants. They are essentially extraneural psychological phenomena dependent only on sufficient substrate integrity of the brain to make perception, memory, and the interrelation of their products possible.

events.* Individuals suffering from senile dementia cannot remember immediately preceding events because the necessary neurophysiological correlates of memory are impaired, but this does not necessarily mean that memory can be explained in terms of its neural substrate.

Although the concept of memory traces is part of the characteristic terminology and theoretical structure of Gestalt psychology, it is by no means indigenous to it. Connectionists and behaviorists implicitly accept the idea that a residue of past experience is represented somehow in the nervous system, and endow this residue with "habit strength" or availability. In behavioristic language, "trace" is conceptually equivalent to "response tendency." Hence, the only aspects of the memory trace concept that are uniquely identifiable with Gestalt theory are the doctrine of isomorphism and the notion that autonomous changes take place within the trace because of the continued operation of dynamic tensions inherent in and derived from its perceptual antecedents. Both behaviorists and Gestalt theorists accept the trace as a neural residue of past perceptual and behavioral experience, as well as the proposition that changes in the integrity and availability of this residue result from interaction (interference, assimilation, consolidation) with new experience and with pre-existing neural residues of prior experience.

Gestalt theory[40] bypasses the problem of explaining cognitive phenomena in terms of psychological processes by first assuming equivalence (isomorphism) between these phenomena and molar** neurophysiological events, and then using the neural events to explain the cognitive phenomena. Simply stated, the doctrine of isomorphism holds that an exact correspondence prevails between the twin domains of experience and neurophysiological process. It attempts to bridge the gap between overt behavior and the observable stimulating environment by setting up a psychophysical field intermediate between the two, which both supersedes the conscious field as the fundamental category of psychology and serves as a dynamic determinant of behavior. The psychophysical field is regarded as a single integral entity in which neural and psychological events are equated. Thus the transition between the designated characteristics of direct experience and the corresponding characteristics of concomitant physiological processes is effected by assuming an identity of process.

The obvious attraction of isomorphic doctrine lies in the fact that neural

---

*For example, knowledge about the localization of mnemonic and amnesic functions in the brain, or the demonstration that "nerve cells have some of their numerous branches turning back to end on the body of the parent cell so that they actually receive samples of their own outgoing messages" (23, pp. 21–22), in the fashion of a "microscopic servo-mechanism," constitute substrate rather than explanatory data about the actual processes underlying memory functioning. The anatomical significance of such data for the understanding of memory is comparable to the functional significance of electroncephalographic waves, which are merely "associated byproducts of brain activity . . . [They] tells us no more about the mysteries of the function of the brain than the waves washing on the shores tell us about the mysteries in the depths of the sea" (23, p. 17).

**Neural processes in extention that are conceived of as dependent on all other processes within the psychophysical field rather than as individually independent and as an additive sum of their parts.

events can be used to explain cognitive phenomena without having to specify the nature of neurophysiological processes. These processes are simply assumed to be metaphorical equivalents or molar projections of consciousness in neural space. Hence the properties of physiological events can be inferred from the data of behavior and consciousness. For every kind of psychological process there is an equivalent physiological process, the number and variety of the two categories necessarily being the same. Corresponding, for example, to the data of memory experience is an analogous temporal-spatial organization of traces existing in fields of stress and manifesting internal tensions. However, the very advantage of isomorphism in circumventing the necessity for specifying independent neurophysiological processes creates the equally great disadvantage of circularity. Such phenomenologically demonstrable properties of memory as leveling, sharpening, and assimilation are simply translated into metaphorical trace terminology; and this latter terminology in turn is used as a neural explanation of the phenomena in question. Similarly, the experienced instability of rotely learned memories is translated into the language of unstable and chaotic traces which, in turn, "explain" why rotely learned memories are quickly forgotten.

Hebb[29] avoids the circularity of isomorphism by positing the existence of independent neurophysiological processes which underlie and account for learning and retention. The initial stages of learning are explained in terms of the formation of closed, reverberating neural circuits ("cell assemblies"). Concept formation, on the other hand, is regarded as a more highly differentiated operation. It is purportedly effected by the separation of those aspects of the cell assembly reflective of the sporadic, variable, and unreinforced components of a given pattern of stimulation (fractionation), and by the corresponding consolidation of those aspects of the cell assembly reflective of the more recurrent and invariable components of the same pattern of stimulation (recruitment). At a later stage of learning, cell assemblies are in turn reorganized into more complex and integrated structures called "phase sequences," which are relatively independent of external stimulation, and which account for the enduring organizational and orienting impact of past experience on new perceptual and learning activity.

It is doubtful, however, whether this type of neurologizing adds much to our understanding of cognitive phenomena. It is both more direct and more parsimonious, in my opinion, to explain cognitive events in terms of their underlying psychological phenomena than in terms of their more distantly related neural correlates which, in all probability, bear a substrate rather than an explanatory relationship to the phenomena in question. It is perfectly legitimate to formulate and test hypotheses about the physiological correlates of cognitive events, providing that one does not assume the existence of a cause-and-effect relationship between the two levels of phenomenology, and providing that the hypothetical neural correlates themselves are closely anchored to known properties of the nervous system. But if the hypothesized neural events themselves are, at least in part, metaphorical constructs and are advanced as explanations of psychological phenomena, one is in large measure speculating about far-fetched speculative relationships.

Computer Models of Cognitive Functioning

In recent years numerous attempts have been made to use the operations and underlying processes of electronic computers as models of cognitive functioning. The analogy has even been extended to include hypothesized neuroanatomical and neurophysiological counterparts of computer mechanisms and to test neurophysiological theories of brain function. "In essence [electronic brains] appear to be electrical systems of memory which at an enormous speed can select specific information in response to the appropriate questions programmed to them by a human operator." (23, p. 22) At least three basic component operations are involved in all forms of thought, human or computer, "namely, memory, language and the capability of recognizing a pattern. The memory may be long or short term depending on the nature of the process. The stimulation which excites the process must be converted into a language which can be interpreted by the system, and the system, biological or mechanical, must be endowed with ability to recognize patterns of language" (57, pp. 38–39).

The particular computer model of human thinking proposed by Newell, Shaw, and Simon,[49] for example, assumes the existence of receptors capable of interpreting coded information, and of a control system consisting of a store of memories, a variety of processes which operate on the information contained in the memories, and a set of rules for combining these latter processes into programs of processing.

"The picture of the central nervous system to which our theory leads is a picture of a more complex and active system than that contemplated by most associationists. The notions of 'trace,' 'fixation,' 'excitation,' and 'inhibition' suggest a relatively passive electro-chemical system (or, alternatively, a passive 'switchboard'), acted upon by stimuli, altered by that action, and subsequently behaving in a modified manner when later stimuli impinge upon it.

In contrast, we postulate an information-processing system with large storage capacity that holds, among other things, complex strategies (programs) that may be evoked by stimuli. The stimulus determines what strategy or strategies will be evoked; the content of these strategies is already largely determined by previous experience of the system. Ability of the system to respond in complex and highly selective ways to relatively simple stimuli is a consequence of this storage of programs and this 'active' response to stimuli" (p. 163).

Similarly, in Miller, Galanter and Pribram's model of cognitive functioning,[46] the basic operational elements are stored information, comparable to the computer's memory ("the Image"), and various strategies (programs) for processing information ("the Plan") that determine cognitive (or computer) operations. These authors also propose a new functional unit of analysis, the "Test-Operate-Test-Exit" sequence in place of the reflex. This sequence involves, first, a search among existing stored representations to find one that is congruous with or fits incoming information. If a test of congruity yields negative results, the incongruity is then resolved by operations that modify either coding mechanisms or the environment.

The theoretical and heuristic value of such models depends, of course, on the tenability of the analogy both between computer and cognitive operations and between their respective underlying processes. Computers certainly seem capable of performing many of the same kinds of cognitive operations performed by humans, e.g., memorizing, abstracting, generalizing, categorizing, problem-solving, purposeful goal seeking, logical decision-making. The crucial question is whether human beings perform these operations by means of the same underlying processes utilized by computers. Engineers have invented many different kinds of information-processing devices that do not in the least resemble human cognitive processes despite the fact that the two sets of operations are overtly similar. Computers, for example, "are particularly good at simulating logical operations. However, machines carry out arithmetic [operations] quite differently from a human being. . . . A human, in performing such [operations] as addition and multiplication, uses stored multiplication and addition tables which have been implanted in his memory in childhood and which subsequently may be regarded almost as conditioned reflexes. But the machine undertakes arithmetical [operations] from first principles because it has been found that such methods are appreciably faster than reference to tables" (57, p. 43).

The processes underlying the operations involved in most computer models of cognitive functioning are incredibly simple when compared to the awesome complexities of the actual processes implied by relevant psychological considerations. Hence the postulated parallelism between the two sets of processes breaks down at innumerable points of comparison. In the first place, computers are able to process and store vast quantities of discrete units of information that are simultaneously or sequentially presented. Human beings can only assimilate and remember a few discrete items at a time. They compensate for this limitation by "chunking,"[45] i.e., by processing longer units composed of sequentially dependent items, by learning generic codes that subsume specific derivative instances (derivative subsumption), and by cataloguing new information under more inclusive subsumers (correlative subsumption). Computers, furthermore, have no forgetting problem. There is no possibility of spontaneous decay or obliterative subsumption, and no problem of proactive interference. Information stored in a computer maintains its availability indefinitely; the entire notion of dissociability strength, of progressive loss of such strength, and of the dependence of rate of loss on such factors as discriminability and the clarity and stability of subsumers, makes little sense in the context of computer memory. Neither is there any problem of developmental change in connection with computers. They do not change with age, in capacity for assimilating and storing information, or in the kinds of information-processing or problem-solving processes they employ.

Second, although computers can be designed to store information in accordance with the principle of progressive differentiation, such an organization of memory is neither a residual product reflective of countless previous instances of subsumption processes, nor a compensatory mechanism designed to overcome inherent limitations in capacity for processing and storing discrete items of simultaneously or sequentially presented information. Unlike human beings, computers can also process new material efficiently even if the information is presented in decreasing order of differentiation or increasing order of inclusiveness. Lastly, as presently engineered, computers lack the human's capacity for imaginative improvisation, for creative inspiration, and for independent thinking.

"The major difference between man and machine in their methods of solving certain types of mathematical problems is that the mathematician, thinking at a high level, frequently discovers short cuts to solutions, but the machine must follow slavishly the sequence of operations decided upon by a human programmer. . . . If a process of thought is regarded as being essentially a creative process, it can be said without fear of contradiction that the mechanization of such a process is not practicable" (57, pp. 43, 36).

As Hovland[35] points out, however, some of these disparities between computer and cognitive processes can be reduced if we *deliberately* "use computing machines to simulate in exact fashion the way a human solves a problem. Both human weaknesses such as limited and fallible memory, and strengths such as the ability to choose an efficient solution out of innumerable alternatives must be represented. We say that we can simulate human problem solving when we are able to specify both the prior information a human possesses and the sequence of steps by which he utilizes this information in the solution of the problem. We are then able to set up a computing machine to carry out this same sequence of operation. . . . The nub of the simulation process involves the use of similar types of 'programs' of 'instructions' to the machine in order to reproduce the steps an individual goes through in thinking out the solution to a difficult problem" (p. 687).

Hovland gives several examples of how machines can be programmed to learn and to use short cuts, but these computer achievements neither equal the complexity, flexibility, improvisation, and autonomy characteristic of human problem-solving, nor eliminate the other differences between computer and cognitive processes listed above. Furthermore, even if completely faithful simulation were presently possible, our lamentable ignorance of human thought processes would render us incapable of constructing valid computer analogues.

Despite these limitations, however, computer simulation of human cognitive functioning can provide us with valuable data and insights. In the first place, simulation forces us to be more precise and explicit in our "formulations concerning mental processes and phenomena."[35] Such precision about a process is obviously necessary before we can hope "to describe it in terms which can be programmed and executed by a machine" (p. 688). Second, "the simulation of human responses has the same overwhelming advantages for our understanding of behavioral phenomena as similar methods in other sciences. For example, the use of the wind tunnel represents a complex set of interacting conditions in actuality which could not be duplicated and whose effects could not be predicted from theory alone. Analogously in the present case, for single factors one can analyze effects without simulation, but when one seeks to understand the combined action of a number of factors interacting in complex ways, no satisfactory way of predicting the exact outcome may be possible" (35, p. 692).

"One may wonder whether we have gained anything by the simulation since we initially derive processes from study of how students work and then program into the computer their ways of proceeding. In fact, at the outset, we may operate in somewhat circular fashion—that is, we may only get out of the machine what we put into it. But as one proceeds new combinations are tested which could not have been predicted from the individual steps" (p. 689).

REFERENCES

1. Allport, G. W. Change and decay in the visual memory image. *Brit. J. Psychol.*, 1930, 21:133–48.

2. Allport, G. W., and Postman, L. *The Psychology of Rumor.* New York: Holt, 1947.

3. Ausubel, D. P. Introduction to a threshold concept of primary drives. *J. gen. Psychol.,* 1956, 56:209–29.

4. Ausubel, D. P. The use of advance organizers in the learning and retention of meaningful verbal material. *J. educ. Psychol.,* 1960, 51:267–72.

5. Ausubel, D. P. A subsumption theory of meaningful learning and retention. *J. gen. Psychol.,* 1962, 66:213–24.

6. Ausubel, D. P., and Blake, E. Proactive inhibition in the forgetting of meaningful school material. *J. educ. Res.,* 1958, 52:145–49.

7. Ausubel, D. P., and Fitzgerald, D. The role of discriminability in meaningful verbal learning and retention. *J. educ. Psychol.,* 1961, 52:266–74.

8. Ausubel, D. P., Robbins, Lillian C., and Blake, E. Retroactive inhibition and facilitation in the learning of school materials. *J. educ. Psychol.,* 1957, 48: 334–43.

9. Ausubel, D. P., Schpoont, S. H., and Cukier, Lillian. The influence of intention on the retention of school materials. *J. educ. Psychol.,* 1957, 48:87–92.

10. Ballard, P. B. Oblivescence and reminiscence. *Brit. J. Psychol., Monogr. Suppl.,* 1913, 1:No. 2.

11. Bartlett, F. C. *Remembering: A Study in Experimental and Social Psychology.* Cambridge: Cambridge University Press, 1932.

12. Brand, H. A study of temporal changes in the organization of retention. *J. gen. Psychol.,* 1956, 54:243–54.

13. Brand, H., and Woods, P. J. The organization of the retention of verbal material. *J. gen. Psychol.,* 1958, 58:55–68.

14. Brown, J. Some tests of the decay theory of immediate memory. *Quart. J. exp. Psychol.,* 1958, 10:12–21.

15. Brown, W. Growth of memory images. *Amer. J. Psychol.,* 1935, 47:90–102.

16. Bruner, J. S. Going beyond the information given. In *Contemporary Approaches to Cognition.* Cambridge, Mass.: Harvard University Press, 1957.

17. Bruner, J. S. Learning and thinking. *Harvard educ. Rev.,* 1959, 29:84–92.

18. Bruner, J. S. *The Process of Education.* Cambridge, Mass.: Harvard University Press, 1960.

19. Burtt, H. E. An experimental study of early childhood memory: Final report. *J. genet. Psychol.,* 1941, 58:435–39.

20. Carmichael, L., Hogan, H. P., and Walter, A. A. An experimental study of the effect of language on visually perceived form. *J. exp. Psychol.,* 1932, 15:73–86.

21. Edwards, A. L., and English, H. B. Reminiscence in relation to differential difficulty. *J. exp. Psychol.,* 1939, 25:100–108.

22. English, H. B., Welborn, E. L., and Killian, C. D. Studies in substance memorization. *J. gen. Psychol.,* 1934, 11:233–60.

23. Feindel, W. The brain considered as a thinking machine. In *Memory, Learning and Language* (W. Feindel, ed.) Toronto: University of Toronto Press, 1960, pp. 11–23.

24. Gibson, J. J. The reproduction of visually perceived forms. *J. exp. Psychol.,* 1929, 12:1–39.

25. Granit, A. R. A study on the perception of form. *Brit. J. Psychol.,* 1921, 12: 223–47.

26. Gomulicki, B. R. The development and present status of the trace theory of memory. *Brit. J. Psychol., Monogr. Suppl.,* 1953, 29:1–94.

27. Hall, V. The effect of a time interval on recall. *Brit. J. Psychol.,* 1936, 27:41–50.

28. Hanawalt, N. G. Memory trace for figures in recall and recognition. *Arch. Psychol.*, 1937, *31:*No. 216.
29. Hebb, D. O. *The Organization of Behavior.* New York: Wiley, 1949.
30. Hebb, D. O., and Foord, E. N. Errors of visual recognition and the nature of the trace. *J. exp. Psychol.*, 1945, *35:*335–48.
31. Heider, F. Trends in cognitive theory. In *Contemporary Approaches to Cognition.* Cambridge, Mass.: Harvard University Press, 1957, pp. 201–10.
32. Hildreth, G. E. The difficulty reduction tendency in perception and problem solving. *J. educ. Psychol.*, 1941, *32:*305–13.
33. Hildreth, G. The simplification tendency in reproducing designs. *J. genet. Psychol.*, 1944, *64:*327–33.
34. Hovland, C. I. Human learning and retention. In *Handbook of Experimental Psychology* (S. S. Stevens, ed.) New York: Wiley, 1951. pp. 613–689.
35. Hovland, C. I. Computer simulation of thinking. *Amer. Psychologist*, 1960, *15:* 687–93.
36. Irwin, F. W., and Seidenfeld, M. A. The application of the method of comparison to the problem of memory changes. *J. exp. Psychol.*, 1937, *21:*363–81.
37. Jenkins, J. G., and Dallenbach, K. M. Oblivescence during sleep and waking. *Amer. J. Psychol.*, 1924, *35:*605–12.
38. Jones, E. E., and de Charms, R. The organizing function of interaction roles in person perception. *J. abnorm. soc. Psychol.*, 1958, *57:*155–64.
39. Kay, H. Learning and retaining verbal material. *British J. Psychol.*, 1955, *46:* 81–100.
40. Koffka, K. *Principles of Gestalt Psychology.* New York: Harcourt, Brace, 1935.
41. McGeoch, J. A. Studies in retroactive inhibition: VII. Retroactive inhibition as a function of the length and frequency of the presentation of the interpolated lists. *J. exp. Psychol.*, 1936, *19:*674–93.
42. McGeoch, J. A., and McGeoch, G. O. Studies in retroactive inhibition: X. The influence of similarity of meaning between lists of paired associates. *J. exp. Psychol.*, 1937, *21:*320–29.
43. McKillop, A. S. *The Relationship between the Reader's Attitude and Certain Types of Reading Response.* New York: Bureau of Publications, Teachers College, Columbia University, 1952.
44. Melton, A. W., and Irwin, J. McQ. The influence of degree of interpolated learning on retroactive inhibition and the overt transfer of specific responses. *Amer. J. Psychol.*, 1940, *53:*173–203.
45. Miller, G. A. Human memory and the storage of information. *I. R. E. Trans. Info. Theory*, 1956, *IT–2:*128–37.
46. Miller, G. A., Galanter, E. H., and Pribam, K. H. *Plans and the Structure of Behavior.* New York: Holt, Rinehart and Winston, 1960.
47. Minami, H., and Dallenbach, K. M. The effect of activity upon learning and retention in the cockroach. *Amer. J. Psychol.*, 1946, *59:*1–58.
48. Nagge, J. W. An experimental test of the theory of associative interference. *J. exp. Psychol.*, 1935, *18:*663–82.
49. Newell, A., Shaw, J. C., and Simon, H. A. Elements of a theory of human problem solving. *Psychol. Rev.*, 1958, *65:*151–66.
50. Northway, M. L. The influence of age and social group on children's remembering. *Brit. J. Psychol.*, 1936, *27:*11–29.
51. Northway, M. L. The concept of the "schema." Parts I and II. *Brit. J. Psychol.*, 1940, *30:*316–25; *31:*22–36.

52. Oldfield, R. C. Memory mechanisms and the theory of schemata. *Brit. J. Psychol.*, 1954, *45*:14–23.
53. Oldfield, R. C., and Zangwill, O. L. Head's concept of the schema and its application in contemporary British psychology. Part III. Bartlett's theory of memory. *Brit. J. Psychol.*, 1942, *33*:113–129.
54. Osgood, C. E. *Method and Theory in Experimental Psychology.* New York: Oxford University Press, 1953.
55. Paul, I. H. *Studies in Remembering: The Reproduction of Connected and Extended Verbal Material. Psychological Issues, 1,* No. 2 (Whole No. 2). New York: International Universities Press, 1959.
56. Perkins, F. T. Symmetry in visual recall. *Amer. J. Psychol.*, 1932, *44*:473–90.
57. Porter, A. The mechanical representation of processes of thought. In *Memory, Learning and Language.* (W. Feindel, ed.) Toronto: University of Toronto Press, 1960. pp. 35–54.
58. Pribram, K. A review of theory in physiological psychology. *Ann. Rev. Psychol.*, 1960, *11*:1–40.
59. Rapaport, D. Cognitive Structures. In *Contemporary Approaches to Cognition.* Cambridge: Harvard University Press, 1957. pp. 157–200.
60. Rosenthal, B. G. Hypnotic recall of material learned under anxiety and non-anxiety producing conditions. *J. exp. Psychol.*, 1944, *34*:369–89.
61. Sharpe, J. F. The retention of meaningful material. *Catholic Univer. Amer. Educ. Res. Monogr.*, 1952, *16*:No. 8.
62. Stevenson, H. W., and Langford, T. Time as a variable in transposition by children. *Child Develpm.*, 1957, *28*:365–70.
63. Summerfield, A., and Steinberg, H. Reducing interfering in forgetting. *Quart. J. exp. Psychol.*, 1957, *9*:146–54.
64. Taft, R. Selective recall and memory distortion of favorable and unfavorable material. *J. abnorm. soc. Psychol.*, 1954, *49*:23–28.
65. Tomlinson, R. M. A comparison of four presentation methods for teaching complex technical material. Unpublished Ed. D. Dissertation. Urbana, Illinois: University of Illinois, 1962.
66. Tresselt, M. E., and Spragg, S. D. S. Changes occurring in the serial reproduction of verbally perceived materials. *J. genet. Psychol.*, 1941, *58*:255–64.
67. Twining, P. E. The relative importance of intervening activity and lapse of time in the production of forgetting. *J. exp. Psychol.*, 1940, *26*:483–501.
68. Underwood, B. J. The effect of successive interpolations on retroactive and proactive inhibition. *Psychol. Monogr.* 1945, *59*:No. 3.
69. Underwood, B. J. Interference and forgetting. *Psychol. Rev.*, 1957, *64*:49–60.
70. Van Ormer, E. B. Retention after intervals of sleep and waking. *Arch. Psychol.*, 1932, *21*:No. 137.
71. Vernon, M. D. The functions of schemata in perceiving. *Psychol. Rev.*, 1955, *62*:180–192.
72. Ward, L. B. Reminiscence and rote learning. *Psychol. Monogr.*, 1937, *49*:No. 220.
73. Williams, O. A study of the phenomenon of reminiscence. *J. exp. Psychol.*, 1926, *9*:368–87.
74. Wulf, F. Über die Veränderung von Vorstellungen (Gedächtnis und Gestalt). *Psychol. Forsch.*, 1922, *1*:333–73.

CHAPTER 5.

Cognitive Structure Variables

FROM THE STANDPOINT of the approach adopted in this book, the structure* of a student's existing knowledge is regarded as the crucial factor influencing new learning, retention, and problem-solving. Only in so far as it is possible to enhance the organizational strength of this structure is it possible to increase the functional retention of new subject-matter knowledge, both as end in itself and for purposes of problem-solving. Cognitive structure itself can be influenced substantively by the generality and integrative properties of the particular organizing and explanatory principles used in a given discipline, and programmatically by methods of presenting, arranging, and ordering units of knowledge that impinge on the clarity, stability, and cohesiveness of that structure.

Potentially meaningful material is always learned in relation to an existing background of relevant concepts, principles, and information which provide a framework for its reception. It is only in this way that interactional cognitive products are formed and that new meanings emerge and are retained. Existing cognitive structure reflects the outcome of all previous subsumption processes, and includes both stable subsumers (*i.e.,* the surviving residue or least common denominators of these prior processes), as well as subsumed material that manifests dissociability strength above threshold value. But all subsuming systems are obviously not equivalent with regard to stability, clarity and organizational properties; and variability in these respects necessarily gives rise to corresponding variability in the validity of emerging meanings and in their dissociability strength. Thus it is a commonplace that the details of a given discipline are learned as rapidly as they can be fitted into a contextual framework consisting of a stable body of general concepts and principles.

However, in searching for knowledge about the processes underlying meaningful reception learning and retention, it is not enough to stress the importance of relevant antecedent experience that is represented in existing cognitive structure. Before fruitful experimentation can be attempted it is necessary to specify and conceptualize those properties (variables) of cognitive structure that influence new learning and retention.

"The ease with which it is possible to suggest new potentially relevant independent variables bears a direct relationship to the rate at which the development of a research area may proceed. . . . Therefore, in addition to the need

---

*"Cognitive structure" refers solely to the stability, clarity, and organization of a learner's subject-matter knowledge in a given discipline. The actual ideas and information embodied in this knowledge are "cognitive content." "Cognitive style" refers to self-consistent inter-individual differences and idiosyncratic trends in cognitive organization and functioning.

for giving more consideration to antecedent conditions, there is a need for a conceptual framework which will suggest those antecedent variables which are most likely to be relevant" (118, p. 64). This chapter is largely concerned with the specification and conceptualization of these variables and with consideration of existing evidence bearing on their functional relationships to meaningful learning and retention.

THE COGNITIVE STRUCTURE APPROACH TO TRANSFER

We have just hypothesized that past experience influences or has positive or negative transfer effects on new meaningful learning and retention by virtue of its impact on relevant properties (variables) of cognitive structure. If this is true, all meaningful learning necessarily involves transfer, because it is impossible to conceive of any instance of such learning that is not affected in some way by existing cognitive structure; and this learning experience, in turn, results in new transfer by modifying cognitive structure. Thus it is apparent that transfer occurs irrespective of whether the influence of or on cognitive structure happens to be deliberate and controlled. A single practice trial, for example, both reflects the influence of existing cognitive structure and induces modification of that structure, thereby affecting the following practice trial. Nevertheless, for purposes of experimental investigation, it is necessary to satisfy the conditions of the transfer paradigm, *i.e.*, variation of particular factors while others are experimentally or statistically controlled, provision of a control group, and definite separation of the training and learning (transfer) periods in terms of the learning tasks involved.

This model of the role of cognitive structure in transfer differs in two significant ways from Bruner's conceptions of structure and transfer. First, structure for Bruner is simply a matter of acquiring "generic coding systems" that have applicability to a wide variety of problems, that enable the learner "to go beyond the information given" and recognize that new phenomena are merely specific variants of existing general formulae.[24,25] "What learning general or fundamental principles does," he says, "is to insure that memory loss will not mean total loss, that what remains will permit us to reconstruct the details when needed" (25, pp. 24–25). As already pointed out, however, relatively little school knowledge conforms to this derivative or "regenerative" model of memory in which the loss of specifics constitutes no great disadvantage in terms of academic achievement. New learning materials more frequently bear a *correlative* rather than a derivative relationship to established concepts in cognitive structure; and the forgetting of meaningfully learned material is largely a disadvantageous process of "obliterative subsumption" in which the identity of newly incorporated specific items is no longer dissociable from the more inclusive and generalized meaning represented by the established concept under which they are subsumed. Second, in accordance with traditional usage, Bruner restricts the use of the term "nonspecific transfer" to those instances in which "a general idea . . . can be used as a basis for recognizing subsequent problems as special cases of the idea originally mastered" (25, p. 17). However, in the vast majority of classroom learning situations where cognitive structure variables play a significant role, the transfer paradigm is more frequently applicable to the incorporation and retention of presented verbal material (*i.e.*, "reception learning") than to "discovery learning" or problem-solving.

SUBSTANTIVE AND PROGRAMMATIC FACTORS INFLUENCING COGNITIVE STRUCTURE

The task of identifying the particular organizing and explanatory principles in the various disciplines that manifest widest generality and integrative properties is obviously a formidable and long-range problem. Experience with various curriculum reform movements, however, indicates that it yields to sustained and resourceful inquiry, especially when it is possible to enlist the cooperative efforts of outstanding subject matter specialists, talented teachers, and imaginative educational psychologists. "Correct and illuminating explanations are no more difficult and are often easier to grasp than ones that are partly correct and therefore too complicated and too restricted. . . . Making material interesting is in no way incompatible with presenting it soundly; indeed a correct general explanation is often the most interesting of all" (25, p. 23).

The substantive principles underlying the choice of subject-matter content in the Physical Science Study Committee Secondary School Physics Program are relevant for most disciplines: "(1) to plan a course of study in which the major developments of physics up to the present time are presented in a logical and integrated whole; (2) to present physics as an intellectual pursuit which is part of present-day human activity and achievement" (46, p. 574). The primary problem in implementing these objectives is "how to construct curricula that can be taught by ordinary teachers to ordinary students and that at the same time reflect clearly the basic or underlying principles of various fields of inquiry. The problem is two-fold: first, how to have the basic subjects rewritten and their teaching materials revamped in such a way that the pervading and powerful ideas and attitudes relating to them are given a central role; second, how to match the levels of these materials to the capacities of students of different abilities at different grades in school" (25, p. 18).

The rationale of the Physical Science Study Committee for its particular choice of subject matter is clearly defensible in terms of providing a stable and widely transferable basis for the assimilation and integration of knowledge.

"The Committee has chosen to select subject matter and organize it with the intent of providing as broad and powerful a base as possible for further learning—further learning both in and beyond the classroom. Through its materials the Committee seeks to convey those aspects of science which have the deepest meaning, the widest applicability. . . .

"The explanatory systems of physics and how they are made have much more forward thrust as educational tools than the individual application and the discrete, unconnected explanation. Thus the PSSC has chosen for its subject matter the big over-arching ideas of physics—those that contribute most to the contemporary physicists' views of the nature of the physical world. . . . The power of the big ideas is in their wide applicability, and in the unity they bring to an understanding of what may appear superficially to be unrelated phenomena. . . . Pedagogically this choice has virtues. . . . Principal among them is the acquisition of criteria by which subject matter can be selected and organized toward the coherence the subject itself strives for."[47]

Once the substantive organizational problem (*i.e.*, identifying the basic organizing concepts in a given discipline) is solved, attention can be directed to the programmatic organizational problems involved in the presentation and sequential arrangement of component units. Here, it is hypothesized, two principles concerned with the efficient programing of content are applicable, irrespective of the subject-matter field—the principle of progressive differentiation and the principle of integrative reconciliation. These principles naturally include and reflect the influence of the previously listed cognitive structure variables, *i.e.*, the availability of a relevant, proximate subsumer, its stability and clarity, and its discriminability from the learning material (see pp. 28–29).

Progressive Differentiation. When subject matter is programed in accordance with the principles of progressive differentiation, the most general and inclusive ideas of the discipline are presented first, and are then progressively differentiated in terms of detail and specificity. This order of presentation presumably corresponds to the natural sequence of acquiring cognitive awareness and sophistication when human beings are exposed either to an entirely unfamiliar field of knowledge or to an unfamiliar branch of a familiar body of knowledge. It also corresponds to the postulated way in which this knowledge is represented, organized, and stored in the human nervous system. The assumption we are making here, in other words, is that an individual's organization of the content of a particular subject-matter discipline in his own mind, consists of a hierarchical structure in which the most inclusive concepts occupy a position at the apex of the structure and subsume progressively less inclusive and more highly differentiated subconcepts and factual data.

Now if the human nervous system as a data processing and storing mechanism is so constructed that both the acquisition of new knowledge and its organization in cognitive structure conform *naturally* to the principle of progressive differentiation, it seems reasonable to suppose that optimal learning and retention occur when teachers *deliberately* order the organization and sequential arrangement of subject matter along similar lines. A more explicit way of stating the same proposition is to say that new ideas and information can be efficiently learned and retained only to the extent that more inclusive and appropriately relevant concepts are already available in cognitive structure to serve a subsuming role or to furnish ideational anchorage.[10] But even though this principle seems rather self-evident it is rarely followed in actual teaching procedures or in the organization of most textbooks. The more typical practice is to segregate topically homogeneous materials into separate chapters, and to present them throughout at a uniform level of conceptualization, in accordance with a logical outline of subject matter organization. This practice, of course, although logically sound is psychologically incongruous with the postulated process whereby meaningful learning occurs, *i.e.*, with the hierarchical organization of cognitive structure in terms of progressive gradations of inclusiveness, and with the mechanism of accretion through a process of progressive differentiation of an undifferentiated field. Thus, in most instances, students are required to learn the details of new and unfamiliar disciplines before they have acquired an adequate body of relevant subsumers at an appropriate level of inclusiveness.[8]

As a result of this latter practice, students and teachers are coerced into treating meaningful materials as if they were rote in character, and consequently experience unnecessary difficulty and little success in both learning and retention. The teaching of mathematics and science, for example, still relies heavily on rote learning of formulas and procedural steps, on recognition of stereotyped "type problems," and on mechanical manipulation of symbols. In the absence of clear and stable concepts which can serve as anchoring points and organizing foci for the incorporation of new meaningful material, students are trapped in a morass of confusion and have little choice but to rotely memorize learning tasks for examination purposes.

One outstanding example of a textbook which is organized in accordance with the principle of progressive differentiation is Boyd's famous "Textbook of Pathology." In this book Boyd parts company with most traditional treatises on pathology, which typically consist of about twenty chapters, each devoted to describing serially the major kinds of pathological processes occurring within the various organs or organ systems. Boyd, in contrast, reserves serial consideration of the pathology of separate organ systems to the second half of his text, and devotes the entire first half to such general organizing and integrative topics as the different categories of pathological processes (e.g., inflammation, allergy, degeneration, neoplasm), and their principal causes and characteristics; the various kinds of etiological agents in disease; types of humoral and tissue resistance to disease; the interaction between genic and environmental factors in the development of pathological processes; and general relationships between pathological lesions and clinical symptoms.

Integrative Reconciliation. The principle of integrative reconciliation in programing instructional material can be best described as antithetical in spirit and approach to the ubiquitous practice among textbook writers of compartmentalizing and segregating particular ideas or topics within their respective chapters or subchapters. Implicit in this latter practice is the assumption (perhaps logically valid, but certainly psychologically untenable) that pedagogic considerations are adequately served if overlapping topics are handled in self-contained fashion, so that each topic is presented in only one of the several possible places where treatment is relevant and warranted, *i.e.*, the assumption that all necessary cross-referencing of related ideas can be satisfactorily performed (and customarily is) by students. Hence little serious effort is made explicitly to explore relationships between these ideas, to point out significant similarities and differences, and to reconcile real or apparent inconsistencies. Some of the undesirable consequences of this approach are that multiple terms are used to represent concepts which are intrinsically equivalent except for contextual reference, thereby generating incalculable cognitive strain and confusion, as well as encouraging rote learning; that artificial barriers are erected between related topics, obscuring important common features, and thus rendering impossible the acquisition of insights dependent on the perception of these commonalities; that adequate use is not made of relevant, previously learned ideas as a basis for subsuming and incorporating related new information; and that since significant differences between apparently similar concepts are not made clear and explicit, these concepts are often erroneously perceived and retain as identical.

Ward and Davis* report a study of meaningful retention in which general science was taught to junior-high-school pupils by means of a textbook that made a special point of reconciling and integrating new ideas with previously learned content. Periodic examinations were also given which tested knowledge of earlier as well as of recently presented material. They found that students retained material as well after sixteen weeks as on tests of immediate retention. Compartmentalization, of course, may be considered a common defence against forgetting. By arbitrarily isolating concepts and information, one prevents interaction with and obliterative subsumption by relevant concepts in cognitive structure. This is a modified variety of rote learning in which new learning material is allowed to interact with only certain of several potential subsumers. Through overlearning, relatively stable retention can be achieved, but the fabric of knowledge as a whole is unintegrated and full of internal contradictions.

THE "ORGANIZER" TECHNIQUE OF DIDACTIC EXPOSITION

In general, the pedagogic strategy proposed in this volume for implementing the programing principles of progressive differentiation and integrative reconciliation involves the use of appropriately relevant and inclusive** organizers that are maximally stable and discriminable from related conceptual systems in the learner's cognitive structure. These organizers are introduced in advance of the learning material itself, and are also presented at a higher level of abstraction, generality, and inclusiveness; and since the substantive content of a given organizer or series of organizers is selected on the basis of their suitability for explaining, integrating, and interrelating the material they precede (see above), this strategy simultaneously satisfies the substantive as well as the programing criteria specified above for enhancing the organizational strength of cognitive structure. Summaries and overviews, on the other hand, are ordinarily presented at the same level of abstraction, generality, and inclusiveness as the learning material itself. They simply emphasize the salient points of the material by omitting less important information, and largely achieve their effect by repetition.

Progressive differentiation in the programing of subject matter is accomplished by using a hierarchical series of organizers (in descending order of inclusiveness), each organizer preceding its corresponding unit of detailed,

---

*A. H. Ward and R. A. Davis, "Acquisition and Retention of Factual Information in Seventh-Grade Science during a Semester of Eighteen Weeks," *J. educ. Psychol.*, 1939, 30:116–25.

**The appropriate level of inclusiveness may be defined as that level which is as proximate as possible to the degree of conceptualization of the learning task— relative, of course, to the existing degree of differentiation of the subject as a whole in the learner's cognitive background. Thus, the more unfamiliar the learning material (*i.e.*, the more undifferentiated the learner's background of relevant concepts), the more inclusive or highly generalized the subsumers must be in order to be proximate.

differentiated material. In this way not only is an appropriately relevant and inclusive subsumer made available to provide ideational scaffolding for each component unit of differentiated subject matter, but the various units in relation to each other are also progressively differentiated, *i.e.*, organized in descending order of inclusiveness.

The advantage of deliberately constructing a special organizer for each new unit of material is that only in this way can the learner enjoy the advantages of a subsumer which both (a) gives him a general overview of the more detailed material in *advance* of his actual confrontation with it, and (b) also provides organizing elements that are inclusive of and take into account most relevantly and efficiently both the *particular content* contained in this material and relevant concepts in cognitive structure. It thereby makes use of established knowledge to increase the familiarity and learnability of new material. Any existing subsumer in the learner's cognitive structure which he could independently employ for this purpose, self-evidently lacks particularized relevance and inclusiveness for the new material, and would hardly be available in advance of initial contact with it. And although students might possibly be able to improvise a suitable subsumer for future learning efforts *after* they become familiar with the material, it is unlikely that they would be able to do so as efficiently as a person sophisticated in both subject matter content and pedagogy.

The pedagogic value of advance organizers obviously depends in part upon how well organized the learning material itself is. If it contains built-in organizers and proceeds from regions of lesser to greater differentiation (higher to lower inclusiveness), rather than in the manner of the typical textbook or lecture presentation, much of the potential benefit derivable from advance organizers will not be actualized. Regardless of how well organized learning material is, however, it is hypothesized that learning and retention can still be facilitated by the use of advance organizers at an appropriate level of inclusiveness. Such organizers are available from the very beginning of the learning task, and their integrative properties are also much more salient than when introduced concurrently with the learning material.

Organizers also undoubtedly facilitate the learning of factual material more than they do the learning of abstract material, since abstractions in a sense contain their own built-in organizers—both for themselves and for related detail items. Northrop[100] showed that internal structuring enhances the learning of factual films, but actually inhibits the learning of ideational films. It would therefore seem advisable to restrict the use of organizers to the learning of material that is relatively factual in nature, and hence offers adequate scope for the ideational scaffolding provided by abstract organizers.

Organizers are also expressly designed to further the principle of integrative reconciliation. They do this by explicitly pointing out in what ways previously learned, related concepts in cognitive structure are either basically similar to or essentially different from new ideas and information in the learning task. Hence, on the one hand, organizers explicitly draw upon and mobilize all available concepts in cognitive structure that are relevant for and can play a subsuming role in relation to the new learning material. This maneuver effects great economy of learning effort, avoids the isolation of essentially similar concepts in separate, noncommunicable compartments, and discourages the confusing proliferation of multiple terms to represent ostensibly different but essentially equivalent ideas. On the other hand, organizers increase the discriminability of genuine differences between the new learning materials and analogous but often conflicting ideas in the learner's cognitive structure. This second way in which organizers purportedly promote integrative reconciliation is predicated on the assumption that if the distinguishing features of the new learning task are not originally salient or readily discriminable from established ideas in cognitive structure, they can be adequately represented by the latter for memorial purposes, and hence would not persist as separately identifiable memories in their own right. It is assumed, in other words, that only discriminable categorical variants of previously learned concepts have long-term retention potentialities.

Thus if an organizer can first delineate clearly, precisely, and explicitly the principal similarities and differences between the ideas in a new learning passage, on the one hand, and existing related concepts in cognitive structure, on the other, it seems reasonable to postulate that the more detailed ideas and information in the learning passage would be grasped later with fewer ambiguities, fewer competing meanings, and fewer misconceptions suggested by the learner's prior knowledge of the related concepts; and that as these clearer, less confused new meanings interact with analogous established meanings during the retention interval, they would be more likely to retain their identity.

In summary, two principal kinds of advance organizers can be employed to facilitate meaningful learning and retention. In the case of completely unfamiliar material, an "expository" organizer is used to provide relevant proximate subsumers. These subsumers primarily furnish ideational anchorage in terms that are already familiar to the learner. In the case of relatively familiar material, a "comparative" organizer is used both to integrate new concepts with basically similar concepts in cognitive structure, as well as to increase discriminability between new and existing ideas which are essentially different but confusable.

LEARNING AND THE AVAILABILITY OF RELEVANT SUBSUMERS

Whether or not a relevant subsumer at an appropriate level of abstraction, generality, and inclusiveness is available in cognitive structure, and the stability and clarity of this subsumer, are obviously important antecedent variables in meaningful learning and retention. In this section I propose to review various short-term studies of meaningful learning, retention, and problem-solving in which these variables are implicated. Such studies exemplify the transfer paradigm providing that the cognitive structure variable is manipulated during a preliminary or training period so that the effect of this manipulation on a new learning task can be ascertained. For example, a study indicating that the over-learning of a given passage results in increased retention would *not* constitute relevant evidence about the influence of cognitive structure on retention; it would merely reflect the influence of amount of practice on retention, inasmuch as practice rather than altered cognitive structure is the only *measurable* independent variable that is relevant under these circumstances. On the other hand, evidence that the overlearning of passage A by an experimental group (as compared to a control group which does not overlearn passage A) leads to superior retention of related passage B, would be relevant evidence of the influence of cognitive structure on retention.

What happens if an appropriate relevant subsumer is not available in cognitive structure when new potentially meaningful material is presented to a learner? If some existing though not entirely relevant and appropriate concept cannot be utilized for subsuming purposes, the only alternative is rote learning. More typically, however, some tangentially relevant subsumer is pressed into service. This type of subsumer obviously cannot provide very adequate or efficient anchorage, thereby giving rise to unclear, unstable, and ambiguous meanings with little longevity. The same outcome may also result when appropriate relevant subsumers are available, if their relevance is not perceived. For both reasons, therefore, in meaningful learning situations, it is advisable to introduce suitable organizers whose relevance is made explicit rather than to rely on the spontaneous availability of appropriate subsumers.

Spontaneous Antecedent Organization

Many different kinds of cognitive functioning are facilitated by the spontaneous (uncontrived) presence and use of organizing concepts within cognitive structure. Poulton[109] showed that memory for short meaningful statements varies directly with the subjects' degree of certainty regarding their truth, which in turn reflects relative degree of subject-matter sophistication in the area covered by the statements in question. Thus the more background knowledge an individual has in a particular discipline, and the more stable this knowledge is, the more successful he is in learning related materials. Memory for a body of items was also found to vary directly with the number of categories subjects were required to use in classifying the items.[94] Associative clustering in the recall of words is a somewhat more spontaneous manifestation of the same tendency to maximize rote retention by organizing discrete items around existing categorical subsumers. The possibility of such clustering is obviously greater if the words themselves are relatively familiar.[19] The facilitation of word-sequence learning by grammatical structure[103] is still another example of the influence of cumulatively learned antecedent organization on cognitive functioning. Finally, ability to learn unfamiliar words in one's mother tongue illustrates the application of a highly established general coding system to the solution of a specific problem.[24]

The relevance of the antecedent organizing elements for the new learning material is also an important factor in cognitive functioning. Concepts are more easily acquired if the specific instances from which they are abstracted are frequently rather than rarely associated with their defining (criterial) attributes, and if subjects have more rather than less relevant information about the nature of this attribute.[141] Relevant and meaningful antecedent context similarly facilitates the perception of connected verbal material when subthreshold tachistoscopic exposure times are used.[64] Saugstad[117] has shown that the solution of problems, such as Maier's two-pendulum problem, is largely dependent on the availability of relevant concepts.

The Effect of Advance Organizers on Learning and Retention

Postman's[106] study of the effect of learned rules of organization on rote learning and retention is an interesting precursor of the use of advance organizers in the meaningful learning of connected verbal discourse. This investigator found that explicit training in the derivation of figural patterns from code models facilitates the retention of the figural material, that the "effectiveness of such preliminary training increases with the retention interval," and that the training reduces the susceptibility of the memory material to retroactive inhibition. In essence then, this experiment involved the facilitation of rote retention by meaningful rules of organization: the learning task was relatively arbitrary, verbatim, and unrelated to cognitive structure as a whole, but was relatable to an explicitly learned code which, in this instance, was analogous to a subsuming principle.

In addition to their practical usefulness as a pedagogic device, organizers can also be used to study programmatically the effects of cognitive structure variables. By systematically manipulating the properties of organizers, it is possible to influence various attributes of cognitive structure (e.g., the availability to the learner of relevant and proximately inclusive subsumers; the clarity, stability, discriminability, cohesiveness, and integrativeness of these subsumers), and then to ascertain the influence of this manipulation on new learning, retention, and problem-solving. Such studies employ control subjects who are exposed to similar introductory materials, except for the particular variable under investigation, and hence follow the transfer paradigm.

The use of expository organizers to facilitate the learning and retention of meaningful verbal material is based on the premise that if the organizational principle of progressive differentiation of an internalized sphere of knowledge does in fact prevail, then new meaningful material becomes incorporated into cognitive structure insofar as it is subsumable under relevant existing concepts. It follows, therefore, that the availability in cognitive structure of appropriate and stable subsumers should enhance the incorporability of such material. If it is also true that "meaningful forgetting" reflects a process of memorial reduction, in which the identity of new learning material is assimilated by the more inclusive meaning of its subsumers, the same availability should also enhance retention by decelerating the rate of obliterative subsumption.

Thus, when undergraduates were first exposed to organizers presenting relevant and appropriately inclusive subsuming concepts, they were better able to learn and retain unfamiliar ideational material dealing with the metallurgy of carbon steel.[8] Differential analysis in another study showed that the facilitating effect of organizers occurred only for those subjects who had relatively poor verbal ability, and who therefore tended spontaneously to structure such material less effectively.[13] General background knowledge in the same subject matter area also facilitated the learning of unfamiliar school material and enhanced the effect of the organizer.[13]

Advance organizers probably facilitate the incorporability and longevity of meaningful verbal material in three different ways. First, they explicitly draw upon and mobilize whatever relevant subsuming concepts are already established in the learner's cognitive structure and make them part of the subsuming entity. Thus, not only is the new material rendered more familiar and meaningful, but the most relevant ideational antecedents are also selected and utilized in integrated fashion. Second, advance organizers at an appropriate level of inclusiveness provide optimal anchorage. This promotes both initial incorporation and later resistance to obliterative subsumption. Third, the use of advance organizers renders unnecessary much of the rote memorization to which students resort because they are required to learn the details of a discipline before having available a sufficient number of key subsuming concepts.

In sequential school learning, knowledge of earlier-appearing material in the sequence plays much the same role as an organizer in relation to later-appearing material in the sequence. It constitutes relevant ideational scaffolding, and hence a crucial limiting condition for learning the latter material when the influence of both verbal ability and general background knowledge is removed.[13] For maximally effective learning, however, a separate organizer should be provided for each unit of material. Thus, sequential organization of subject matter can be very effective, since each new increment of knowledge serves as an anchoring post for subsequent learning. This presupposes, of course, that the preceding step is always clear, stable and well-organized. If it is not, the learning of all subsequent steps is jeopardized. Hence new material in the sequence should never be introduced until all previous steps are thoroughly mastered. Perhaps the chief pedagogic advantage of the teaching machine lies in its ability to control this crucial variable in sequential learning.

Most complex learning tasks, particularly those which are sequential in nature, can be analyzed into a hierarchy of component learning sets or units.[*] The rate of learning these units and the extent to which they can be recalled are more highly related to final achievement on the learning task than are general intellectual ability or more specific cognitive aptitudes. Serious breakdowns in learning can often be attributed to inadvertent omission of a logically essential component unit from the total task or to its inadequate integration with other components.

Little reliable evidence is available regarding the effect of overlearning on the relative stability of subsumers in cognitive structure, and hence on their relative ability to enhance meaningful verbal learning and retention. Heterogeneous presentation of stimulus material that does not provide sufficient repetition to allow for mastery is not only less effective than homogeneous presentation in learning a principle, but also does not facilitate the learning of a reversal principle during the transfer period.[116] Reversal learning in rats is similarly facilitated when the first of two discrimination problems is overlearned.[28,110,111] According to Bruner, "learning often cannot be translated into a generic form until there has been enough mastery of the specifics of the situation to permit the discovery of lower-order regularities which can then be recombined into higher-order more generic coding systems" (24, p. 60). In serial and paired-associate rote learning, under conditions comparable to stimulus generalization, increased practice on the training task tends to in-

---

[*]R. M. Gagné and N. E. Paradise, "Abilities and Learning Sets in Knowledge Acquisition," *Psychol. Monogr.*, 1961, 75, No. 14.

crease positive transfer;[23,26] and under conditions typically associated with negative transfer, increased prior training tends to reduce and even reverse the direction of negative transfer.[6,23,93,120,140,149]

Evidence is also lacking with respect to the effect of multicontextual learning on the stability and transferability of subsuming concepts. Insofar as concept formation itself is concerned, the weight of the evidence indicates that the defining attributes of a concept are learned most readily when the concept is encountered in a large number of different contexts;[29,71,119] the only evidence to the contrary is contained in a study by Adams.[2] It would seem reasonable to suppose that by de-emphasizing particularity, multicontextual learning facilitates the abstraction of commonality, strengthens the generality of the resulting concept, and endows it with greater stability.

Mediational Organization

Various kinds of verbal and nonverbal pretraining facilitate learning and problem-solving by providing an organizing subsumer or general coding principle. Reference has already been made to the facilitation of reversal learning when the first of two principles or discrimination problems is overlearned. [28,110,111,116] Bilateral transfer effects[98] similarly depend on the acquisition of a generally applicable pattern of neuromuscular coordinations at the disposal of any bodily member. Verbal prefamiliarization with the content of films by means of a pretest[125] or by exposure to key words[143] also facilitates learning and retention. In concept formation, the facilitating effect of verbal pretraining is relative to subjects' mastery of discriminative verbal cues during pretraining.[57,148]

The "learning set" phenomenon, i.e., "learning to learn," "successive transfer" or progressive intra-problem improvement in performance,[62] also illustrates the gradual acquisition of a general coding principle which facilitates the solution of a given class of problems. Both Duncan[37] and Morrisett and Hovland[96] have demonstrated that transfer in Learning Set problems is a function of mastery (practice) within a given type of problem, as well as of experience with a large number of specific variants of this problem type. These experiments, therefore, further substantiate the value of overlearning and multicontextual experience in learning generic coding systems.

Much positive transfer in problem-solving is attributable to the carry-over of general elements of strategy, orientation, and adaptation to the problem. Systematic instruction in approach to a given task has been shown to facilitate both motor learning[37] and memorization.[147] Overlearning of the training task tends to reduce negative transfer in serial rote learning,[6,23,93,120140,148] because it establishes the particular relevance of specific elements for specific instances, while at the same time permitting the positive transfer of general factors. The same basic phenomenon can also be observed in rat maze learning.[72,145]

More explicit facilitation of the learning of skills by deliberately making a transferable general principle (e.g., the nature of refraction) available, is seen in Judd's classical experiment on learning how to shoot submerged targets.[65,75] Ervin[42] also found that verbal instruction in relevant physical principles underlying a given motor performance increases transfer to an analogous motor performance. However this effect does not occur unless subjects are able to perceive both the similarity between the two motor tasks and the link between verbal principles and performance. In solving puzzle-type problems, both Katona[77] and Hilgard and others[66,67] have demonstrated that understanding a general principle is more transferable than is rote memorization of the solution for a given class of problems. French[48] obtained similar findings in a study which required subjects to learn sequentially dependent concepts.

The importance of organization, generalization, and the understanding of basic relationships for positive transfer in such school subjects as arithmetic[22,91,133,135] and spelling[52] has been amply demonstrated. For transfer of principles to extend beyond the confines of the particular discipline in which they are encountered, a deliberate effort must be made to appreciate their relevance in other contexts. Thus geometry can be deliberately taught so as to cultivate critical and reflective thinking in other fields,[44,63,139] and the teaching of genetics can be so organized as to modify superstitious thinking and racial prejudice.[*][18]

Recognition of the role of cognitive structure in symbolic learning—and even in rote and simple discrimination learning—is implicit in such neobehavioristic mediational hypotheses as those offered by Osgood[102,103] and Mowrer.[97][**] The formation of such mediating cognitive structures as response-produced cues and covert verbal responses has been postulated to explain the facilitating influence of verbal pretraining on concept formation,[30,81] paired-associate learning,[99] and reversal learning.[16,80,116] Goss and Moylan[57] and Yarcozower[148] have shown that this facilitating effect is relative to the extent to which subjects have mastered discriminative verbal cues during pretraining.

Evidence continues to accumulate regarding the mediating function of implicit verbal processes in concept formation. Liublinskaya,[89] Kendler and Karasik,[81] and Carey and Goss[30] have demonstrated that the availability of distinctive verbal responses facilitates concept formation and conceptual transfer; and, confirming earlier findings in this area, Weir and Stevenson[142] reported that explicit instructions to verbalize enhances transposition learning in children, and that this effect is unrelated to chronological age within the age range of three to nine. Mere ability to verbalize, however, may constitute no advantage in simple transposition problems; "preverbal" preschool children seem to do as well as "verbal" preschool children.[55,114] The interposition of a time delay between training and test problems enhances transposition behavior,[127] presumably by de-emphasizing the importance of absolute differences and by making relational principles more salient. Even when the trans-

---

*This does not imply that a grand heuristic strategy is discoverable which can be applied to all disciplines, or that critical thinking ability can be enhanced by teaching general principles of logic apart from specific subject-matter content. It simply means that in certain instances specific models or analogies may have interdisciplinary heuristic value, and that certain substantive or methodological principles have applicability to more than one discipline provided that the interdisciplinary relevance and implications are made explicit. (see pp. 92, 126, and 157)

**The organizing function of Bartlett's schemata in the perceptual and reproductive phases of meaningful learning and retention has been considered elsewhere. (pp. 64–67) Goss[56] offers an elaborate theoretical discussion of the acquisition of "conceptual schemes" and of their mediating and organizing uses.

fer task requires reversal of the training principle, further training on the original form of the principle, accompanied by mediating symbolic processes, has facilitating rather than inhibitory effects.[16,116]

THE ROLE OF DISCRIMINABILITY IN MEANINGFUL LEARNING AND RETENTION

The discriminability of new learning material from previously learned concepts in cognitive structure is a major variable in meaningful learning and retention. In the effort to simplify the task of apprehending the environment and its representation in cognitive structure, new stimulus material that resembles existing knowledge often tends to be perceived and understood as identical to the latter, despite the fact that objective identity does not exist. Existing knowledge, in other words, tends to pre-empt the cognitive field and to superimpose itself on similar potential meanings. Under these circumstances, the resulting meanings obviously cannot conform to the objective content of the learning material. In other instances, the learner may be cognizant of the fact that new propositions differ somehow·from established principles in cognitive structure, but is unable to specify wherein the difference lies. When this situation exists, ambiguous meanings emerge, permeated by doubt, confusion, and alternative or competing meanings. In either case, however, the newly learned meanings have relatively little initial dissociability strength. In addition, because of the natural tendency for even clearly discriminable meanings to undergo memorial reduction to established subsumers in cognitive structure, nondiscriminable meanings quite understandably manifest little longevity. If new meanings cannot be readily distinguished from established meanings, they can certainly be adequately represented by them for memorial purposes. This is especially true for longer retention periods. Over short retention intervals, nondiscriminable material can be retained on a purely rote basis.

The discriminability of a new learning task is in large measure a function of the clarity and stability of existing concepts in the learner's cognitive structure to which it is relatable. In learning an unfamiliar passage about Buddhism, for example, subjects with greater knowledge of Christianity make significantly higher scores on the Buddhism test than do subjects with less knowledge of Christianity.[11,12] This significantly positive relationship between Christianity and Buddhism test scores holds up even when the effect of verbal ability is eliminated.[12] Thus, much of the effect of overlearning—both on retaining a given unit of material and on learning related new material—is probably a reflection of enhanced discriminability, which can be accomplished by increasing the clarity and stability of either the learning material itself or of its subsumer. Reference has already been made to the effect of overlearning in increasing positive transfer and decreasing negative transfer in rote learning situations (see pages 86 and 87). Amount of retroactive inhibition also tends to vary inversely with the number of presentations given the original test.[92]

When discriminability between new learning material and established concepts in cognitive structure is inadequate because of the instability or ambiguity of prior knowledge, comparative organizers that explicitly delineate similarities and differences between the two sets of ideas can significantly increase discriminability and hence facilitate learning and retention.[12] This method of facilitating learning and retention is probably more effective than overlearning of the new material, since such overlearning does not in any way strengthen or clarify the subsuming concepts which provide the anchorage for long-term retention. When established ideas in cognitive structure are *already* clear and stable, however, organizers do not have a facilitating effect.[12] Under these latter circumstances, overlearning of the new material is the only feasible way of further enhancing discriminability. In conceptual learning, sequences of presenting stimuli that provide successive contrasts between relevant and irrelevant criterial attributes tend to facilitate concept formation.[34]

Attempts to increase the discriminability of verbal learning materials through techniques other than overlearning or the use of advance organizers have not been strikingly successful. Merely establishing a set to perceive differences between two related passages does not, in and of itself, enhance retention;[146] and the inclusion of explicit comparisons within the learning passage itself produces somewhat equivocal results.[11] For several plausible reasons, advance organizers are more effective:

First [they] provide advance ideational scaffolding. Second, they provide the learner with a generalized overview of *all* of the major similarities and differences between the two bodies of ideas *before* he encounters the new concepts individually in more detailed and particularized form. Finally, they create an advance set in the learner to perceive similarities and differences, and, by avoiding overly explicit specification, encourage him *actively* to make his own differentiations in terms of his own particular sources of confusion (12, p. 267).

In some instances of meaningful learning and retention, the principal difficulty is not one of discriminability, but of apparent contradiction between established ideas in cognitive structure and new propositions in the learning material. Under these conditions the learner may dismiss the new propositions as invalid, may try to compartmentalize them as isolated entities apart from previously learned knowledge (*i.e.*, retain them on a rote basis), or may attempt integrative reconciliation under a more inclusive subsumer. The function of an advance organizer in this type of learning situation would be to provide just such a subsumer.

Perhaps the most important feature of the automated teaching device, insofar as the facilitation of meaningful learning and retention is concerned, is not the incentive and drive-reducing effects of immediate feedback,* but the extent to which these devices influence learning by enhancing the stability and clarity of cognitive structure. By deferring the introduction of new material until prior material in the learning sequence is consolidated, they maximize the effect of stability of cognitive structure on new learning; and

---

*The reinforcement value of feedback, as conceived by Skinner is discounted by the fact that subjects who make no spontaneous overt response which can be reinforced (i.e., who respond covertly or merely read the correct response), generally learn and retain programed verbal material just as well as subjects who independently and overtly construct their responses.[33,43,87]

by supplying immediate feedback, these devices rule out and correct alternative wrong meanings, misinterpretations, ambiguities, and misconceptions before they have an opportunity to impair the clarity of cognitive structure and thereby inhibit the learning of new material. Because of the rigor with which such variables as degree of consolidation and amount and immediacy of feedback can be controlled, teaching machines can be very useful in studying the effects of stability and clarity of cognitive structure on sequential learning.

Several investigators, as a matter of fact, have used automated teaching devices in short-term studies of learning and retention, but have generally restricted their attention to the relative effectiveness of these devices as compared to conventional classroom instruction. Both Coulson and Silberman[31] and Evans, Glaser, and Homme,[43] for example, reported that university students, using simulated teaching machines and programmed textbooks, respectively, are better able to learn small units of meaningful material than are control groups employing comparable conventional methods. These studies also isolated the effects of such variables as size of step and mode and overtness of response. But until the transfer paradigm is followed (*i.e.*, until the effect of prior exposure to such factors is related to the learning of *new* material), the rich potentialities of these devices for increasing our knowledge of cognitive structure variables will not be realized.

LONG-TERM STUDIES OF COGNITIVE STRUCTURE VARIABLES

Despite their self-evident significance for school learning, long-term studies of cognitive structure variables involving subject matter achievement are extremely sparse. Very little research in this area conforms to the minimally necessary research design (*i.e.*, the transfer paradigm) which requires that a single attribute of cognitive structure first be deliberately manipulated, using adequate experimental and/or statistical control procedures, and that this altered cognitive structure then be related to long-term achievement outcomes in an extended program of new studies in the same field.

Improvement of Thinking

Promising attempts to enhance critical-thinking ability by influencing cognitive structure in particular subject matter areas have been made by Abercrombie,[1] Suchman[129,130] and Smith.[122] Abercrombie tried to improve medical students' ability to reason more effectively by providing them with opportunities for "therapeutic" group discussion in an unstructured, nonauthoritarian atmosphere. Analysis of X-rays was used as the criterion measure for assessing the effects of this training. Abercrombie's findings were generally in the predicted direction but are vulnerable on the grounds of failure to control for the so-called "Hawthorne Effect."

Suchman[130] has been "experimenting with the teaching of strategies and tactics of scientific inquiry to children who learn to apply them in question-and-answer investigations." Preliminary findings[129] indicate that although such training increases the number of valid questions children ask in the test (criterion) situation, it does not significantly enhance the quality of the questions or facilitate grasp of concepts. Hence, more definitive evidence of the transfer value of such training to new situations is being sought; and the new criteria of transfer being employed are not only more independent of the particular training procedures used, but are also more reflective of the ultimate purpose of such training, *i.e.*, greater knowledge of the content and/or the method of science.

Smith and Henderson developed instructional materials "designed to develop critical-thinking abilities, and . . . helped the teachers learn how to handle these materials in the classroom. . . . [They] found wide differences among teachers with respect to improvement of their students in critical thinking,"[122] but refrained from drawing definitive conclusions because they had not as yet devised a technique for describing and measuring what teachers were *actually* doing in this situation. Their next step, therefore, was to devise a method of categorizing the logical operations in thinking. The great promise of this approach is twofold: First the attempt to influence critical thinking is based on the simultaneous teaching of the logic of a particular subject-matter field along with its content, rather than on instruction in general principles of logic. Second, by quantifying the crucially important but elusive teaching variable, this category system can do much to place long-term classroom studies of cognitive structure variables on a sound experimental basis. Aschner[5] has developed another useful "category system for clarifying thought processes that are reflected in verbal behavior. . . . [based] on Guilford's conception of the structure of intellect."

Improvement of Instruction

Many of the curriculum reform movements attempt to enhance long-term learning and retention by influencing cognitive structure variables. The University of Illinois Committee on School Mathematics,[15] for example, stresses initial self-discovery of generalizations by students, followed by precise, consistent, and unambiguous verbalization of modern concepts. The Secondary School Physics Program of the Physical Science Study Committee[46] places great emphasis on the more integrative and widely generalizable concepts in modern physics; on inquiry in depth rather than on broad, superficial coverage of the field; on careful, sequential programing of principles; and on conveying to the student something of the spirit and methods of physics as a developing experimental science. Implicit in each program is the assumption that whatever ultimate superiority in academic attainment is achieved by following these pedagogic principles, is attributable to cumulative changes in the organization, stability and clarity of cognitive structure.

Achievement test data provided by evaluative studies of such programs offer presumptive evidence regarding the long-term effects of cognitive structure variables. Nevertheless, this type of research does not conform to our transfer paradigm, since the learning of *new* material in the same subject-matter field is not studied as a function of modified cognitive structure. Furthermore not only is it impossible in such programs to isolate the effects of the individual variables involved, but only rarely is any effort made to obtain comparable achievement data from control groups or to control for the "Hawthorne Effect." Measurement is also a difficult problem because standardized achievement tests both cover various traditional subject-matter units deliberately ignored by these new curricula, as well as fail to measure knowledge of the more modern concepts which they emphasize. All of these difficulties point up the unfeasibility of using curriculum development research as a source of rigorous experimental evidence bearing on a single cognitive structure variable.

Automated Teaching

Similar kinds of presumptive evidence regarding the long-term effects of cognitive structure variables come from studies of automated teaching. Pressey[108] systematically used a self-instructional (punchboard) device as an integral part of a course in educational psychology. This device both provides immediate feedback and guides the student to the correct answer if he is wrong. Students using the punchboard make higher midterm and final examination scores than do control Ss. Little[88] and Stephens[126] reported similar findings. But although control groups were employed in these studies, the transfer paradigm was not followed, the effects of the drill and feedback variables were not isolated from each other, the "Hawthorne Effect" was disregarded, and no attempt was made to equate experimental and control groups with respect to actual degree of exposure to relevant learning material.

Long-term experimental evidence derived from more modern teaching machine procedures is equally sparse. The study conducted by Skinner and Holland[121] on the effectiveness of programed instruction in introductory psychology, for example, is subject to all of the methodological criticisms listed above in addition to the fact that control groups were not used. A better controlled study in the same subject-matter area shows no advantage for programed instruction.[101] Porter's study of programed instruction in spelling[105] and Meyer's[95] vocabulary study are notable for the use of matched control groups and demonstrate a consistent advantage in favor of the automated techniques. A well-controlled experiment on the automated teaching of fourth-grade arithmetic yielded negative findings except for low IQ pupils.[74] But despite the paucity of rigorous experimental work in this area, it is evident that with proper controls, manipulation of single variables, and the use of the transfer paradigm, automatic teaching devices could provide much valuable evidence on the long-term effects of cognitive structure variables.

INFLUENCE OF EXISTING DEGREE OF KNOWLEDGE ON ACADEMIC ACHIEVEMENT

Studies in which degree of existing knowledge of subject matter at one level of educational attainment is related to performance at subsequent educational levels, also conform to the long-term transfer paradigm. Constancy of academic attainment is, of course, partly attributable to constancy of academic aptitude and motivation. But especially when these latter factors are controlled, it is reasonable to attribute some of the obtained relationship between earlier and later educational levels to the cumulative effects of cognitive structure variables.[51,132] Swenson,[132] for example, found that, holding academic aptitude constant, students from the upper two-fifths of their graduating classes made significantly higher quality-point averages in college courses than did students from the lower three-fifths. Engle[41] demonstrated that university grades in psychology for students who had psychology in high school were no higher than the grades of students who did not have psychology in high school. This lack of relationship reflected, in part, significant differences in content and emphasis between high school and college psychology courses. From the standpoint of rational principles of curriculum development, however, introductory courses in a given field of knowledge might normally be expected to establish the type of cognitive structure that would facilitate the later assimilation of more advanced and highly differentiated material in the same field.

Reference has already been made to short-term research evidence on the relationship between existing degree of knowledge and the learning of unfamiliar material in the same subject-matter field. Students with a more extensive knowledge of Christianity are better able to learn principles of Buddhism than are students of equal academic aptitude who have less knowledge of Christianity.[12] Similarly, subjects who have more general background knowledge in endocrinology learn and retain more unfamiliar material about the endocrinology of pubescence than do a matched control group with less general background knowledge of endocrinology.[13] In the first instance, where new learning material is substantively relatable to existing knowledge, the facilitating effect of increased knowledge can be attributed to higher discriminability. In the second instance, where the new learning material is not substantively relatable to previously learned principles, general background knowledge probably facilitates learning and retention by increasing the familiarity of the new material, and hence the learner's confidence in coping with it.

The use of automated teaching and other organizing, clarifying and integrative techniques appears to exert a leveling influence on the relationship between degree of existing knowledge and new learning in the same subject-matter area. Meyer[95] obtained a correlation of $-.52$ between pretest scores on knowledge of English prefixes and gain in such knowledge after ten days of self-instruction with a programed workbook. Little[88] similarly found that drill machines giving immediate knowledge of results of practice tests in an educational psychology course, as well as opportunity to correct mistakes by drill, benefits those students most who usually score in the lower half of the distribution. As a result of such teaching, both the more and the less knowledgeable Ss move upwards in attainment, but the terminal achievement of the two groups tends to converge. Organizers also tend differentially to benefit only those subjects whose existing relevant knowledge is unclear and unstable;[12] but when the new learning material is not explicitly relatable to previously learned concepts, subjects with greater background knowledge seem to benefit more from organizers.[13]

It also seems reasonable to suppose that organizational aids and other improved methods of teaching would tend to benefit the average and dull student more than the bright student. The latter, after all, could be expected more successfully to structure and organize unfamiliar learning material by himself. The research evidence in this area, however, tends to be equivocal. The lucid integrative teaching in the PSSC high-school physics program not only brings it well within the ability of most high-school physics students,[45] but also tends to produce progressively decreasing correlations between academic aptitude and physics achievement as the course progresses. Both Porter[105] and Detambel and Stolurow[34] obtained almost zero correlations between general ability measures and achievement on programed learning tasks;[*] and Joos[74] showed that automated teaching programs in arithmetic differentially benefits low IQ children. Keislar,[79] on the other hand, found that programed instruction in elementary arithmetic was more successful for the brighter pupils. By emphasizing the outline of a film, Northrop[100] differentially increased learning in a low ability group; but in another study, increased patterning of the learning material through underlining had precisely the opposite effects.[83] The use of organizers was suggestively more beneficial for low ability subjects in the learning of completely unfamiliar material,[13] but was unrelated to academic aptitude when the learning material was substantively relatable to existing knowledge.[12]

When pupils are permitted to learn at their own rate of speed in sequentially organized subjects such as mathematics, initial individual differences in rate of achievement tend to increase rather than decrease over time.[15] This phenomenon apparently reflects both the increased learning opportunities given the more able pupils, as well as the reciprocal circular relationship between relative success and failure, on the one hand, and interest and motivation, on the other. Despite this divergence, however, dull pupils who are permitted to learn at their own speed obviously acquire a sounder foundation of knowledge, and also maintain higher educational morale than when forced to proceed and flounder at a rate exceeding their ability level.

COGNITIVE STYLE

"Cognitive style" refers to self-consistent and enduring individual differences in cognitive organization and functioning. Cognitive style includes individual differences in general principles of cognitive organization (e.g., simplification and consistency trends), and self-consistent idiosyncratic tendencies that are not reflective of human cognitive functioning in general (e.g., intolerance for ambiguity; memory for particular kinds of experience). It reflects differences in personality organization as well as in genically and experientially determined differences in cognitive capacity and functioning; in a very real sense, it mediates between motivation and emotion, on the one hand, and cognition, on the other.[104] A serious methodological weakness common to many of the studies in this area is the fact that they utilize measures of cognitive style, its determinants, and its functional consequences for which adequate intra- or intertask generality of function has not been established.

Many cognitive style variables reflect self-consistent individual differences with respect to certain general properties or attributes of cognitive organization and functioning that characterize human beings as information storing and processing mechanisms. These tendencies occur in the same direction and apply to all individuals and all age levels, but are consistently more or less accentuated in particular persons. Among the various general attributes of cognitive organization and functioning that have already been considered in this volume are: (a) the tendency for the learner's acquisition of entirely new bodies of knowledge or of new components of familiar bodies of knowl-

---

[*]For additional evidence in the same direction see L. M. Stolurow, *Teaching by Machine* (1961), pp. 124, 126, 136–138. For additional negative evidence see p. 212.

edge to follow the principle of progressive differentiation; (b) the tendency toward cognitive reductionism or simplification—for purposes of easing the cognitive burden—as manifested in such processes as abstraction, concept formation, categorization, generalization, and obliterative subsumption; and (c) the tendency toward achieving greater internal consistency or congruence of meaning within cognitive structure, by means of selective forgetting or selectively misperceiving or misunderstanding unfamiliar or incongruous new ideas in accordance with established meanings. Bartlett's "rationalization," "fit," and "effort after meaning" can be explained as manifestations of both the simplification and consistency trends. These mechanisms render unfamiliar new experience both simpler (more manageable, meaningful, comprehensible) and more consistent with existing cognitive content.

The following aspects of cognitive style have been identified and studied: intolerance for ambiguity (tendency toward premature closure); intolerance for unrealistic experience; leveling-sharpening; need for simplification (skeletonizing, rationalizing); explication and importing of detail in memory (embroidery); vividness of memory; long-term or short-term memory; memory for particular kinds and sense modality of experience; constriction or flexibility in problem solving. Other possible and suggested aspects of cognitive style include strategy preferences in problem-solving (focusing or scanning; whole or part hypotheses); strategy preferences in processing, acquiring and organizing information; memory for details or concepts; integration versus compartmentalization in memory; degree of openness to new information after closure is achieved.

The tendency more or less to simplify the representation and storage of information in cognitive structure, and thus to reduce cognitive strain, is an important aspect of cognitive style. Although it is a commonplace that some individuals tend to remember unimportant anecdotal detail, whereas other individuals tend more to remember only the substantive import of past experience, little direct research evidence is available on this point. In general, because of the trend toward obliterative subsumption in memory, "skeletonization" is a more common occurrence than "importation" in the recall of narrative material. Holzman and Gardner[69] used the Schematizing Test, with an odd-even reliability coefficient of .84 to .90, to measure leveling-sharpening tendencies. They found that "sharpeners" surpass "levelers" in ability to recall anecdotal material. Berkowitz[17] showed that leveling tendencies manifest significant generality of function, and that "levelers" tend to prefer simple to complex phenomenal experience. Partially trained teachers (i.e., teachers with an average degree of knowledge) tend to use fewer dimensions "in perceiving and evaluating complexities of environmental stimuli" than do teachers with either low or high levels of knowledge (115, p. 261). Anxiety in male teachers has the same effect as partial training.[115]

Although it is probably true that human beings tend to "organize the world of ideas, people, and authority along the lines of belief congruence, [and that] what is congruent is further organized in terms of similarity to what is congruent" (113, p. 395), interindividual differences obviously exist with respect to the need for internal consistency within belief systems. Some individuals are undoubtedly more content than others to internalize contradictory propositions in logic-tight compartments rather than to subject them to integrative reconciliation. However, direct research evidence regarding the stability and generality of such individual differences is presently unavailable. Another way of maintaining ideational self-consistency is peremptorily to reject all new propositions that appear incongruent with existing beliefs. Rokeach[113] obtained evidence of a generalized "open-closed" dimension of belief systems measured by Dogmatism and Opinionation Scales, with respective reliability coefficients of approximately .80 and .70. In validating these scales he found that Catholics make high Dogmatism and Right Opinionation scores, whereas Communists and religious disbelievers make high Dogmatism and Left Opinionation scores. Only the Right Opinionation groups, however, tend to score high on the Berkeley F and E Scales.

Intolerance of ambiguity is a characteristic manifestation of the relatively "closed mind" and is symptomatic of high anxiety level.[7,124] The anxious individual, who requires immediate and clear-cut answers and is impatient with conflicting evidence and tentative conclusions, tends to exhibit either excessive impulsiveness or excessive cautiousness in decision making.[124] Both early and late decision makers "manifested significantly more response perseveration and shorter latency of response" on an object recognition test than did a middle group (124, p. 35).

Individuals also differ consistently with respect to tendency to use "affect labels" in categorizing stimuli, and to emphasize conceptual or perceptual-motor components in their response to cognitive tasks. In an investigation of intra-individual consistency in the use of affect labels in describing and categorizing social and ink blot stimuli, Kagan, Moss, and Sigel[76] were able to demonstrate significantly positive intercorrelations among their four measures. Broverman[20,21] identified "conceptual versus perceptual-motor dominance" and "strong versus weak automatization" styles on a word-color interference test. He then demonstrated that "conceptually dominant" Ss are less distracted than "perceptual-motor dominant" Ss on a difficult conceptual task, and that "strong automatizers" are less distracted than "weak automatizers" both on an automatized conceptual and on an automatized perceptual-motor task.[20] Parallel kinds of results were also reported for the effects of these same cognitive style variables on intra-individual differences in response strength.[21] The significance of these findings, however, is diminished by the failure to consider intra- or intertask generality of function either for the measures of cognitive style or for the measures of their effects.

Gardner and others,[49] employing a factor analytic approach, isolated a limited number of control principles reflective of individual consistencies in cognitive behavior. This study was later broadened to include tests of intellectual ability and personality variables.[50] On the basis of their findings, these investigators conclude that "intellectual abilities and cognitive controls are not isolated aspects of cognitive organization but are mutually interrelated. The arbitrary distinction that has sometimes been maintained between intelligence and the broad scale organization of cognition thus seems inappropriate" (50, p. 123).

"Retention style" was studied by Paul[104] who found general and consistent individual differences with respect to importation, amount of material retained, and the use and retention of imagery:

"Importing sometimes was clearly explicatory in function (assimilating and connecting), at other times merely decorative and extraneous (sharpening). Interestingly enough, for the nonimporters it *rarely* seemed to be the latter; most of the decorative importations were contributed by the importers" (p. 144).

"The reproductions of nonimporters and importers were stylistically different: the former were generally leaner in structure, more disconnected and more abbreviated than those of the importers; the latter seemed more continuous and coherent" (p. 135).

Contrary to general belief among teachers and students, James[73] found that the use of a preferred method of learning meaningful material (*i.e.*, reading versus lecture) makes no difference whatsoever in learning outcomes.

It is quite probable that consistent individual differences exist with regard to strategy of and general approach to problem-solving. Although a particular strategy of concept acquisition (simultaneous scanning, successive scanning, conservative focusing, or focus gambling) is generally more likely to occur under some experimental conditions than under others,[27] it is also possible that self-consistent and generalized individual preferences are concomitantly operative. The issue of flexibility-rigidity in problem-solving has also received considerable attention. Luchins and Luchins,[90] in reviewing the literature on rigidity of behavior and the effect of Einstellung, asserted that no conclusions are possible at this time as to whether a general and self-consistent factor of rigidity exists. The intratask generality of individual differences in the Water-Jar Einstellung Test has not yet been determined, and the validity of this measure, as well as its relationship both to other measures of rigidity and to other personality traits, are highly equivocal. Rokeach,[113] on the other hand, has presented evidence which suggests that "closed" and rigid individuals experience difficulty in synthetic and analytic thinking, respectively.

CREATIVITY

Like cognitive style, creativity constitutes a significant intrapersonal variable influencing individual differences in meaningful learning and retention, problem-solving, and academic achievement.* It also reflects enduring differences in personality organization as well as in various aspects of intellectual capacity and functioning. What is actually meant by creativity, however, is a very moot point. Few terms used in psychology and education today are quite as vague. This vagueness is particularly unfortunate in view of the fact that "teaching for creativity" is the latest and most flourishing educational fad, panacea and catch-phrase.

---

*The general facilitating effect of intellectual ability, as measured by conventional IQ scores, on learning, problem-solving and academic achievement is too well-known to require any explicit consideration in this context. It has also been shown that the rate of acquiring learning sets is a function of IQ,[40,70,78,128] and that intelligence significantly influences strategy of problem-solving.[14,86] When arithmetic learning tasks are graded to pupils' current achievement levels, however, no significant differences are found among children of low, average, and high IQ, in learning, retention, and transfer.[84,85] Longer exposure times can similarly compensate for the effects of low intelligence on level of perceptual organization.[3]

Much of the semantic confusion regarding the term "creativity" stems from failure to distinguish between "creativity" as a trait inclusive of a wide and continuous range of individual differences, and the "creative person" as a unique individual possessing a rare and singular degree of this trait, *i.e.*, a degree sufficient to set him off *qualitatively* from most other individuals in this regard. This same difficulty also exists with respect to "intelligence," but gives rise to less confusion because the term is more familiar. Everyone agrees that all degrees of intelligence exist, that even an imbecile exhibits some manifestations of intelligent behavior. But when we refer to an "intelligent person," we mean only someone who is at the upper end of the distribution of IQ scores, someone who exceeds a hypothetical cut-off point separating intelligent individuals from the general run of mankind. Thus, although creativity undoubtedly varies along a continuum, only the rare individual who makes a singularly original and significant contribution to art, science, literature, philosophy, government, etc., can be called a creative person. The creative person is, by definition, a much rarer individual than the intelligent person. Thousands of intelligent individuals exist for everyone who is truly creative.

It is important, therefore, to preserve the criterion of unique and singular originality in designating a person as creative. All discovery activity is not qualitatively of one piece. In the course of growing older, for example, every infant inevitably discovers that objects continue to exist even when they are out of sight; this discovery, however, hardly manifests the same *quality* of creativity as Einstein's formulation of the theory of relativity. Similarly, a sixth-grade pupil may exhibit some degree of creativity in composing a song or writing a poem, but this does not mean that his accomplishments differ from Bach's and Shakespeare's merely in degree rather than in kind. The fact that it is often difficult to measure originality, and that great discoveries may frequently go unrecognized for decades or centuries, does not detract in the least from the existence of qualitative differences in creative achievement. A creative person must do more than simply produce something that is novel or original in terms of his *own* life history.

A second source of semantic confusion regarding the concept of creativity reflects the failure to distinguish between creativity as a highly *particularized and substantive capacity* (*i.e.*, a rare and unique manifestation of talent in a particular field of endeavor), and as a *general constellation of intellectual abilities, personality variables, and problem-solving traits*. Typical of the latter conception of creativity is Torrance's definition of creative thinking as the "process of sensing gaps or disturbing, missing elements; forming ideas or hypotheses concerning them; testing these hypotheses; and communicating the results, possibly modifying and retesting the hypotheses" (138, p. 3). These latter aspects of intellectual functioning presumably include such component traits or abilities as originality, redefinition, adaptive flexibility, spontaneous flexibility, word fluency, expressional fluency, associational fluency, and problem sensitivity.[60,61,82] Much stress, also, is currently laid on divergent thinking as the distinctive attribute of creative thinking; and such Guilford-type tests as unusual uses, consequences, impossibilities, problem situations, and improvements[61] have been employed to measure this ability. Considered as a constellation of general intellectual abilities and personality traits that are not measured by conventional intelligence tests, it is small wonder that creativity correlates just as highly with academic achievement as does IQ[53,54,136] and even more highly than IQ with quality of research accomplishment and vocational productivity.[134]

However, without denying in any way the existence of general creative abilities, it must be insisted that such abilities do not constitute the essence of creativity. It is true that they are more intrinsically related to creative achievement than is IQ. Genuinely creative talent, nevertheless, is a particularized intellectual-personality capacity related to the substantive content of a given field of human endeavor, rather than a set of general content-free intellectual and personality traits; and with increasing age it probably becomes increasingly particularized in its expression. Creative achievement, in other words, reflects a rare capacity for developing insights, sensitivities, and appreciations in a circumscribed content area of intellectual or artistic activity.* This capacity is obviously not coextensive with any one general ability such as divergent thinking, although the possession of this latter ability, and of other general creative abilities as well, undoubtedly facilitates the actualization of particularized and substantive creativity. It should also be recognized that high scores on tests that purportedly measure divergent thinking also reflect the influence of such contaminating factors as verbal fluency and glibness, uninhibited self-expression, and deficient self-critical ability.

To summarize, *creativity* per se is a particularized, substantive capacity, whereas the commonly measured *creative abilities* are general intellectual-personality functions which, like general intelligence and capacity for disciplined concentration, implement the expression of creativity, i.e., convert creative potentialities into creative achievement. The general creative abilities are normally distributed in the population; differences among individuals, like differences in IQ, are differences in degree rather than in kind. Varying degrees of creativity also exist, but the creative person differs *qualitatively* from individuals manifesting lesser degrees of creativity. Hence, although general creative abilities manifest considerable intersituational generality,[54,82,144] there is no reason to believe that creativity per se exhibits any generality of function. Because of their implementing or enabling function, high scores on both tests of general intelligence and of general creative ability are more generously distributed among creative than noncreative individuals.[35,112] Neither type of test, however, measures creativity itself. As a matter of fact, by definition, no general test of creativity is possible. Assessments of creative potentiality can only be based on expert judgments of actual work products, suitably tempered by considerations of age and experience.

Until these distinctions between creativity, general creative abilities, and the creative person are clearly understood by those who use the terms so glibly, existing semantic confusion will remain and probably worsen. It is claimed, for example, that an elementary-school pupil behaves creatively in arithmetic when he proposes alternative approaches to the solution of problems, grasps concepts intuitively, or displays autonomy, flexibility, and freedom from perseverative rigidity in his discovery efforts.[68] What is actually

---

*It may sometimes happen, of course, that a single individual possesses more than one creative talent.

meant, however, is not that he is manifesting even a moderate degree of mathematical creativity or that he has potentialities for becoming a creative mathematician, but that he is exhibiting some general creative abilities in his mathematics work. Quite frequently also, research workers who ordinarily use "creativity" in the more "democratic" sense of the term (*i.e.*, to refer to general creative abilities) also imply in other contexts that the encouragement of true creativity (*i.e.*, in the sense of original accomplishment) in *every* child is one of the major functions of the school. This view is implicit in Bruner's position that the school should help every child reach discontinuous realms of experience so that he can create his own interior culture.[26] It is also implicit in the goal that Suchman proposes for his inquiry training program; namely, that children should be trained to formulate the same kinds of unifying concepts in science which are produced by our most creative scientists.[131] And it is made unambiguously explicit in the following statement by Bruner:

"A small part, but a crucial part of discovery of the highest order is to invent and develop models or "puzzle forms" that can be imposed on difficulties with good effect. It is in this area that the truly powerful mind shines. But it is interesting to what degree perfectly ordinary people can, given the benefit of instruction, construct quite interesting and, what a century ago, would have been considered greatly original models" (26, p. 30).

General Creative Ability and IQ

Tests of general creative ability tap a somewhat different spectrum of intellectual abilities than do the traditional tests of intelligence. The two measures are therefore only slightly correlated.[35,53,54,58,138] The degree of overlap between individuals with high IQ's and individuals with high scores on tests of creativity is approximately 30 per cent.[58,138] Thus, "if an IQ test is used to select top level talent, about 70 per cent of the persons who have the highest 20 per cent of the scores on a creativity test battery would be missed" (134, pp. 68–69). On the basis of his own and other research, Torrance estimates that beyond a cut-off point of 120 IQ, "a higher IQ makes little difference, and the creative thinking abilities become determiners of success. . . . Many of the most creative children tested by our staff achieve IQ's in the 120's or slightly under, and most of these children generally achieve quite well. Most such children would not be included in most special programs for gifted children, however." (138, p. 15) The same relationship probably prevails between IQ and true creativity as between IQ and general creative abilities: above a certain minimum level of IQ, the relationship is approximately zero. The noncreative high IQ individual who does well on academic tasks, but never generates an original idea, is a very familiar figure in our culture.

Getzels and Jackson studied "two groups of adolescents representing two types of cognitive giftedness, the one group very high in 'intelligence' but lower in 'creativity,' the other very high in 'creativity' but lower in 'intelligence' (54, p. 60). They summarize their findings as follows:

"When they were so differentiated, despite a variation of 23 points in average IQ, the two groups were found to be equally superior in scholastic achievement to the population from which they were drawn, but they themselves differed significantly in a number of social-personal variables including perception by their teachers; their values and attitudes, their fantasies and imaginative productions, and their career aspirations.

"The data with respect to both cognitively-oriented and socially-oriented behavior were found to be consistent, and the characteristics that describe the one describe the other. The high IQ's tend to converge on stereotyped meanings, to perceive personal success by conventional standards, to move toward the model provided by teachers, to seek out careers that conform to what is expected of them. The high creatives tend to diverge from stereotyped meanings, to move away from the model provided by teachers, to seek out careers that do not conform to what is expected of them (54, pp. 60–61).

"The family environments of our subjects, at least as portrayed in the mothers' interviews, are consonant with these formulations. It is the parents of the high IQ's rather than the parents of the high creatives who seem to be, in Schachtel's phrase, 'more worried about the dangers of the world.' It is they who more frequently recall financial insecurity during their own childhood, and presumably this may still be at least a latent concern. It is the high IQ parents who are more 'vigilant' about their children's behavior and academic performance. They tend to be more critical of their children and of the education the school is providing. Nor is their vigilance limited only to concerns about their children's educational progress. They are vigilant too about their children's friends. The qualities they would like to see in these friends, which may be conceived of as projections of the qualities they are the most concerned with in their own children, focus on such conventional and immediately visible virtues as 'cleanliness,' 'good manners,' and 'studiousness.' In contrast, the parents of the high creativity adolescents focus on such less conventional qualities as the child's 'openness to experience,' his 'values,' and his 'interests and enthusiasm for life'" (54, p. 75).

"Teaching for Creativity"

Much militant sentimentality underlies the currently popular educational objective of making *every* child a creative thinker and of helping him discover discontinuously new ideas and ways of looking at things. This objective, is in part a wish-fulfilling extension of our present-day preoccupation with actualizing the creative potentialities of gifted children. But it also harks back to the official environmentalistic bias of Progressive Education and to the naive *tabula rasa* conception of human plasticity which holds that, even if a child has no creative potentialities, inspired teaching can create them anyway. True creativity, it is alleged, is not the exclusive property of the rare genius among us, but a tender bud that resides in some measure within every child, requiring only the gentle, catalytic influence of sensitive, imaginative teaching to coax it into glorious bloom. This notion has received some support from recent developments in the mental measurement movement. If, for example, we accept the premise that the structure of intellect can be analyzed into a multiplicity of separately identifiable cognitive abilities or factors [as many as 120 according to Guilford,[59]] the conclusion seems inescapable that simply on the basis of probability, almost every child is destined to become a genius or a near-genius with respect to at least one factor; and even if a particular child were to receive an unlucky shake of the genic dice, a benevolent educational environment would certainly make up for the difference.

How reasonable then is the goal of 'teaching for creativity,' that is, in the sense of singularly original achievement? A decent respect for the realities of the human condition would seem to indicate that the training possibilities with respect to creativity are severely limited. The school can obviously help in the realization of existing creative potentialities by providing opportunities for spontaneity, initiative, and individualized expression; by making room in the curriculum for tasks that are sufficiently challenging for pupils with creative gifts; and by rewarding creative achievement. But it cannot actualize potentialities for creativity if these potentialities do not exist in the first place. Hence it is totally unrealistic, in my opinion, to suppose that even the most ingenious kinds of teaching techniques that we could devise could stimulate creative accomplishment in children of average endowment. Since creative potentialities are, by definition, sparsely distributed in the population, instances of true creativity can be anticipated no more frequently among the clientele of our schools than among any other population of human beings. Actually, creativity is a rare gift. The school can only help in actualizing its expression in those rare individuals who already possess the necessary potentialities.

It is probably true, however, that general creative abilities, in contrast to creativity per se, are more widely distributed and also more susceptible to training. In this sense it can be validly claimed that some creative traits are present in all children; enthusiasts about creativity training,[4] however, tend to imply that potentialities for *creativity* reside in every child, but that their expression is stifled by the culture. It would be more precise and defensible, in my opinion, to state that *general creative abilities* exist in most children, but that the educational system tends to discourage their development.

"Research tells us that children and adults develop along the lines that they find rewarding. If schools are to develop the creative thinking abilities, they must find ways of rewarding this kind of thinking or achievement (137, p. 69).

. . . In the main, current school curricula at all levels of education are designed to develop and make use of the kinds of thinking abilities reflected in traditional tests of intelligence. No one is suggesting that the development of these abilities be eliminated. It is only suggested that parallel treatment be given the creative thinking abilities, as well as other abilities not adequately represented in our present tests of intelligence" (137, p. 68).

REFERENCES

1. Abercrombie, M. L. J. *Learning to Think.* New York: Basic Books, 1960.
2. Adams, J. A. Multiple versus single problem training in human problem solving. *J. exp. Psychol.,* 1954, 48:15–19.
3. Allen, D. C., Tyrell, Sybil, Schulz, R. E., and Koons, Roberta G. The effect of exposure time on the relation between perceptual organization and intelligence. *Amer. J. Psychol.,* 1958, 71:573–77.
4. Anderson, H. H. Creativity in perspective. In *Creativity and its Cultivation.* (H. H. Anderson, ed.). New York: Harper, 1959.
5. Aschner, Mary Jane Mc. The productive thinking of gifted children in the classroom. Urbana, Ill.: Institute for Research on Exceptional Children, University of Illinois, 1961.
6. Atwater, S. K. Proactive inhibition and associative facilitation as affected by degree of prior learning. *J. exp. Psychol.,* 1953, 46:400–404.

7. Ausubel, D. P. Ego development and the learning process. *Child Develpm.*, 1949, *20*:173–90.
8. Ausubel, D. P. The use of advance organizers in the learning and retention of meaningful verbal material. *J. educ. Psychol.*, 1960, *51*:267–72.
9. Ausubel, D. P. Learning by discovery: rationale and mystique. *Bull. Natl. Assoc. Sec. School Principals*, 1961, *45*:18–58.
10. Ausubel, D. P. A transfer of the training approach to improving the functional retention of medical knowledge. *J. med. Educ.*, 1962, *37*:647–55.
11. Ausubel, D. P., and Blake, E. Proactive inhibition in the forgetting of meaningful school material. *J. educ. Res.*, 1958, *52*:145–49.
12. Ausubel, D. P., and Fitzgerald, D. The role of discriminability in meaningful verbal learning and retention. *J. educ. Psychol.*, 1961, *52*:266–74.
13. Ausubel, D. P., and Fitzgerald, D. Organizer, general background, and antecedent learning variables in sequential verbal learning. *J. educ. Psychol.*
14. Battig, W. F. Some factors affecting performance on a word formation problem. *J. exp. Psychol.*, 1957, *54*:96–104.
15. Beberman, M. *An Emerging Program of Secondary School Mathematics.* Cambridge, Mass.: Harvard University Press, 1958.
16. Bensberg, G. J. Concept learning in mental defectives as a function of appropriate and inappropriate "attention sets." *J. educ. Psychol.* 1958, *49*: 137–43.
17. Berkowitz, L. Leveling tendencies and the complexity-simplicity dimension. *J. Pers.*, 1957, *25*:743–51.
18. Bond, A. D. *An Experiment in the Teaching of Genetics.* New York: Bureau of Publications, Teachers College, Columbia University, 1940.
19. Bousfield, W. A., Cohen, B. H., and Whitemarsh, G. A. Associative clustering in the recall of words of different taxonomic frequencies of occurrence. *Psychol. Repts.*, 1958, *41*:39–44.
20. Broverman, D. M. Dimensions of cognitive style. *J. Pers.*, 1960, *28*:167–85.
21. Broverman, D. M. Cognitive style and intraindividual variation in abilities. *J. Pers.*, 1960, *28*:240–56.
22. Brownell, W. A., and Moser, H. E. Meaningful versus mechanical learning: A study in Grade III subtraction. *Duke Univer. Res. Stud. Educ.*, 1949, No. 8.
23. Bruce, R. W. Conditions of transfer of training. *J. exp. Psychol.*, 1933, *16*: 343–61.
24. Bruner, J. S. Going beyond the information given. In *Contemporary Approaches to Cognition.* Cambridge, Mass.: Harvard University Press, 1957.
25. Bruner, J. S. *The Process of Education:* Cambridge, Mass.: Harvard University Press, 1960.
26. Bruner, J. S. The act of discovery. *Harvard educ. Rev.*, 1961, *31*:21–32.
27. Bruner, J. S., Goodnow, Jacqueline J., and Austin, G. A. *A Study of Thinking.* New York: Wiley, 1956.
28. Bruner, J. S., Mandler, J. M., O'Dowd, D., and Wallach, M. A. The role of overlearning and drive level in reversal learning. *J. comp. physiol. Psychol.* 1958, *51*:607–13.
29. Callantine, M. F., and Warren, J. M. Learning sets in human concept formation. *Fyschol. Repts.*, 1955, *1*:363–67.
30. Carey, J. E., and Goss, A. E. The role of mediating verbal responses in the conceptual sorting behavior of children. *J. genet. Psychol.*, 1957, *90*:69–74.
31. Coulson, J. E., and Silberman, H. F. Results of an initial experiment in automated teaching. *Teaching Machines and Programmed Learning* (A. A.

Lumsdaine and R. Glaser, eds.). Washington D. C.: National Education Association, 1960, pp. 452–68.

32. Cox, J. W. Some experiments on formal training in the acquisition of skill. *Brit. J. Psychol.*, 1933, *24*:67–87.

33. Della-Piana, G. *An Experimental Evaluation of Programmed Learning: Motivational Characteristics of the Learner, His Responses, and Certain Learning Outcomes.* Salt Lake City, Utah: University of Utah, 1961.

34. Detambel, M. H., and Stolurow, L. M. Stimulus sequence and concept learning. *J. exp. Psychol.*, 1956, *51*:34–40.

35. Drevdahl, J. E. Factors of importance for creativity. *J. clin. Psychol.* 1956, *12*:21–26.

36. Duncan, C. P. Transfer in motor learning as a function of degree of first-task learning and inter-task similarity. *J. exp. Psychol.*, 1953, *45*:1–11.

37. Duncan, C. P. Transfer after training with single versus multiple tasks. *J. exp. Psychol.*, *1958*, 55:63–72.

38. Duncan, C. P. Recent research on human problem solving. *Psychol. Bull.* 1959, 56:397–429.

39. Duncan, C. P. Description of learning to learn in human subjects. *Amer. J. Psychol.*, 1960, 73:108–14.

40. Ellis, N. R. Objective-quality discrimination learning sets in mental defectives. *J. comp. physiol. Psychol.*, 1958, *51*:79–81.

41. Engle, T. L. High school psycholgy courses as related to university college courses. *Bull. Natl. Assoc. Sec. School Principals*, 1957, *41*:38–42.

42. Ervin, Susan M. Transfer effects of learning a verbal generalization. *Child Develpm.*, 1960, *31*:537–54.

43. Evans, J. L., Glaser, R., and Homme, L. E. A preliminary investigation of variation in the properties of verbal learning sequences of the "teaching machine" type. In *Teaching Machines and Programmed Learning* (A. A. Lumsdaine and R. Glaser, eds.). Washington D. C.: National Education Assn., 1960, pp. 446–51.

44. Fawcett, H. P. Teaching for transfer. *Math. Teacher*, 1935, *28*:465–72.

45. Ferris, F. L. An achievement test report. In *Review of the Secondary School Physics Program of the Physical Science Study Committee.* 1959 Progress Report. Watertown, Mass.: Educational Services Inc., 1960. pp. 26–28.

46. Finlay, G. C. Physical Science Study Committee: a status report. *Science Teacher*, 1959, *26*:574–81.

47. Finlay, G. C. Secondary school physcis: the Physical Science Study Committee. *Am. J. Physics*, 1960, *28*:286–93.

48. French, R. S. The effect of instructions on the length-difficulty relationship for a task involving sequential dependency. *J. exp. Psychol.*, 1954, *48*:89–97.

49. Gardner, R. W., Holzman, P. S., Klein, G. S., Linton, H. B., and Spence, D. P. *A Study of Individual Consistencies in Cognitive Behavior. Psychological Issues*, *1*, No. 4. New York: International Universities Press, 1959.

50. Gardner, R. W., Jackson, D. N., and Messick, S. J. *Personality Organization in Cognitive Controls and Intellectual Abilities. Psychological Issues*, *2*, No. 4. New York: International Universities Press, 1960.

51. Garside, R. F. The prediction of examination marks of mechanical engineering students at King's College, Newcastle. *Brit. J. Psychol.*, 1957, *48*:219–20.

52. Gates, A. I. *Generalization and Transfer in Spelling.* New York: Bureau of Publications, Teachers College, Columbia University, 1935.

53. Getzels, J. W., and Jackson, P. W. The highly intelligent and the highly crea-

tive adolescent: a summary of some research findings. In *The Third (1959) University of Utah Research Conference on the Identification of Creative Scientific Talent.* (C. W. Taylor, ed.). Salt Lake City, Utah: University of Utah Press, 1959. pp. 46–57.

54. Getzels, J. W., and Jackson, P. W. *Creativity and Intelligence.* New York: Wiley, 1962.

55. Gonzalez, R. C., and Ross, S. The basis of solution of preverbal children of the intermediate-size problem. *Amer. J. Psychol.,* 1958, 71:742–46.

56. Goss, A. E. Acquisition and use of conceptual schemes. In *Verbal Learning and Verbal Behavior* (C. N. Cofer, ed.) New York: McGraw Hill, 1961. pp. 42–68.

57. Goss, A. E., and Moylan, Marie C. Conceptual block sorting as a function of degree of mastery of discriminative verbal responses. *J. genet. Psychol.,* 1958, 93:191–98.

58. Guilford, J. P. Creativity. *Amer. Psychol.,* 1950, 9:444–54.

59. Guilford, J. P. Three faces of intellect. *Amer. Psychol.,* 1959, 14:469–79.

60. Guilford, J. P., and Merrifield, P. R. The structure of the intellect model: Its uses and implications. *Reps. psychol. Lab.,* No. 24. Los Angeles: University of Southern California, 1960.

61. Guilford, J. P., Wilson, R. C., Christensen, P. R., and Lewis, D. J. A factor-analytic study of creative thinking. I. Hypotheses and description of tests. *Reps. psychol. Lab.* No. 4. Los Angeles: University of Southern California, 1951.

62. Harlow, H. F. The formation of learning sets. *Psychol. Rev.,* 1949, 56:51–65.

63. Hartung, M. L. Teaching of mathematics in senior high school and junior college. *Rev. educ. Res.,* 1942, 12:425–34.

64. Haselrud, G. M. Transfer from context by sub-threshold summation. *J. educ. Psychol.,* 1959, 50:254–58.

65. Hendrickson, G., and Schroeder, W. H. Transfer of training in learning to hit a submerged target. *J. educ. Psychol.,* 1941, 32:205–13.

66. Hilgard, E. R., Edgren, R. D., and Irvine, R. P. Errors in transfer following learning with understanding: further studies with Katona's card-trick experiments. *J. exp. Psychol.,* 1954, 47:457–64.

67. Hilgard, E. R., Irvine, R. P., and Whipple, J. E. Rote memorization, understanding and transfer: an extension of Katona's card-trick experiments. *J. exp. Psychol.,* 1953, 46:288–92.

68. Hohn, F. E. Teaching creativity in mathematics. *Arith. Teacher,* 1961, 8: 102–106.

69. Holzman, P. S., and Gardner, R. W. Leveling-sharpening and memory organization. *J. abnorm. soc. Psychol.,* 1960, 61:176–80.

70. House, B. J., and Zeaman, D. Positive discrimination and reversals in low grade retardates. *J. comp. physiol. Psychol.,* 1959, 52:564–65.

71. Hull, C. L. Quantitative aspects of the evolution of concepts. *Psychol. Monogr.,* 1920, 28 (Whole No. 123).

72. Jackson, T. A. General factors in transfer of training in the white rat. *Genet. Psychol. Monogr.,* 1932, 11:1–59.

73. James, N. E. Personal preference for method as a factor in learning. *J. educ. Psychol.,* 1962, 53:43–47.

74. Joos, L. W. Utilization of teaching machine concept to elementary school arithmetic. Baltimore, Md.: Board of Education of Baltimore County, 1961.

75. Judd, C. H. Practice and its`effects on the perception of illusions. *Psychol. Rev.*, 1902, 9:27–39.

76. Kagan, J., Moss, H. A., and Sigel, I. E. Conceptual style and the use of affect labels. *Merrill-Palmer Quart. Behav. Developm.*, 1960, 6:261–78.

77. Katona, G. *Organizing and Memorizing.* New York: Columbia University Press, 1940.

78. Kaufman, M. E., and Peterson, W. M. Acquisition of a learning set by normal and mentally retarded children. *J. comp. physiol. Psychol.*, 1958, 51:619–21.

79. Keislar, E. R. The development of understanding in arithmetic by a teaching machine. *J. educ. Psychol.*, 1959, 50:247–53.

80. Kendler, H. H., and D'Amato, M. F. A comparison of reversal shifts and non-reversal shifts in human concept formation behavior. *J. exp. Psychol.*, 1955, 49:165–74.

81. Kendler, H. H., and Karasik, Alan D. Concept formation as a function of competition between response produced cues. *J. exp. Psychol.*, 1958, 55: 278–83.

82. Kettner, N. W., Guilford, J. P., and Christensen, P. R. A factor-analytic study across the domains of reasoning, creativity, and evaluation. *Psychol. Monogr.*, 1959, 73, No. 9 (Whole No. 479).

83. Klare, G. R., Mabry, J. E., and Gustafson, Lenore M. The relationship of patterning (underlining) to immediate retention and to acceptability of technical material. *J. appl. Psychol.*, 1955, 39:40–42.

84. Klausmeier, H. J., and Check, J. F. Retention and transfer in children of low, average and high intelligence. Paper presented to American Educational Research Assoc., Atlantic City, N. J., 1961.

85. Klausmeier, H. J., and Feldhusen, J. F. Retention in arithmetic among children of low, average, and high intelligence at 117 months of age. *J. educ. Psychol.*, 1959, 50:88–92.

86. Klausmeier, H. J., and Loughlin, L. J. Behavior during problem solving among children of low, average, and high intelligence. *J. educ. Psychol.*, 1961, 52:148–52.

87. Krumboltz, J. D. Meaningful learning and retention: practice and reinforcement variables. *Rev. educ. Res.*, 1961, 31:535–46.

88. Little, J. K. Results of use of machines for testing and for drill upon learning in educational psychology. In *Teaching Machines and Programmed Learning* (A. A. Lumsdaine and R. Glaser, Eds.) Washington D. C.: National Education Ass'n., 1960, pp. 59–65.

89. Liublinskaya, A. A. The development of children's speech and thought. In *Psychology in the Soviet Union* (B. Simon, ed.). Stanford, Calif.: Stanford University Press, 1957. Pp. 197–204.

90. Luchins, A. S., and Luchins, Edith H. *Rigidity of Behavior: A Variational Approach to the Effect of Einstellung.* Eugene, Ore.: University of Oregon Books, 1959.

91. McConnell, T. R. Discovery *vs.* authoritative identification in the learning of children. *Univer. Iowa Stud. Educ.*, 1934, 9, No. 5.

92. McGeoch, J. A. Influence of degree of learning upon retroactive inhibition. *Amer. J. Psychol.*, 1929, 41:252–62.

93. Mandler, G. Transfer of training as a function of degree of response overlearning. *J. exp. Psychol.*, 1954, 47:411–17.

94. Mathews, R. Recall as a function of number of classificatory categories. *J. exp. Psychol.*, 1954, 47:241–47.

95. Meyer, Susan R. Report on the initial test of a junior high-school program. In *Teaching Machines and Programmed Learning.* (A. A. Lumsdaine and R. Glaser, eds.) Washington D. C.: National Education Ass'n., 1960. pp. 229–46.

96. Mortisett, L., and Hovland, C. I. A comparison of three varieties of training in human problem solving. *J. exp. Psychol.*, 1959, 58:52–55.

97. Mowrer, O. H. *Learning Theory and the Symbolic Processes.* New York: Wiley, 1960.

98. Munn, N. L. Bilateral transfer of training. *J. exp. Psychol.*, 1932, 15:343–53.

99. Norcross, K. J., and Spiker, C. C. Effects of mediated associations on transfer in paired-associate learning. *J. exp. Psychol.*, 1958, 55:129–34.

100. Northrop, D. S. Effects on learning of the prominence of organizational outlines in instructional films. *Human Engineering Report*-SDC 269-7-33. Pennsylvania State College, Instructional Films Research Program, October 1952.

101. Oakes, W. F. Use of teaching machines as a study aid in an introductory psychology course. *Psychol. Reps.*, 1960, 7:297–303.

102. Osgood, C. E. *Method and Theory in Experimental Psychology.* New York: Oxford University Press, 1953.

103. Osgood, C. E. A behavioristic analysis of perception and language as cognitive phenomena. In *Contemporary Approaches to Cognition.* Cambridge, Mass.: Harvard University Press, 1957.

104. Paul, I. H. *Studies in Remembering: The Reproduction of Connected and Extended Verbal Material. Psychological Issues,* 1, No. 2. New York: International Universities Press, 1959.

105. Porter, D. Some effects of year long teaching machine instruction. In *Automatic Teaching: the State of the Art.* (E. Galanter, ed.) New York: Wiley, 1959. pp. 85–90.

106. Postman, L. Learned principles of organization in memory. *Psychol. Monogr.* 1954, 68 (whole No. 374).

107. Postman, L. The present status of interference theory. In *Verbal Learning and Verbal Behavior.* (C. N. Cofer, ed.). New York: McGraw-Hill, 1961, pp. 152–178.

108. Pressey, S. L. Development and appraisal of devices providing immediate automatic scoring of objective tests and concomitant self-instruction. In *Teaching Machines and Programmed Learning* (A. A. Lumsdaine and R. Glaser, eds.). Washington D. C.: National Educ. Association, 1960.

109. Poulton, E. C. Previous knowledge and memory. *Brit. J. Psychol.*, 1957, 48: 259–70.

110. Pubols, B. H. Successive discrimination reversal learning in the white rat: a comparison of two procedures. *J. comp. Physiol. Psychol.*, 1957, 50:319–22.

111. Reed, L. S. The development of non-continuity behavior through continuity learning. *J. exp. Psychol.*, 1953, 46:107–12.

112. Roe, Anne. Crucial life experiences in the development of scientists. In *Education and Talent* (E. P. Torrance, ed.) Minneapolis: University of Minnesota Press, 1960.

113. Rokeach, M. *The Open and Closed Mind.* New York: Basic Books, 1960.

114. Rudel, Rita G. Transposition of response to size in children. *J. comp. physiol. Psychol.*, 1958, *51*:386–90.

115. Runkel, P. J., and Damrin, Dora E. Effects of training and anxiety upon teachers' preferences for information about students. *J. educ. Psychol.*, 1961, *52*:254–61.

116. Sassenrath, J. M. Learning without awareness and transfer of learning sets. *J. educ. Psychol.*, 1959, *50*:205–12.

117. Saugstad, P. Problem-solving as dependent on availability of functions. *Brit. J. Psychol.*, 1955, *46*:191–98.

118. Schulz, R. W. Problem solving behavior and transfer. *Harvard educ. Rev.* 1960, *30*:61–77.

119. Shore, E., and Sechrest, L. Concept attainment as a function of number of positive instances presented. *J. educ. Psychol.*, 1961, *52*:303–307.

120. Siipola, E. M., and Israel, H. E. Habit-interference as dependent upon stage of training. *Amer. J. Psychol.*, 1933, *45*:205–27.

121. Skinner, B. F., and Holland, J. G. The use of teaching machines in college instruction. In *Teaching Machines and Programmed Learning* (A. A. Lumsdaine and R. Glaser, eds.) Washington D. C.: National Education Association, 1960, pp. 159–72.

122. Smith, B. O. Critical thinking. In *Recent Research Developments and their Implications for Teacher Education.* Thirteenth Yearbook, American Association of Colleges for Teacher Education. Washington, D. C.: The Association, 1960. pp. 84–96.

123. Smith, M. K. The PSSC physics course. In *Review of the Secondary School Physics Program of the Physical Science Study Committee.* 1959 Progress Report, Watertown, Mass.: Educational Services Inc., 1960, pp. 33–36.

124. Smock, C. D. The relationship between "intolerance of ambiguity," generalization, and speed of perceptual closure. *Child Develpm.*, 1957, *28*:27–36.

125. Stein, J. J. The effect of a pre-film test on learning from an educational sound motion picture. *Technical Report—SDC.* 269-7-35. Pennsylvania State College, Instructional Film Research Program, November 1952.

126. Stephens, A. L. Certain special factors involved in the law of effect. In *Teaching Machines and Programmed Learning* (A. A. Lumsdaine and R. Glaser, eds.) Washington, D. C.: National Education Ass'n. 1960, pp. 89–93.

127. Stevenson, H. W., and Langford, T. Time as a variable in transposition of children. *Child Develpm.*, 1957, *28*:365–70.

128. Stevenson, H. W., and Swartz, J. D. Learning set in children as a function of intellectual level. *J. comp. physiol. Psychol.*, 1958, *51*:755–57.

129. Suchman, J. R. Training children in scientific inquiry. Urbana: College of Education, University of Illinois, 1959.

130. Suchman, J. R. Inquiry training in the elementary school. *Science Teacher,* 1960, *27*:42–47.

131. Suchman, J. R. Inquiry training: building skills for autonomous discovery. *Merrill-Palmer Quart. Behav. Develpm.*, 1961, *7*:148–69.

132. Swenson, C. H. College performance of students with high and low school marks when academic aptitude is controlled. *J. educ. Res.*, 1957, *50*:597–603.

133. Swenson, Esther J. Organization and generalization as factors in learning, transfer, and retroactive inhibition. In *Learning Theory in School Situations.*

University of Minnesota Studies in Education. Minneapolis: University of Minnesota Press, 1949. Pp. 9–39.

134. Taylor, C. W. A tentative description of the creative individual. In *Human Variability and Learning*. (W. W. Waetjen, ed.) Washington, D. C.: Association for Supervision and Curriculum Development, 1961, pp. 62–79.

135. Thiele, C. L. *The Contribution of Generalization to the Learning of the Addition Facts*. New York: Bureau of Publications, Teachers College, Columbia University, 1938.

136. Torrance, E. P. Eight partial replications of the Getzels-Jackson study. *Research Memorandum* BER-60-15. Minneapolis: Bureau of Educational Research, University of Minnesota, 1960.

137. Torrance, E. P. Gifted children. In *Recent Research and Developments and their Implications for Teacher Education*. Thirteenth Yearbook, American Association of Colleges for Teacher Education. Washington, D. C.: The Association, 1960, pp. 64–72.

138. Torrance, E. P., Yamamoto, K., Schenetzki, D., Palamutlu, N., and Luther, B. Assessing the creative thinking abilities of children. Minneapolis: Bureau of Educational Research, University of Minnesota, 1960.

139. Ulmer, G. Teaching geometry to cultivate reflective thinking: an experimental study with 1239 high school pupils. *J. exp. Educ.*, 1939, 8:18–25.

140. Underwood, B. J. Proactive inhibition as a function of time and degree of prior learning. *J. exp. Psychol.*, 1949, 39:24–34.

141. Underwood, B. J., and Richardson, J. Verbal concept learning as a function of instructions and dominance level. *J. exp. Psychol.*, 1956, 51:229–38.

142. Weir, M. W., and Stevenson, H. W. The effect of verbalization in children's learning as a function of chronological age. *Child Develpm.*, 1959, 30: 143–49.

143. Weiss, W., and Fine, B. J. Stimulus familiarization as a factor in ideational learning. *J. educ. Psychol.*, 1956, 47:118–24.

144. Wilson, R. C., Guilford, J. P., and Christensen, P. R. The measurement of individual differences in originality. *Psychol. Bull.*, 1953, 50:362–70.

145. Wiltbank, R. T. Transfer of training in the white rat upon various series of mazes. *Behav. Monogr.*, 1919, 4, No. 1.

146. Wittrock, M. C. Transitional Materials in Verbal Learning. Unpublished Ph. D. dissertation. Urbana, Illinois, University of Illinois, 1960.

147. Woodrow, H. The effect of type of training upon transference. *J. educ. Psychol.*, 1927, 18:159–72.

148. Yarcozower, M. Conditioning test of stimulus-predifferentiation. *Amer. J. Psychol.*, 1959, 72:572–76.

149. Young, R. K., and Underwood, B. J. Transfer in verbal materials with dissimilar stimuli and response similarity varied. *J. exp. Psychol.* 1954, 47:153–59.

CHAPTER 6.

Readiness

READINESS—BOTH IN TERMS of manifesting the necessary level of cognitive functioning for handling specified kinds of cognitive operations, and in terms of possessing adequate background knowledge and sophistication in particular subject-matter areas for specified learning tasks—is obviously a crucial cognitive structure variable. It can, in fact, be considered the principal developmental dimension of cognitive structure.

General theories of intellectual development, such as those advanced by Piaget and his collaborators,[32,55,57] include age-level changes in at least four major areas of cognitive functioning, namely, perception, objectivity-subjectivity, the structure of ideas or knowledge, and the nature of thinking or problem-solving. The major focus of our concern in this chapter, however, will be restricted to those developmental changes in the acquisition and organization of knowledge that affect the learning and retention of meaningful verbal material. For example, as children increase in age, they tend to perceive the stimulus world more in general, abstract, and categorical terms and less in tangible, time-bound, and particularized contexts;[32,55,57,62] they demonstrate increasing ability to comprehend and manipulate abstract verbal symbols and relationships, and to employ abstract classificatory schemata;[32,55,57,68] they are better able to understand ideational relationships without the benefit of direct, tangible experience, of concrete imagery, and of empirical exposure to numerous particular instances of a given concept or proposition[32,55,57,68]; they tend more to infer the properties of objects from their class membership rather than from the direct experience of proximate, sensory data;[27,59,64,68,72] they tend more to use remote and abstract than immediate and concrete criterial attributes in classifying phenomena, and to use abstract symbols rather than concrete imagery to represent emerging concepts;[2,32,55,57,72] and they acquire an ever increasing repertoire of more inclusive and higher-order abstractions.[32,62,70,72]

Readiness is a cumulative developmental product reflecting the influence of all prior genic effects, all prior incidental experience, and all prior learning (i.e., specific practice) on cognitive patterning and the growth of cognitive capacities, as well as the interactions among these different variables. In any particular instance of readiness, any one or all of these latter factors may be involved. Readiness can be general in the sense of an individual manifesting a certain level of cognitive functioning required for a wide range of intellectual activities, or understanding certain fundamental principles that are broadly applicable to the comprehension of many subsidiary facts and sub-principles in a given discipline. On the other hand, it may be limited to highly particularized background knowledge necessary for the learning of a narrow segment of new subject matter, and even to the particular teaching method employed in acquiring that knowledge.

111

Pedagogically, therefore, recognition of the principle of readiness implies both that methods of teaching take account of general developmental changes in cognitive functioning, and that the curriculum be organized along sequential lines, i.e., that pupils acquire readiness for each new unit of subject matter as a result of mastering the preceding sequentially related unit. The acquisition of particularized readiness, in other words, is co-extensive with the acquisition and consolidation of relevant, and proximate subsumers in cognitive structure (see pages 30, 83–89). Thus the occurrence of positive transfer in most school learning situations is simply a manifestation of the particularized readiness of existing cognitive structure for the new learning task at hand. General and unqualified statements about the readiness of individuals or age groups obviously make little pedagogic sense, since readiness is always relative to a particular subject matter, topic, level of difficulty, and method of teaching. A pupil who is not ready to read may be ready to learn arithmetic; and within the area of arithmetic he may be ready for multiplication but not for division. Similarly, he may be ready for mutliplication taught by one method but not by another.

STAGES OF INTELLECTUAL DEVELOPMENT

Piaget's delineation of qualitatively distinct stages of intellectual development has been a powerful stimulus to research in this area, as well as a perennial source of theoretical controversy. Despite the general cogency and hueristic promise of his formulations, however, the issue of stages remains unresolved for a number of reasons. Some of these reasons unfortunately inhere in Piaget's unsystematic and faulty methods of conducting his research and reporting his findings.* In the first place, he is almost totally indifferent to problems of sampling, reliability, and statistical significance. He fails to present adequate normative data on age level, sex, and IQ differences, to use uniform experimental procedures for all subjects, to designate unambiguous criteria for classifying the responses of his subjects, and to determine inter-rater reliability. In place of statistical analysis of data and customary tests of statistical significance, he offers confirmatory illustrations selectively culled from his protocols. Second, he tends to ignore such obvious and crucial considerations as extent of intersituational generality and relative degree of intra-and inter-stage variability in delineating stages of development. Third, the cross-sectional observations he uses to measure developmental change (i.e., observations on different age groups of children) are particularly ill-adapted for his purposes. The transitional stages and qualitative discontinuities he purports to find can only be

---

*In the past few years the findings of other investigators[11,20,23,24,42,43,45,47,51,73] have, on the whole, been in general agreement with Piaget's more recent formulations regarding stages of intellectual development. They differ from Piaget's findings less in terms of the developmental sequences involved than in the specification of different age levels for particular stages, in exhibiting greater intra-stage variability, and in manifesting less intersituational and intertask generality.[11,20,21,42,43,45,,47,51] Nevertheless, much more rigorous developmental data than have been presented to date, especially of a longitudinal nature, are required to substantiate Piaget's conclusions.

convincingly demonstrated by longitudinally extended studies of the *same* children. Logical inference is not an adequate substitute for empirical data in naturalistic investigation. Finally, he refines, elaborates, and rationalizes the subdivision of his stages to a degree that goes far beyond his data. Hence the psychological plausibility and freshness of the general outlines of his theory tend to become engulfed in a welter of logical gymnastics, prolix detail, tedious repetition, and abstruse, disorganized speculation.

Criteria of Developmental Stages

Even more important than Piaget's methodological shortcomings in preventing resolution of the disagreement with respect to stages of intellectual development, are the unwarranted and gratuitous assumptions made by his critics regarding the criteria that *any* designated stage of development must meet. Many American psychologists and educators, for example, have been sharply critical of Piaget's designation of stages for the concrete-abstract dimension of cognitive development. They argue that the transition between these stages occurs gradually rather than abruptly or discontinuously; that variability exists both between different cultures and within a given culture with respect to the age at which the transition takes place; that fluctuations occur over time in the level of cognitive functioning manifested by a given child; that the transition to the abstract stage occurs at different ages both for different subject-matter fields and for component subareas within a particular field; and that environmental as well as endogenous factors have a demonstrable influence on the rate of cognitive development. For all of these reasons, therefore, they deny the validity of Piaget's designated stages.

Actually, developmental stages imply nothing more than identifiable sequential phases in an orderly progression of development that are *qualitatively* discriminable from adjacent phases and generally characteristic of most members of a broadly defined age range. As long as a given stage occupies the same sequential position in all individuals and cultures whenever it occurs, it is perfectly compatible with the existence of intraindividual, interindividual, and intercultural differences in age level of incidence and in subject-matter field. It reflects the influence of both genic and environmental determinants, and can occur either gradually or abruptly. Hence all of the aforementioned arguments disputing the legitimacy of Piaget's stages of intellectual development seem quite irrelevant.

Although stages of development are qualitatively discontinuous in *process* from preceding and succeeding stages, there is no reason why their *manner of achievement* must necessarily be abrupt or saltatory. This is particularly true when the factors that bring them into being are operative over many years and are cumulative in their impact. Unlike the situation in physical, emotional, and personality development, cognitive development is not marked by the sudden, dramatic appearance of discontinuously new determinants.

It is also unreasonable to insist that a given stage must always occur at the same age in every culture. Since rate of development is at least in part a function of environmental stimulation, the age range in which a stage occurs tends to vary from one culture to another. Thus, considering the marked differences between the Swiss and American school systems, it would be remarkable indeed if comparable stages of development took place at the same ages. Similarly, within a given culture, a particular stage cannot be expected to occur at the same age for all individuals. When a particular age level is designated for a given stage, it obviously refers to a mean value and implies that a normal range of variability prevails around the mean. This variability reflects differences in intellectual endowment, experiential background, education, and personality. Thus a certain amount of overlapping among age groups is inevitable. A particular stage may be generally characteristic of five- and six-year-olds, but also typically includes some four- and seven-year-olds and even some three- and eight-year-olds. Piaget's age levels, like Gesell's, are nothing more than average approximations set for purposes of convenience. Hence to attack the concept of developmental stages on the grounds that a given stage includes children of varying ages, instead of taking place at the precise age designated by Piaget, is simply to demolish a straw man.

One also cannot expect complete consistency and generality of stage behavior within an individual from one week or month to another, and from one subject matter or level of difficulty to another. Some overlapping and specificity are inevitable whenever development is determined by multiple variable factors. A particular twelve-year-old may use abstract logical operations in his science course in October, but may revert for no apparent reason to a concrete level of cognitive functioning in November, or even several years later when confronted with an extremely difficult and unfamiliar problem in the same field. Furthermore, he may characteristically continue to function at a concrete level for another year or two in social studies and literature. Since transitions to new stages do not occur instantaneously but over a period of time, fluctuations between stages are common until the newly emerging stage is consolidated. In addition, because of intrinsic differences in level of subject-matter difficulty, and because of intra-and interindividual differences in ability profiles and experiential background, it is hardly surprising that transitions from one stage to another do not occur simultaneously in all subject-matter areas and subareas. Abstract thinking, for example, generally emerges earlier in science than in social studies because children have more experience manipulating ideas about mass, time, and space than about government, social institutions, and historical events. However, in some children, depending on their special abilities and experience, the reverse may be true. In any developmental process where experiential factors are crucial, age per se is generally less important than degree of relevant experience. Finally, stages of development are always referable to a given range of difficulty and familiarity of the problem area. Beyond this range, individuals commonly revert (regress) to a former stage of development.

Neither is the concept of developmental stages invalidated by the demonstration that they are susceptible to environmental influence. It is erroneous to believe that stages of intellectual development are exclusively the products of "internal ripening," and hence that they primarily reflect the influence of endogenous factors. Gesell's embryological model of development has little applicability to human development beyond the first year of life when environmental factors become increasingly more important determinants of variability in developmental outcomes. In fact, as the educational system improves, we can confidently look forward to earlier mean emergence of the various stages of cognitive development.

Quantitative and Qualitative Changes in Intellectual Development

Still another reason for confusion and conflict about the problem of stages in intellectual development is the tendency to adopt an all-or-none position regarding the existence of such stages. Actually the evidence suggests that some aspects or dimensions of intellectual development are characterized by quantitative or continuous change whereas others are characterized by qualitative or discontinuous change. Hence, if the issue is no longer approached from the standpoint of an all-or-none proposition, much truth can be found on both sides.

Changes in learning ability, thought processes, and approach to problem-solving appear to differ in degree rather than in kind. No qualitative transitions in learning ability occur at any age; and the evidence indicates that the same kinds of logical operations and problem-solving techniques are employed at all age levels, differing principally in degree or complexity.[15,40,41,71] As Munn[49] points out, the age differences are partly attributable to disparity in previous experience, motivation, and neuromuscular coordination. Perhaps an even more important source of these age level differences, however, is the child's growing ability to generalize and use abstract symbols. Both trial-and-error and insightful problem-solving are found in pre-school children, elementary-school children, adolescents, and adults; the choice between these approaches depends on the inherent difficulty of the problem, the individual's prior background of experience, and the problem's amenability to logical analysis. It is true that insightful approaches tend to increase with age, but only because increasing ability to generalize and use abstract symbols permits a more hypothesis-oriented approach.

Two dimensions of intellectual development characterized by gradually occurring qualitative change, on the other hand, are the transition from subjective to objective thought and the transition from concrete to abstract cognitive operations. Acquisition of the ability to separate objective reality from subjective needs and preferences results in the gradual disappearance of autistic, animistic, anthropomorphic, magical, absolutistic, and nominalistic thinking.[52,53,54] Reference has already been made to studies (see footnote on p. 112) supporting Piaget's findings[32,55,56,57] regarding the transition from concrete to abstract thought. These findings will be discussed in greater detail below.

Reflective of both kinds of qualitative change is evidence indicating that children seem to pass through gross qualitative stages of causal thinking[17,18,28,60] and rarely appreciate antecedent-consequent relationships in the adult sense of the term prior to the age of eight to ten.[16,39] Even Piaget's severest critics concede that there is gradual improvement with increasing age in the quality of children's causal explanations.[17,50] On the other hand, much overlapping prevails between age groups. All kinds of causal explanations are found at all age levels;[19,28,50] some adolescents and adults even give responses characteristic of young children.[18,29,50] Furthermore, changes tend to occur gradually, and the quality of causal thinking shows much specificity and dependence on particular relevant experience.[17,19,50] None of these latter facts, however, are incompatible with the existence of stages in children's thinking as defined above.

The Concrete-Abstract Dimension of Cognitive Development*

The concrete-abstract dimension of intellectual development may be divided into three qualitatively distinct developmental stages—the preoperational stage, the stage of concrete operations, and the stage of abstract operations—which occur respectively during the preschool, elementary-school, and adolescent-adult periods of development. During the preoperational stage, the child is capable of using language to represent objects and experience, but is unable to manipulate or relate these verbal representations to each other meaningfully in solving problems or comprehending new ideas. Lacking the ability to relate verbal symbols internally, he relies instead on the direct manipulation of objects, i.e., on overt trial and error. Thus he manipulates relations between objects per se rather than relations between their symbolic representations.

In the sense that the learning behavior of the preoperational child is largely regulated by overt action rather than by verbal mediation, it is very similar to that manifested by infra-human mammals.[36,37,38,46] Because logical operations during this period are not internalized, and also lack the quality of reversibility that characterizes an internalized operation, the child in this developmental stage cannot grasp the concept of conservation of mass (i.e., the idea that mass remains constant even though its shape changes). This same inability internally to relate ideas to each other obviously precludes the correlative type of meaningful reception learning—the kind of learning that requires an individual to relate presented new ideas to existing concepts in his cognitive structure in an elaborative, correlative, or qualifying sense—unless concurrent overt manipulation is possible. The derivative type of meaningful reception learning, however, is entirely compatible with cognitive capacity during the preoperational stage, even in the absence of such manipulation; in this kind of learning the new idea is simply a symbolic representation of an existing concrete image or an illustration of an established concept or proposition in cognitive structure.

The stage of concrete operations is inaugurated when behavior and learning finally come under predominantly verbal or symbolic control. During this stage the child is able to manipulate relations between ideas internally, that is, without overt manipulation of the objects represented by the ideas. In solving problems and in meaningful reception learning, he tends to work exclusively with ideational representations of ideas and with the relations between them. Thus he is thoroughly capable both of solving problems either by internal (covert) trial-and-error or by testing hypotheses, and of meaningfully understanding presented new ideas that imply correlative relationships with existing concepts in cognitive structure.

It is also important to realize that logical operations at this stage of intellectual development are not really concrete in the sense that concrete images of objects are relationally manipulated in problem-solving or meaningful reception learning. The elementary-school child actually manipulates relations between the verbal representations of objects. The concreteness of the oper-

---

*The following description of this aspect of cognitive development is a modified version and somewhat idiosyncratic interpretation of the account given by Piaget and Inhelder.[32,55,56,57]

ations merely inheres in the fact that they are dependent upon current or re-cently prior concrete-empirical experience, and are constrained in their logical implications by the particularity of this experience. The logical operations per-formed at this point of development are relational extensions of and make ex-plicit reference to particular and tangible empirical data; unlike the situa-tion in the abstract stage, they cannot be considered logical transformations of hypothetical relationships between general abstract variables.* Never-theless they constitute a significant advance over the preceding preoperational stage when correlative relations between ideas could not be handled at all in reception or discovery learning, even with the aid of concrete-empirical props, and required direct manipulation of objects.

The elementary-school child is, of course, no more dependent on immediate concrete-empirical experience than is the preoperational child in understand-ing and manipulating simple abstractions or ideas about objects and phen-omena. It is true that the emergence of such ideas must always be preceded by an adequate background of direct, nonverbal experience with the use of empirical data from which they are abstracted. But once their meaning becomes firmly established as a result of this background of past experience, the child can meaningfully comprehend and use them without any *current* reference to concrete-empirical data.

The meaningful understanding or manipulation of relationships between abstractions or of *ideas about ideas,* on the other hand, is quite another mat-ter. In this kind of operation the elementary-school pupil is still dependent upon current or recently prior concrete-empirical experience: when such ex-perience is not available, he finds abstract relational propositions unrelatable to cognitive structure and hence devoid of meaning. This dependence upon concrete-empirical props self-evidently limits his ability meaningfully to grasp and manipulate relationships between abstractions, since he can only acquire those understandings and perform those logical operations which do not go beyond the concrete and particularized representation of reality implicit in his use of props. Thus, where complex relational propositions are involved, he is largely restricted to a subverbal, concrete, or intuitive level of cognitive functioning, a level that falls far short of the clarity, precision, explicitness, and generality associated with the more advanced abstract stage of intellectual development.

It is clear, therefore, that until they consolidate a sufficiently large working

---

*Brown[12] argues that the cognitive processes of adults are more abstract than those of children only in the sense that they manifest more discriminative generaliza-tion—that children actually exhibit more simple stimulus generalization than do adults (*i.e.,* generalization not requiring prior discriminative analysis). Hence he claims that adults do not really use a wider range of generic concepts in their thinking, but merely employ a more highly differentiated repertoire of subcategories within existing categories. Simple stimulus generalization, however, can hardly be considered a form of abstract thinking reflecting the use of generic concepts. Thus it seems more plausible to believe that adults also characteristically use a greater number of generic *categories* than do children, as well as more differentiated sub-categories.

body of key verbal concepts based on appropriate experience, and until they become capable of directly interrelating abstract propositions without reference to specific instances, children are closely restricted to basic empirical data in the kinds of logical operations they can relate to cognitive structure. Thus in performing "class inclusive and relational operations," they generally require direct experience with the actual diverse instances underlying a concept or generalization, as well as proximate, nonverbal (rather than representational) contact with the objects or situations involved. During the elementary-school years, directly presented and general verbal propositions are too distantly removed from empirical experience to be relatable to cognitive structure. This does not necessarily mean, however, that autonomous discovery experience is required before meaningfulness is possible. As long as direct, nonverbal contact with the data is an integral part of the learning situation, both derivative and correlative verbal concepts and generalizations may be meaningfully apprehended even though they are presented rather than discovered.

Beginning in the junior-high school period, however, children become increasingly less dependent upon the availability of concrete-empirical experience in meaningfully relating complex abstract propositions to cognitive structure. Eventually, after sufficient gradual change in this direction, a qualitatively new capacity emerges: the intellectually mature individual becomes capable of understanding and manipulating relationships between abstractions without any reference whatsoever to concrete, empirical reality. Instead of reasoning directly from a particular set of data, he uses indirect, second-order logical operations for structuring the data; instead of merely grouping data into classes or arranging them serially in terms of a given variable, he formulates and tests hypotheses based on all possible combinations of variables. Since his logical operations are performed on verbal propositions, he can go beyond the operations that follow immediately from empirical reality (equivalence, distinctiveness, reversibility and seriation), and deal with all possible or hypothetical relations between ideas. He can now transcend the previously achieved level of subverbal, intuitive thought and understanding, and formulate general laws relating general categories of variables that are divorced from the concrete-empirical data at hand. His concepts and generalizations, therefore, tend more to be second-order constructs derived from relationships between previously established verbal abstractions already one step removed from the data itself. And since he is freed from dependence on direct, nonverbal contact with data in independently discovering meaningful new concepts and generalizations, he is obviously also liberated from this same dependence in the much less rigorous task of merely apprehending these constructs meaningfully when they are verbally presented to him.

Although abstract operations are typically verbal, and concrete operations are typically nonverbal, the verbal-nonverbal distinction is not the distinguishing difference between the two kinds of operations.

". . . The mean feature of propositional logic is not that it is verbal logic but that it requires a combinatorial system. . . . Formal [abstract] thought is a system of second-degree operations. Concrete operations may be called first-degree operations in that they refer to objects directly. . . . But it is also possible to structure relations between relations. . . . This notion of second-degree operations also expresses the general characteristic of [abstract] thought—it goes beyond the framework of transformations bearing directly on empirical reality (first-degree operations) and *subordinates* it to a system of hypothetico-deductive operations—*i.e.*, operations which are possible" (32, p. 254).

General and Specific Aspects of the Transition. We have already rejected complete generality over subject-matter areas and levels of difficulty as a legitimate criterion of a developmental stage. Too much unevenness exists in any individual's experiential background and pattern of abilities for the transition from concrete to abstract functioning to occur simultaneously in all areas. A stage of development, also, is always referable to a typical range of difficulty and familiarity of the problem at hand; beyond this range, regression to an earlier stage of development commonly occurs. Nevertheless, it is apparent that the transition from concrete to abstract cognitive functioning takes place specifically in each subject-matter area, and presupposes a certain necessary amount of sophistication in each of the areas involved. This specificity, however, does not invalidate the existence of qualitatively distinct stages of development. It is still possible to designate an individual's over-all developmental status as concrete or abstract on the basis of an estimate of his characteristic or predominant mode of cognitive functioning.

This distinction between specific and general aspects of developmental status is important for two reasons: First, the individual necessarily continues to undergo the same transition from concrete to abstract cognitive functioning in each *new* subject matter area he encounters—even *after* he reaches the abstract stage of development on an over-all basis. Second, once he attains this latter general stage, however, the transition to abstract cognitive functioning in unfamiliar new subject-matter fields takes place much more readily and presupposes less specific subject-matter sophistication. For example, a cognitively mature adult who has never studied astronomy is not in the same developmental position as a nine-year-old with respect to the concrete-abstract dimension when both begin an introductory course in astronomy.

Thus, even though an individual characteristically functions at the abstract level of cognitive development, when he is first introduced to a wholly unfamiliar subject-matter field he tends initially to function at a concrete, intuitive level. But since he is able to draw on various transferable elements of his more *general* ability to function abstractly, he passes through the concrete stage of functioning in this particular subject-matter area much more rapidly than would be the case were he still generally in the concrete stage of cognitive development. These facilitating transferable elements presumably include transactional terms, higher-order concepts, and successful experience in *directly* understanding and manipulating relationships between abstractions (*i.e.*, without the benefit of props), which, although acquired in specific subject matter contexts, are generally applicable to other learning situations. (see below) Hence, in contrast to the cognitively immature child who continues to use concrete-empirical data in relating abstractions to each other, he only uses the concrete props initially—to develop the necessary higher-order abstractions—and then proceeds to dispense with props entirely in acquiring additional abstractions. His dependence on concrete-empirical props, in other words, is temporary and reflective of specific subject-matter unsophistication, rather than developmental and reflective of general cognitive immaturity.

Determinants of Change. It is hypothesized that the combined influence of three concomitant and mutually supportive developmental trends accounts for the transition from concrete to abstract cognitive functioning. In the first place, the developing individual gradually acquires a working vocabulary of transactional or mediating terms that makes possible the more efficient juxtaposition and combination of different relatable abstractions into potentially meaningful propositions. Second, he can relate these latter propositions more readily to cognitive structure, and hence render them more meaningful, in view of his growing fund of stable, higher-order concepts and principles encompassed by and made available within that structure. A sufficient body of abstract ideas that are clear and stable is obviously necessary before he can hope efficiently to manipulate relationships between them so as to develop meaningful general propositions. The possession of a working body of inclusive concepts also makes possible the formulation of more general statements of relationship that are less tied to specific instances; greater integration of related ideas and different aspects of the same problem; the elaboration of more precise distinctions and finer differentiations; and less dependence on complete concrete-empirical data in reaching warranted inferences. Finally, it seems reasonable to suppose that after many years of practice in meaningfully understanding and manipulating relationships *with* the aid of concrete-empirical props, he gradually develops greater facility in performing these operations, so that eventually (after acquiring the necessary transactional and higher-order concepts) he can perform the same operations just as effectively *without* relying on props. The same sequence of events is seen in acquiring many other neuromuscular and cognitive skills, *e.g.*, walking without "holding on," bicycling "without hands," talking a foreign language without internal translation from one's mother tongue, transmitting Morse code in sentences rather than in word or letter units.

This is probably an adequate explanation of the transition from concrete to abstract thought at a proximate or immediate level of causality, but it begs the more *ultimate* issue of causality, *i.e.*, what is it that accounts for these three enabling changes in cognitive structure that eventually effect developmental transition? The ultimate cause of this transition undoubtedly inheres in genic potentiality and the necessary experience to actualize it. Human beings have a genic capacity for developing the kinds of information-processing and storing mechanisms that use abstract categories, and can directly relate these abstract categories to each other in meaningful fashion. They also have a genic capacity for processing and storing information at a concrete-empirical and noncategorical level. Now, given these two genic capacities, one of which is more complex than the other, the concrete level constituting a developmental prerequisite for and precursor of the abstract level, and the abstract level constituting a more stable, efficient, and economical form of information processing and storage, then the direction of development from concrete to abstract levels of functioning is inevitable providing that the necessary degree of experiential stimulation and support is forthcoming. This latter environmental component includes sufficient experience at the concrete level to permit the emergence of abstractions and abstract operations, and living in a culture in which abstractions are part of the language and are in common use.

To what extent, however, does this more remote explanation go beyond the statement that we develop the way we do because we are so constituted that this is the way we develop? Are we seeking to answer a question of causality by simply restating the question in declarative form and equating a vague, nonspecifiable generality with "cause"? Actually, an explanation of the course of developmental direction in terms of genic potentialities and the experience necessary to actualize them is not scientifically tautological. In the first place, genes are not reified abstractions but specific entities that exist in the real world, entities whose existence in the real world can be demonstrated independently of their effects. Second, the highly general nature of this explanation is also mitigated by the designation of two more specific and proximate (mediating) determinants, i.e., the gradual acquisition of a sufficient member of stable, higher-order concepts and transactional terms, and the gradual increase in facility to relate abstractions to each other with the aid of props so that eventually the same relational process can be performed without the use of props.

This still leaves two causal questions unanswered. How, in greater detail, is the influence of genic potentialities actually mediated in the acquisition of concrete and abstract cognitive capacities? How can a change from one qualitative level to another be effected at a certain critical point in the cumulation of quantitative changes? Someday we may obtain more precise answers as to how genes affect the nervous system in ways that make different kinds of cognition possible. The answer to the second question, however, will probably always remain in the realm of metaphysical speculation.

Piaget and Inhelder[58] largely embrace a maturational position in explaining how developmental transition is effected during the earlier stages of intellectual development. Their view of maturation, however, which they call "equilibration," is inclusive of both internal (genic) factors and incidental experience. It is therefore closer to the empirical concept of maturation than it is to Gesell's notion of maturation as a process of internal ripening. Maturation accounts for the universality of the sequential stages and the order in which they occur, whereas specific learning experience accounts for interindividual, intraindividual, and intercultural differences in age level and subject-matter field. Suitable training can undoubtedly accelerate to some extent the rate at which the various stages of intellectual development succeed each other. Inevitably, however, maturational considerations impose a limit on such acceleration. For example, training children in the preoperational stage to appreciate the notion of conservation of mass tends to produce an unstable understanding of this principle which is hardly equivalent to that acquired by older children.[65] Similarly, young children who receive laboratory training in learning the principle of a teeter-totter (i.e., that the longer side from the fulcrum falls when both ends are equally weighted), fail to acquire any resistance to learning a spurious causal relationship about the operation of a teeter-totter (i.e., that the color of the blocks placed at either end of the teeter-totter is the determining factor.[9] Older children, on the other hand, who are both cognitively more mature and have more incidental experience with teeter-totters, resist learning the spurious causal relationship.[9]

Both general and specific motivational explanations[32] have been advanced to account for the transition from concrete to abstract cognitive functioning. Desire to obtain greater meaning out of experience is not a convincing explanation since this desire does not arise suddenly or uniquely at adolescence. Furthermore, although motivation may energize and facilitate cognitive change, it cannot explain either its occurrence or direction. Desire to identify with and participate in the adult world has more specific relevance for this age period; but again no amount of motivation would suffice to effect the change in question in the absence of the necessary genic potentialities and supportive experience.

EDUCATIONAL IMPLICATIONS OF THE INTUITIVE-CONCRETE LEVEL

Intuitive cognitive functioning refers to an implicit, relatively unprecise and informal type of understanding or thought process in which the individual is only vaguely aware of the parameters of a problem or its solution and of the logical operations involved. In contrast to formal abstract thought, it is nonanalytic and unsystematic in its approach, relies on immediate apprehension, and defies explicit formulation. The principal difficulty with the concept is the failure, on the part of those who use it, to differentiate between four very different kinds of intuitive processes, i.e., developmental, unsophisticated, sophisticated, and creative, and to treat all four types as if they were identical. This obviously leads to incalculable semantic and pedagogic confusion.

Types of Intuitive Processes

The *developmental* type of intuitive process occurs in the child who is in the preoperational stage or in the stage of concrete operations. The lack of explicitness and precision and the unsystematic, nonanalytic approach in this case reflect the semi-abstract and relatively nonverbal character of the elementary-school child's cognitive functioning, the paucity of his higher-order concepts and transactional terms, and the particularity of his logical operations and their dependence on overt manipulation or concrete-empirical props. In addition, these cognitive attributes reflect a general lack of sophistication in all subject-matter fields. The *unsophisticated* type of intuitive process, on the other hand, occurs in the cognitively mature individual who happens to be a complete novice in a *particular* subject-matter field. It is phenomenologically similar to the developmental type, but is a self-limited condition lasting only until the individual acquires some minimal sophistication in the area in question.

Intuitive processes also occur in *cognitively mature* individuals who are confronted with a difficult new problem in a given subject-matter field in which they *are* highly sophisticated. In fact, it is this very sophistication and thorough familiarity with the field as a whole which enable them to explore the problem informally without systematic analysis of the data, to develop hunches, and to use short-cuts. Although the probings are unsystematic and the formulations are unprecise and lack explicitness, the logical operations, in contrast to those of the two previously described types of intuition, are conducted on an abstract and completely verbal level and are not limited by the particularity of specific instances. Sophisticated intuitive processes become *creative* when they reflect notable degrees of perceptiveness, sensitivity, originality, and insight, in addition to thorough familiarity with the subject-matter field.

Bruner[13] tends to treat the developmental and sophisticated kinds of intuitive process as if they were synonymous. Anderson[1] and Page (13, pp. 39-40) go even further and contend that the concrete-intuitive approach of young children is more creative than the abstract-verbal approach of older individuals, and is comparable to the creative type of intuitive thinking found among creative scholars and scientists. Actually, however, there is no necessary or intrinsic relationship between intuitive thinking and creativity—either among children or adults. The only existing relationship is a chronological one: if a given individual happens to be creative, whether he is a child or an adult, he will obviously first manifest his creativity during the intuitive phase, because this phase invariably precedes the abstract-verbal phase; and contrariwise, if he is not creative, either as a child or an adult, he will not manifest any creativity during either phase.

Hence there is a world of difference between the intuitive thinking of elementary-school children and the intuitive thinking of sophisticated scholars or scientists. The preschool or elementary-school child, irrespective of whether or not he is creative, thinks intuitively about many abstract ideas because this is *the best he can do* at his particular stage of intellectual development. He is incapable of understanding relationships between complex abstractions in abstract-verbal terms and without the benefit of overt manipulation or concrete-empirical props. The intuitive expressions of creative or just ordinarily competent scholars or scientists, on the other hand, consist of tentative and roughly formulated hunches or exploratory germs of ideas which are merely preparatory to more rigorous thought. Thus they are reflective of a preliminary phase in a particular problem-solving sequence—when full information and precise ideas about the problem in question are not yet available—rather than of gross developmental limitations in level of intellectual functioning. Furthermore, although the hunches themselves are only makeshift approximations that are not precisely stated, they presuppose both a high level of abstract verbal ability as well as sophisticated knowledge of a particular discipline.

Can Any Subject Be Taught Intuitively at Any Age Level?

By suitably adapting methods of teaching to the child's level of cognitive functioning, Bruner believes that it is possible to teach preschool and elementary-school children any subject that can be taught to adolescent and adult students.

"At each stage of development the child has a characteristic way of viewing the world and explaining it to himself. The task of teaching a subject to a child at any particular age is one of representing the structure of that subject in terms of the child's way of viewing things. The task can be thought of as one of translation (13, p. 33). . . . If one respects the ways of thought of the growing child, if one is courteous enough to translate material into his logical forms, and challenging enough to tempt him to advance, then it is possible to introduce him at any early age to the ideas and styles that in later years make an educated man (p. 54). . . . Any idea can be represented honestly and usefully in the thought forms of children of school age and . . . these first representations can later be made more powerful and precise the more easily by virtue of this early learning (p. 33).

"Experience over the past decade points to the fact that our schools may be wasting precious years by postponing the teaching of many important subjects on the ground that they are too difficult (p. 12) . . . [Actually] any subject can be taught effectively in some intellectually honest form to any child at any stage of development (p. 33). . . . The basic ideas that lie at the heart of all science and mathematics and the basic themes that give life to literature are as simple as they are powerful. To be in command of these basic ideas, to use them effectively, requires a continual deepening of one's understanding of them that comes from learning to use them in progressively more complex forms. It is only when such basic ideas are put in formalized terms as equations or elaborated verbal concepts that they are out of reach of the young child, if he has not first understood them intuitively and had a chance to try them out on his own. The early teaching of science, mathematics, social studies and literature should be designed to teach these subjects with scrupulous intellectual honesty but with an emphasis upon the intuitive grasp of ideas and upon the use of these basic ideas. A curriculum as it develops should revisit these basic ideas repeatedly, building upon them until the student has grasped the full formal apparatus that goes with them" (pp. 12-13).

Inhelder expresses very similar views:

". . . It is possible to draw up methods of teaching the basic ideas in science and mathematics to children considerably younger than the traditional age. It is at this earlier age that systematic instruction can lay a groundwork in the fundamentals that can be used later and with great profit at the secondary level (13, pp. 44-45).

". . . It seems highly arbitrary and very likely incorrect to delay the teaching, for example, of Euclidian or metric geometry until the end of the primary grades, particularly when projective geometry has not been given earlier. So too with the teaching of physics which has much in it that can be profitably taught at an inductive level much earlier. Basic notions in these fields are perfectly accessible to children of seven to ten years of age, *provided they are divorced from their mathematical expression and studied through materials* that the child can handle himself" (13, p. 43).

It is quite possible, of course, that prior intuitive understanding of certain concepts during childhood can facilitate their learning and stabilize their retention when they are taught at a more formal, abstract level during adolescence. In fact, this procedure may be the most effective means of discouraging rote memorization of verbally presented propositions in the secondary school. However, confirmatory empirical evidence is still unavailable. Further, one must balance against these possible advantages of early intuitive learning the excessive time-cost involved in many instances. In certain cases it may be more feasible in the long run to postpone entirely the introduction of particular subject-matter fields until children are cognitively mature. No general answer can be given to this problem. The decision in each case must be based on the findings of particularized research. Some studies[10,25] indicate that kindergarten attendance facilitates academic performance during the first grade and that evidence of this facilitation can even be found in the eleventh grade. On the other hand, children in one progressive school who learned no formal arithmetic until the fifth grade equalled matched controls in computation by the seventh grade, and surpassed them in arithmetic reasoning.[61]

In addition, it undoubtedly overstates the case to claim that *any* subject can be taught to children in the preoperational stage or in the stage of concrete logical operations provided that the material is presented in a nonformal, intuitive fashion with the aid of overt manipulation or concrete-empirical props. It is readily conceivable that some topics, such as "set theory" in mathematics, can be successfully learned by fourth-grade pupils when recast in accordance with their characteristic ways of thinking and conceptualizing experience. This hardly rules out the possibility, however, that the comprehension of many other ideas presupposes a certain minimal level of life experience, cognitive maturity, and subject-matter sophistication, or that some ideas simply cannot be expressed without the use of certain higher-order abstractions. These latter kinds of concepts would be *intrinsically* too difficult for preschool or elementary-school children irrespective of the method of presentation. Moreover, even assuming that all abstract-verbal concepts could be restructured on an intuitive basis, it would be unreasonable to expect that they could *all* be made comprehensible to children at *any* grade level. Although the intuitive comprehensibility of any given restructured idea is best determined empirically, it would surely be plausible on *a priori* grounds to expect that a certain proportion of these ideas could not be rendered comprehensible to typical pupils in some of the preschool and elementary grades.

Specificity or Generality of Intuitive Learnings

Still another difficulty with the intuitive elementary-school curriculum proposed by Bruner or Inhelder is its generality and separation from the content of the various disciplines. It is oriented toward certain universal and recurrent principles of science which, when learned once in general form, are supposedly applicable to the more specific problems of the particular sciences, *e.g.,* "categorization and its uses, the unit of measure and its development, the indirectness of information in science and the need for operational definition of ideas, . . . the attitude that things are connected and not isolated, . . . the idea of multiple determination of events in the physical and social world" (13, pp. 26-27). Inhelder suggests that we:

". . . devote the first two years of school to a series of exercises in manipulating, classifying and ordering objects in ways that highlight basic operations of logical addition, multiplication, inclusion, serial ordering and the like. For surely these logical operations are the basis of more specific operations and concepts of all mathematics and science. It may indeed be the case that such an early science and mathematics 'precurriculum' might go a long way toward building up in the child the kind of intuitive and more inductive understanding that could be given embodiment later in formal courses in mathematics and science. The effect of such an approach would be, we think, to put more continuity into science and mathematics, and also to give the child a much better and firmer comprehension of the concepts, which until he has this early foundation, he will mouth later without being able to use them in any effective sense" (13, p. 46).

In the first place, it is questionable whether general, content-free principles of science have any applicability to the understanding of ideas in a particular science. The philosophy and fundamental concepts of a given discipline are largely shaped by its unique content, history and methodology. Scientific method is not readily transferable across different disciplines. Hence principles that hold true for a wide range of sciences are more likely to constitute basic postulates of a general philosophy of science than to have relevance for the substantive content or methodology of any particular science. Second, general principles of scientific inquiry consist, by definition, of higher-order abstractions far removed from and exceedingly difficult to relate to the concrete-empirical experience of an elementary-school child. In order to be made comprehensible to him they would first have to be presented in multiple particularized contexts from which their generality could then be abstracted. But it is precisely this type of higher-order abstraction and hypothetico-deductive reasoning in general terms that is beyond the developmental capacity of the elementary-school child. As we shall see later in another context (see p. 156), although the content, organization, objectives and methods of the elementary-school curriculum must obviously be adapted to the cognitive capacities of pupils, the curriculum must systematically come to grips with the actual substantive content and methodology of the various disciplines.

Can Children Learn Anything More Efficiently than Adults?

Related to the proposition that children can learn anything that adults can, (provided that it is suitably presented), is the contention that they can also do so more efficiently. David Page, for example makes the following assertion:

"In teaching from kindergarten to graduate school, I have been amazed at the intellectual similarity of human beings at all ages, although children are perhaps more spontaneous, creative, and energetic than adults. As far as I am concerned, young children can learn almost anything *faster* than adults do if it can be given to them in terms they understand" (13, pp. 39-40).

In my opinion, although this propostion is generally untrue and unsupportable, it is nevertheless valid in a very limited sense of the term. Even more important, however, it is, in many instances, partially true for reasons that are very different from those offered by its advocates.

Many reasons exist for believing that under *certain* conditions young children *can* learn more efficiently than older and intellectually more mature persons. In the first place, older individuals, particularly if miseducated, must often first unlearn what they have previously been taught before they are ready for new learning. This is frequently the case when a student's knowledge is unclear, unstable, or disorganized because of a prior history of rote or nonmeaningful learning. Second, older individuals are more apt to have "emotional blocks" with respect to particular subject matter areas. Finally, there is a marked falling off of intellectual enthusiasm as children move up the academic ladder.

Generally speaking, however, adolescents and adults have a tremendous advantage in learning any new subject matter—even if they are just as unsophisticated as young children in that particular discipline. This advantage inheres in the fact that they are able to draw on various transferable elements of their *over-all* ability to function at an abstract-verbal level of logical operations. Hence they are able to move through the concrete-intuitive phase of intellectual functioning very rapidly; and, unlike the comparably unsophisticated child, who is tied to this latter stage developmentally, they are soon able to dispense entirely with concrete-empirical props and with intuitive understandings. These facilitating transferable elements, as indicated above, include the possession of transactional terms and higher-order concepts, as well as successful past experience in *directly* manipulating relationships between abstractions (*i.e.*, without the benefit of concrete-empirical props).

But according to the advocates of the child superiority proposition, this more rapid shift on the part of the older learners from a concrete-intuitive to an abstract-verbal level of intellectual functioning in the unfamiliar new subject-matter area, results in *less* efficient learning processes and outcomes. Research findings, however, suggest precisely the opposite conclusion, namely, that as long as abstract-verbal understandings are meaningful rather than rote, they constitute a more complete, explicit, inclusive and transferable form of knowledge. For example, numerous experiments on the effects of verbalization on children's ability to solve transposition problems[66,69] demonstrate that verbal concepts are more manipulable and transferable than their sub-verbal equivalents. The availability of distinctive verbal responses has also been shown to facilitate rather than inhibit concept formation and conceptual transfer (see p. 88). We have already observed that there is no necessary or intrinsic relationship between intuitive thinking and creativity, and that the developmental type of intuitive process bears little relationship to the intuitive thinking of sophisticated or creative scholars (see p. 123).

A final argument sometimes advanced for the child superiority proposition is that since there are allegedly optimal (*i.e.*, "critical") periods of readiness for all kinds of developmental acquisitions, many intellectual skills can be acquired more easily by younger than by older pupils. But although this argument is supported by some aspects of motor, physical and perceptual development, it has still to be validated in the field of intellectual development.° Of course, one would hardly attempt to justify the postponement of any subject-matter content on the grounds that older children generally learn more efficiently than do young children; the resulting waste of precious years in which reasonably economical learning could have taken place if attempted, would in this instance more than offset the waste attributable to less efficient learning. But by the same token this wasted opportunity cannot be used as an argument in support of the proposition that the occurrence of optimal periods of readiness renders the learning of younger pupils more efficient than that of older pupils in certain subject-matter areas.

Acceleration of the Concrete Stage

Is it possible to accelerate children's progress through the stage of concrete logical operations by taking account of their characteristic cognitive limita-

---

°Elementary-school children, on the average, learn less French in three years than do college freshmen in a single semester.[22] However there is a low but consistent negative relationship between chronological age and the Spanish achievement test scores of elementary-school pupils.[33] Johnson, in a personal communication, attributes this relationship to the younger learner's greater facility in pronunciation, listening comprehension, and rote linguistic expression, despite less mastery of the grammatical structure of the language.

tions, and by providing suitably contrived experience geared to their cognitive capacity and mode of functioning? Can we, for example, train them, as Inhelder suggests,[13] to focus on more than one aspect of a problem at a time or to acquire genuine appreciation of the concept of conservation of mass? If stages of development have any true meaning, the answer to this question can only be that although some acceleration is possible, it is necessarily limited in extent. In general, transitions from one stage of development to another presuppose the attainment of a critical threshold level of capacity that is reflective of extended and cumulative experience. This does not mean, of course, that development occurs spontaneously as a result of internal ripening. In addition to the operation of genic patterning factors, the necessary environmental stimulation must be forthcoming; and as children increase in age and cognitive capacity, teaching methods can place increasingly less reliance on concrete-empirical props.* Also, since rate of development is partly a function of quantity and appropriateness of relevant experience, it is quite conceivable that suitable long-term training procedures might produce more stable developmental acceleration than the previously reported studies of short-term training (see p. 121).

Dependence on Concrete-Empirical Experience

The elementary-school child is completely dependent upon current or recently prior concrete-empirical experience for the meaningful understanding or manipulation of relational propositions. He tends to appreciate relationships between abstractions intuitively—as rather immediate logical extensions of his own personal experience—rather than in the truly abstract sense of relationships between general variables. Hence general laws and methodological canons of science, in their own right, have little meaning and intellectual appeal for him; they make sense only insofar as they are relatable to more tangible types of experience. "Utility" is a major example of this type of experience, but is certainly not the only possible example.

As far as elementary-school children are concerned, therefore, one cannot hope to reduce science to "first principles" and basic abstract laws.** At the very best one can strive for a semiabstract, intuitive grasp of these laws on a descriptive or perhaps semianalytic level that is tied to particularized experience. On the methodological side, abstract principles of scientific inquiry and strategy also have much less meaning for children than a purely concrete-empirical explanation of how it is possible for mankind to know the facts and generalizations under discussion.***

---

*Galperin[26] describes a method of teaching arithmetic to slow-learning pupils in which concrete-empirical props are eliminated very gradually and are replaced by abstract-verbal representations.

**Both Karplus[34] and Shamos[63] deplore the emphasis in elementary-science education upon the practical utilitarian aspects of science and the attempt "to relate science primarily to everyday experience." They advocate, instead, stress upon the concepts and methods of science.

***Atkin and Wyatt[3] emphasize the "how we know" aspects of astronomy, using didactic exposition and simple exercises and demonstrations.

The teacher's task of translating ideas into language that is compatible with the elementary-school child's cognitive capacities and level of cognitive functioning is difficult indeed. First, in teaching others, his natural tendency is to adopt the same level of discourse he himself characteristically uses in learning new ideas. Second, once he has acquired difficult concepts, he tends to regard them as self-evident and to forget both the psychological steps involved in the learning process, as well as the numerous misconceptions and ambiguities he had to overcome in the course of learning; and after he has mastered a particular discipline, he tends to think of its structure only in terms of the logical relationships between component ideas, forgetting the psychological process of progressive differentiation involved in acquiring any new body of knowledge. Lastly, because of his more sophisticated and highly differentiated cognitive structure, he is aware of various subtleties, connotations, ramifications, and qualifications connected with even simple ideas, and often fails to realize that they would only confuse his pupils.

Although the preschool child is dependent on overt manipulation of objects and situations for the understanding of correlative relational propositions, it is *not* necessary that all teaching during this period be conducted on a nonverbal, problem-solving, or self-discovery basis in order to be meaningful. Derivative propositions can be directly apprehended when presented verbally, and correlative propositions can be verbally presented and understood as long as an opportunity for preliminary or concurrent overt manipulation exists. Self-discovery of the proposition to be learned might conceivably enhance current learning and provide additional motivation for future learning, but is certainly not indispensable for meaningful understanding.

The elementary-school child's dependence on concrete-empirical experience for the meaningful understanding of abstract propositions also requires that much teaching be directed toward a semiabstract or intuitive type of learning. This does not mean, however, that all or even most teaching must necessarily be conducted on an inductive, problem-solving (discovery), and nonverbal basis. The only essential condition for learning relational concepts during this period is the availability of first-hand, nonrepresentational, and empirical experience. Didactic verbal exposition can easily be combined with such concrete-empirical props in the form of demonstrations and exercises, and usually suffices for the presentation of most subject matter that is neither excessively complex nor unfamiliar. In some instances, it might be desirable to enhance verbal exposition with a semiautonomous type of problem-solving in which discovery is accelerated by the use of prompts, hints, and Socratic questioning.

It is a serious mistake, therefore, to believe that intuitive learning during the stage of concrete logical operations must necessarily be restricted to nonverbal, concrete manipulation of objects. Abstract verbal relationships between ideas can be adequately comprehended—in a somewhat particularized sense—as long as concrete-empirical props are available. Hence, concurrently with providing elementary-school children with "particularly informative and suggestive experiences as a base for their abstractions," one must provide them "with a conceptual framework that permits them to perceive the phenomena in a meaningful way and to integrate their inferences into generalizations of lasting value" (35, pp. 243-44).

Although it is true that the intuitive thinking of children is relatively unprecise and inexplicit, we tend to exaggerate both aspects of children's cognitive functioning in our culture. It is part of our folk-lore that children are inherently incapable of precise thinking and observation. Because of this belief
we are unduly lax and indulgent in our demands on children that they observe and execute acts carefully. We encourage an attitude of approximation
throughout the period of childhood, and then suddenly at adolescence demand
rigorous adherence to precise standards of work and statement. The Manus,
on the other hand, do not arbitrarily identify precision as an attribute of adult
personality; and by demanding and receiving it from children, they demonstrate that the latter are not developmentally incapable of adhering to it.[48]
Thus not only is their standard of childrens' performance much higher than
our own, but they are also spared the sudden need for a reformation of work
standards on approaching adulthood. In any society, such as our own, which
places such a high premium on precision and accuracy, early training in these
attributes would seem to be a self-evident goal of education. Yet the influence
of folklore is so great that our deficiency in this respect first becomes striking
when seen in contrast to another society whose adult values closely parallel
our own.

The developmental characteristics of the elementary-school child's cognitive
functioning do not require that we restrict the pedagogic use of these years
to teaching the fundamental intellectual skills. His cognitive equipment is adequate enough for acquiring an intuitive grasp of many concepts in the basic
disciplines. Thus, for example, the psychological argument for teaching science
in the elementary school is extremely convincing.[34] First, it is well-known that
young children spontaneously acquire many animistic and subjectivistic conceptions about the physical and biological universe.[54] These notions also tend
to persist and often compete with more mature conceptions, especially when
not counteracted by early scientific training. Second, without early and satisfactory instruction in science, it is difficult for children both to assimilate positive interests in and attitudes toward the scientific enterprise, and to avoid
being negatively conditioned to scientific subject matter. Lastly, since elementary-school pupils can easily acquire an intuitive grasp of many scientific
concepts, failure to provide suitable opportunities for them to do so not only
wastes available readiness for such learning, but also wastes valuable time
in junior and senior high school that could be used for more advanced instruction in science.

However the suggestion that sciences be studied in the order of their
phenomenological complexity, i.e., that one start with "the basic concepts of
physics and chemistry before tackling the complex phenomena of biology and
geology"[63] although logically sound, is psychologically unfeasible. More important pedagogically than the logical structure of knowledge is the pupil's intellectual readiness to handle different kinds of subject matter; and from the
standpoint of relevant experience and readiness, the phenomenologically "simple" laws of physics are far more abstract and difficult than the phenomenologically "complex" laws of biology and geology which are so much closer to
everyday experience. This is not to deny the possibility that some aspects of
physics might be profitably introduced in the elementary-school curriculum.
However, before this could be done in the "rigorous fashion [physics] de-

serves," the teaching of elementary-school mathematics would first have to be sufficiently improved to make possible a more functional intuitive understanding of the quantitative relationships that figure so prominently in the physical sciences.[63]

The problem of facilitating intuitive understanding in elementary-school children, *i.e.*, of developing techniques of presenting (translating) abstract subject matter in ways that are meaningful to them, must not be confused with the vastly different problem of enhancing intuitive processes in cognitively sophisticated individuals who may or may not be creative. Bruner[13] offers the following suggestions for promoting the latter objective: the teacher himself setting an example of intuitive problem-solving; teaching students the fundamental unifying and integrative principles of a discipline; encouraging students to guess intelligently, and rewarding them for originality and spontaneity; and training students in such general heuristic procedures as constructing models, using analogies, examining the limiting conditions of a problem, searching for symmetry, and trying to visualize solutions. The last-mentioned approach will be considered in greater detail in another context (see p. 157).

EDUCATIONAL IMPLICATIONS OF THE TRANSITION FROM CONCRETE TO ABSTRACT COGNITIVE FUNCTIONING

From the standpoint of the secondary-school teacher, the most significant development in cognitive functioning that occurs during the preadolescent and early adolescent years is the gradual transition from a predominantly concrete to a predominantly abstract mode of understanding and manipulating complex relational propositions. This developmental shift, in turn, has far-reaching implications for teaching methods and curricular practices in the secondary school.

Once the developing indivudal reaches the abstract stage of cognitive functioning, he becomes in large measure an abstract verbal learner. He now forms most new concepts and learns most new propositions by *directly* apprehending verbally or symbolically stated relationships between previously learned abstractions. To do so meaningfully, he need no longer refer to first-hand, non-representational experience, nor actually perform any of the abstracting or generalizing operations on the underlying empirical data. With his developmental dependence on concrete-empirical props removed, the only condition necessary for the meaningful understanding and manipulation of higher-order concepts and relational propositions is that their substantive import be non-arbitrarily relatable to his particular cognitive structure, and that he adopt a set to learn them in this fashion. Hence, on developmental grounds, he is ready at the secondary-school level for a new type of verbal expository teaching that uses concrete-empirical experience primarily for *illustrative* purposes, *i.e.*, to clarify or dramatize truly abstract meanings rather than to generate intuitive meanings.

Many features of the activity program were based on the quite defensible premise that the elementary-school child perceives the world in relatively specific and concrete terms, and requires considerable firsthand experience with diverse concrete instances of a given set of relationships before he can abstract genuinely meaningful concepts and relate them meaningfully to cognitive structure. Thus, an attempt was made to teach factual information and intellectual skills in the "real-life" functional contexts in which they are customarily encountered, rather than through the medium of verbal exposition supplemented by artificially contrived drills and exercises. This approach has real merit provided that a fetish is not made of naturalism and incidental learning, that adequate use is made of appropriate expository teaching, that drills and exercises are provided in instances where opportunities for acquiring skills do not occur frequently and repetitively enough in more natural settings, and that deliberate or guided effort in most learning situations is not regarded as incompatible with incidental learning in others. Even more important, however, is the realization that in older children, once a sufficient number of basic concepts is consolidated, new concepts are primarily abstracted from verbal rather than from concrete experience. Hence in secondary school it may be desirable to reverse both the sequence and the relative balance between abstract concepts and supportive data. There is good reason for believing, therefore, that much of the time presently spent in cookbook laboratory exercises in the sciences could be much more advantageously employed in formulating precise definitions, making explicit verbal distinctions between concepts, generalizing from hypothetical situations, etc.

It would be very misleading, however, to assert that secondary-school and even older students can *never* profit either from the use of concrete-empirical props to generate intuitive meanings, or from the use of inductive discovery and deductive problem-solving techniques to enhance such meanings. As previously suggested, generally mature students tend to function at a relatively concrete level when confronted with a particular new subject-matter area in which they are as yet totally unsophisticated. But since abstract cognitive functioning in this new area is achieved with the attainment of a minimal degree of subject-matter sophistication, these special auxiliary techniques should only be employed for the aforementioned purposes during the early stages of instruction. Continued use for other purposes, however, (*i.e.*, to illustrate abstract meanings, to improve problem-solving skills, to foster appreciation of scientific method, or to test verbal understanding) is quite another matter.

Since a largely verbal type of expository teaching is both more economical in terms of time-cost, and also makes possible a qualitatively superior kind of abstract meaningful understanding, one might reasonably ask why the secondary school has not placed greater emphasis on more abstract and verbal techniques of effecting meaningful verbal learning. In the first place, by unwarrantedly extrapolating childhood learning conditions to adolescence and adult life, the Progressive Education movement fostered widespread acceptance of the proposition that all verbal concepts and generalizations are *necessarily* nothing more than rotely memorized glib verbalisms unless they both reflect current or recently prior concrete experience and are products of independent problem-solving or discovery. This belief led, in turn, to summary rejection of verbal exposition, and to paradoxical endorsement of such inherently rote problem-solving and discovery practices as the teaching of "type problems," the wholly mechanical manipulation of mathematical symbols, and the performance of cookbook laboratory experiments.

Second, the tendency among educational psychologists uncritically to extrapolate findings from laboratory studies of nonverbal or verbal rote learning to meaningful verbal learning in the classroom, reinforced the educator's perception of verbal learning as necessarily rote in character, and further encouraged him to repudiate expository verbal teaching. Lastly, the failure of educational psychologists to investigate the nature and conditions of meaningful verbal learning and retention, delayed the discovery of more effective techniques of verbal exposition, as well as helped perpetuate the use of traditional rote techniques. Only within the last few years have curriculum specialists and educational psychologists concerned themselves with substantive and programmatic aspects of the problem of facilitating the meaningful acquisition and retention of viable bodies of knowledge.

DEVELOPMENTAL CONSIDERATIONS REGARDING BREADTH OF CURRICULUM

One of the chief complaints of the critics of public education in the United States is that contemporary children fail to learn "the fundamentals" because of the broadening of the elementary-school curriculum to include such subjects as social studies, art, science, music, and manual arts in addition to the traditional "three R's." This, of course, would be a very serious charge if it were true, because the wisdom of expanding a child's intellectual horizons at the expense of making him a cripple in the basic intellectual skills is highly questionable, to say the least. Fortunately, however, the benefits of an expanded curriculum have thus far not been accompanied by a corresponding deterioration in the standard of the three R's. Evidently, the decreased amount of time spent on the latter subjects has been more than compensated for by the development of more efficient methods of teaching, and by the incidental learning of "fundamentals" in the course of studying these other subjects. Nevertheless, the issue of breadth versus depth still remains because there *is* obviously a point beyond which increased breadth could only be attained by sacrificing mastery of the fundamental skills; and even if we agreed to maintain or improve the present standard of the three R's, we would still have to choose between breadth and depth in relation to other components of the curriculum, particularly at the junior- and senior-high school levels. It is at these points of choice that developmental criteria can be profitably applied.

Concrete-Intuitive Stage

Generally speaking, maximal breadth of the curriculum consistent with adequate mastery of its constituent parts is developmentally desirable at all ages because of the tremendously wide scope of human abilities. The wider the range of intellectual stimulation to which pupils are exposed, the greater are the chances that all of the diverse potentialities both within a group of children and within a single child will be brought to fruition. By the same token a broad curriculum makes it possible for more pupils to experience success in the performance of school activities and thus to develop the necessary self-confidence and motivation for continued academic striving and achievement. The very fact that elementary-school children are able to make significant progress in science and social studies also indicates that myopic concentration on the 3 R's would waste much available readiness for these types of learnings, and thus compel junior- and senior-high schools to devote much of their instructional time to materials that are easily learnable in the lower grades. In fact, one of the major failings of the secondary-school curriculum today is that because it still has not adequately adjusted to the expansion of the elementary-school syllabus, entering pupils are not only subjected to much stultifying repetition but also fail to break the new ground for which they are obviously ready.

Other factors also counsel a choice of breadth over depth in the content of elementary-school curriculum. First, from a logistical standpoint, the young child is not prepared for depth of subject-matter coverage. His limited attention span and his dependence on concrete-empirical props slow down greatly his rate of learning new material, thereby making it difficult for him to assimilate a wide array of information about a given topic; and the particularized, semiabstract, and relatively unprecise nature of his concepts detracts from his ability to organize and integrate this material in usable fashion.

Second, the relationship between breadth and depth must also take into account the progressive differentiation of intelligence, interests, and personality structure with increasing age. The elementary-school child is a "generalist" because both his intellect and personality are still relatively unstable and uncrystallized and lack impressive internal consistency. Thus many different varieties of subject matter are equally compatible with his interest and ability patterns. Furthermore, unless he has experience with many different fields of knowledge and gives each a "provisional try," he is in no position to judge which kinds of intellectual pursuits are most congruent with his major ability and value systems. Hence, quite apart from the future life-adjustment values of a broad educational background, it is appropriate on developmental grounds for elementary- and early high-school curricula to stress breadth rather than depth.

Breadth, of course, inevitably implies a certain amount of superficiality. This superficiality, however, is not necessarily opprobrious. Whether it is desirable or undesirable cannot be judged in absolute terms, but only in relation to the student's intellectual readiness for depth. It should also be pointed out in this connection that superficiality itself is always a relative state of affairs; the graduate school curriculum is just as superficial to the post-doctoral scholar as the elementary-school curriculum is to the college undergraduate. The spiral curriculum—the reintroduction of the same topics in progressively greater depth as intellectual readiness and maturity increase—is predicated on this assumption.

Superficiality is also not synonymous with triviality or with slipshod, unsystematic, or outdated teaching. Good teaching is as thorough as is possible at the appropriate level of breadth and depth; and even at the elementary-school level it allows for the occasional introduction of atypical depth, both substantively and methodologically, to give the student a taste of scholarship and of research inquiry. But, as will be pointed out later, the probing in depth of isolated areas, apart from the systematic presentation of subject matter—merely as a means of enhancing inquiry skills or methodological sophistication—is indefensible at any age level, and particularly in the elementary school. It is a type of activity suitable for the scholar and research scientist—*after* he has acquired substantive and methodological sophistication in his field.

Abstract-Verbal Stage

Toward the latter portion of the junior-high-school period, however, precisely the opposite kind of developmental situation begins to emerge. Interests have crystallized and abilities have undergone differentiation to the point where greater depth and specialization are possible and desirable. Many students at this stage of intellectual development are ready to sink their teeth into more serious and solid academic fare, but, unfortunately, suitable instructional programs geared at an intermediate level of systematic presentation of the fundamental principles of a discipline are rarely available. The changes that have taken place in secondary-school curricula since the academy days have been primarily characterized by the belated and half-hearted addition of more up-to-date and topical information. Very little has been done in the way of providing the student with a meaningful, integrated and systematic view of the major ideas in a given field of knowledge.

The transition from concrete to abstract cognitive functioning enables the secondary-school student to master a much greater volume of subject-matter knowledge. To begin with, the logistics of the learning situation become more favorable. His ability to understand abstract relational propositions directly (*i.e.*, to dispense with the time-consuming operations of using both concrete-empirical props and discovery and problem-solving experience to generate and enhance intuitive insights) permits the teacher to present much more subject matter in the same period of time. In addition, his qualitatively higher level of abstract understanding makes possible a more efficient means of organizing and integrating the materials that are presented. Because his higher-order concepts and relational propositions are no longer intuitive, but are meaningfully formulated in truly abstract and general terms, they become clearer, more stable, more precise, and sufficiently inclusive to subsume a wider array of differentiated facts and subconcepts.

In view of these latter developments and of the greater differentiation of his abilities and interests, the secondary-school student is prepared to cope with a greater depth as well as with a greater volume of subject matter. He 'is ready for more intensive and differentiated coverage of smaller areas of knowledge as opposed to more global and superficial coverage of larger areas. "Depth" in this context, however, implies greater substantive density of knowledge rather than greater degree of autonomy in discovering the principles and obtaining the information to be learned. If the secondary-school student is required to discover most principles autonomously, to obtain most subject-matter content from primary sources, and to design his own experiments, he only has time to acquire methodological sophistication. In terms of *substantive* depth, he has simply moved from previously superficial coverage of broad areas to comparably superficial coverage of more circumscribed areas. The aim of secondary-school and undergraduate education is not to produce substantively ignorant junior scholars and scientists, but to produce students who are knowledgeable both in breadth and depth of subject matter.

REFERENCES

1. Anderson, H. H. Preface. In *Creativity and its Cultivation* (H. H. Anderson, ed.) New York: Harper, 1959.

2. Annett, M. The classification of instances of four common class concepts by children and adults. *Brit. J. educ. Psychol.*, 1959, 29:233–36.
3. Atkin, J. M., and Wyatt, S. P. *Astronomy: Charting the Universe*, trial edition. Urbana, Ill.: Elementary-School Science Project, University of Illinois, 1961.
4. Ausubel, D. P. *Theory and Problems of Child Development*. New York: Grune & Stratton, 1958.
5. Ausubel, D. P. Viewpoints from related disciplines: human growth and development. *Teachers Coll. Rec.*, 1959, 60:245–54.
6. Ausubel, D. P. Can children learn anything that adults can—and more efficiently? *Elem. Sch. J.*, 1962, 62:270–72.
7. Ausubel, D. P. Implications of preadolescent and early adolescent cognitive development for secondary school teaching. *High Sch. J.* 1962, 45:268–75.
8. Ausubel, D. P. Some psychological considerations in the objectives and design of an elementary-school science program. *Science Educ.*, 1963, in press.
9. Ausubel, D. P., and Schiff, H. M. The effect of incidental and experimentally induced experience in the learning of relevant and irrelevant causal relationships by children. *J. genet. Psychol.*, 1954, 84:109–23.
10. Baer, C. J. The school progress and adjustment of underage and overage students. *J. educ. Psychol.*, 1958, 49:17–19.
11. Braine, M. D. S. The ontogeny of certain logical operations: Piaget's formulations examined by nonverbal methods. *Psychol. Monogr.*, 1959, 73, No. 4 (Whole No. 475).
12. Brown, R. W. *Words and Things*. Glencoe, Ill.: The Free Press, 1958.
13. Bruner, J. S. *The Process of Education*. Cambridge, Mass.: Harvard University Press, 1960.
14. Bruner, J. S. After Dewey What? *Saturday Review*, June 17, 1961, 58–59; 76–78.
15. Burt, C. The development of reasoning in children. *J. exp. Pedag.* 1919, 5: 68–77.
16. Cohen, J., and Hansel, C. E. M. The idea of independence. *Brit. J. Psychol.*, 1955, 46:178–90.
17. Dennis, W. Piaget's questions applied to a child of known environment. *J. genet. Psychol.*, 1942, 60:307–20.
18. Dennis, W. Animism and related tendencies in Hopi children. *J. abnorm. soc. Psychol.*, 1943, 38:21–36.
19. Deutsche, J. M. *The Development of Children's Concepts of Causal Relationships*. Minneapolis: University of Minnesota Press, 1937.
20. Dodwell, P. C. Children's understanding of number and related concepts. *Can. J. Psychol.*, 1960, 14:191–205.
21. Dodwell, P. C. Children's understanding of number concepts: characteristics of an individual and of a group test. *Can. J. Psychol.*, 1961, 15:29–36.
22. Dunkel, H. B., and Pillet, R. A. A second year of French in the elementary school. *Elem. Sch. J.*, 1957, 58:143–51.
23. Elkind, D. The development of quantitative thinking: a systematic replication of Piaget's studies. *J. genet. Psychol.*, 1961, 98:37–48.
24. Ervin, Susan M. Experimental procedures of children. *Child Develpm.*, 1960, 31:703–19.
25. Fast, I. Kindergarten teaching and Grade I reading. *J. educ. Psychol.*, 1957, 48:52–57.

26. Galperin, P. Ya. An experimental study in the formation of mental actions. In *Psychology in the Soviet Union* (B. Simon, ed.) Stanford Calif.: Stanford University Press, 1957, pp. 213–25.

27. Gollin, E. S. Organizational characteristics of social judgment: a developmental investigation. *J. Pers.*, 1958, *26*:139–54.

28. Grigsby, O. J. An experimental study of the development of concepts of relationship in preschool children as evidenced by their expressive ability. *J. exp. Educ.*, 1932, *1*:144–62.

29. Hazlitt, V. Children's thinking. *Brit. J. Psychol.*, 1930, *20*:354–61.

30. Hibbs, A. R. Science for elementary students. *Teachers Coll. Rec.*, 1962, *43*: 136–42.

31. Hunt, J. McV. *Intelligence and Experience.* New York: Ronald, 1961.

32. Inhelder, Bärbel, and Piaget, J. *The Growth of Logical Thinking from Childhood to Adolescence.* New York: Basic Books, 1958.

33. Johnson, C. E., Ellison, F. P., and Flores, J. S. A summary of the major findings at the close of the first year of the study of the development of methods and materials to facilitate foreign language instruction in elementary schools. Urbana, Ill.: University of Illinois, 1960.

34. Karplus, R. Beginning a study in elementary-school science. *Amer. J. Physics,* 1962, *30*:1–9.

35. Karplus, R. The science curriculum—one approach. *Elem. Sch. J.*, 1962, *62*: 243–52.

36. Kendler, H. H. Vertical and horizontal processes in problem solving. *Psychol. Rev.*, 1962, *69*:1–62.

37. Kendler, T. S., and Kendler, H. H. Reversal and nonreversal shifts in kindergarten children. *J. exp. Psychol.*, 1959, *58*:56–60.

38. Kendler, T. S., Kendler, H. H., and Wells, D. Reversal and nonreversal shifts in nursery school children. *J. comp. physiol. Psychol.*, 1959, *52*:387–89.

39. Lacey, J. I., and Dallenbach, K. M. Acquisition by children of the cause-effect relationship. *Amer. J. Psychol.*, 1940, *53*:575–78.

40. Long, L., and Welch, L. The development of the ability to discriminate and match numbers. *J. genet. Psychol.*, 1941, *59*:377–87.

41. Long, L., and Welch, L. Influence of level of abstractness on reasoning ability. *J. Psychol.*, 1942, *13*:41–59.

42. Lovell, K. A follow-up study of some aspects of the work of Piaget and Inhelder on the child's conception of space. *Brit. J. educ. Psychol.*, 1959, *29*: 104–17.

43. Lovell, K., and Ogilvie, E. A study of the conservation of substance in the junior school child. *Brit. J. educ. Psychol.*, 1960, *30*:109–18.

44. Lovell, K., and Slater, A. The growth of the concept of time: a comparative study. *Child Psychol. Psychiat.*, 1960, *1*:179–90.

45. Lunzer, E. A. Some points of Piagetian theory in the light of experimental criticism. *Child Psychol. Psychiat.*, 1960, *1*:192–202.

46. Luria, A. R. The role of language in the formation of temporary connections. In *Psychology in the Soviet Union.* (B. Simon, ed.) Stanford, Calif.: Stanford University Press, 1957, pp. 115–29.

47. Mannix, J. B. The number concepts of a group of E. S. N. children. *Brit. J. educ. Psychol.*, 1960, *30*:180–81.

48. Mead, Margaret. *From the South Seas.* New York: William Morrow, 1939.
49. Munn, N. L. Learning in Children. In *Manual of Child Psychology.* (L. Carmichael, ed.), ed. 2. New York. Wiley, 1954, pp. 374–458.
50. Oakes, M. E. *Children's Explanations of Natural Phenomena.* New York: Bureau of Publications, Teachers College, Columbia University, 1946.
51. Peel, E. A. Experimental examination of some of Piaget's schemata concerning children's perception and thinking and a discussion of their educational significance. *Brit. J. educ. Psychol.,* 1959, 29:89–103.
52. Piaget, J. *Judgment and Reasoning in the Child.* New York: Harcourt, Brace, 1928.
53. Piaget, J. *The Child's Conception of the World.* London: Routledge and Keagan, Paul, 1929.
54. Piaget, J. *The Child's Conception of Physical Causality.* New York: Harcourt, Brace, 1932.
55. Piaget, J. *The Psychology of Intelligence.* New York: Harcourt, Brace, 1950.
56. Piaget, J. *Logic and Psychology.* Manchester, England: University of Manchester Press, 1953.
57. Piaget, J. *The Construction of Reality in the Child.* New York: Basic Books, 1954.
58. Piaget, J., and Inhelder, Bärbel. *La Genesè des Structures Logiques Élémentaires: Classifications et Seriations.* Neuchâtel: Editions Delachaux and Niestlé, 1959.
59. Reichard, S., Schneider, M., and Rapaport, D. The development of concept formation in children. *Amer. J. Orthopsychiat.,* 1944, 14:156–62.
60. Russell, R. W. Studies in Animism. II. The development of animism. *J. genet. Psychol.,* 1940, 56:353–66.
61. Sax, G., and Ottina, J. P. The arithmetic reasoning of pupils differing in school experience. *Calif. J. educ. Res.,* 1958, 9:15–19.
62. Serra, M. C. A study of fourth grade children's comprehension of certain verbal abstractions. *J. exp. Educ.,* 1953, 22:103–18.
63. Shamos, M. H. Science for citizens. *Saturday Review,* September 16, 1961, 68–69.
64. Sigel, I. E. Developmental trends in the abstraction ability of children. *Child Develpm.,* 1953, 24:131–44.
65. Smedslund, J. The acquisition of conservation of substance and weight in children. *J. Scan. Psychol.,* 1961, 2:11–20; 71–87; 153–60; 203–10.
66. Spiker, C. C., and Terrell, G. Factors associated with transposition behavior of preschool children. *J. genet. Psychol.,* 1955, 86:143–58.
67. Szuman, S. Comparison, abstraction, and analytic thought in the child. *Enfance,* 1951, 4:189–216.
68. Wallon, H. Precategorical thinking in the child. *Enfance,* 1952, 5:97–101.
69. Weir, M. W., and Stevenson, H. W. The effect of verbalization in children's learning as a function of chronological age. *Child Develpm.,* 1959, 30, 143–49.
70. Welch, L. A preliminary investigation of some aspects of the hierarchical development of concepts. *J. gen. Psychol.,* 1940, 22:359–78.
71. Welch, L., and Long, L. Comparison of the reasoning ability of two age groups. *J. genet. Psychol.,* 1943, 62:63–76.
72. Werner, H. *Comparative Psychology of Mental Development.* Chicago: Follett, 1948.
73. Wohlwill, J. F. A study of the development of the number concept by scalogram analysis. *J. genet. Psychol.,* 1960, 97:345–77.

CHAPTER 7.

Learning by Discovery

LEARNING BY DISCOVERY has its proper place among the repertoire of accepted pedagogic techniques available to teachers. For certain designated purposes and for certain carefully specified learning situations, its rationale is clear and defensible. But learning by discovery also has its own elaborate mystique. Its legitimate uses and advantages have been unwarrantedly extrapolated to include both educational goals and levels of intellectual maturity, levels of subject-matter sophistication, and levels of cognitive functioning for which it is ill-adapted—and for reasons which derive from sheer dogmatic assertion; from pseudonaturalistic conceptions about the nature and conditions of intellectual development; from outmoded ideas about the relationship between language and thought; from sentimental fantasies about the nature of the child and the aims of education; and from uncritical interpretation of the research evidence. The chief aim of this chapter is to distinguish between the rationale and mystique of the so-called discovery method of teaching.

HISTORICAL ANTECEDENTS

Before attempting to set forth the rationale and mystique of the discovery method, I think it might be helpful briefly to consider the more important of the numerous educational movements and currents of thought from which it has evolved. Some of its historical antecedents are relatively recent, whereas others have flourished for centuries. Unfortunately, also, not all of these precursory trends are logically compatible with each other.

The Progressive Education movement obviously furnished several major strands in the design of the discovery method. One aspect of this movement was a growing dissatisfaction with the empty formalism of much educational content in the latter part of the nineteenth century and the early part of the twentieth century; with stultifying drill and catechism-like methods of teaching; with the curriculum's lack of relatedness to the everyday experience of the child, his physical world, and social environment; and with pupils' rote verbalization and memorization of ideas for which they had no adequate referents in experience. Overstatement of the realities underlying this dissatisfaction constituted the basis of the later mystique that *all* verbal learning is little more than glib verbalism and parrot-like recitation. This led, in turn, to the exaggerated emphasis that progressivists placed on relating the curriculum to the physical and social environment of the child; on direct, immediate, and concrete experience as a prerequisite for meaningful understanding; on active learning and inquiry; and on incidental learning and learning in natural, uncontrived situations. From this type of emphasis grew activity programs and project methods, and the credo of "learning for and by problem-solving" as the principal objective and method, respectively, of the educational enterprise. Two final by-products of this point of view were deification of the act of discovery associated with the inductive and incidental learning methods of teaching, and extrapolation to the secondary-school and university student of the elementary-school child's dependence on recently prior concrete, empirical experience in the comprehension and manipulation of ideas. As we shall see later, both of these developments became extremely impotrant components of the mystique of learning by discovery.

Such modern proponents of the discovery method as Gertrude Hendrix acknowledge their historical and ideological kinship to the Progressive Education movement, but are quick to disassociate themselves from some of the basic assumptions made by the inductive and incidental learning approaches to instruction. Hendrix quite rightly points out that the main fallacy of the inductive approach lies in the teacher's use of the pupil's ability to verbalize a discovery as the "criterion by which [she] recognizes that discovery has taken place" (29, p. 296). And in referring to the incidental learning that purportedly occurs in the course of a pupil's involvement in a project or activity program, Hendrix correctly berates the advocates of this method because "all too often they took no responsibility for seeing that instances of the same generalization came along close enough together for the learner to become aware of either concepts or principles" (29, p. 293).

A second aspect of the Progressive Education movement relevant to the evolution of the discovery method was the child-centered approach to instruction that originated in the educational philosophies of Rousseau and Froebel. The adherents of this approach emphasized the importance of structuring the curriculum in terms of the nature of the child and his participation in the educative process, that is, in terms of his current interests, his endogenously derived needs, and his state of intellectual and emotional readiness. According to this point of view, the educational environment promotes development best by providing a maximally unstructured field that does not interfere with the predetermined process of internal ripening. The child himself, it is asserted, is the person best qualified to know and select those educational ingredients that correspond most closely with his prevailing developmental needs, and hence are most beneficial for his optimal growth. Propositions such as these obviously make a fetish of autonomy and self-discovery, and regard as little short of sacrilege any form of guidance or direction in learning, and particularly the communication of insights or generalizations by teachers to pupils. Herein lies in part the origin of the mystique that expository teaching is inherently authoritarian, and that self-discovered insights are uniquely and transcendentally endowed with meaning and understanding that can be achieved through no other means. Hendrix, for example, castigates didactic exposition of generalizations as "authoritarian" and as only "satisfying to someone who is already aware of the ideas being presented. (29, p. 296)" This same mystique also underlies the quite different educational doctrine that it is authoritarian and undemocratic for a knowledgeable person to communicate his knowledge to other persons lacking his particular background of thought and study, and that the latter individuals can learn more through "democratic discussion," that is, by talking off the tops of their heads and pooling their ignorance.

These two strands of the Progressive Education movement—emphasis on the child's direct experience and spontaneous interests, and insistence on autonomously achieved insight free of all directive manipulation of the learning environment—set the stage for the subsequent deification of problem-solving, laboratory work, and naive emulation of the scientific method. Many mathematics and science teachers were rendered self-conscious about systematically presenting and explaining to their students the basic concepts and principles of their fields, because it was held that this procedure would promote glib verbalism and rote memorization. It was felt that if students worked enough problems, and were kept busy pouring reagents into a sufficient number of test tubes, they would somehow spontaneously discover in a meaningful way all of the important concepts and generalizations they needed to know in the fields they were studying.

Of course, one had to take pains to discourage students from rotely memorizing formulas, and then mechanically substituting for the general terms in these formulas the particular values of specified variables in given problems. This would naturally be no less rote than formal didactic exposition. Hence, in accordance with the new emphasis on *meaningful* problem-solving, students ceased memorizing formulas, memorizing instead type problems. They learned how to work exemplars of all of the kinds of problems they were responsible for, and then rotely memorized both the form of each type and its solution. Thus equipped, it was comparatively easy to sort the problems with which they were confronted into their respective categories, and "spontaneously proceed to discover meaningful solutions"—provided, of course, that the teacher played fair and presented recognizable exemplars of the various types.°

Similarly, as the terms "laboratory" and "scientific method" became sacrosanct in American high schools and universities, students were coerced into mimicking the externally conspicuous but inherently trivial aspects of scientific method. They wasted many valuable hours collecting empirical data which, at the very worst, belabored the obvious, and at the very best, helped them rediscover or exemplify principles which the teacher could have presented verbally and demonstrated visually in a matter of minutes. Actually, they learned precious little subject matter and even less scientific method from this procedure. The unsophisticated scientific mind is only confused by the natural complexities of unsystematized empirical data, and learns much more from schematic models and diagrams; and following laboratory manuals in cookbook fashion, without adequate knowledge of the relevant methodological and substantive principles involved, confers about as much genuine appreciation of scientific method as putting on a white "lab" coat and doing a TV commercial for a patent remedy.

Partly as a result of the superstitious faith of educators in the very uncritical efficacy of problem-solving and laboratory methods, we have produced in the past four decades millions of high-school and college graduates who *never* had the foggiest notion of the meaning of a variable, of a function, of an exponent, of calculus, of molecular structure, or of electricity, but who have done all of the

---

°In some instances, transferability did not even extend to a change in algebraic notation. Thorndike[63] found that some students who could square $(x + y)$ could not square $(B_1 + B_2)$.

prescribed laboratory work, and have successfully solved an acceptable percentage of the required problems in differential and integral calculus, in logarithms, in molar and normal solutions, and in Ohm's Law.

One basic lesson that some modern proponents of the discovery method have drawn from this educational disaster is that problem-solving *per se* is not conducive to meaningful discovery. Problem-solving can be just as deadening, just as formalistic, just as mechanical, just as passive, and just as rote as the worst form of verbal exposition. The type of learning outcomes that emerges is largely a function of the structure, the substance, the organization, and the spirit of the problem-solving experiences one provides. However, an equally important lesson which these same proponents of the discovery method refuse to draw is that, because of the educational logistics involved, even the best program of problem-solving experience is no substitute for a minimally necessary amount of appropriate didactic exposition. But this minimum will never be made available as long as we adhere to the standard university formula of devoting one hour of exposition to every four hours of laboratory work and paper-and-pencil problem-solving.

Historically, the discovery method may also be considered, in part, a revolt against the prevailing educational psychology of our time, which is largely an eclectic hodge-podge of logically incompatible theoretical propositions superimposed upon a sterile empiricism. Perhaps the most significant example of this self-defeating eclecticism has been the stubborn attempt made by various psychologists to integrate Thorndikian connectionism and a widely extrapolated neo-Behaviorism with the major tenets of Progressive Education. But the glaring contradictions that resulted from the effort to reconcile such antithetical sets of principles as the Law of Effect, drive reduction, stimulus-response and rote learning theory, the transfer of identical elements, and trial-and-error learning, on the one hand, and progressivist viewpoints regarding meaningful understanding of ideas, active inquiry, and autonomous discovery, on the other, tended to alienate some of the more independent-minded educational psychologists in the Progressive Education camp. Some defected to psychoanalysis, spawning a weird synthesis of Deweyism and Freudianism, whereas others were attracted by the greater emphasis on cognition and insightful problem-solving which characterized such field theorists and Gestalt theoreticians as Tolman, Lewin, Köhler, Wertheimer, and Katona. Also included among the defectors were many vigorous supporters of the discovery method, who viewed the extrapolation of rote learning theory to verbal classroom learning as sufficient proof of the essentially rote nature of verbal learning, and as ample justification for designing nonverbal discovery techniques of teaching.

A final current of educational thought influencing the evolution of the discovery method is the currently fashionable educational goal of making *every* child a critical and creative thinker. The general untenability of this approach has already been considered in another context (see pp. 102–103).

PSYCHOLOGICAL AND EDUCATIONAL RATIONALE OF THE DISCOVERY METHOD

An all-or-none position regarding use of the discovery method is warranted neither by logic nor evidence. The method itself is very useful for certain pedagogic purposes and in certain educational circumstances. The objectionable aspects of the method are some of its unwarranted assumptions, overstated claims, inadequately tested propositions, and, above all, some of the reasons advanced for its efficacy.

"It is evident that the young human being must receive considerable instruction but also that he should be eternally vigilant in making additional observations. His life is a complicated blending of instruction and discovery. Many facts will be handed to him outright. At the same time, during every day of his life, he will be engaged, almost unknowingly, in inductive reasoning, the process of bringing together a number of experiences and extracting from them some common factor. The issue becomes, then, not instruction versus discovery. since both are essential, but a consideration of the relative importance to be accorded each in the educative process" (55, p. 457).

What are some of the legitimate claims, the defensible uses, and the palpable advantages of the discovery method? In the early, unsophisticated stages of learning any abstract subject matter, particularly prior to adolescence, the discovery method is extremely helpful. It is also indispensable for testing the meaningfulness of knowledge and for teaching scientific method and effective problem-solving skills. Furthermore, various cognitive and motivational factors undoubtedly enhance the learning, retention, and transferability of meaningful material learned by discovery.

Occasional use of inductive discovery techniques for teaching subject matter content is didactically defensible when pupils are in the *concrete* stage of cognitive development. It is true, of course, that only the availability of concrete-empirical experience is necessary to generate the semi-abstract or intuitive level of meaningfulness characteristic of this stage of cognitive development. Hence, either simple verbal exposition, using concrete-empirical props, or a semi-autonomous type of discovery, accelerated by the judicious use of prompts and hints, is adequate enough for teaching simple and relatively familiar new ideas. But when the learning task is more difficult and unfamiliar, autonomous discovery probably enhances intuitive meaningfulness by intensifying and personalizing both the concreteness of experience and the actual operations of abstracting and generalizing from empirical data. In these circumstances also, the time-cost disadvantage of discovery learning is relatively less serious, since the time-consuming concrete-empirical aspects of learning must take place anyway, and since a large volume of subject matter cannot be covered in any case during the elementary-school period.

In lesser degree, this same rationale also applies to adolescents and adults who are relatively unsophisticated in the basic concepts and terminology of a given discipline. The older individual, however, has the benefit of greater general cognitive sophistication and linguistic facility, as well as of past successful experience in meaningfully relating abstractions to each other without the aid of concrete, empirical experience. Hence, he will move through the intuitive, subverbal phase of insightful understanding much more rapidly than the comparably unsophisticated child, and, unlike the latter, will soon dispense with this phase entirely.

The discovery method also has obvious uses in evaluating learning outcomes and in teaching problem-solving techniques and appreciation of scientific method. There is no better way of developing effective skills in hypothesis making and testing; desirable attitudes "toward learning and inquiry, toward guessing and hunches, toward the possibility of solving problems on one's own. . . ., [and] attitudes about the ultimate orderliness of nature and a conviction that order can be discovered" (11, p. 20). As a matter of fact, this is the major rationale for laboratory work. Except in the case of children and unsophisticated older persons, subject-matter content can be both transmitted and illustrated much more efficiently by means of exposition, demonstration, and schematic models. In addition, independent problem-solving is one of the few feasible ways of testing whether students *really* comprehend meaningfully the ideas they are able to verbalize (see p. 155).

Finally, in spite of the inconclusive empirical evidence, when all is said and done, and one has properly discounted the exaggerated claims made for the unique virtues of learning by discovery, as well as the fanciful reasons offered for same, it still seems plausible to suppose that the greater effort, motivation, and vividness associated with independent discovery lead to somewhat greater learning and retention. One might expect the advantages conferred by discovery techniques to be even greater with respect to transferability, since the experience gained from formulating a generalization from diverse instances obviously facilitates the solution of problems involving this generalization.

The crucial points at issue, however, are not whether learning by discovery enhances learning, retention, and transferability, but (a) whether it does so *sufficiently*, for learners who are capable of learning principles meaningfully *without* it, to warrant the vastly increased expenditure of time it requires; and (b) whether, in view of this time-cost consideration, the discovery method is a feasible technique for transmitting the substantive content of an intellectual or scientific discipline to cognitively mature students who have already mastered its rudiments and basic vocabulary. It is largely to an exploration of these issues that the remainder of this chapter is devoted.

PSYCHOLOGICAL AND EDUCATIONAL LIMITATIONS OF LEARNING BY DISCOVERY

For purposes of analysis, the psychologically and educationally untenable arguments advanced in support of learning by discovery can be conveniently considered under nine propositions.

"All Real Knowledge Is Self-Discovered"

The most general and metaphysical of the nine propositions is the familiar assertion that to possess knowledge *really* or to acquire an idea, the learner must discover it by himself or through his own insight. This proposition stems in part from the deification of the act of creative discovery in the problem-solving, activity program approach to teaching, and from John Dewey's extreme preference for problem-solving ability, rather than ability to acquire knowledge, as the proper criterion of intelligence. It is also partly derived from the child-centered and client-centered doctrines that the individual himself is best equipped to regulate the process of learning about himself and his universe, and therefore, that any tampering with this autonomy, is, by definition, detrimental to learning outcomes.

More recently, a sentimental type of Rousseauean mysticism and primitivism has become fashionable, and has been superimposed upon the aforementioned

ideological substrate. It is best exemplified by Jerome Bruner's statement that:
". . . if man's intellectual excellence is the most his own among his perfec-
tions, it is also the case that the most uniquely personal of all that he knows is
that which he has discovered himself . . . [Discovery creates] a special and
unique relation between knowledge possessed and the possessor (12, p. 22)
. . . The transition to adulthood involves an introduction to new realms of experience, the discovery and exploration of new mysteries, the gaining of new
powers. This is the heady stuff of education and it is its own reward" (13,
p. 76).

In accordance with this conception of the true nature of genuine knowledge,
Bruner formulates the objectives of education as follows:

"Schools should provide not simply a continuity within the broader community or with everyday experience. It is the special community where one
experiences discovery by the use of intelligence, where one leaps into new
and unimagined realms of experience, experience that is discontinuous with
what went before. . . . Education must also seek to develop the processes of
intelligence so that the individual is capable of going beyond the cultural
ways of his social world, able to innovate, in however modest a way, so that
he can create an interior culture of his own. For whatever the art, the science,
the literature, the history, and the geography of a culture, each man must be
his own artist, his own scientist, his own historian, his own navigator" (13,
pp. 76, 59).

It is perfectly true, of course, that one cannot simply soak up one's culture
like a piece of blotting paper and expect it to be meaningful. But who advocates doing anything of the kind? The very processes of perception and cognition necessarily require that the cultural stimulus world must first be filtered
through each individual's personal sensory apparatus and cognitive structure
before it can have any meaning. Meaning can never be anything more than a
personal phenomenological product that emerges when potentially meaningful
ideas are integrated within an individually unique cognitive structure. Invariably, therefore, the achievement of meaning requires translation into a personal
frame of reference, and reconciliation with established concepts and propositions. All of this goes on in any program of meaningful expository teaching, and
is obviously a far cry from the straw-man picture of passive absorption which
Bruner draws to disparage this method and thereby enhance the relative attractiveness of learning by discovery. Most of what anyone *really* knows consists of insights discovered by *others* which have been communicated to him
in meaningful fashion.

Quite apart from its lack of face validity, the proposition that every man
discover for himself every bit of knowledge that he *really* wishes to possess
is, in essence, a repudiation of the very concept of culture. For perhaps the
most unique attribute of human culture, which distinguishes it from every
other kind of social organization in the animal kingdom, is precisely the fact
that the accumulated discoveries of millennia can be transmitted to each
succeeding generation in the course of childhood and youth, and need not
be discovered anew by each generation. This miracle of culture is made
possible only because it is so much less time-consuming to communicate and
explain an idea meaningfully to others than to have them rediscover it by
themselves.

"The infant is born into a logically ordered world, abounding in problem solutions accumulated during the long span of mankind's sojourn on earth, and this distilled wisdom, called 'culture,' constitutes his chief heritage. Were it wiped away, he would become, in all respects, a wild animal, even less well equipped to cope with nature than are the instinct-aided beasts of the jungle. An individual is sagacious in direct proportion to the facility with which he can acquire and use existing knowledge; for even the most brilliantly endowed person can make but few valuable original discoveries" (55, p. 455).

Within each generation, therefore, we can only expect a given individual to internalize meaningfully a reasonable fragment of the total fabric of the culture that is expounded to him by the various educational agencies. If we are at all concerned with the breadth of his knowledge, we cannot possibly expect him to discover everything he is expected to know. The obligation of going beyond one's cultural heritage and contributing something new is an obligation that applies to an entire generation, not to each of its individual members. Hence, as we shall see later, the school cannot realistically set for itself the goal of having *each* child "leap into new and unimagined realms of experience" and emerge with ideas that are "discontinuous with what went before." The school can only hope to help one child in a thousand do this, or, more likely, one child in a million.

Meaning as an Exclusive Product of Creative, Nonverbal Discovery

A related proposition that relies somewhat less on flat epistemological assertion, and is more naturalistically grounded, holds that abstract concepts and propositions are forms of empty verbalism unless the learner discovers them directly out of his own concrete, empirical, nonverbal experience. Another slightly different way of expressing the same idea is to say that "generalizations are products of problem-solving . . . and are attainable in no other way" (10, p. 119).

The assertion that abstract concepts and generalizations are forms of glib verbalism unless the learner discovers them himself is predicated in my opinion, (a) on a misrepresentation of verbal learning as a passive, rote phenomenon; (b) on confusion between the reception-discovery and the rote-meaningful dimensions of learning; and (c) on unwarranted generalization to adolescents and adults of children's dependence on concrete-empirical props in comprehending and manipulating abstract ideas (see pp. 19–20). Meaningful knowledge is not an exclusive product of creative nonverbal discovery. For potentially meaningful *presented* material to become meaningful knowledge, the learner need only adopt a set to relate and incorporate its substantive import nonarbitrarily within his cognitive structure. As every elementary-school teacher knows, meaningful verbal reception learning—without any problem-solving or discovery experience whatsoever—is perhaps the most common form of classroom learning, provided that the necessary props are available.

Discovery enthusiasts tend to confuse the act of discovery with the act of understanding. Hilda Taba, for example, states that "the act of discovery occurs at the point in the learner's efforts at which he gets hold of the organizing principles embedded in any concrete instance, can see the relationship of the facts before him, understands the why of the phenomena, and can relate what he sees to his prior knowledge."[61] Actually this is a definition of all meaningful learning irrespective of whether it is reception or discovery learning. Discovery enthusiasts also tend to deny the transition from concrete to abstract cognitive functioning, and insist that mature learners cannot understand a verbal proposition without relating it to concrete-empirical experience and translating it into subverbal terms. Thus Gertrude Hendrix asserts that a cognitively sophisticated student, who is sufficiently skillful in interpreting sentence structure as well as referential symbols, can read a sentence which expresses a generalization and then construct or find enough examples of his own to make the generalization an organic part of himself— that is, to acquire the subverbal thing prerequisite to meaning of the sentence" (28, p. 337).

Subverbal Awareness as the Key to Transfer

We have seen, up to this point, that the reasoning underlying the argument that discovery is a prerequisite for meaning has rested either upon bald metaphysical assertion, or upon unwarranted pseudonaturalistic assumptions regarding the nature of understanding and knowledge. Gertrude Hendrix tried to fill this theoretical void by constructing a more systematic and sophisticated pedagogic rationale for the discovery method than had been attempted heretofore. She did this by adapting to the problem of transfer the time-honored labeling theory of the function of language in thought. Hendrix denies that "verbal generalizing is the primary generator of transfer power. . . . As far as transfer power [is] concerned the whole thing [is] there as soon as the non-verbal awareness [dawns]. . . . The separation of discovery phenomena from the process of composing sentences which express those discoveries is the big new breakthrough in pedagogical theory (29, pp. 292, 290).

The "key to transfer," Hendrix states, is a "subverbal internal process—something which must happen to the organism before it has any new knowledge to verbalize" (27, p. 200). Verbalization, she asserts further, is not only unnecessary for the generation and transfer of ideas and understanding, but is also positively harmful when used for *these* purposes. Language only enters the picture because of the need to attach a symbol or label to the emerging subverbal insight so that it an be recorded, verified, classified, and communicated to others; but the entire substance of the idea inheres in the subverbal insight itself. The resulting problem then, according to Hendrix, becomes one of how to plan and execute teaching so that language can be used for these necessary secondary functions "*without* damage to the dynamic quality of the learning itself" (29, p. 292).

How plausible is this proposition? Let us grant at the outset that a subverbal type of awareness or insight exists, and that this type of insight is displayed by rats, monkeys, and chimpanzees in experimental learning situations, and by household pets, saddle horses, barnyard animals, wild beasts, children, and adults in a wide variety of everyday problem-solving situations. But is it because of this type of insight that human beings have evolved a culture, and have achieved some progress in such fields as philosophy, chemistry, physics, biology, and mathematics, quite beyond anything yet approached by horses, chickens, or apes? Or is it because of the qualitatively superior transfer power of verbal or symbolic generalization?

The principal fallacy in Gertrude Hendrix' line of argument, in my opinion, lies in her failure to distinguish between the labeling and process functions of language in thought. She writes:

"We have been a long time realizing that subverbal awareness of a class, or a property, or a relation *had* to be in *someone's* mind before anyone could have thought of inventing a word for it anyway. In the natural order of events, the abstraction forms first, and then a name for it is invented" (28, p. 335).

Now what Hendrix is referring to here is simply the labeling or naming function of language in thought. The choice of a particular arbitrary symbol to represent a *new* abstraction obviously comes *after* the *process* of abstraction, and is not organically related to it. But this is not the *only* role of language in the abstraction process, nor is it the *first* time that it is used in this process. Verbalization does more than verbally gild the lily of subverbal insight; it does more than just attach a symbolic handle to an idea so that one can record, verify, classify, and communicate it more readily. In constitutes, rather, an integral part of the very process of abstraction itself. When an individual uses language to express an idea, he is not merely encoding subverbal insight into words. On the contrary, he is engaged in a process of generating a higher level of insight that transcends by far—in clarity, precision, generality, and inclusiveness—the previously achieved stage of subverbal awareness.

The old philosophical notion that words merely mirror thought or clothe it in outer garments is charmingly poetic but has little functional utility or explanatory value in the modern science of psycholinguistics. Even the seemingly simple act of making a choice of words in developing an idea involves complex processes of categorization, differentiation, abstraction, and generalization; the rejection of alternative possibilities; and the exclusion of less precise or overinclusive meanings. All of these processes contribute to and help account for the qualitatively superior transfer power of symbolic generalization.

Although the transfer power of symbolic generalization operates at many different levels of complexity and sophistication, even the simplest level transcends the kind of transfer that can be achieved with subverbal insight. Consider, for example, the transfer power of the word "house," which most preschool children can use correctly. Obviously, before the child ever uses this word, he has some unverbalized notion of what a house is. But once he attains and can meaningfully use the verbal concept of "house," he possesses an emergent new idea that he never possessed before—an idea that is sharper, clearer, more precise, more inclusive, more transferable, and more manipulable for purposes of thinking and comprehension that its crude subverbal precursor. He can now talk about the idea of "house" in the abstract, devoid of all particularity, and can combine this idea with concepts of form, size, color, number, function, *etc.* to formulate relational propositions that could hitherto be formulated with only the greatest difficulty.

The unqualified generalization that verbalization of an insight prior to use inhibits transfer, lacks both logical cogency and empirical support. Nonverbal understanding undoubtedly exists, especially in children and unsophisticated adults, as a precursor to some verbal understandings.[32,41] But several experiments on children's ability to solve transposition problems[53,67] show that verbal insights are more transferable than subverbal insights. Knowledge of underlying verbal principles also enhances problem-solving[20] and the learning of relevant motor skills (see p. 87); and when distinctive verbal responses are available, they tend to facilitate concept acquisition and conceptual transfer (see p. 88). Verbal generalization is particularly important for concept attainment in cognitively sophisticated learners.[26] In a well-controlled recent experiment Gagné and Smith demonstrated the facilitating effect of verbalization on the discovery of general principles and their use in problem-solving.[23] Finally, merely informing learners verbally that previous learnings might be useful in other situations, tend to increase transfer significantly.[16]

Not all ideas, however, are acquired quite as easily as the concepts of "house." As he enters school, the child encounters other concepts of much greater abstractness and complexity, e.g., concepts of addition, multiplication, government, society, force, velocity, digestion, that transcend his immediate experience and language ability. Before he can hope to acquire a meaningful grasp of such abstractions directly, that is, through direct verbal exposition, he must first acquire a minimal level of sophistication in the particular subject-matter area, as well as graduate into the higher level of intellectual development, i.e., the stage of abstract logical operations. In the meantime he is limited to an intuitive, subverbal kind of understanding of these concepts; and, even though convincing empirical evidence is still lacking, it is reasonable to suppose that preliminary acquisition and utilization of this subverbal level of insight both facilitates learning and transferability, and promotes the eventual emergence of *full* verbal understanding. (Gertrude Hendrix, of course, would say that *full* understanding was already attained in the subverbal phase, and that verbalization merely attaches words to subvebral insight.)

Now, assuming for the moment that Hendrix' experimental findings are valid, how can we explain the fact that immediate verbalization of newly acquired subverbal insight renders that insight less transferable than when verbalization is not attempted?[27] First, it seems likely that verbalization of nonverbal insight, before such insight is adequately consolidated by extensive use, may interfere with consolidation at this level, as well as encourage rote memorization of the ineptly stated verbal proposition, especially in pupils who are anxiety ridden or over-anxious to please. Even more important, however, is the likelihood that a verbally expressed idea—when ambiguous, unprecise, ineptly formulated, and only marginally competent—possesses less functional utility and transferability than the ordinarily more primitive and less transferable subverbal insight. This is particularly true in the case of children because of their limited linguistic facility and their relative incompetence in formal propositional logic.

Drawing these various strands of argument together, what can we legitimately conclude at this point? First, verbalization does more than just encode subverbal insight into words. It is part of the very process of thought which makes possible a qualitatively higher level of understanding with greatly enhanced transfer power. Second, direct acquisition of ideas from verbally presented propositions presupposes both that the learner has attained the stage of abstract logical operations, and that he possesess minimal sophistication in the particular subject matter in question. The typical elementary-school child, therefore, tends to be limited to an intuitive, subverbal awareness of difficult abstractions. The older, cognitively mature individual, how-

ever, who is also unsophisticated in a particular subject matter area is able
to dispense with the subverbal phase of awareness rather quickly, *i.e.*, as
soon as he attains the necessary degree of sophistication; and once he attains
it, he probably short-circuits the subverbal phase completely. Lastly, immediate
verbalization of a nonverbal insight, when this latter insight is newly acquired
and inadequately consolidated, probably decreases its transferability. This
phenomenon can be explained by citing the general developmental principle
that an ordinarily higher and more efficient stage of development, while still
embryonic and only marginally competent, is less functional than an ordinarily
more primitive and less efficient phase of development. Running, for example,
is eventually more efficient than creeping, but if a one-year-old infant had to
run for his life, he would make better progress creeping.

Gertrude Hendrix, however, comes out with somewhat different and more
sweeping conclusions from the same set of data. First, she regards nonverbal
awareness as containing within itself the entire essence of an emerging idea,
and insists that language merely adds a convenient symbolic handle to this
idea. Second, she generalizes children's dependence on a preliminary subverbal
stage of awareness, to all age levels, to all degrees of subject-matter sophistication, and to all levels of ideational difficulty. Actually, this subverbal stage is
highly abbreviated, both for young children learning less difficult kinds of
abstractions and for older, cognitively mature individuals working in a particular subject-matter area in which they happen to be unsophisticated; and it is
bypassed completely when this latter sophistication is attained. Finally, she
interprets her experimental findings regarding the inhibitory effects of immediate verbalization on the transferability of subverbal insight, as providing
empirical *proof* of her thesis that both the substance of an idea and the essential basis of its transfer power are present in their entirety as soon as nonverbal awareness emerges. In my opinion, these findings do nothing of the
kind. They merely show that a relatively clear subverbal insight, even when
only partially consolidated, is more functional and transferable than an ambiguous, inept, and marginally competent verbally expressed idea.

Unlike Gertrude Hendrix, therefore, I would conclude that secondary-
school and college students, who already possess a sound, meaningful grasp
of the rudiments of a discipline like mathematics, can be taught this subject
meaningfully and with maximal efficiency through the method of verbal exposition, supplemented by appropriate problem-solving experience; and that
the use of the discovery method in these circumstances is inordinately time-
consuming, wasteful, and rarely warranted. Why, then, do discovery techniques seem to work so well in programs such as the one devised by the University of Illinois Committee on School Mathematics? For one thing, the students entering the program, being victims of conventional arithmetic teaching
in the elementary schools, do *not* have a sound, meaningful grasp of the rudiments of mathematics and have to be re-educated, so to speak, from scratch.
For another, I have a very strong impression that as the program develops,
the discovery element becomes progressively attenuated, until eventually it is
accorded only token recognition. Lastly, stripped of its quite limited discovery
aspects, the UICSM approach is a much more systematic, highly organized,
self-consistent, carefully programed, abstractly verbal system of verbal exposition than anything we have known to date in secondary-school mathematics.

If it proves anything, the success of this program is a testimonial to the feasibility and value of a good program of didactic verbal exposition in secondary-school mathematics, which program is taught by able and enthusiastic instructors and, in its early stages, makes judicious use of inductive and discovery techniques.

The Discovery Method in Transmitting Subject-Matter Content

Educators who are convinced that abstractions are mere glib verbalisms unless independently discovered by the learner, have no other logical alternative than to advocate the use of discovery techniques—in high school and university as well as in the elementary school—as a principal method of transmitting the *substantive content* of subject matter. Easley,[18,19] for example, argues strenuously for reorganizing, in whole or in part, the curriculum of science, mathematics, and other secondary-school and college level subjects along the lines of inductive discovery. He also insists that nonverbal understanding and application of principles should be required of and demonstrated by students before they are permitted to use them in verbal form.

From a practical standpoint, however, it is impossible to consider the pedagogic feasibility of learning by discovery as a primary means of teaching subject-matter content without taking into account the inordinate time-cost involved. This disadvantage is not only applicable to the type of discovery where the learner is thrown entirely on his own resources, but also applies in lesser degree to the "contrived" or "arranged" type of discovery. Considerations of time-cost are particularly pertinent in view of our aforementioned developmental conclusions that the discovery approach offers no learning advantages except in the very limited case of the more difficult learning task, when the learner is either in the concrete stage of cognitive development, or, if generally in the abstract stage, happens to lack minimal sophistication in a particular subject-matter field. Also, once students reach secondary school and university, the time-cost disadvantage can no longer be defended on the dual grounds that the time-consuming aspects of learning must take place anyway, and that in any case elementary-school pupils cannot be expected to cover a great deal of subject matter. Subverbal, intuitive techniques have more general applicability during the elementary-school period, but are also more time-consuming and confer a qualitatively inferior type of understanding than does the verbal expository approach which can be successfully employed once students reach the abstract stage of cognitive development.

Thus, whereas the use of discovery and subverbal techniques in the transmission of complex and abstract subject matter content can be defended in the elementary school, it is difficult to rationalize the same practices in high school and beyond. It is true, as already pointed out, that the utilization of discovery learning and subverbal insight by older individuals might be temporarily helpful in the early, unsophisticated stages of learning a difficult new discipline. Nevertheless, since discovery and subverbal methods are incomparably more time-consuming than didactic verbal exposition, and since the cognitively mature individual does not linger very long in the unsophisticated state that is benefited by discovery and the prior acquisition of subverbal insight, the use of these methods as a *primary* means of transmitting subject-matter content is as unfeasible as it is unnecessary. If secondary-school and university students were obliged to discover for themselves every concept and principle in the syllabus, they would never get much beyond the rudiments of any discipline. However, as is similarly the case in the elementary school, teachers who do not regard completely *autonomous* discovery as sacrosanct, could greatly mitigate the time-consuming disadvantage of discovery methods by the judicious use of prompts or hints.

Some discovery enthusiasts[11,58] grudgingly admit that there is not sufficient time for pupils to discover everything they need to know in the various disciplines, and hence concede that there is also room for good expository teaching in the schools. In practice, however, this concession counts for little, because in the very next breath they claim that the acquisition of actual knowledge is less important than the acquisition of ability to discover knowledge autonomously, and propose that pedagogy and the curriculum be reorganized accordingly. Hence, in spite of the formal bow they made to didactic exposition, it is clear that they regard the acquisition of problem-solving ability[13,58] as more basic than the acquisition of subject matter. There is, after all, only so much time in a school day. If the school takes as its principal function the development of discovery and inquiry skills, how much time could possibly remain for the teaching of subject matter? The things that the school can do best, after all "are likely to belong in one or more of the following classes: ... (1) learning ... that requires organization and distribution of practice over considerable periods of time; ... (2) learning in which the central factors are not obvious to one observing the phenomenon and where basic principles, concepts, and meanings must be brought especially to the attention of the learner; ... (3) learning ... where the experiences cannot be provided directly; ... (4) learning which requires experiences of higher quality than are commonly available in the environment of the student; ... and (5) learning where examination and interpretation of experiences are essential; where it is not enough simply to have had more contact with, but where periodically there is need for reflection upon and examination of experience and an effort to interpret it to have it become more meaningful."[66]

Discovery methods of teaching are often based on the naive premise that autonomous problem-solving necessarily proceeds on the basis of inductive reasoning from empirical data. Actually, even young children usually start with some preconceptions or spontaneous models derived from their own experience or from the prevailing folklore. Hence when they are supposedly discovering principles inductively, they are really attempting to use empirical experience to confirm their existing preconceptions. It is "unpromising to base a teaching program on the expectation that children can invent ... modern scientific concepts, because their spontaneously invented concepts ... present too much of a block" (2, p. 4). A more realistic approach "is for the teacher to *introduce* ... modern scientific concepts ... [and] follow the introduction with opportunities for the children to discover that new observations can also be interpreted by use of the concept" (2, p. 4).

Still another disadvantage in using a discovery approach for the presentation of subject matter content inheres in the difficulties caused by children's subjectivism and by their exaggerated tendency to jump to conclusions, to overgeneralize on the basis of limited experience, and to consider only one aspect of a problem at a time.[34,35,47] It is true that one objective of the elementary-science curriculum (*i.e.*, to enhance appreciation of scientific method) implies an effort to educate them out of these tendencies. But it is one thing to do so as part of a limited laboratory program, and quite another to struggle full-time with this handicap as children are required to self-discover everything they have to learn.

Finally, one might reasonably ask how many students have the ability to discover everything they need to know. Although the ability to understand original ideas worth remembering is widely distributed, the ability to generate comparably original ideas autonomously is manifested by relatively few persons, that is, by gifted individuals.

In conclusion, after the elementary-school years, verbal reception learning constitutes the most effective method of meaningfully assimilating the substantive content of a discipline. Problem-solving and subverbal methods are developmentally and pedagogically unnecessary and are too time-consuming to accomplish this objective efficiently. However, the method of verbal reception learning will be restored to its rightful place in classroom instruction only when it is related to relevant but still-to-be-conducted research on the nature and conditions of long-term meaningful learning of large bodies of verbally presented material.

Problem-Solving Ability as the Primary Goal of Education

A fourth proposition underlying the learning by discovery thesis is the belief that the development of problem-solving ability is the primary goal of education. Implicit in this proposition is the assumption that the objectives involved in developing problem-solving ability, on the one hand, and in acquiring a body of knowledge, on the other, are more or less coextensive, and, therefore, that the learner somehow manages to acquire all of the important subject-matter content he needs to know in the course of learning how to discover knowledge automously. Actually, however, although these two sets of objectives are related and in a sense mutually supportive, they are far from being identical. Hence it cannot be assumed that methods promoting one objective necessarily promote the other, and that the process and goal of education are "one and the same thing" as Bruner (12, p. 77) claims they are.

In the first place, quite apart from its frequent usefulness in problem-solving, the acquisition of knowledge as an end in itself must be considered a major goal of education. Despite the fact that a large proportion of what human beings learn in the course of a lifetime has no immediate utility and is not applicable to any pressing problem of adjustment, people are nevertheless strongly motivated to learn so that they can better understand themselves, the universe, and the human condition. Much of this kind of knowledge, however, would have to be dismissed as worthless, if utility for problem-solving purposes were invariably held to be implicit in designating worthwhileness for learning. Hence, if we are concerned with achieving this particular aim of education, we cannot leave its implementation to problem-solving and discovery techniques. The use of these techniques, as already pointed out, furthers the problem-solving objective of education, but, except in the elementary school and under other special circumstances, is not very efficient for transmitting subject-matter content.

Second, the actual objective of typical problem-solving activity in most individuals is the solution of various *everyday* problems of living rather than the discovery of ideas or insights sufficiently important to be included in their permanent store of knowledge.* Although the ability to understand original ideas worth remembering is widely distributed, the ability to generate comparably original ideas autonomously is manifested by only relatively few persons, that is, by gifted individuals. It is true, of course, that "arranged" or "contrived" rediscovery would require considerably less giftedness; but even the use of this expedient on the part of the relatively more able (if not gifted) segment of the population would be so time-consuming as to render learning by discovery an impractical method of learning everything they need and have to know.

In the realm of educational theory, if not in actual practice, the impact of Dewey's exaggerated emphasis on problem-solving still continues to disturb the natural balance between the "transmission of the culture" and the problem-solving objectives of education. Enthusiastic proponents of the discovery method still assert that "more basic than the attainment of concepts is the ability to inquire and discover them autonomously."[58]

These somewhat extreme value judgments regarding the principal function of the school inspire, in turn, correspondingly one-sided proposals with respect to curriculum and pedagogy. Suchman, for example, contends that "the schools must have a new pedagogy with a new set of goals which subordinates retention to thinking. . . . Instead of devoting their efforts to storing information and recalling it on demand, they would be developing the cognitive functions needed to seek out and organize information in a way that would be most productive of new concepts."[58]

The development of problem-solving ability is, of course, a legitimate and significant educational objective in its own right. Hence it is highly defensible to utilize a certain proportion of classroom time in developing appreciation of and facility in the use of scientific methods of inquiry and of other empirical, inductive, and deductive problem-solving procedures. But this is a far cry from advocating that the enhancement of problem-solving ability is the major function of the school. To acquire facility in problem-solving and scientific method, it is not necessary for learners to rediscover every principle in the syllabus. Since problem-solving ability is itself transferable, at least within a given subject matter field,** facility gained in independently formulating and applying one generalization is transferable to other problem areas in the same discipline. Furthermore, overemphasis on developing problem-solving ability would ultimately defeat its own ends. It would leave students with insufficient time in which to learn the content of a discipline; and, hence, despite their adeptness at problem-solving, they would be unable to solve simple problems involving the application of such content. Hence, although actual practice in the process of formulating and testing hypotheses and in applying general principles to particular problem situations is necessary for enhancing

---

*The inductive derivation of concepts and generalizations from diverse instances is an exception to this statement, but is only a conspicuous feature of concept attainment during childhood (before a really large quantity of subject matter is incorporated.)

**See reference to Harlow's "learning set" experiments (p. 87).

problem-solving ability, much "teaching for problem-solving" necessarily involves the efficient transmission of fundamental, widely generalizable principles that are clearly understood and can be stably retained (see p. 78).

"Teaching for *critical* thinking" and "teaching for problem-solving" are really somewhat grandiose slogans, although obviously much more realistic than "teaching for creative thinking." To be sure, the critical thinking and problem-solving abilities of most pupils can be improved. But this is a far cry from saying that most pupils can be trained to become good critical thinkers and problem-solvers. Potentialities for developing high levels of these abilities are admittedly much less rare than corresponding potentialities for developing creativity. Nevertheless, there are no good reasons for believing that they are any commoner than potentialities for developing high general intelligence. Variability in genic endowment is probably responsible for more of the measured variance in critical thinking or problem-solving ability than is variability in educational experience.

Aptitude in problem-solving also involves a much different pattern of abilities than those required for understanding and retaining abstract ideas. The ability to solve problems calls for qualities (*e.g.*, flexibility, resourcefulness, improvising skill, originality, problem sensitivity, venturesomeness) that are less generously distributed in the population of learners than the ability to comprehend verbally presented materials. Many of these qualities also cannot be taught effectively. Although appropriate pedagogic procedures can improve problem-solving ability, relatively few good problem-solvers can be trained in comparison with the number of persons who can acquire a meaningful grasp of various subject-matter fields. Thus, to ignore the latter individuals and concentrate solely on producing talented problem-solvers would be educationally indefensible.

Hence a valid distinction can be drawn between "doing" and "understanding." Understanding is a necessary but not a sufficient condition for meaningful problem-solving (*i.e.*, the kind that involves genuine appreciation of underlying principles—not trial-and-error procedures or simply pragmatic rules of practice). Thus pupils can genuinely understand a proposition without being able to apply it successfully in particular problem situations, because such application requires additional knowledge, skill, ability, experience, or personality traits that are not inherent in the understanding per se. Conversely, "doing" does not necessarily either presuppose or enhance understanding if it is rote or mechanical in nature.

Many current writers[13,20,30,58] in the field of science education express the view that the principal objectives of science instruction are the acquisition of general inquiry skills, appropriate attitudes about science, and training in the "heuristics of discovery." Implicit or explicit in this view is the belief either that the particular choice of subject matter chosen to implement these goals is a matter of indifference (as long as it is suitable for the operations of inquiry), or that somehow in the course of performing a series of unrelated experiments in depth, the learner acquires all of the really important subject matter he needs to know. Thus, Hibbs states:

"It does not matter whether the student learns any particular set of facts, but it does matter whether he learns how much fun it is to learn—to observe and experiment, to question and analyze the world without any ready-made set of answers and without any premium on the accuracy of his factual results, at least in the field of science."[30]

In my opinion, any science curriculum worthy of the name must be concerned with the systematic presentation of an organized body of knowledge as an explicit end in itself. Even if it is relatively superficial and organized on an intuitive basis, as it must be in the elementary school, the science curriculum should make a start in this direction and give the student a feeling for science as a selectively and sequentially organized structure. This is no less important than imparting the view that science is a method of inquiry. It is also completely unrealistic to expect that subject-matter content could be acquired incidentally as a by-product of problem-solving or discovery experience, as in the typical activity program or project method. Such incidental learning pays too little attention to graded and systematically organized content, to substantive and programmatic factors, and to practice variables, when the aim is to transmit a specific body of knowledge rather than simply to enhance general problem-solving ability.

Another significant difficulty with this approach is that its proponents tend to confuse the goals of the scientist with the goals of the science student. They assert that these objectives are identical, and hence that students can learn science most effectively by enacting the role of junior scientist. But are the goals of the research scientist and of the science student really identical? The scientist is engaged in a full-time search for new general or applied principles in his field. The student, on the other hand, is primarily engaged in an effort to learn the same basic subject matter in this field which the scientist had learned in his student days, and also to learn something of the method and spirit of scientific inquiry. Thus, while it makes perfectly good sense for the scientist to work full-time formulating and testing new hypotheses, it is quite indefensible, in my opinion, for the student to be doing the same thing—either for real, or in the sense of rediscovery. Most of the student's time should be taken up with appropriate expository learning, and the remainder devoted to sampling the flavor and techniques of scientific method. It is the scientist's business to formulate unifying explanatory principles in science. It is the student's business to learn these principles as meaningfully and critically as possible, and *then*, after his background is adequate, to try to improve on them if he can. If he is ever to discover, he must first learn; and he cannot learn adequately by pretending he is a junior scientist. By so pretending, he would fail to acquire the minimal degree of subject-matter sophistication in a given discipline that is necessary for abstract intellectual functioning in that discipline, much less make original research contributions to science.

Rationale of laboratory work. Science courses at all academic levels are traditionally organized so that students waste many valuable hours in the laboratory collecting and manipulating empirical data which at the very best help them rediscover or exemplify principles that the instructor could present verbally and demonstrate schematically in a matter of minutes. Hence, although laboratory work can easily be justified on the grounds of giving students some appreciation of the spirit and methods of scientific inquiry, and of promoting problem-solving, analytic, and generalizing ability, it is a very time-consuming and inefficient practice for routine purposes of teaching subject-matter content or illustrating principles, where didactic exposition or simple demonstration are perfectly adequate. Knowledge of the methods whereby data and principles in a particular discipline are acquired also need not necessarily be gained through self-discovery in the laboratory. In many instances this purpose can be accomplished much more efficiently through didactic exposition in conjunction with demonstrations and exercises.

Laboratory work in this context refers to inductive discovery experience and should not be confused with demonstrations and simple exercises. Nevertheless it involves a contrived type of discovery that is very different from the truly autonomous discovery activities of the research scholar and scientist. The immature or unsophisticated student tends to be overwhelmed by the complexities of raw, unselected, and unsystematized data. Before he can discover concepts and generalizations efficiently, the problem must be structured for him, and the available procedures and methods of handling data must be skillfully "arranged" by others, that is, simplified, selectively schematized, and sequentially organized in such a way as to make ultimate discovery almost inevitable. Occasional independent design of experiments may have a salutary effect in conveying the actual spirit of scientific inquiry, but should hardly be a routine procedure.

Thus, in dividing the labor of science instruction, the laboratory typically carries the burden of conveying the method and spirit of science, whereas the textbook and teacher assume the burden of transmitting subject-matter content. The laboratory, however, should be carefully integrated with the textbook, that is, it should deal with methodology related to the subject matter of the course, and not with experiments chosen solely because of their suitability for illustrating various strategies of discovery. It goes without saying, of course, that laboratory methods can only be used where the underlying methodology and substantive principles are thoroughly understood rather than followed mechanically in cookbook fashion.

Training in the "Heuristics of Discovery"

Some advocates of the discovery method favor a type of guided practice in the "heuristics of discovery" that is reminiscent of the faculty psychology* approach to improving over-all critical thinking ability through instruction in the general principles of logic. Once the heuristics of discovery are mastered, they constitute, according to Bruner, "a style of problem solving or inquiry that serves for any kind of task one may encounter" (12, p. 31). Similarly, Suchman's Inquiry Training Program "is not proposed as a new way to teach science,

---

*The doctrine of formal discipline is still very much alive as evidenced by the stubborn persistence of studies purporting to improve critical thinking ability or general academic performance by means of instruction in general principles of logic or the study of foreign languages. Hyram,[33] for example, concluded that upper-grade elementary-school pupils could be taught to "think critically and therefore logically through the use of instructional procedures" emphasizing principles of logic. His findings, however, provided no evidence of gain in critical thinking ability beyond the actual area of training, since it was to be expected that pupils instructed in general principles of logic would make significantly higher scores than a matched control group on a test of reasoning based on these principles.

but as a way of teaching basic cognitive skills. . . . [that belong] in the science program and in every other curriculum area that requires . . . reasoning and the formulation and testing of hypotheses."[58]

The principal difficulty with this approach, as the faculty psychologists discovered, is that critical thinking ability can only be enhanced within the context of a specific discipline. Grand strategies of discovery, like scientific method, do not seem to be transferable across disciplinary lines—either when acquired within a given discipline, or when learned in a more general form apart from specific subject-matter content. This principle has been confirmed by countless studies and is illustrated by the laughable errors of logic and judgment committed by distinguished scientists and scholars who wander outside their own disciplines. The only kinds of transfer that have been empirically demonstrated in problem-solving situations are the transfer of specific skills, the transfer of general principles, and the transfer of general approach or orientation to a specified class of problems (see pp. 87–89). Hence critical thinking cannot be taught as a generalized ability; in practice, it can only be enhanced by adopting a precise, logical, analytic, and critical approach to the teaching of a particular discipline, an approach that fosters appreciation of scientific method in that discipline. Also, from a purely theoretical standpoint alone, it hardly seems plausible that a strategy of inquiry, which must necessarily be broad enough to be applicable to a wide range of disciplines and problems, can ever have, at the same time, sufficient particular relevance to be helpful in the solution of the specific problem at hand. And from the standpoint of elementary-school children, one wonders whether principles of inquiry pitched at this level of abstraction could be meaningful enough to be used successfully in problem-solving.

"Every Child a Creative and Critical Thinker"

Discovery methods are often rationalized in terms of the currently fashionable slogan that the school's chief responsibility is to make every child (or nearly every child) a critical and creative thinker. This incredible notion is based on the highly questionable assumption that all discovery activity, irrespective of degree of originality, is qualitatively of one piece; on a watered-down, more "democratic" definition of creativity, broad enough to include any type of independent discovery; on the belief that the very multiplicity of human abilities gives every individual a good chance, genically speaking, of being creative in at least one area; and on naive tabula rasa conceptions of human plasticity which maintain that even if a given child has no creative potentialities, good teachers can take the place of missing genes.

Bruner is an eloquent spokesman for this point of view:

"Intellectual activity anywhere is the same, whether at the frontier of knowledge or in a third-grade classroom. What a scientist does at his desk or in the laboratory, what a literary critic does in reading a poem are of the same order as what anybody else does when he is engaged in like activities—if he is to achieve understanding. The difference is in degree, not in kind. The schoolboy learning physics is a physicist, and it is easier for him to learn physics behaving like a physicist than doing something else" (11, p. 14).

Suchman also explains that the ultimate goal of his Inquiry Training Program is for children to discover and formulate explanations which represent "the causality of a single instance in terms of broad universal principles and generalizations. This is the unification of concepts for which the scientist strives. It can, and, in our opinion, should be the ultimate goal of children's inquiry as well."[58]

We have already considered in some detail the over-all plausibility of this proposition (see pp. 102 and 145). It only remains to point out that from the standpoint of enlightened educational policy in a democracy, the school should concentrate its major efforts on teaching both what is most important in terms of cultural survival and cultural progress, and what is most teachable to the majority of its clientele. As improved methods of teaching become available, most students will be able to master the basic intellectual skills as well as a reasonable portion of the more important subject-matter content of the major disciplines. Is it not more defensible to shoot for this realistic goal, which lies within our reach, than to focus on educational objectives that presuppose exceptional endowment and are impossible of fulfillment when applied to the generality of mankind? Would it not be more realistic to strive first to have each pupil respond meaningfully, actively, and critically to good expository teaching before we endeavor to make him a good critical thinker and problem-solver?

I am by no means proposing a uniform curriculum and pedagogy for all children irrespective of individual differences. By all means let us provide all feasible special opportunities and facilities for the exceptional child. But in so doing, let us not attempt to structure the learning environment of the *non*-exceptional child in terms of educational objectives and teaching methods that are appropriate for either one child in a hundred or for one child in a million.

There is a pressing need in these troubled times to dispense with sentimental fantasy and euphoric slogans and to get on with the realistic business of education. This means helping schools do well the kinds of jobs that schools can *really* do, namely, developing more efficient and appropriate ways of selecting, organizing, and presenting significant knowledge to students so that they can learn and retain it meaningfully—both as an end in itself and as a basis for future learning and problem solving.

Expository Teaching as Authoritarianism

Advocates of the discovery method also take advantage of the opprobrium associated with authoritarianism in education to discredit didactic exposition and to further their own cause. In doing this, they not only rely on the straw-man technique of representing a highly exaggerated "tell'm and drill" approach as typical of expository teaching, but also assert that expository teaching is *inherently* authoritarian. When a teacher stands in front of a classroom and presents facts, concepts, and principles, he is, according to Gertrude Hendrix[29] and others, behaving in an authoritarian fashion. This is presumably so because he is allegedly coercing pupils, by the prestige of his position and by his power to dispense reward and punishment, into unquestioningly accepting on faith his own version of "the truth," instead of giving them an opportunity to discover it for themselves. Bruner puts it this way:

"Insofar as possible, a method of instruction should have the objective of leading the child to discover for himself. Telling children and then testing them on what they have been told inevitably has the effect of producing bench-bound learners whose motivation for learning is likely to be extrinsic to the task at hand—pleasing the teacher, getting into college, artificially maintaining self-esteem" (13, p. 77).

In the first place, I submit that this distressing picture of expository teaching is a bit overdrawn. I do not deny that schools and colleges abound in such teachers. But this characterization is certainly not true of all didactic exposition, nor is it inherent in the method itself. Second, there is nothing inherently authoritarian in presenting or explaining ideas to others as long as they are not obliged, either explicitly or implicitly, to accept them on faith. Didactic exposition has always constituted the core of any pedagogic system, and, I suspect, always will, because it is the only feasible and efficient method of transmitting large bodies of knowledge. The deference to authority implied in accepting already discovered relationships has been condemned out of all reason. If students were required independently to validate every proposition presented by their instructors before accepting it, they would never progress beyond the rudiments of any discipline. We can only ask that established knowledge be presented to them as rationally and nonarbitrarily as possible, and that they accept it tentatively and critically as only the best available approximation of the "truth."

Discovery Organizes Learning Effectively for Later Use

I turn now to four propositions recently propounded by Jerome Bruner[12] which, taken together, may be said to constitute a proposed psychological rather than philosophical rationale for the discovery method. First, Bruner hypothesizes that, emphasis upon discovery in learning has precisely the effect upon the learner of leading him to be a constructionist, to organize what he is encountering in a manner not only designed to cover regularity and relatedness, but also to avoid the kind of information drift that fails to keep account of the uses to which information might have to be put (12, p. 26).

However, learning by discovery, in my opinion, does not *necessarily* lead to more orderly, integrative, and viable organization, transformation, and use of knowledge. It does so only insofar as the learning situation is highly structured, simplified, and skillfully programed to include a large number of diversified exemplars of the same principle, carefully graded in order of difficulty. But under these circumstances, one must, in all fairness, attribute these latter outcomes to the teacher's or textbook writer's organization of the data from which the discovery is to be made, rather than to the act of discovery itself.

As a matter of fact, *pure* discovery techniques, as employed by scholars and scientists, could only lead to utter chaos in the classroom. Put a young physics student into a bathtub and he is just as likely to concentrate on the soap bubbles and in the refraction of light as on the displacement principle that he is supposed to discover. In the UICSM program, therefore, students are given a prearranged sequence of suitable exemplars, and from these they "spontaneously self-discover" the appropriate generalization. Elementary-school pupils in the Inquiry Training Program are similarly shown a carefully prepared demonstration film illustrative of a given principle in physics, and are then permitted to ask questions answerable by "yes" or "no." Under both of these conditions pupils are engaging in "true," autonomous discovery in the same sense that a detective independently "solves" a crime after a benevolent Providence kindly gathers together all of the clues and arranges them for him in the correct sequence. This type of discovery is obviously a far cry from the kind of discovery that takes place in research laboratories, as Stanley observes.

"If, as a few ultra-progressive educators seem to imply, education were solely discovery, then teachers would no longer be necessary. Usually these theorizers are thinking of classroom situations in which the process of discovery resembles an Easter-egg hunt or the piecing together of a jigsaw puzzle: the participants make discoveries that could hardly have come about without previous 'structuring' of the situation. The teacher activity which is involved in setting up good learning situations is as truly a form of instruction as is direct teaching from lesson plans. Simply turning children loose without direction and expecting each of them to discover for himself important relationships, such as the fact that the first letter of the first word in every sentence is capitalized, would probably prove decidedly ineffective and wasteful of time" (55, p. 455).

Now in making these observations, I certainly do not wish to create the impression that I quarrel with the UICSM method of inducing discovery, or that I favor the use of raw, unselected, and unorganized data in discovery programs. I quarrel only with Bruner's interpretation that the organizing and integrative effects of learning by discovery are attributable to the act of discovery *per se*, rather than to the structure and organization which are put there by the programers of such curriculums as the UICSM and the Physical Science Study Committee courses in secondary-school mathematics and physics respectively.

Concern with the "structure" of a discipline is certainly not indigenous to the discovery method as Taba[61] seems to imply. It is also the basis of all modern approaches to expository teaching or reception learning. In fact, concern with presenting the unifying principles of a discipline is the main substantive rationale of expository teaching. The more unstructured discovery methods, on the other hand, tend to ignore the particular substantive content of a discipline as long as it can be used to further problem-solving or inquiry processes. In Suchman's Inquiry Training, for example, there is no attempt to present systematically the content of a scientific discipline. Content is largely a matter of indifference, or incidental to the process of discovery. Any kind of content is as good as any other as long as it lends itself to discovery and inquiry. Hence, unsystematic and haphazard sampling of scientific content is characteristic of his Inquiry Training Program.

Thus, contrary to Taba's assertion,[61] learning by discovery does not develop autonomous intellectual power and transfer because it *uniquely* enables the learner to get at the underlying structure of ideas of a subject. Expository teaching can give the learner the same kind of mastery of these ideas. If learning by discovery promotes transfer in some unique way, it probably does so through the transferable experience of independently formulating and testing alternative hypotheses and through the transferable attitude of independent search. It still has to be demonstrated, however, that such experience and attitudes are transferable across disciplinary lines.

Learning by discovery is not necessarily antithetical to programed instruction, despite the howls of anguish which teaching machines frequently elicit from discovery enthusiasts. True, the more unstructured kinds of discovery methods (e.g., the Inquiry Training Program), which demand more genuinely autonomous (unprompted) discovery on the part of the learner, are incompatible with the "ruleg" type of programing,[31] in which a verbal rule is stated at the outset, and the learner is then tested on his ability to apply this rule correctly to various relevant examples. These kinds of discovery methods also prefer to give the learner greater scope for independent thinking than is implied in the use of closely graduated steps in programed sequences. On the other hand, highly structured discovery methods, such as the UICSM, which lead the learner to a desired generalization through the use of carefully graded problem examples, are quite compatible with a programing technique that follows the same general procedure. Gagné and Brown[22] recently conducted an experiment in which one group of learners ("guided discovery") were required to discover a principle after working a hierarchy of problems which reduced the learning task to a graduated series of sequential steps.

Discovery as a Unique Generator of Motivation and Self-Confidence

Bruner[11,12,13] and other discovery enthusiasts[29,58] perceive learning by discovery as a unique and unexcelled generator of self-confidence, of intellectual excitement, and of motivation for sustained problem-solving and creative thinking. I have already acknowledged that discovery techniques are valuable for acquiring desirable attitudes toward inquiry, as well as firm convictions about the existence and discoverability of orderliness in the universe. It is also reasonable to suppose that successful discovery experience enhances both these attitudes and convictions and the individual's feeling of confidence in his own abilities. On the other hand, there is no reason to believe that discovery methods are unique or alone in their ability to effect these outcomes.

As every student who has been exposed to competent teaching knows, the skillful exposition of ideas can also generate considerable intellectual excitement and motivation for genuine inquiry, although admittedly not quite as much perhaps as discovery. Few physics students who learn the principle of displacement this way will run half-naked through the streets shrieking, "Eureka." But then again, how many students of Archimedes' ability are enrolled in the typical physics or mathematics class? How comparable to the excitement of Archimedes' purely autonomous and original discovery is the excitement generated by discovering a general formula for finding the number of diagonals in an n-sided polygon after working problems one through nine in the textbook? And what happens to Archimedes Junior's motivation and self-confidence if, after seventeen immersions in the tub, he has merely succeeded in getting himself soaking wet?

Careful study of the psychological experiment cited by Bruner[12] by way of illustrating the allegedly unique motivational and inspirational values of discovery methods, leaves me no more convinced than I was before. Bruner describes a psychological experiment in probability learning with a two-choice apparatus in which "the payoff sequence is arranged at random and there is no pattern." Some subjects quickly begin to catch on to the fact (and rightly so in this case), that "things are happening quite by chance . . . [and] very soon revert to a much more primitive [and empirically more successful] strategy wherein *all* responses are allocated to the side that has the greater payoff." Other more trusting and optimistic souls, however, persist in believing that "there *is* some pattern to be found in the sequence . . . *i.e.*, that regularities are discoverable," and hence keep trying one unsuccessful hypothesis after another, in each of which "the number of responses given to each side is roughly equal to the proportion of times it pays off."

"What has [all] this to do with the subject at hand?" asks Bruner?

"For the person to search out and find regularities and relationships in his environment, he must be armed with an expectancy that there will be something to find and, once aroused by expectancy, he must devise ways of searching and finding. One of the chief enemies of expectancy is the assumption there is nothing one can find in the environment by way of regularity or relationship" (12, p. 24).

I can thoroughly appreciate the logic of this argument, but I still cannot see what relevance it has for the issue regarding the unique motivational virtues of the discovery method. All Bruner is saying here is that, in the absence of a firm conviction about the existence of discoverable regularities in a particular problem-solving situation, one will resort to simple trial-and-error behavior—just like Thorndike's cats in the puzzle-box. But why should discovery methods necessarily inspire any more confidence in the existence of discoverable regularities in the universe than the method of didactic exposition which, after all, is dedicated to the presentation and explication of these regularities? It is true that successful discovery experience strengthens such confidence; but unsuccessful experience has precisely the opposite effect—as demonstrated by the resurgence of magical and superstitious thinking that follows in the wake of failure to find patterns of orderliness in nature.

Discovery as a Prime Source of Intrinsic Motivation

A related motivational proposition put forth by Bruner states that "to the degree that one is able to approach learning as a task of discovering something rather than 'learning about it,' to that degree will there be a tendency for the child to carry out his learning activities with the autonomy of self-reward or, more properly, by reward that is discovery itself" (12, p. 26). Bruner feels that learning by discovery frees the child from the immediate control of such extrinsic motives as high marks, desire for parental and teacher approval, and a need to conform to the expectations of authority figures. In support of this hypothesis, he cites research data showing that early "over-achievers" in school tend to be conformists, to overdevelop rote abilities, and to be deficient in analytic and critical-thinking ability.[12]

In my opinion, however, there is no existing or necessary association between a discovery approach to learning and intrinsic motivation, on the one hand, and a reception approach to learning and extrinsic motivation, on the other. But because of certain cultural influences on personality development in our type of social system, I would tend to postulate precisely the opposite kind of relationship, namely, that discovery learning is more often associated with extrinsic motivation than is reception learning. Whether an individual primarily manifests intrinsic or extrinsic motivation in learning, it seems to me, is largely a function of two factors: (a) how much intrinsic self-esteem he possesses, and hence how great his relative need is for compensatory extrinsic status; and (b) the strength of his cognitive needs in their own right, that is, his need to acquire knowledge and to understand his environment, as influenced by genic and temperamental determinants and by previous satisfactory learning experience.

On these grounds, I would think that a more plausible interpretation of Bruner's data is that it is the learner who is lacking in intrinsic self-esteem who develops an overpowering need, both for such external symbols of achievement as high grades and teacher approval and for the glory and prestige associated with independent discovery in our culture. Hence the overachiever is typically a child who is deficient in intrinsic self-esteem. He relies unduly on rote memorization both because it is the surest route to the high marks and the teacher approval he craves, and because (on account of his anxiety and impaired self-esteem) he lacks the courage and self-confidence to improvise in novel, problem-solving test situations.[9] At the same time, however, to bolster his impaired self-esteem, he aspires to the prestige and status which, in our culture, can only be achieved through the exercise and hypertrophy of White's so-called "competence motive," which Bruner equates with the drive to discover.[12]

What I am suggesting, therefore, is that rather than being uniquely powered by intrinsic motives, learning by discovery or over-vigorous exercise of the drive for competence typically reflects in our culture a lack of intrinsic self-esteem and a compensatory need to overachieve with respect to the external symbols and trappings of successful accomplishment. To be sure, there are individuals who are driven to discover principally because of a compelling need to express their individuality or creative urges, to find the answers to haunting problems, or to discharge their feelings of moral obligation to the social community. But in our particular culture with its emphasis on status, prestige, ego aggrandizement, and material rewards—especially among individuals who lack intrinsic self-esteem—such motives for discovery tend to be the exception rather than the rule.

Discovery and the "Conservation of Memory"

In the last of his four propositions, Bruner claims unique retention advantages for material learned by the discovery method. And again he illustrates his point by citing an experiment of questionable relevance to the principle he proposes. Pairs of words are presented to twelve-year-old children:

"One group is simply told to remember the pairs, that they will be asked to repeat them later. Another is told to remember them by producing a word or idea that will tie the pair together in a way that will make sense to them. A third group is given the mediators used by the second group when presented with the words, to aid them in tying the pairs into working units" (12, p. 31).

The wholly predictable results were that the uninstructed chidlren remembered least, and that the "children who developed their own [mediators] for relating the members of each word pair . . . did better than the children" who were given the mediators by exposition (12, p. 31).

Why don't these findings support Bruner's proposition regarding the beneficial influence of discovery on retention? First, the learning task in this experiment is hardly comparable to the situation where children must discover a generalization inductively and autonomously. In Bruner's experiment, the entire content of what is to be learned is *given* and the child need only supply a mediating link from his own cognitive structure which is sufficiently inclusive to subsume both members of the word pair. Now is this not precisely the paradigm for meaningful reception learning in which materials are presented, and the learner then tries to incorporate them into his own cognitive structure by relating them to more inclusive established ideas? The superior retention of the children who used mediators, as compared to those who were uninstructed, is attributable to the facilitating effect on retention which occurs when one helps learners convert an ostensibly rote reception learning task into a more meaningful type of reception learning. The discovery variable, in my opinion, is not implicated at all in this experiment.

Second, the superior retention of the word pairs related to the *self*-constructed mediators simply reflects the value of using more stable, relevant, and familiar subsumers within cognitive structure as anchoring posts for new learning materials. Mediators that children choose themselves are obviously more relevant and familiar to them than mediators suggested to them by others. The fact that they are self-constructed is quite beside the point.

Lastly, even within the framework of a reception learning interpretation, we should be careful about generalizing these findings to classroom pedagogy. In a short and easy learning task dealing with familiar materials, it is quite feasible for children to construct their own organizing concepts. But one could not legitimately conclude from this experiment that it would also be feasible for them to construct their own organizers for large bodies of complex and unfamiliar learning materials in subject-matter areas where their level of sophistication is necessarily low.

RESEARCH EVIDENCE

I now propose to examine a representative sample of the more significant published research bearing on the discovery method. The professional literature on"learning by discovery" regrettably exemplifies, as clearly as any research in education, the all too frequent hollowness of the hallowed phase, "research shows."* Careful examination of what research supposedly "shows" in this instance yields these three disheartening conclusions: (a) that most of the articles most commonly cited in the literature as reporting results supportive of discovery techniques actually report no research findings whatsoever, consisting mainly of theoretical discussion, assertion, and conjecture; descriptions of existing programs utilizing discovery methods; and enthusiastic but wholly subjective testimonials regarding the efficacy of discovery approaches; (b) that most of the reasonably well-controlled studies report negative findings; and (c) that most studies reporting positive findings either fail to control other significant variables or employ questionable techniques of statistical analysis. Thus, actual examination of the research literature allegedly supportive of learning by discovery reveals that valid evidence of this nature is virtually nonexistent. It appears that the various enthusiasts of the discovery

---

*See Martin Mayer (44, p. 67) for a critique of the phrase, "research shows."

method have been supporting each other research-wise, by taking in each other's laundry, so to speak; that is, by citing each other's opinions and assertions as evidence and by generalizing wildly from equivocal and even negative findings.

In view of the apparently sound theoretical reasons listed earlier (under "rationale") for predicting modest advantages in learning, retention, and transferability attributable to the use of discovery techniques, these largely equivocal and negative findings are somewhat disappointing. In many cases, of course, findings are equivocal simply because of failure to control such other relevant variables as the rote-meaningful, the inductive-deductive, the verbal-nonverbal, and the intra-material organization dimensions of learning, while varying the reception-discovery factor. In other instances, it is quite possible that negative findings are less indicative of inadequacies in the underlying theory than of inadequacies in research design, which unfairly load the dice against the possibility of confirming hypotheses. And as far as long-term curriculum studies are concerned, one might anticipate that any short-term advantages accruing from the use of discovery techniques *per se* would be more than offset by its time-consuming aspects, and the consequent low rate of acquiring subject-matter content.

Long-Term Studies

Despite their frequent espousal of discovery principles, the various curriculum reform projects have failed thus far to yield any research evidence in support of the discovery method. This is not to say that the evidence is negative, but rather that there just is not any evidence, one way or the other—notwithstanding the fact that these projects are often cited in the "discovery" literature under the heading, "research shows." For one thing, the sponsors of some of these projects have not been particularly concerned about *proving* the superior efficacy of their programs, since they have been thoroughly convinced of this from the outset. Hence, in many instances they have not even attempted to obtain comparable achievement test data from matched control groups. And only rarely has any effort been expended to prevent the operation of the crucial "Hawthorne Effect," that is, to make sure that evidence of superior achievement outcomes is attributable to the influence of the new pedagogic techniques or materials in question, rather than to the fact that the experimental group is the recipient of *some* form of conspicuous special attention; that *something* new and interesting is being tried; or that the teachers involved are especially competent, dedicated, and enthusiastic, and receive special training, attend expense-free conventions and summer institutes, and are assigned lighter teaching loads.

But even if the sponsors of the curriculum reform movements were all imbued with missionary research zeal, it would still be impossible to test the discovery hypothesis within the context of curriculum research. In the first place, a large number of other significant variables are necessarily operative in such programs. The UICSM program, for example, not only relies heavily on the principle of self-discovery of generalizations, but also on an inductive approach, on nonverbal awareness, on abundant empirical experience, on careful sequential programing, and, above all, on precise, self-consistent, unambiguous, and systematic verbal formulation of basic principles.

To which variable or to which combination of these variables and the "Hawthorne Effect," should the success of this program be attributed? Personally, for reasons enumerated earlier in this chapter, I would nominate the factor of precise and systematic verbal formulation rather than the discovery variable. (Students enrolled in the UICSM program learn more mathematics, in my opinion, *not* because they are required to discover generalizations *by themselves*, but because they have at their disposal a systematic body of organizing, explanatory, and integrative principles which are not part of the conventional course in secondary-school mathematics. These principles illuminate the subject for them and make it much more meaningful, coherent, and exciting.) Finally, "'measurement is [always] a difficult problem [in such research] because standardized achievement tests both cover various traditional subject-matter units deliberately ignored by these new curricula, as well as fail to measure knowledge of the more modern concepts, which they emphasize."[8]

A number of long-term curriculum studies in the older literature are frequently cited as providing empirical support for the discovery method. Using basically identical research designs, McConnell,[42] Thiele,[62] and Swenson[60] compared the so-called "drill" and "generalization" methods of teaching number facts to second-grade pupils. The drill approach emphasized rote memorization and mechanical repetition of authoritatively presented facts and rules, whereas the generalization method stressed meaningful perception of relationships and derivation of generalizations. Pupils taught by the generalization method also had the added benefit of concrete props in the McConnell study, and of organized grouping of materials in the Swenson study. A well-known study by G. Lester Anderson[1] was also conducted along very similar lines, but used fourth-grade pupils.

Needless to say, the generalization method was found to be superior in all four studies, except in criterion situations calling for immediate and automatic recall of knowledge relatively unchanged in form from that learned in the training situation. Much more salient than the discovery variable in each of these studies, however, was the rote-meaningful factor; and in two of the studies, the differential availability to the "generalization" group of concrete visual aids or of organized grouping of learning materials, further complicated interpretation of the findings. It should also be remembered that it is precisely in relation to this age group of young learners first entering the stage of concrete logical operations, and still completely unsophisticated in a new, difficult, and abstract subject matter, that the efficacy and feasibility of the discovery method are least disputed. The time-cost factor is relatively unimportant at this age level, both because large bodies of subject matter cannot be learned through expository teaching anyway, and because a transitional phase of subverbal, intuitive understanding is developmentally necessary in the acquisition of complex abstractions. However, it would be quite unwarranted to generalize from these findings that meaningful expository teaching of twelfth-grade mathematics is less efficacious than learning by discovery.

Preliminary findings of the Inquiry Training Program also fail to support the discovery hypothesis.[56,59] Inquiry training did not significantly improve the quality of the questions asked by the subjects or facilitate their grasp of concepts. It is true that those pupils who were trained in the particular inquiry techniques employed did ask a significantly greater number of questions and more of the right kinds of questions (verification rather than implication) in the criterion situation than did pupils in the control group. But is this not precisely what they were trained to do? Pupils who are trained to ask certain kinds of questions in one situation will naturally tend to ask more of the same kinds of questions in an analogous criterion situation than will pupils who do not receive this particular inquiry training. The transfer value of such training can only be demonstrated by using criteria which are both more independent of the particular training procedures employed, and more reflective of its goals than of its techniques.

Short-Term Studies

The well-known Gestalt writings on insightful problem-solving by Köhler,[40] Wertheimer,[68] Duncker,[17] and Katona,[36] are traditionally cited in the "discovery" literature as supportive of the discovery method of teaching. Actually, however, the Gestalt emphasis on insight deals only with the rote-meaningful dimension of problem-solving and has no bearing whatsoever on the relative efficacy of the expository (reception) and discovery approaches. As pointed out earlier, both reception and discovery learning may each be rote or meaningful, depending on the conditions under which learning occurs. The Gestalt theorists merely insist that the concept of insight is more valid than the Thorndikian trial-and-error or the Hullian point of view in explaining problem-solving behavior that lies within an organism's verbal or subverbal reasoning ability.

Köhler's, Wertheimer's, and Duncker's monographs also do not really report research findings in the usual sense of the term. They are, rather, elaborate and sophisticated analyses of the nature and conditions of insightful problem-solving from the Gestalt point of view, which use observations, informal experiments, anecdotes, and demonstrations to illustrate the principles under discussion. Katona's studies, on the other hand, are more genuinely experimental but, at the very most, demonstrate that understanding of a principle, as opposed to rote memorization, leads to superior retention° and transfer. One experiment in particular shows that a rotely memorized verbal principle is less transferable to new problems than is mere empirical experience with problems exemplifying the principle in question. (36, p. 89) But this only indicates that meaningful understanding of a principle, even when unverbalized, is more transferable than rote memorization. It does not suggest that newly emerging nonverbal awareness is always more transferable than verbal understanding.

This latter study by Katona is reminiscent of Gertrude Hendrix' previously discussed experiment,[27] but Hendrix carried the design and argument one

---

°A neo-behaviorist explanation of this "superior retention" finding is that understanding of a principle reduces the sheer volume of what has to be remembered by rendering the details of the learning task reconstructable from memory of the principle itself (46 p. 570). The writer's own interpretation stresses the nonarbitrary and substantive incorporability (anchorability) of meaningfully learned material within cognitive structure.[6]

step further. She also included another control group of subjects who *first* acquired *meaningful* nonverbal awareness of a principle, and *then* attempted immediate verbalization. She showed that her experimental subjects, who were sent out of the room while these control subjects were attempting to verbalize nonverbal awareness, were not only superior in transfer power to the control subjects who had merely learned the principle through verbal exposition, but were also superior to this other control group as well, which had acquired nonverbal awareness *prior* to verbalization. Hendrix interpreted her findings to mean that the full transfer power and substance of an idea are already present in the emerging subverbal insight, and that this dawning subverbal awareness, when left unverbalized, is *invariably* more transferable than when put into words. I have already explained in detail why I think that immediate verbalization of insight reduces transferability *only* when cognitively immature pupils are in the process of learning difficult abstract propositions, or when older individuals are in the early unsophisticated stages of learning a new discipline, and why I believe that verbalization enhances transferability under *all other* circumstances. At this point, I only wish to consider methodological and statistical aspects of Hendrix' experiment.

In reporting her study, Hendrix frankly acknowledged the difficulty of devising both "a good behavioral test for the achievement of unverbalized awareness," and a suitable test of transfer. There was also the formidable problem of deciding "whether subjects were obtaining the correct answers through counting or through applying the generalization" (27, p. 203). With respect to the maintenance of necessary controls, Hendrix freely admitted, furthermore, that it was difficult to prevent "communication and discussion among members of the different method groups in the time interval between learning and testing," and to administer the various tests and experimental procedures without revealing to the subjects that an experiment was in progress (27, pp. 203-204).

In addition to all of these acknowledged measurement, evaluation, and control problems, only forty subjects were available for all three groups, and even this relatively small number was achieved only by pooling results from three very different kinds of experimental populations, for whom a test of homogeneity of variance was not even reported. Both the small experimental population, and the undetermined comparability of its three separate components, rendered untenable Hendrix' assumption that random assignment of subjects to the three treatment groups equalized these groups with respect to the influence of the uncontrolled variables.

Lastly, the difference on the transfer test between the "verbal exposition" group and the "nonverbal awareness group" was only significant at the .12 level, and the corresponding difference between the "nonverbal awareness" group and the group which had verbalized their nonverbal awareness was only significant at the .33 level. Neither of these levels of significance is regarded very seriously by either statisticians or educational research workers. Taking all of these factors into consideration, therefore, the experimental foundations for the far-reaching conclusions which Hendrix draws from these findings can hardly be considered impressively firm.

We come finally to a series of experimental studies in which varying amounts of guidance were furnished to different groups of subjects in problem-solving situations. Stacey[54] studied the effects of directed *versus* independent discovery on solving a group of meaningful problems, each of which required subjects to identify the one item in a set of five that did not "belong." He found that active participation and self-discovery were more efficacious for learning than was "passive participation involving only recognition or identification of information" presented to the learner. This finding, of course, was wholly predictable, since the fostering of such complete passivity in problem-solving experience as providing the correct answer for each problem as well as the reason for same is self-evidently inadvisable and is seldom if ever practiced today. But even so, surprisingly enough, significant differences were *not* found between these extreme treatment groups on a transfer test.

Using similar kinds of material, but with college students rather than sixth-grade pupils, Craig[15] obtained results even less favorable for the discovery method. His "directed" group, which received a brief verbal explanation of principles during the training period, learned and retained significantly more principles than did his "independent group" which had no help whatsoever in the training situation. As in the Stacey study, however, the two groups were not significantly different with respect to mean score on a transfer test. Kittell's findings in a similar type of experiment with sixth-grade pupils[39] were, if anything, even more damaging to the discovery cause than were Craig's. The group in his experiment which received an "intermediate" amount of guidance, but nevertheless an amount which was somewhat *greater* than that received by Craig's "directed" group (*i.e.*, explanation of principles *plus* organization of materials) was superior in learning, retention, *and* transfer to groups receiving either less or more direction. Pooling the findings of these three studies, therefore, the evidence seems to support the conclusion that in this type of problem-solving exercise, guidance in the form of providing information about underlying principles facilitates learning, retention, and possibly transfer more than either the provision of less guidance or the furnishing of specific rules for each of the problems.

Haselrud and Meyers[25] recently conducted a coding study, with college students, which was explicitly designed to rebut the Craig and Kittell findings. However, their subjects exhibited significantly better learning on problems where the coding rule was given than where it had to be independently derived. Furthermore, on a delayed transfer test, there was *no* difference whatsoever in the number of correct code identifications made for the problems learned originally with the rule given and the problems learned originally by independent derivation of the code. Nevertheless, on the grounds that the gain from the first to the second test was greater for those problems where the rule had been independently derived, the investigators concluded that principles which are independently derived are more transferable than principles for which the rule is given. This, in my opinion, is equivalent to saying that, of two matched race horses trained by methods A and B respectively, who are tied at the end of the criterion race, the horse trained by method B is *really* superior because at the half-way mark he was one lap behind the horse trained by method A, but nevertheless caught up to him by the end of the race.

Another study in this area by Kersh[37] yielded results practically identical to those of Craig, Kittell, and Haselrud and Meyers on the test of original learning, but results opposite to those of Kittell on the delayed retest. By using an ingenious research design, however, Kersh was able to explain this latter finding on the basis of the greater interest and motivation, on the part of the "independent discovery" group, to continue practicing the task during the test-retest interval. Kersh concluded that discovery experience *per se* does not enhance understanding or meaningfulness.*

In another group of studies on the effects of varying amounts of guidance on problem-solving, either no differences were found between treatment groups, or a limited amount of guidance ("guided discovery") was found to be superior both to no guidance whatsoever or to complete guidance. Moss,[45] Maltzman and others,[43] Tomlinson,[65] and Forgus and Schwartz[21] reported no significant differences in delayed retention and transfer between "direct-detailed"** and "guided discovery" types of learning groups. Ray[50] and Rowlett,[51] on the other hand, found that guided discovery was superior to direct-detailed instruction in remembering and transferring principles of micrometer use and orthographic projection. In a recent study of programed learning, Gagné and Brown[22] reported that a small-step, guided-discovery method of programing was superior both to the "ruleg" method and to a large-step prompted-discovery procedure.*** Corman's findings[14] were differentiated with respect to the ability level of his subjects: highly explicit instructions were most effective with his more able subjects, whereas his less able subjects benefited equally from more and less explicit instructions. Grote[24] found that the direct-detailed method was superior for high-ability students and that the guided discovery procedure was superior for average-ability students in learning a lever principle.

The issue of expository teaching versus independent discovery in the learning, retention, and transfer of principles is still very much in doubt because of the non-comparability of the various studies, serious deficiencies in research design, and the failure to hold constant or take into account rote-meaningful, inductive-deductive, verbalization, ability level, cognitive maturity, subject-matter sophistication, and motivational variables. In general the research findings support Thorndike's well-known conclusion that "refusal to supply information on the ground that the learner will be more profited by discovering the facts himself, runs the risk not only of excessive time-cost but also the strengthening of wrong habits" (64, p. 147). Providing guidance to the learner in the form of verbal explanation of the underlying principles almost invariably facilitates learning and retention and sometimes transfer as well. *Self*-discovery methods and the furnishing of completely explicit rules, on the other hand, are relatively less effective.

The most efficacious type of guidance (guided discovery) is actually a

---

*In a more recent experiment, Kersh[38] confirmed these findings.

**A relatively complete, explicit, step-by-step type of guidance.

***Ervin (see p. 87) used a similar "guided discovery" approach in teaching elementary-school children the verbal principles underlying various motor performances. The children were helped by leading questions to formulate the principles from their own observations. This method of instruction resulted in greater transfer than did a nonverbal type of guidance.

variant of expository teaching that is very similar to Socratic questioning. It demands the learner's active participation and requires him to formulate his own generalizations and integrate his knowledge in response to carefully programed leading questions; and it is obviously much more highly structured than most discovery methods, with the possible exception of the UICSM. Further research is needed to determine whether guided discovery is superior to simple didactic exposition in terms of relative effectiveness for the time-cost involved when such factors as cognitive maturity, subject-matter sophistication, and verbal ability are varied.

REFERENCES

1. Anderson, G. L. Quantitative thinking as developed under connectionist and field theories of learning. In *Learning Theory in School Situations*. University of Minnesota Studies in Education. Minneapolis: University of Minnesota Press, 1949, pp. 40–73.

2. Atkin, J. M., and Karplus, R. Discovery or invention? Urbana, Ill.: College of Education, University of Illinois, 1962.

3. Ausubel, D. P. In defense of verbal learning. *Educ. Theor.*, 1961, *11*:15–25.

4. Ausubel, D. P. Learning by discovery: rationale and mystique. *Bull. Natl. Assoc. Sec. Sch. Principals,* 1961, *45*:18–58.

5. Ausubel, D. P. Implications of preadolescent and early adolescent cognitive development for secondary school teaching. *High Sch. J.*, 1962, *45*:268–75.

6. Ausubel, D. P. A subsumption theory of meaningful verbal learning and retention. *J. gen. Psychol.*, 1962, *66*:213–24.

7. Ausubel, D. P. Some psychological considerations in the objectives and design of an elementary-school science program. *Science Educ.*, 1963, in press.

8. Ausubel, D. P., and Fitzgerald, D. Meaningful learning and retention: intrapersonal cognitive variables. *Rev. educ. Res.*, 1961, *31*:500–510.

9. Ausubel, D. P., Schiff, H. M., and Goldman, M. Qualitative characteristics in the learning process associated with anxiety. *J. abnorm. soc. Psychol.*, 1953, *48*:537–47.

10. Brownell, W. A., and Hendrickson, G. How children learn information, concepts, and generalizations. In *Learning and Instruction*. Forty-ninth Yearbook, Natl. Soc. Stud. Educ., Part I, 1950, pp. 92–128.

11. Bruner, J. S. *The Process of Education*. Cambridge, Mass.: Harvard University Press, 1960.

12. Bruner, J. S. The Act of discovery. *Harvard educ. Rev.*, 1961, *31*:21–32.

13. Bruner, J. S. After Dewey what? *Saturday Review*, June 17, 1961, pp. 58–59; 76–78.

14. Corman, B. R. The effect of varying amounts and kinds of information as guidance in problem solving. *Psychol. Monogr.*, 1957, *71*, No. 2 (Whole No. 431).

15. Craig, R. C. Directed versus independent discovery of established relations. *J. educ. Psychol.*, 1956, *47*:223–34.

16. Dorsey, M. N., and Hopkins, L. T. The influence of attitude upon transfer. *J. educ. Psychol.*, 1930, *21*:410–17.

17. Duncker, K. On problem-solving. *Psychol. Monogr.*, 1945, *58*, (Whole No. 270).

18. Easley, J. A. Is the teaching of scientific method a significant educational objective? In *Philosophy and Education* (I. Scheffler, ed.). Boston: Allyn and Bacon, 1958.
19. Easley, J. A. The Physical Science Education Committee and educational theory. *Harvard educ. Rev.*, 1959, 29:4–11.
20. Ewert, P. H., and Lambert, J. F. Part II. The effect of verbal instructions upon the formation of a concept. *J. gen. Psychol.*, 1932, 6:400–13.
21. Forgus, R. H., and Schwartz, R. J. Efficient retention and transfer as affected by learning method. *J. Psychol.*, 1957, 43:135–39.
22. Gagné, R. M., and Brown, L. T. Some factors in the programing of conceptual material. *J. exp. Psychol.*, 1961, 62:313–21.
23. Gagné, R. M., and Smith, E. C. A study of the effects of verbalization on problem solving. *J. exp. Psychol.*, 1962, 63:12–16.
24. Grote, C. N. A comparison of the relative effectiveness of direct-detailed and directed discovery methods of teaching selected principles of mechanics in the area of physics. Unpublished Ed. D. Dissertation. Urbana, Ill.: University of Illinois, 1960.
25. Haselrud, G. M., and Meyers, Shirley. The transfer value of given and individually derived principles. *J. educ. Psychol.*, 1958, 49:293–98.
26. Heidbreder, E., and Zimmerman, C. The attainment of concepts: IX. Semantic efficiency and concept attainment. *J. Psychol.*, 1955, 40:325–35.
27. Hendrix, Gertrude. A new clue to transfer of training. *Elem. Sch. J.* 1947, 48:197–208.
28. Hendrix, Gertrude. Prerequisite to meaning. *Math. Teacher*, 1950, 43:334–39.
29. Hendrix, Gertrude. Learning by discovery. *Math. Teacher*, 1961, 54:290–299.
30. Hibbs, A. R. Science for elementary students. *Teachers Coll. Rec.*, 1961, 63:136–42.
31. Homme, L. E., and Glaser, R. Problems in programing verbal sequences. In *Teaching Machines and Programmed Learning* (A. A. Lumsdaine and R. Glaser, eds.), Washington, D. C.: National Education Ass'n., 1960, pp. 486–96.
32. Hull, C. L. Quantitative aspects of the evolution of concepts. *Psychol. Monogr.*, 1920, 28 (Whole No. 123).
33. Hyram, G. H. An experiment in developing critical thinking in children. *J. exp. Educ.*, 1957, 26:125–32.
34. Inhelder, Bärbel, and Piaget, J. *The Growth of Logical Thinking from Childhood to Adolescence.* New York: Basic Books, 1958.
35. Karplus, R. Beginning a study in elementary school science. *Amer. J. Physics.*, 1962, 30:1–9.
36. Katona, G. *Organizing and Memorizing.* New York: Columbia University Press, 1940.
37. Kersh, B. Y. The adequacy of "meaning" as an explanation for the superiority of learning by independent discovery. *J. educ. Psychol.* 1958, 49:282–92.
38. Kersh, B. Y. The motivating effect of learning by directed discovery. *J. educ. Psychol.*, 1962, 53:65–71.
39. Kittell, J. E. An experimental study of the effect of external direction during learning on transfer and retention of principles. *J. educ. Psychol.*, 1957, 48:391–405.

40. Köhler, W. *The Mentality of Apes*. New York: Harcourt, Brace, 1925.
41. Luchins, A. S., and Luchins, Edith H. A structural approach to the teaching of the concept of area in intuitive geometry. *J. educ. Res.*, 1947, 40:528–33.
42. McConnell, T. R. Discovery *vs.* authoritative identification in the learning of children. University of Iowa Studies, *Stud. Educ.*, 9, No. 5, 1934.
43. Maltzman, I., Eisman, E., and Brooks, L. O. Some relationships between methods of instruction, personality variables, and problem-solving behavior. *J. educ. Psychol.*, 1950, 47:71–78.
44. Mayer, M. *The Schools*. New York: Harper, 1961.
45. Moss, J. An experimental study of the relative effectiveness of the direct-detailed and the directed discovery methods of teaching letterpress imposition. Unpublished Ed. D. Dissertation. Urbana, Ill.: University of Illinois, 1960.
46. Osgood, C. E. *Method and Theory in Experimental Psychology*. New York: Oxford University Press, 1953.
47. Piaget, J. *The Child's Conception of Physical Causality*. New York: Harcourt, Brace, 1932.
48. Piaget, J. *The Psychology of Intelligence*. New York: Harcourt, Brace, 1950.
49. Piaget, J. *The Construction of Reality in the Child*. New York: Basic Books, 1954.
50. Ray, W. E. An experimental comparison of direct-detailed and directed discovery methods of teaching micrometer principles and skills. Unpublished Ed. D. Dissertation. Urbana, Ill.: University of Illinois, 1957.
51. Rowlett, J. D. An experimental comparison of direct-detailed and directed discovery methods of teaching orthographic projection principles and skills. Unpublished Ed. D. Dissertation. Urbana, Ill.: University of Illinois, 1960.
52. Serra, Mary C. A study of fourth-grade children's comprehension of certain verbal abstractions. *J. exp. Educ.*, 1953, 22:103–18.
53. Spiker, C. C., and Terrell, G. Factors associated with transposition behavior of preschool children. *J. genet. Psychol.*, 1955, 86:143–58.
54. Stacey, C. L. The law of effect in retained situations with meaningful material. In *Learning Theory in School Situations*. University of Minnesota Studies in Education. Minneapolis: University of Minnesota Press, 1949, pp. 74–103.
55. Stanley, J. C. The role of instruction, discovery, and revision in early learning. *Elem. Sch. J.*, 1949, 49:455–58.
56. Suchman, J. R. Training children in scientific inquiry. Urbana, Ill.: College of Education, University of Illinois, 1959.
57. Suchman, J. R. Inquiry training in the elementary school. *Science Teacher*, 1960, 27:42–47.
58. Suchman, J. R. Inquiry training: building skills for autonomous discovery. *Merrill-Palmer Quart. Behav. Develpm.*, 1961, 7:148–69.
59. Suchman, J. R. The inquiry process and the elementary school child. Paper presented to the American Educational Research Association, Atlantic City, N. J., February 1962.
60. Swenson, Esther J. Organization and generalization as factors in learning, transfer, and retroactive inhibition. In *Learning Theory in School Situations*. University of Minnesota Studies in Education. Minneapolis: University of Minnesota Press, 1949, pp. 9–39.
61. Taba, Hilda. Learning by discovery: psychological and educational rationale. Paper presented to the American Educational Research Association, Atlantic City, N. J., February 1962.

62. Thiele, C. L. *The Contribution of Generalization to the Learning of Addition Facts.* New York: Bureau of Publications, Teachers College, Columbia University, 1938.

63. Thorndike, E. L. The effect of changed data upon reasoning. *J. exp. Psychol.,* 1922, 5:33–38.

64. Thorndike, E. L. *The Psychology of Wants, Interests, and Attitudes.* New York: D. Appleton-Century, 1935.

65. Tomlinson, R. M. A comparison of four presentation methods for teaching complex technical material. Unpublished Ed. D. Dissertation. Urbana, Ill.: University of Illinois, 1962.

66. Tyler, R. W. The education of teachers: A major responsibility of schools and colleges. *Educ. Rec.,* 1958, 39:253–61.

67. Weir, M. W., and Stevenson, H. W. The effect of verbalization in children's learning as a function of chronological age. *Child Develpm.,* 1959, 30:143–49.

68. Wertheimer, M. *Productive Thinking,* enl. ed., New York: Harper, 1959.

CHAPTER 8.

Task Variables: Practice and Instructional Materials

MEANINGFUL LEARNING REFERS to nontransitory organizational changes in cognitive structure as the learner responds to initial and successive presentations of the learning task. Although much significant learning obviously occurs during initial presentation of the stimulus material, most learning situations in both laboratory and school settings presuppose multiple presentations or trials (i.e., practice); and both learning process and outcome customarily encompass various quantitative and qualitative changes that take place during the course of these several trials. Learning, therefore, ordinarily implies practice. Such practice, furthermore, is typically specific (restricted to the learning task) and deliberate (intentional). Long-term organizational changes in cognitive structure that occur in the demonstrable absence of specific and deliberate practice experience (i.e., incidental learning) may be more properly considered manifestations of maturation (see p. 31). Short-term fluctuations in the availability of learned material, on the other hand, are reflective of changes in the threshold of availability (see p. 57).

As previously suggested, the effects of practice both reflect the influence of existing cognitive structure and also modify that structure. The cognitive impact of initial presentation of new learning material is largely determined by the organizational attributes of existing cognitive structure; and by altering these attributes, such presentation influences, in turn, the learner's response to subsequent trials. Practice therefore affects learning and retention by modifying cognitive structure. Generally speaking it increases the stability and clarity of newly learned materials in cognitive structure and hence enhances dissociability strength and retention.

Practice, in other words, is not a cognitive structure variable itself but is one of the principal variables influencing cognitive structure. The most immediate effect of practice is to increase the stability and clarity and hence the dissociability strength of the new learning material. In turn, these organizational changes in the newly learned material that occur within the context of its subsumer, facilitate the learner's assimilation of the stimulus material during the subsequent trial, i.e., "sensitize" him to its potential meanings and thereby enhance the facilitating effect of the next trial on dissociability strength. In addition, consolidation of this new material makes available in cognitive structure a clear and stable subsumer for other related learning tasks introduced at a later date. Practice therefore influences cognitive structure in at least three different ways: it increases the dissociability strength of the current learning task for a given trial, it enhances the learner's responsiveness to subsequent presentations of the same material, and it facilitates the learning and retention of related new learning tasks.

176

But even though each learning trial influences subsequent learning trials by virtue of its sensitizing effect on cognitive structure, the mediating influence of this effect on the next practice trial is not experimentally measurable. The transfer paradigm (*i.e.*, comparing learning outcomes of the two groups after the experimental group receives two trials and the control group receives only one trial) is inapplicable under these circumstances, because as long as training and criterion tasks are identical (*ie.*, consist of two presentations of the same material), it is impossible to distinguish between the practice effect per se (the direct effect of an additional presentation upon learning) and the indirect mediating (sensitizing) influence of altered cognitive structure in accounting for the superiority of the experimental group on the second learning trial. In classical transfer situations, on the other hand, inasmuch as criterion and training tasks differ, the superiority of the experimental group on the criterion task can be unequivocally attributed to the modification of cognitive structure induced by the training task. It goes without saying, however, that simply because the influence of a cognitive structure variable is not demonstrable under certain conditions, we cannot warrantedly infer that it does not affect learning-retention outcomes. The reality of a variable's effect on a phenomenon cannot be denied just because the variable itself currently defies reliable and valid measurement, or because experimental or statistical procedures are not yet available to isolate this effect from that of other variables.

In this chapter we will *not* be concerned with the problem of how different dimensions of the practice variable (*e.g.*, overlearning, multicontextual exposure) affect transfer, that is, influence the meaningful learning and retention of *new* material by altering cognitive structure (see pp. 86 and 87). We will consider instead the effects of repeated presentations of the *same* learning task (practice) on the learning and retention of *that* task. Relevant dimensions of the practice variable to be considered include the number, type, and distribution of practice trials; the method and general conditions of practice; and the learner's awareness of the effect of practice on learning-retention outcomes (feedback). It should be appreciated, however, that only a slight alteration in experimental design would be necessary to make the relevant studies in this area conform to the transfer paradigm and thus shed light on the pedagogically more significant issue of how different aspects of practice influence the meaningful learning and retention of related *new* material.

Also to be considered in this chapter are other related non-practice dimensions of the task variable such as various general properties of the instructional material used in meaningful learning tasks, *e.g.*, the amount and difficulty of the material, its degree of internal organization, and the rate of presenting new ideas and information. Treatment of the more specific aspects of the instructional material variable, *e.g.*, textbooks, laboratory manuals, teaching machines, educational television, audio-visual aids, is more properly left to specialized monographs devoted to these topics and to treatises on the methodology of teaching the various school subjects.

THE ROLE OF FREQUENCY IN LEARNING AND RETENTION

Theoretical Issues. The role and importance of frequency (number of trials or presentations) in learning and retention have received varying emphases over the years in psychology and education. Traditionally both folklore and pedagogy have taken the position that "practice makes perfect," particularly in the learning of motor skills. For the most part, in the history of psychological thought, frequency has been regarded as one of the cardinal laws of associative learning, and, more recently, of classical conditioning as well. In the early Thirties, however, "the law of frequency" received a severe setback at the hands of E. L. Thorndike who concluded after much experimentation that frequency per se has little or no impact on the learning process, and that its supposed influence must really be attributed to reinforcement (satisfying effect), knowledge of results, belongingness, or intention.[153,154] The authority of Thorndike's pronouncement was subsequently bolstered by the influence of such nonfrequency conceptions of learning as the Guthrian "contiguity-single-trial" model of learning,[31,32,49,125] the Hullian emphasis on drive reduction as the principal variable determining habit strength,[62] the Skinnerian preoccupation with reinforcement in operant conditioning,[140] Tolman's view of learning as the gradual acquisition of cognitive sophistication,[158] and the Gestalt formulation of learning as the abrupt emergence of "insight."[78] The combined influence of these theoretical developments in the psychology of learning and of the prevailing progressivist and child-centered trends in the philosophy of education led to a widespread de-emphasis of the value of practice or drill in the teaching-learning process. Drill was unwarrantedly stigmatized as necessarily rote in nature, and a fetish was made of uncontrived, unstructured, and incidental learning experience.

The progressivists, of course, did not entirely deny the value of practice. As a matter of fact both their espousal of activity programs and their battle cry of "learning by doing" carried an implied endorsement of the importance of appropriate practice. But by appropriate practice they meant repeated encounters with different exemplars of the same principle in uncontrived, real-life situations. Their mistake lay in assuming that all structured practice (drill) is necessarily rote, that unstructured (incidental) practice is maximally effective for school learning tasks, and that "doing" necessarily leads to learning (understanding) simply because it occurs repeatedly in natural situations. Actually, for practice to result in meaningful mastery of material, the only really essential conditions are that the learning task be potentially meaningful, that the learner exhibit a meaningful learning set and possess the necessary relevant background concepts, and that the number, distribution, sequence, and organization of intra-and inter-task trials conform to empirically validated principles of efficient learning and retention. Not only is the uncontrived or unstructured quality of practice an unessential condition of meaningful, effective learning, but it also often leads to no meaningful mastery whatsoever. This is so because incidental practice is typically haphazard in terms of frequency and distribution of trials, and because the spontaneous, unstructured organization of learning experiences is more frequently than not inconsistent with established criteria of effective programing. Problem-solving and laboratory exercises may similarly lead to little or no meaningful learning if a student's learning set is simply rotely to memorize type problems or techniques of manipulating symbols, and if he has inadequate background in or appreciation of the methodological principles illustrated by specific laboratory procedures. It should also be realized, finally, that just as "doing" does not necessarily lead to understanding, understanding does not necessarily imply ability successfully to solve problems involving meaningful appreciation of the principles in question. Factors other than understanding are also implicated in the outcome of problem-solving activities (see p. 155).

Despite the tendency among many learning theorists and progressive educators to denigrate the frequency variable in learning, both classroom teachers and athletic coaches have continued to place implicit reliance on practice as an essential condition of learning. Overlearning is still regarded by most psychologists as a major variable enhancing the retention of rote learning, increasing positive transfer, decreasing negative transfer, and increasing resistance to retroactive interference (see pp. 44 and 86); and by way of counter-offensive, the incremental or gradual concept of associative rote learning as opposed to the "one-trial" concept has recently received much vigorous support.[94,116,163,164,173] Advocates of the incremental position of course, insist, that typically, with each successive trial, associative strength is gradually increased until it reaches or exceeds threshold level, rather than that the entire gain in associative strength is necessarily acquired in the single trial preceding the appearance of the correct response. They implicitly assume, in other words, that the increment in associative strength is attributable, in whole or in part, to the effect of repeated presentations of the learning task, i.e., to the influence of frequency per se; and Underwood has more explicitly defended the role of frequency as such in rote verbal learning, insisting that at the very least it is related to "familiarity," and thus accounts in part for the "availability of response," if not for the "associative strength" aspect of paired-associate learning.[162]

It is apparent therefore that three principal issues must be considered in evaluating the role of frequency in learning and retention. First, is repetition typically required both in gradually establishing associative or dissociability strength at or above threshold level (learning), and in sufficiently enhancing such strength so that the span of retention is extended, or is all effective learning and retention actually accomplished in a single trial? Is frequency, in other words, organically related to the learning-retention process, or is gradual improvement with repetition merely an artifactual consequence of various circumstances involved in the investigation, measurement, and representation of learning-retention outcomes? Second, does frequency affect learning and retention in any distinctive way apart from affording repeated opportunities for other variables such as contiguity, drive reduction, and confirmation-clarification to operate in cumulative fashion? Lastly, in what ways, if any, does frequency affect meaningful learning and retention differently than rote learning and retention?

Importance of Frequency. Prima-facie evidence in support of the incremental (continuity) conception of learning and of the importance of frequency can be derived from the overwhelming majority of research studies in the field, irrespective of the type of learning involved. In addition to these studies of practice per se, evidence has already been presented which suggests that prior *over*learning of relevant material during a training period facilitates the learning of related new material (i.e., induces positive transfer) by enhancing the stability and clarity of the training concepts in cognitive structure (see pp. 86–87). But theorists who deny that frequency intrinsically influences learning-retention outcomes do not seem at all impressed by the apparently irrefutable evidence implicit in the very shape of the learning curve. They attribute the gradual improvement that occurs with repetition to various methodological artifacts. Gestalt and field theorists,[77,78,79,80,91] for example, typically assert that learning (insight) occurs suddenly, and that the trials preceding the attainment of insight have no real effect on its emergence. Learning, they contend, only appears to be incremental either because the grossness of existing measuring instruments obscures the abrupt acquisition of partial insights, or because the pooling of data from many subjects who achieve insight on an all-or-none basis during different trials, results in a smooth and gradual group learning curve. Guthrie[49] also espouses an all-or-none concept of learning for any particular stimulus-response connection, attributing the apparent improvement with practice to unavoidable variability in the stimulus situation over a series of trials which, in turn, leads to ever increasing stimulus generalization and correspondingly greater probability of response elicitation. Lastly, according to Rock,[125] frequency appears to be necessary in learning a list of paired associates because "only a limited number of associations can be formed on any one trial" (p. 186).

Frequency and Rote Learning. Until relatively recently, most of the empirical evidence bearing on the frequency issue in rote learning had been conducted by E. L. Thorndike.[153,154] In amassing experimental evidence against the role of frequency, however, he chose highly atypical learning tasks that could not possibly be mastered in the absence of either explicit intention or knowledge of results, respectively, and then deliberately failed to provide these conditions. Hence, since the minimally necessary conditions for learning were lacking in his particular experiments, he did not find it very difficult to demonstrate that numerous repetitions of the task under the same impossible conditions he set were just as ineffective for learning as was the provision of a single trial. Needless to say, despite the fact that such evidence is almost universally cited in educational psychology textbooks as definitively proving the negligible influence of frequency *per se* on learning, it merely demonstrated that certain atypical kinds of learning cannot take place in the absence of explicit intention or feedback, no matter how frequently the learning task is repeated.

In one series of experiments, for example, Thorndike endeavored to prove that frequency has no effect in the absence of belongingness, and by eliminating this latter condition successfully demonstrated that frequency was in fact ineffective. This result was hardly surprising because although contiguity is an essential condition of associative learning, not all contiguous events are necessarily associated: some selectivity based on belongingness is always involved in the particular items that are associated. In the case of meaningful learning material, belongingness is a reflection of functional or logical relatedness. In rote learning tasks, however, where the association to be formed is purely arbitrary, belongingness is established either by explicit instruction (and the formation of corresponding explicit sets or intentions), or by habitual expectancies based on previous experience. Hence much "incidental learning" (*i.e.*, learning in the absence of explicit instruction and intention) can occur either if the learning material is meaningful, or if the rote learning task is constituted in accordance with habitual expectancies.* But if a particular rote learning task is unrelated to or inconsistent with habitual expectancies (e.g., associating the second member of one paired associate with the first member of the next paired associate in the series), it is understandable that little or no learning will occur in the absence of explicit intention, despite numerous contiguous repetitions.[153,154]

From the latter experiments, therefore, one could warrentedly infer that in addition to contiguity, belongingness is essential for associative learning, and that belongingness can either be established implicitly (in potentially meaningful material or in familiar rote tasks) or by explicit intention (in unfamiliar rote tasks). One could not justifiably conclude either that explicit intention is necessary for *all* learning, or that frequency per se has no effect whatsoever on learning. True, in the absence of belongingness, frequency is ineffective because no learning at all can occur. This does not mean, however, that when belongingness *is* present, the improvement that occurs with repetition must necessarily be attributed to belongingness rather than to frequency.

Similarly, in another widely cited series of experiments, Thorndike[153,154] showed that in the absence of knowledge of results, frequency of repeating certain tasks (e.g., drawing a line of specified length, estimating the length of paper strips) bears no relation to learning (improvement). In instances where a constant stimulus situation is repeated but the response is variable or indeterminate, it is obvious that some knowledge of results is essential for learning. Feedback, however, is not indispensable for learning in situations either where *both* stimulus and response are specified, or where the learner's task is simply to reproduce the material that is presented to him. Furthermore, not only is frequency effective in these latter instances where feedback is *not* required for learning, but it also enhances learning in those situations where feedback *is* essential and is provided.

What applies to the role of frequency in the case of learning characterized by knowledge or ignorance of results, also applies to the role of frequency in learning situations where other kinds of drives, and rewards through drive reduction, may or may not be present. Although experimental evidence is equivocal and subject to conflicting interpretations, it appears that problems are commonly solved and their solutions are selectively remembered, either through trial-and-error variation of responses or through acquisition of insight into a means-end relationship, despite the fact that a drive state is neither present before and during the problem-solving act nor is reduced by the successful goal-achieving responses. Even where drives and drive reduction do play a role in human learning, the drives in question are rarely homeostatic in nature since such drives are quickly satiated and, when accompanied by intense affect, tend to disrupt learning.[51] Both in humans and infra-human primates, much learning is motivated by curiosity, urge to ex-

---

*Children, for example, acquire much specific information about objects irrelevant to the solution of particular incentive-motivated problems[150] and, without any obvious motivation for so doing, effectively retain, over long periods of time, information presented in motion pictures.[53] Experimenters who administer lists of nonsense syllables to subjects, incidentally learn many of these syllables themselves.[66]

plore and manipulate, and desire to know. Thus responses that satisfy these urges are drive reducing, and hence both motivate further learning, and, under certain circumstances, may be selectively reinforced.* So much of the learning is motivated (both proactively and retroactively) and reinforced on this basis that, unlike the situation of "latent learning" in rats,[159] the later provision of material rewards makes little or no difference in learning outcomes.[1,6] It should also be realized that knowledge of results, (feedback) which satisfies (reduces) the cognitive drive, also facilitates learning and retention on purely nonmotivational and nonreinforcement cognitive grounds (e.g., confirmation, clarification, correction).

Some evidence against the role of frequency in rote learning has been adduced from various experiments on "single-trial" paired-associate learning.[31,32,125] Rock[125] modified the conventional paired-associate technique of presentation so that his experimental subjects would have only a single trial in which to learn any given pair. This was accomplished by removing from the list (i.e., on the subsequent trial) all pairs that were not learned on the previous trial, and substituting new pairs. He found that subjects who learned lists of paired associates presented in this manner, learned them just as rapidly to a criterion of one errorless trial as did control subjects who, by following the conventional procedure, had one or more additional trials in which to learn those pairs missed on the first trial. Estes et al[32] have also shown that when a list of paired associates were studied only once, items which were incorrect on the first trial almost invariably tended to be incorrect on the second test trial. Since the probability of making a correct response under these circumstances apparently did not increase from the first test trial to the second, they concluded that associative strength either increases from zero to 100 per cent on a given trial or shows no increase whatsoever.

These latter studies, however, neither provide more definitive evidence than Thorndike's aforementioned research in ruling out the effect of frequency per se on learning, nor demolish the incremental conception of learning. In addition to such methodological difficulties in both studies as failure to control for item difficulty,**[94,116,163,164,173] Estes' interpretation of his findings did not allow for the possibility that frequency may result in gradual *subliminal* increments in associative strength, i.e., in increments below threshold value that are not reflected in performance. If, for example, a single study trial increases the associative strength of a given item in a

---

*The position is adopted in this volume (see p. 234), that reinforcement through drive reduction occurs, if at all, only in the case of rote learning (the learning of discrete, arbitrary, and verbatim stimulus or stimulus-response connections). In meaningful learning, the satisfying effect of drive reduction does not lead to reinforcement since it has no conceivable way of influencing dissociability strength or thresholds of availability. However, drive reduction may retroactively generate further motivation to learn in either instance.

**It seems highly probable on *a priori* grounds that the particular items in a series of paired associates which a given subject fails to learn, are more difficult for *him* than those items which he succeeds in learning, even if the two sets of items can be considered equally difficult when some *average* criterion of difficulty such as Glaze value is applied.

list of paired associates but `does not do so to threshold level, the sub-threshold strength of the item is no more likely to lead to a correct response on a second test trial than on the first test trial, provided that no study has intervened between the two test trials. Hence the fact that the particular items incorrect on the first test trial also tend to be incorrect on the second test trial does not warrant the conclusion that the first study trial produces no increase in associative strength. The notion of incremental learning in which frequency plays a significant role is, of course, by no means incompatible with the possibility that later trials may have a differentially greater effect on the yet unlearned components of a total learning task than on those items already above threshold level. On *a priori* grounds it would also appear that this differential effect is less likely to occur when trials are distributed rather than massed, inasmuch as a longer interval between trials leads to some forgetting of the learned items and hence to less difference in associative strength between learned and unlearned items.

In many military and industrial training situations involving perceptual-motor skills (*e.g.*, gunnery) and the learning of sequential procedures, practice of the task itself apparently has no facilitating effect.[39] This is so because the *real* learning task under these circumstances does not involve the acquisition of appropriate responses or stimulus-response connections (which in fact are already highly familiar or overlearned), but rather appreciation of underlying principles or memorization of a correct sequence of activities. In the first instance, therefore, instruction and guidance in the relevant principles are more effective than practice in bringing about improvement; and in the second instance, memorization of a sequential list and use of it in conjunction with practice are similarly more effective than mere practice of the task.[39] This does not mean, of course, that the principle of practice or frequency does not apply to these types of learning, as Gagné[39] asserts. It simply means that for frequency to be effective the learner must practice *the actual task that needs learning*—not overt responses that are already thoroughly mastered.

Frequency and Rote Retention. The effect of frequency on rote retention is considerably less controversial than its effect on rote learning. Both Luh[96] and Krueger[82] have shown that overlearning enhances the absolute level of retention and makes review less necessary, even though the retention curve under these circumstances is similar in form to that obtained when material is learned to a criterion of a single perfect repetition. Greater degrees of overlearning lead to higher levels of retention than do lesser degrees of overlearning, but the resulting gains in retention are not proportionate to the increase in learning trials. Overlearning also undoubtedly accounts for whatever superiority in retention slow learners manifest over fast learners, for when degree of learning is held constant, the latter's retention is superior.[44]

One-trial learning theorists are divided on the relationship between frequency and retention. Estes *et al*[32] claim that their experimental evidence refutes the traditional finding that overlearning enhances retention; but Rock,[125] while insisting that "repetition plays no role in the formation . . . of associations other than that of providing the occasion for new ones to be formed, each in a single trial," concedes that "repetition *after* the association is formed is effective in strengthening it" (p. 193).

Conclusion. It is quite apparent that the issue regarding the role and importance of frequency in learning and retention is far from being settled. Nevertheless the weight of the evidence and logic suggests that learning is typically a gradual (continuous) rather than an all-or-none (discontinuous) phenomenon; that it reflects a summation of increments in associative or dissociability strength wrought by repeated presentations of the learning task; and that the apparent abruptness of some learning outcomes ("insight") really masks the occurrence of much prior hypothesis-formulation, -testing, -rejection, and -confirmation activity which is organically related to the supposedly sudden emergence of the correct insight. Even conceding that learning may sometimes occur in a single trial, and that frequency seldom operates alone in learning and retention but rather in conjunction with other variables (e.g., the stability and clarity of related concepts in cognitive structure, intention to learn, reinforcement, knowledge of results or feedback, internal organization of the learning task), we can tentatively conclude that the frequency factor both *actively* interacts with these other variables as well as constitutes a significant variable in its own right in influencing learning-retention outcomes. Evidence indicating that in certain kinds of learning tasks frequency has no effect in the absence of belongingness, explicit intention, reward, or feedback, does not warrant the conclusion that when these factors are *present*, most of the improvement accompanying repetition must be attributed to them rather than to frequency per se; as a matter of fact there is much suggestive evidence that frequency can often enhance learning in the absence of explicit intention, knowledge of results, or drive reduction.

It is not asserted, of course, that increments in learning necessarily occur at a uniform rate over a series of trials, or that those components of a task that are already learned are benefited as much by later trials as are the yet unlearned components. But even after a given association is established or a given meaning or means-end relationship is correctly apprehended, additional repetition increases associative or dissociability strength still further, thereby enhancing retention.

Frequency: Mechanism of Action

We would also insist that frequency has a distinctive effect of its own on learning and retention, that operates in addition to and cannot simply be reduced to the opportunity which additional trials provide for *other* effective variables to influence, in *cumulative* fashion, the process and outcome of learning and retention. That is, we would hold that frequency does more than merely make possible a summation of the repeated effects of some other variable such as reinforcement through drive reduction, or cognitive confirmation and clarification. Frequency does admittedly provide opportunity for the recurrent operation of drive reduction and the cognitive aspects of feedback. But since learning can and does occur in the absence of both of these variables, frequency must also serve as more than a vehicle for the cumulation of their repeated effects.

According to the traditional associationist philosophers, as well as more contemporary learning theorists such as Tolman,[158] the residual effect of frequency on learning that cannot be attributed to the recurrent influence of drive reduction or cognitive confirmation-clarification, merely reflects the cumulative impact of temporal contiguity on learning over a series of trials.

Temporal contiguity, of course, refers to the juxtaposition of two stimulus, response, or ideational elements (x contiguous with y or xcy) in the same psychological field so that the formation of an arbitrary, verbatim association (x'-y') or a meaningful relationship (x'-y' as a dissociable component of a more inclusive idea) between them in consciousness is facilitated; and obviously each additional trial creates an additional opportunity for contiguity (xcy) to interact with and strengthen the previously formed association or meaning (x'-y'), namely, to convert x'-y' into a clearer and more stable representation of itself (i.e., into x'-y').

But the learning effects of frequency, it is postulated, are greater than the mere summated influence of successive instances of contiguity, because not only do repeated presentations of the learning task determine and enhance new cognitive content, but the newly acquired cognitive content itself reciprocally induces changes in the *perceived* learning task which make it more learnable. The newly formed association or meaningful subsumption product (x'-y'), in other words, particularly after its stability and clarity are enhanced by repeated presentations, transforms the learning task (xcy) so that it is actually perceived as x-y. The effect of additional trials (frequency), therefore, transcends the cumulative influence of the contiguity variable as such on associative or dissociability strength (x'-y'); *also* involved in the effect of frequency is the mediating influence of the newly formed cognitive content which sensitizes the learner (increases his responsiveness) to the next presentation of the contiguous elements (xcy) by transforming the actual stimulus content into the perceived content x-y, and thus makes possible the interaction between x-y and x'-y'. Hence, since x-y is already a perceived associative entity or meaningful unit that is closer to the ultimate goal of learning (x'-y') than is xcy (two contiguous elements that still have to be related to each other), the interaction between x-y and x'-y' has a self-evidently greater facilitating effect on associative or dissociability strength than the interaction between xcy and x'-y'. It is this first-mentioned interaction between x-y and x'-y', which cannot be reduced to the cumulative effect of contiguity or other variables over a series of trials, that constitutes the distinctive effect of frequency on learning and retention.* Because of *both* this distinctive mediating consequence of repeated presentations of the learning task, *and* the summation of the repeated effects induced by the operation of *each* of several *other* variables over multiple trials, frequency per se may be considered a variable in its own right.

Frequency: Meaningful versus Rote Learning-Retention

The last important issue is whether the role and significance of frequency is different for meaningful than it is for rote learning. In order to be consistent with our previously made distinction between rote and meaningful learning processes (see pp. 42–44), we would have to assign quite different roles to frequency in these two kinds of learning situations. Repeated encounters

---

*Frequency also has a distinctive mediating effect on learning and retention insofar as the experience of forgetting material presented on a previous trial enables the learner to cope better with decremental processes operative in the learning situation (see p. 189).

with the same array of stimulation presumably enhance rote learning and retention by increasing the strength of discrete, arbitrary, and verbatim associative linkages, *i.e.*, their resistance to the short-term interfering effects of prior and subsequent stimulation. The same repetitiveness presumably enhances meaningful learning and retention, on the other hand, by increasing the dissociability strength of nonarbitrary, nonverbatim relationships that have been substantively incorporated (on a nonarbitrary, nonverbatim basis) within a larger subsuming concept or principle in existing cognitive structure. On *a priori* grounds one might assume that sheer repetition would play a more significant role in the learning and short-term retention of discrete and arbitrary associations largely isolated from cognitive structure than it would in the learning and longer-term retention of materials that can be meaningfully incorporated within that structure. In the latter as opposed to the former circumstances, such other factors as the availability of clear and stable subsumers, the discriminability between these subsumers and the learning task, and the internal logic and lucidity (the potential meaningfulness) of the learning task would presumably overshadow the effect of repetition on simple learning and retention. Nevertheless, the influence of repetition cannot be dismissed in any case as either inconsequential or as basically extrinsic to the process whereby increments in strength are effected.

Empirical Studies. Despite its immense practical significance for pedagogy and classroom learning, amazingly little experimental research has been conducted on the relationship between frequency and meaningful learning-retention. As far as the effect of repetition on meaningful learning is concerned, most educational psychologists seem content to cite the relevant rote learning studies, and to suggest on theoretical grounds that less practice is required for learning if the subject can acquire clear, unambiguous, and discriminable meanings from the learning task.* Paralleling Thorndike's research on the effect of repetition on the estimation of length of lines, it has been demonstrated that frequency of writing themes, in the absence of feedback, has little effect on the acquisition of composition skills.[27,132] Although the provision of suitable feedback does result in improvement of these skills,[14,111] the role of frequency under these latter conditions has yet to be empirically determined.

More is known about the effect of overlearning on meaningful retention than about its effect on meaningful learning. The degree of delayed retention of poetry[29] and connected discourse[142] is directly related to the number of repetitions of the learning materials,** but diminishing returns set in more rapidly than in the case of rote retention. McTavish,[101] for example, showed that the first repetition of a film on general science substantially increases retention, but that second and third repetitions add little or nothing to the effect of the first. As is also true of rote retention, the slope of the retention

---

*In a recent study, Maier and Hoffman[102] have shown that a group's second solution of a human relations problem in industry tends to be superior to its first solution in terms of speed, integrativeness, and acceptability to group members.

**In these studies there was actually a combination of meaningful retention and of rote retention of meaningful material, inasmuch as verbatim recall of the material was demanded.

curve for meaningful materials is not altered by degree of overlearning.[43] Review (delayed practice) enhances meaningful retention, particularly when an attempt is made to integrate old and new materials,[169] but is generally less necessary for meaningful than for rote memory.

DISTRIBUTION OF PRACTICE: EFFECT ON LEARNING AND RETENTION

The distribution of practice has long been a favorite topic of research and theoretical inquiry in the psychology of learning. In fact, more empirical evidence is available regarding the effects of distributed practice on learning and retention than regarding the comparable effects of simple frequency of practice. Generally speaking, the evidence supports the conclusion that distributed practice is more effective than massed practice for both learning and retention. The relative efficacy of distributed practice, however, depends on such factors as the age and ability of the learner, and the nature, quantity, and difficulty of the learning task. The advantages of distributed over massed practice, for example, are greater for younger and less able learners, and for long, rote, and difficult tasks, than they are for older and more able learners, and for short, meaningful, and easy tasks; and for tasks requiring a prolonged warm-up period or considerable concentrated effort, distributed practice is demonstrably *less* effective than when it is massed. Although the effects of distributed practice are similar (*i.e.*, in direction, not in degree) for both rote and meaningful learning and retention, it will be convenient to consider each type separately.

Rote Learning and Retention

Short practice periods are more effective than long practice periods for rote learning tasks.[72,74,149] But since units of practice must obviously be long enough to permit learning to take place, there is naturally a lower limit of length below which they are inefficient.[120,121] In learning lists of nonsense syllables, distributed practice is relatively more effective for longer than for shorter lists,[59,97] for items in the middle than toward the ends of the list,[59,112] and at faster than at slower rates of presentation.[56] Distributed practice is also relatively more effective for serial than for paired-associate learning.[57,60] Meaningfulness of material does not significantly reduce the advantage of distributed over massed practice in rote learning.[30,166]

The length of the rest period between practice trials also influences rote learning but, except for the results of one study,[73] does not appear to be linearly related to rate of learning. Trials should not be spaced so far apart that all previously acquired learning is forgotten; later trials in the series, however, can be spaced more widely than earlier trials.[93] Apart from these specifications, the actual length of the rest period is not consistently related to the effectiveness of practice.[95,119]

Distributed practice facilitates the retention as well as the learning of rote materials.[15,58,68,112,122] The effect of distribution is greater for the longer than for the shorter retention intervals,[15,122] probably because the occurrence of reminiscence, shortly after the completion of massed practice trials, counterbalances the facilitating influence of distributed practice during the initial phase of retention. The distribution of practice has also been shown to facilitate rote retention only in those instances where the subject has learned previous lists in the laboratory, *i.e.*, where adequate sources of proactive interference exist.[165] For maximum retention of rote material, reviews should be spaced like original practice, that is, relatively frequently at first and later at progressively greater intervals.[97,161]

Meaningful Learning and Retention

Distribution of practice also facilitates meaningful learning. For reasons that will be specified later, however, it has *less effect* on meaningful than on rote learning.[*5,12,13] Massed practice is more effective for the immediate retention of meaningfully learned materials (probably because of reminiscence), but distributed practice is superior when delayed tests of retention are administered.[48] Review of meaningfully learned material by rereading facilitates retention most when it is delayed for about two weeks;[114,139,146] when the review is conducted by testing, however, it is most advantageously given shortly after original learning.[146,148,157] The reason for this latter difference is quite self-evident: If the material to be reviewed must be supplied from the learner's memory, he must be able to recall enough of it to make review profitable. Hence review by testing must be undertaken soon after learning, before very much is forgotten. But if the learner is not dependent on memory for his review material, he can wait for the most advantageous moment which, according to Jost's laws (see p. 189), would be after the original learning has been appreciably but not completely forgotten.

Mechanism of Action

The facilitating effect of distributed practice has been explained in terms of perseveration, work decrement, motivational, and forgetting theories. According to perseveration theorists, massed trials provide no opportunity for the necessary "fixation" of the neural activity accompanying and following practice. However, in addition to being vague and relying on empirically unvalidated and metaphorical neural phenomena, this theory fails to account for the differential effectiveness of distributed practice in relation to length, difficulty, and meaningfulness of the learning task, to prior relevant learning, and to length of the retention interval. *Rehearsal,* a psychological variant of perseveration involving implicit practice, does not require any unparsimonious neurological assumptions, and may very well explain part of the effect of distributed practice in certain instances; but it definitely does not offer a complete explanation of the value of distributed practice, because the provision of inter-trial rests has also been shown to facilitate learning in animals, in motor activities where rehearsal is improbable, and in practice schedules where rest intervals are filled with sleep[147] or other activities precluding rehearsal.[56,57,58,60]

Fatigue or boredom (manifestations and causes of work decrement) do not provide very satisfactory explanations of the effects of distributed practice because few learning tasks in the laboratory are long or strenuous enough

---

*It will be remembered that meaningfulness reduces the facilitating effect of distributed practice on *rote* learning, but not significantly.

to give rise to either phenomenon. Neither aspect of work decrement, further-more, can account for the differential learning task and temporal position findings associated with distributed practice. A somewhat more sophisticated work decrement explanation, couched in terms of "reactive inhibition" (the postulated self-inhibitory potential produced by a given response following its elicitation, which supposedly dissipates with rest), is hardly more en-lightening; inasmuch as the postulated mechanism of reactive inhibition invokes a purely hypothetical behavioral or neurophysiological process that enjoys no independently validated existence, and is merely metaphorically descriptive of the empirical facts it purports to explain (i.e., the facilitation of learning when practice trials are distributed), the theory tends to be circular. Motivational theories stress the decline in interest and drive accompanying fatigue or boredom, and are vulnerable, of course, to the same criticisms that have been applied to the latter theories.

Forgetting theories are both theoretically most cogent and most in accord with the experimental evidence. They specify the following ways in which inter-trial rests can facilitate later learning and/or retention trials: (a) If it is true that on any given trial, repetition primarily strengthens those components of the learning task that are yet unlearned (see p. 183), the forgetting of previously learned components that occurs between trials in distributed prac-tice schedules, makes it possible for these latter components, as well as for the yet unlearned components, to profit from the strengthening effect of later trials. (b) Rest provides an opportunity both for the dissipation of the con-fusion attributable to initial learning shock (see p. 58), and for the forgetting of interfering (wrong, alternative, competing) responses or meanings. The dissipation of initial learning shock is comparable to that underlying the reminiscence effect in retention, except that it occurs in relation to numerous rest intervals rather than to a single rest interval; whereas the dissipation of the inhibition caused by incorrect competing alternatives, reflects the dif-ferentially faster rate of forgetting for these latter relatively weak elements than for their stronger correct counterparts.[28] (c) Finally, the forgetting that takes place during inter-trial rests, enhances the facilitating influence of later trials because, as a result of experiencing and becoming aware of the inter-fering and subsuming processes that underlie the loss of associative and dis-sociability strength and bring about forgetting, the learner is better able to cope with and resist the decremental effects of these processes when he en-counters them again during and after subsequent learning trials. Previous obliterative experience with interfering and subsuming processes, in other words, appears to confer some degree of "immunity" to the recurrence of their detrimental effects on learning, and hence to promote a higher residual level of associative or dissociability strength.

The "immunizing" effect of prior forgetting on later relearning and re-tention can be inferred from Jost's laws, which state that the older of two associations of equal strength both profits more from additional repetition and is retained longer.[68,175] These laws are obviously implicated in the ad-vantages conferred by distributed practice since, for any given trial, inter-trial rest intervals render the component associations or meanings of a learn-ing task older than corresponding associations or meanings learned by means of massed practice. Prior forgetting has this "immunizing effect because the experience of learning and trying to remember makes the learner aware of the relevant subsuming concepts and indicates areas of weakness, ambiguity, confusion, and lack of discriminability. Thus forearmed, he can take the necessary steps to strengthen appropriate subsuming concepts and particularly weak components of the learning task, as well as to increase discriminability between established ideas and related new propositions. This facilitating effect of forgetting on relearning and retention can also be considered one of the distinctive mediating mechanisms through which frequency increases associative or dissociability strength. Prior experience with the learning task modifies cognitive structure in ways that enhance both the learner's responsiveness to the task and his ability to counteract the effects of decremental processes: on subsequent trials he not only perceives component elements of the associations to be formed or the meanings to be comprehended as "belonging together" or constituting integrated wholes (see p. 185), but he is also better able to contend with factors promoting interference or obliterative subsumption.

The forgetting theory of the mechanism underlying distributed practice effects is not quite as applicable to retention as it is to learning. True, the "immunizing" effect of distributed practice, i.e., the protection against future interference or obliterative subsumption provided by prior forgetting, applies to delayed as well as to immediate associative or dissociability strength. But other aspects of the forgetting theory, namely, the notions that distributed practice allows learned components to be forgotten (so that they too can profit from later practice trials), and also makes possible the differentially more rapid dissipation of initial learning shock and incorrect competing meanings than of their correct counterparts, obviously apply to the intertrial rest intervals rather than to the retention period. Furthermore, as can be plainly seen from examination of the comparative *meaningful* retention curves after massed and distributed practice,[48] respectively, the massing of practice trials is *initially* followed by greater retention, because the reminiscence effect under these circumstances cannot occur during the inter-trial rest intervals, but only during the first phase of the retention period.° Hence the superiority of *delayed* retention following distributed as against massed practice must be attributed either to the *direct* "immunizing" effect of prior forgetting on the retention process *per se*, or to the *indirect* enhancement of retention that necessarily takes place when learning itself is enhanced (*i.e.,* to the fact that if more material is learned under conditions of distributed than massed practice, more will also be retained).

The forgetting theory of distributed practice effects is supported by research evidence showing that the relative effectiveness of distribution increases under conditions producing maximum interference or obliterative subsumption. Experimental studies have already been cited which indicate that distributed practice is relatively more effective for longer than for shorter lists of nonsense syllables; for centrally placed than for end-of-list items in

---

° *Rote* retention *immediately* after distributed practice is greater than after massed practice, but the difference is less than the corresponding difference for *delayed* retention, presumably because of the reminiscence effect that occurs *shortly after* massed trials (see p. 187).

serial learning; for serial than for paired-associate learning; for faster than for slower rates of nonsense syllable presentation; for rote than for meaningful learning; and for rote learning tasks preceded by similar tasks in the laboratory than for completely novel rote tasks. Youtz[175] has also demonstrated that subjects make fewer errors in central portions of *older* series of nonsense syllables than they do in central portions of more recently learned series. The principal reason why the facilitating effect of distributed practice is less striking for meaningful than for rotely learned material is probably the fact that less inter-trial forgetting occurs when material is meaningfully learned. Fatigue, boredom, and motivational factors are also presumably less relevant for meaningful than for rote learning, and rehearsal is obviously less beneficial when less inter-trial forgetting takes place.

METHOD OF PRACTICE

Method of practice refers to those factors concerned with the arrangement or ordering of practice trials, apart from the distribution of trials and rest intervals. It includes the following variables: (a) the relative proportions of study trials (presentation of the material) and test trials (recitation or recall); (b) the nature of the response, *i.e.*, overt or covert, constructed or multiple-choice, verbatim recall or reformulated, prompted or unprompted; (c) whether practice trials are so organized that each trial encompasses either the learning task as a whole or merely parts of same; and (d) whether the number of repetitions and the rate of presenting new material is or is not related to the success of prior performance.

Recitation versus Recapitulation

In reception learning, where the learning task is to internalize presented materials (*e.g.*, facts, propositions, arbitrary associations) so that they are available for later reproduction, the learner may either be presented with numerous study trials or repetitions of the task, or he may elect or be required to spend varying proportions of the total practice time in attempting to recall (recite) the material in test trials, with or without the benefit of prompting. The relevant research findings support the conclusion that whereas increasing proportions of recitation tend to facilitate *rote* learning and retention[37,41,61] (retention more than learning), the facilitating effect of recitation on *meaningful* learning and retention is both less striking and more equivocal.[41,108,113]

The effectiveness of recitation, particularly for rote material, may be attributed to several factors. First, since the attempt to recall presented material actually tests whether and to what extent internalization (learning) has taken place, the feedback that is provided in the next trial is therefore a much more significant factor after recitation than after recapitulation: it indicates explicitly and systematically what the correct associations or meanings are, in relation to the internalized learning that has already taken place. Under these circumstances, all of the effects of feedback—as an incentive condition; as cognitive confirmation, correction, clarification, and evaluation of the adequacy of learning; and as reinforcement following reduction of cognitive and ego-enhancing drives—are considerably intensified. A closely related immediate consequence of feedback in this context is that as a result of discovering which parts of the learning task have not yet been sufficiently mastered, the subject is better able to focus his attention and effort selectively on these latter aspects. Second, the more active kind of participation involved in recitation than in rereading, implies greater learning effort which, in addition to exerting a general facilitating influence on learning, differentially salvages items at or near threshold strength, and leads to more active and meaningful organization of the learned material (e.g., use of rhythm, mnemonic devices and conceptual organizers). Lastly, the conditions of recitation more nearly resemble the conditions under which the learning will eventually be exercised than do those of recapitulation.

For rote learning, where prompting is used, recitation is most effective if it is introduced after only a few study trials.[139] Without the benefit of prompting, however, recitation is more advantageously introduced at a later stage of practice.[81,83] Recitation apparently cannot prove helpful until enough material is learned so that a test trial can provide almost as much practice as a study trial; but if prompts are furnished to fill in gaps of knowledge, recitation obviously becomes feasible at an earlier point in a series of practice trials. Thus the principle governing the optimal temporal position for introducing recitation is similar to the principle determining the optimal spacing of reviews: if, on any given trial, the learner himself has to provide from what he has previously learned, the stimulus material to be used for that trial (i.e., if he is given a test trial), the temporal arrangements must be such as to ensure the existence of sufficient learning or retention, respectively, to make practice or review profitable. If, on the other hand, the learning task is *presented* to the learner, in whole or in part, sufficiency of learning or retention is a less important temporal consideration than Jost's laws (see p. 188).

The markedly reduced effectiveness of recitation with respect to meaningful learning and retention is not difficult to understand. To begin with, the logical sequential structure of connected meaningful discourse, makes implicit recitation possible during the same trial; that is, in the course of rereading, subjects typically tend to anticipate the remembered facts and propositions that follow logically from the material they are currently perusing. In the case of meaningful material, also, where the achievement of understanding is both a reward and an incentive in its own right, less effort is required for learning, and the incentive and ego-enhancement values of feedback are less important. Explicit testing is similarly less necessary for the confirmation, correction, clarification, and evaluation effects of feedback in view of the fact that the internal logic of the material partly provides its own feedback, i.e., enables subjects to appreciate whether they have grasped meanings correctly and, in any case, implicitly to test their understandings against the next presentation of the material. Finally, meaningful learning tasks benefit less from the organizing effects of recitation since they possess an inherent organization of their own.

Nature of the Response

Overtness. Closely related to but not completely coextensive with the recitation-recapitulation issue is the problem of whether the subject's mode of response during practice is overt or covert. Overtness of response does not necessarily imply recall or construction, as does recitation, but merely some measure of activity and externality (observability). Hence either reading, listening to, or "mentally composing" answers to questions can be regarded as "covert" responses, whereas both the construction of an appropriate answer and the selection of a suitable multiple-choice alternative must be categorized as "overt." Admittedly, however, constructed responses rank higher on a scale of overtness than do selected responses.

The overt-covert dimension of practice has been explored principally in relation to a limited variety of automated instruction contexts, *i.e.*, those involving meaningful learning, using programs of short duration, and, for the most part, requiring short-term retention. The research findings, under these conditions indicate that subjects who respond covertly not. only learn and retain verbal material as well as or better than subjects who construct their responses, but also do so more efficiently in terms of learning time.[*46,47,85,117, 126,135,138,172] Overt selection of multiple-choice answers, *e.g.*, by pushing a button, is similarly no more effective than listening to or reading the correct underlined answers.[69,71,100] Under certain circumstances, however (see below), overtness of response may facilitate learning and retention.

In trying to understand these findings and to reconcile them with the research on recitation, it is necessary to consider the various ways in which overtness of response influences or allegedly influences learning and retention. In the first place, it is self-evident that overtness of response facilitates perceptual-motor learning in instances where the overtly practiced response itself is one of the objects of learning (*i.e.*, part of the learning task). But where the overt response (*e.g.*, writing, pressing a lever) is already a well-established component of the learner's response repertory, and consitutes merely a nonspecific means of responding to test questions, it is obvious that the response-acquisition advantage of overtness is irrelevant, and that overt responses are more time-consuming and less efficient than their covert counterparts.[39,168]

Second, it is widely asserted that behavior must be "emitted" in order to be properly reinforced through drive reduction.[54,141] Nevertheless, although this notion is a key assumption of the more orthodox brands of behaviorism, there is little theoretical justification for believing that associations and response dispositions (sets) cannot be similarly reinforced.

Third, overtness of response plainly makes more explicit testing of knowledge possible which, in turn, enhances the cognitive, drive-reduction, and motivational effects of feedback (see p. 191). This consideration is probably very important for rote learning, and undoubtedly accounts for much of the value of recitation when rote materials are used; but, for reasons already specified (see p. 192), it has little applicability to meaningful learning. Thus, since practically all of the research in this area has been conducted with

---

*See also footnote on p. 90. Krumboltz and Weisman[86] found the overt response mode more effective in delayed (two-week) retention, but Wittrock,[172] using a one-year retention criterion, failed to confirm their findings. Hillix and Marx[52] reported that subjects who actively made their own trial-and-error responses in learning light circuits, learned less efficiently than subjects who observed others making the very same responses.

meaningful programed materials, it is not surprising that the findings have been almost uniformly negative. The facilitating effect of overtness of response on meaningful learning is further reduced in an automated instruction context inasmuch as the provision of feedback tends to make relatively little difference when the error rate is low:[34] if, because of small step-size (*i.e.*, slow rate of introducing new material), the subject's responses are almost invariably correct in any case, he obviously does not stand to profit very much from the potentially facilitating cognitive effects of feedback. In support of this interpretation is the fact that overtness of response is differentially more effective for difficult than for easy programed material,[45] and for intellectually less able than for intellectually more able students.[172]

Meaningfulness of material, as previously explained (see p. 192), also counteracts a fourth possible reason for the effectiveness of overt responses, *i.e.*, the fact that they imply greater activity, and hence greater effort and more efficient organization of learning* (see p. 192). It is interesting to note in this connection that when overtly and covertly responding subjects do not differ in motivation, they also do not differ in learning outcomes.[100,172] This suggests but does not confirm the possibility that the facilitating effects of overtness, when they do occur, are partly mediated by motivational variables.

Lastly, overt response during practice could conceivably facilitate learning by resembling more closely than covert response the response mode that is typically required in the criterial situation. In an empirical test of this hypothesis, however, response mode had no more effect on learning outcomes when the overt response was directly relevant to the behavior sampled on the post-test,[172] than when such relevance was lacking.[71]

Constructed or Multiple-Choice. The rationale for constructing rather than selecting answers during practice trials is precisely the same as that already specified for overtness of response (see above), plus the fact that exposing subjects to wrong answers presumably engenders and strengthens undesired competing responses.[141] These considerations, of course, apply primarily to the learning of rote materials, both because overtness of response is not particularly advantageous in meaningful learning (see above), and because the presence of competing responses affects meaningful learning differently than it does rote learning. In the case of arbitrary, verbatim learning, the increased availability of competing responses is self-evidently harmful inasmuch as the desired response is correct by definition, and only has to be discriminated from similar rote responses that *actually* occur in recent proximity (rather than from all other logically plausible alternatives); in these circumstances, furthermore, one response is inherently just as plausible as another. In the case of meaningful learning, however, where the new learning task largely consists of discriminating the correct meaning from other relevant alternatives, and where built-in criteria exist in cognitive structure and in the learning material itself for assessing relative degrees of plausibility, identification of the relevant alternatives constitutes the first step in enhancing the discriminability of the newly presented ideas (see pp. 29 and 89).

---

*According to Holland,[54] automated instruction even leads to a more active type of covert learning, inasmuch as the material "stands still," instead of moving past the learner (as in a book or lecture), when his attention wanders.

The clarification of meaningful new ideas, in other words, is primarily a process of differentiating the propositions in question from related established propositions in cognitive structure and from other plausible alternatives in the learning material.[117,118] But before the comparative and evaluative aspects of such differentiation can be successfully undertaken, it is first necessary to identify as precisely as possible the nature and source of the confusion, that is, to make explicit the various relevant alternatives.* Pressey's "adjunct auto-instruction[117,118] uses multiple-choice items to sharpen meanings *after* initial presentation and learning of the material. Crowder,[24] on the other hand, employs the multiple-choice format as part of the programming procedure itself ("intrinsic programming"): the subject chooses one of several presented alternatives for a given test item and, depending on the particular wrong alternative he chooses, is then given a differential set of corrective materials which both explain the nature of his error and retest him for evidence of clarification.

Research on the relative efficacy of constructed and selected responses[10,22,34,126] generally indicates that the two response modes are not significantly different in terms of learning and retention outcomes, but that the constructed mode is less efficient (requires more time). Since all of the above-cited studies used meaningful programed materials to which the advantages of the constructed response are least applicable, it is not surprising that the latter response mode was not shown to be superior. In the one study reporting a significant difference in favor of constructed responses,[38] it is notable that the learning task (Spanish vocabulary) was both more rotelike and relatively difficult (high error rate). On the other hand, the hypothesized superiority of the multiple-choice format for the learning and retention of meaningful materials also failed to be empirically substantiated by these studies. It is conceivable, however, that the discriminability advantage inherent in the multiple-choice response mode was counteracted by the greater learning time and effort involved in constructing responses.

Prompting and Guidance. The learner's responses during the course of practice may be completely unaided, on the one hand, or receive the benefit of varying degrees of external assistance, on the other. The nature and significance of such assistance obviously differ greatly depending on whether reception or discovery learning is involved. In a discovery learning situation, assistance takes the form of *guidance, i.e.,* providing cues which detract from the learner's opportunity for autonomous discovery. Hence guidance refers to and affects the reception-discovery dimension of learning. The provision of complete guidance is tantamount to presenting the learner with the essential content of the learning task (reception learning), whereas the absence of any guidance whatsoever requires completely autonomous discovery. The degree of guidance furnished in most instances of discovery learning typically falls between these two extremes.

⟩ *That learners can profit from the exposure to and mistaken choice of wrong alternatives is shown by the fact that the percentage of correct answers increased on retest one month later for subjects in an experimental group who were given auto-instruction with multiple-choice items after studying the learning task.[67] This increase did not occur in the case of control subjects, who did not receive any auto-instruction.

In a reception learning situation, external assistance takes the form of *prompting* during the test trials. This assistance does not affect the autonomy of discovery, since the content of the learning task is wholly presented in any case, but does influence the autonomy of reproduction. The learner is assisted, in whole or in part, to reproduce previously presented material which as yet has not been internalized above the threshold of availability. If the entire and explicit substance of the information demanded by the test item is furnished, the stimulus support can be regarded as a *prompt;* if the stimulus support is less complete and explicit during the test trial, it can be considered a *cue.*

Prompting is more necessary and effective in the earlier stages of reception learning because at this time the learner has not yet internalized sufficient material to receive much practice benefit from unaided recitation. Furthermore, the provision of prompts at this early point of practice can prevent the learning of errors (incorrect competing responses), and thus obviate the necessity for costly unlearning. For these reasons, prompting is more efficacious than confirmation (feedback) for relatively short periods of practice in reception learning.[10,21,61,69,136,137,143] During the later stages of practice, however, these considerations are obviously less relevant. In addition, it is important that the conditions of practice gradually begin to approximate the desired (unprompted) end-point of the learning product. Hence, as the amount of correct learning increases, both reduction of the completeness and explicitness of the prompts[54,65,115] and their replacement by confirmation[3,151] are advantageous for further learning. On theoretical grounds it also seems plausible that prompting could be profitably dispensed with earlier in the case of meaningful than of rote reception learning because of the more rapid rate of acquisition and the different role played by competing responses (see p. 194).

In reviewing short-term studies of the role of guidance in meaningful discovery learning (see p. 168), it was concluded that guided or semi-autonomous discovery (*i.e.,* either providing the learner with a verbal explanation of the underlying principles and permitting him to apply them autonomously to specific examples, or encouraging him to discover the principles himself after working a carefully graded series of relevant problems) is more efficacious for learning, retention, and transfer than is either completely autonomous discovery or the provision of complete guidance. Wittrock[171] further substantiated this conclusion recently in a well-controlled study in which college students were taught to decipher transposition codes. Although more learning, retention, and transfer occurred when the rule was provided than when it was not provided, an "intermediate" type of guidance (furnishing either the rule itself or a worked example of it) was more effective than furnishing both rule and worked example or furnishing neither rule nor example. Guidance under these circumstances apparently sensitizes the learner to the salient aspects of the problem, orients him to the goal, and promotes economy of learning by preventing misdirected effort.

From such studies, however, it cannot be warrantedly concluded that guided discovery is necessarily more effective for teaching subject-matter content than is simple didactic exposition. The learning of a novel and relatively isolated principle for largely problem-solving purposes is hardly comparable to the learning of a large body of sequentially organized subject matter. Much also depends on the relative time-cost of the two approaches, on the cognitive maturity of the learner, on his degree of subject-matter sophistication, on the nature of the learning task (descriptive information, representational equivalents, or principles that are discoverable by stating and testing hypotheses), and on whether the purpose of the learning experience is to acquire knowledge, enhance problem-solving ability, or obtain insight into scientific method.

Some opportunity for autonomous discovery is obviously necessary in those instances where the object of learning is not merely the acquisition of knowledge, but also the development of skill in formulating general principles and in applying them to particular problem situations. Verbally presented principles, it is true, are transferable to such situations even if they are not self-discovered; but the ability to solve a particular class of problems efficiently also pre-supposes experience in coping with the distinctive features of that class of problems, in hypothesis formulation and testing, in the strategy of application, in identifying fruitful approaches that minimize costly risk and unnecessary cognitive strain, in using systematic and economic methods of inquiry, and in maintaining a flexible and meaningful learning set. Actual discovery experience is even more important in trial-and-error learning and in the learning of perceptual-motor skills. Adaquate learning in these circumstances also requires the individual to learn what *not* to do, and for this he needs first-hand experience in making mistakes and correcting them. Thus, although appropriate guidance helps the learner avoid unnecessary error in the early stages of practice, its value tends to diminish as it increases in amount or extends into the later stages of practice.[16,42] Since he must eventually perform the learning task unaided, he must also avoid becoming overdependent on guidance.

Verbatim Recall versus Reformulated Response. In measuring the learner's comprehension and retention of meaningful verbal content, test items can be appropriately constructed either to encourage verbatim recall of the presented material, or to lead him to reformulate his understanding of the material in terms of his own vocabulary and ideational background. Although explicit empirical evidence is lacking on this issue, the reformulation approach has at least three theoretical arguments in its favor. It not only constitutes a more valid measure of genuine understanding, but also requires the more active participation of the learner in the testing situation and tends to discourage the adoption of a rote learning set in future learning efforts. Other ways of accomplishing the same purposes in a formal testing context include the use of a multiple-choice format, employing application or problem-solving items, and measuring ability to learn a new set of propositions presupposing mastery of the content being tested. In a less formal testing context, the substitution of appropriate recitation trials for study trials tends to encourage reformulation rather than verbatim reproduction.

Whole versus Part Learning*

Whether it is more effective to practice a given learning task as a whole or to practice various component parts separately, depends on the interaction

---

*Because of the voluminous and somewhat antiquated character of the research literature in this area, specific studies are not cited. Excellent reviews of the literature can be found in McGeoch and Irion (99, pp. 499–507) and Woodworth (174, pp. 216–223).

between a large number of complex variables. Each method possesses certain
inherent advantages and disadvantages. Hence neither method can be said
to be *invariably* superior to the other. Their relative efficacy varies with the
amount, difficulty, and organization of the learning material; with the age,
intelligence, motivation, and subject-matter sophistication of the learner; and
with the stage and distribution of practice.

The basic advantages of the whole method are both that the learner can
better grasp the relationship of each part to every other part as well as to
the learning task in its entirety, and that he does not have to forge connecting links between separately learned parts. The part method, in turn,
has both motivational and logistical advantages. First, it enables the learner
to enjoy early, tangible experience of successful progress toward the goal,
thereby rewarding his current learning efforts, enhancing his self-confidence,
and encouraging him to persevere. Second, subdivision of a long task into
several parts reduces its over-all difficulty, inasmuch as the number of trials
necessary for learning a task tends to decrease disproportionately as the
amount of material it encompasses decreases (see p. 206). For example, it
takes considerably fewer trials to learn two short tasks, each consisting of ten
units, than to learn one long task of twenty units. Since the relative weight of
the aforementioned advantages of each method varies, depending on many
task, practice, cognitive, motivational, and developmental factors, it is impossible to predict whether the whole or part method will be superior in any
particular learning task unless the relevant variables are specified.

Amount of learning material is a crucial variable in the part-whole problem
because of the tendency for learning difficulty to increase much more rapidly
than the time required for combining separately learned parts as amount of
material is increased. Hence, the part method tends to become increasingly
superior as the learning task exceeds the size of unit that the learner can
conveniently manage in one practice trial. But since the optimal size of the
latter unit tends to increase with cognitive maturity, subject-matter sophistication, intelligence, and degree of motivation, the increment in amount of
material required to weigh the balance in favor of the part method must
necessarily be greater in the case of older, more sophisticated, more intelligent,
and more highly motivated individuals. Further, the disproportion between
increase in amount of material and increase in learning trials becomes less
marked when practice trials are distributed rather than massed.

The organization of the learning task and its evenness of difficulty level
also affect the relative superiority of whole and part methods. The "whole"
approach is superior only if there is continuity of meaning from one part to
the next, *i.e.*, if the component units blend into a more inclusive and better
integrated whole. If the separate parts, on the other hand, constitute natural,
logically self-contained subdivisions with little relationship to each other, the
part method is more effective. The feasibility of the whole method similarly
depends on the existence of a relatively uniform level of difficulty throughout
the task. If this is not the case, the learner will devote too little time to difficult portions of the material and too much time to easy portions.

Lastly, the importance of immediate learning rewards varies with the learner's drive and level of maturity. Highly motivated individuals are less discouraged by deferred reward of learning effort, and older, more mature

individuals manifest greater frustration tolerance and capacity for delayed gratification. The motivational advantages of the part over the whole method also tend to decrease during the later stages of practice as the cumulative learning effects of the whole method begin to exceed threshold value, and hence to bolster the learner's confidence in this approach.

To summarize, the whole method is superior to the part method when the amount of learning material does not exceed the size of the practice unit that the learner can conveniently handle, and when continuity of meaning and uniformity of difficulty level are maintained throughout the task. The whole method also becomes more feasible when learners are older, brighter, more highly motivated, and intellectually more mature, and when they possess considerable background experience in the learning task. Finally, the whole method is more likely to succeed in the later stages of practice, and when practice trials are distributed rather than massed. When the opposite set of conditions prevail, the advantage naturally tends to lie with the part method. Depending on the prevailing conditions of learning, various combinations of the two methods may be successfully employed, e.g., beginning with several "whole" trials, then concentrating selectively on the more difficult parts, and concluding with a review of the material as a whole.

Differential Practice Schedules

Should all learners complete uniform practice schedules irrespective of the quality of prior performance, or should the content and step size of subsequent practice trials be differentially adjusted in terms of the individual learner's success or failure and type of error on preceding learning tasks or test items? Three types of differential adjustment are possible. First, in a constructed response program the successful learner simply proceeds to the next item, whereas the unsuccessful learner is repeatedly confronted with the same item and is not permitted to advance further in the program until he obtains the correct answer. Second, in a multiple-choice type program the successful learner similarly proceeds to the next set of items, and the unsuccessful learner is given another easier series of items or a differential set of corrective materials related to the nature of his error. Lastly, in either type of program, size of step can be increased on subsequent items for the successful individual and decreased for the unsuccessful individual. The non-differential program, in which all learners proceed through the same sequence of steps, is conventionally referred to as "linear," in contrast to the "branching" or "multiple-track" type of differential program. Available research evidence regarding this issue is far from being definitive. The weight of the evidence suggests that branching programs, requiring either simple repetition of incorrectly answered items or more differential corrective exercises, are not only more efficient in terms of learning time,[10,22] but also result in learning outcomes that are either equal[10,22,104,137] to or better[23,55,64] than those of linear programs.

On purely theoretical grounds the branching procedure should be superior to the linear procedure because it ensures mastery (consolidation) of a prior item of knowledge in a sequentially organized program before the learner can proceed to the next step in the sequence. It accomplishes this objective by adapting both to *intra*-individual differences with respect to the relative difficulty level of different portions of the program, and to *inter*-individual differences in general intellectual ability and in particular subject-matter sophistication. The branching program, in other words, requires both that all learners devote selectively greater learning effort to those items they find more difficult, and that generally less able learners, on the average, take more practice trials than generally more able learners in mastering a given unit of material.

Skinner[141] argues, on the other hand, that consolidation can be assured for all practical purposes, without requiring repetition of incorrectly answered items, by using a linear program with small task and step size and correspondingly low error rate. Under these circumstances differential programs are allegedly unnecessary for different ability levels, since even low ability students do not make an appreciable number of errors, and high ability students can simply move through the program mpre rapidly. Shay's study[133] provides some support for this position by indicating that differential adjustment of step size to ability level does not significantly enhance learning outcomes; his findings, however, have no bearing whatsoever on the repetition or correction issue. In this latter connection is should be noted that previously cited evidence (see p. 199) suggests that learning outcomes are adversely affected by lack of opportunity to correct errors. This is particularly true for low ability students who, despite an ostensibly low error rate, actually learn considerably less than high ability students after completing the same linear program.[7,70,133,137,172] It is therefore unsafe to assume that dull students necessarily learn as much as bright students from the linear programs that both complete, and that the only difference between them lies in the number of programs each group is able to master in a given unit of time.

GENERAL CONDITIONS OF PRACTICE

In addition to frequency, distribution, and various specific aspects of method of practice (recitation versus recapitulation, nature of the response, size of the practice unit, linear versus branching programs), many *general* conditions of practice undoubtedly influence learning and retention outcomes. These conditions include learning set, naturalness of the practice setting, and degree of task homogeneity. Unfortunately, however, relatively little research evidence is available regarding the effects of these important variables.

Natural versus Structured Settings

How desirable is it that practice takes place in natural (*i.e.*, real-life, uncontrived) settings? Enthusiastic supporters of project and activity methods, as we have already seen, take a rather extreme position on this issue, rejecting all kinds of highly structured practice (drill) and advocating, in effect, an incidental type of learning. It is true, of course, (providing that all other factors are equal) that learning is enhanced when the conditions of practice closely resemble the conditions under which the skill or knowledge in question will eventually be used. Wholly natural settings, however, rarely provide the practice conditions that are either necessary or optimal for efficient learning. Generally it is only during the latter stages of learning, *after* component aspects of the learning task have already been identified and mastered in structured practice sessions, that naturalistic "dress rehearsals" become feasible. In the first place, uncontrived learning experiences typically fail to include a sufficient number of properly spaced practice trials as well as adequate opportunity for differential repetition of particularly difficult components. Second, unstructured practice does not receive the benefit of skilled pedagogic selection, presentation, and organization of material; of careful sequencing, pacing, and gradation of difficulty; and of optimal balancing of intra-task repetition, intra-task variability, and inter-task variability. Lastly, most learning effort is enhanced by deliberate intention to learn.

Task Homogeneity

Relative degree of task homogeneity is often an important practical consideration in the learning of skills and inductively acquired concepts and principles. The issue is whether such learnings can be acquired most efficiently as a result of intensive practice with just a few exemplars, or as a result of less intensive practice with a large variety of exemplars. We have already concluded in an earlier chapter that, other factors being equal, the defining attributes of a given concept are learned most readily when the concept is encountered in many diverse contexts (see p. 87). Such experience obviously lessens the particularity and enhances the generality of abstract knowledge and transferable skills. It is important to qualify this conclusion, however, by pointing out that if this multi-contextual experience is acquired at the expense of attaining adequate mastery of the particular component tasks which comprise it, its over-all effect on learning is detrimental. In learning general concepts, principles, and skills inductively, experience with a particular exemplar has a positive transfer effect on other exemplars only if it is adequately consolidated; and similarly, it is only by mastering several exemplars in the same fashion that the total experience can be successfully utilized in formulating a transferable generalization. Thus transfer in Learning Set problems requires mastery *within* a given type of problems, as well as experience with many variants of this problem type (see p. 87). Also, if the supportive empirical instances of a concept[89] or a proposition (see p. 86) are too heterogeneous in content or sequence of presentation, learning is impeded.

It seems therefore that efficient learning of transferable skills and knowledge demands a proper balance between the over-learning of particular intra-task instances, on the one hand, and adequate exposure to intra- and inter-task diversity, on the other. These two conditions of practice are complementary and mutually supportive rather than antithetical or mutually preclusive, although it is quite probable that their optimal proportions vary in different learning tasks. Many cases of disability in particular academic skills can undoubtedly be attributed to overemphasis on the importance of diversified experience in unstructured learning situations, with consequent insufficiency of practice and failure to attain mastery of the component habit exemplars from which the skill in question is derived. Hence we should not lose sight of the fact that the acquisition of general skills is dependent upon the prior consolidation of more particular habit exemplars*, and that these skills are therefore not efficiently or satisfactorily established unless learners practice the underlying exemplars sufficiently to master them thoroughly.

Another obvious advantage of multi-contextual learning, providing it does not interfere with intra-task mastery, is that it prevents boredom and enhances the exploratory drive. This is particularly true in the case of more intelligent learners; less inter-task variability is required to sustain the interest of duller pupils.[4] Learning set considerations bearing on desirable degree of inter-task variability in practice will be considered in the next section.

Learning Set

The term "learning set" refers to current disposition to learn or perform in a particular way. Hence in its broader meaning it also includes the learner's disposition to learn in a rote or meaningful fashion. Meaningful learning set, as one of the major prerequisites for meaningful learning, is obviously an important general condition of practice, but has already been fully discussed in another context (see p. 22).

In the present context, therefore, we will only consider learning set insofar as it reflects the influence of *recent* past learning experience or activity. This aspect of learning set reflects both (a) the manifestation of general methodological sophistication in approaching a given learning task or attacking a particular type of problem ("learning to learn"), and (b) the manifestation of an appropriate performance attitude or momentary state of readiness for engaging in a particular kind of activity ("warm-up" effect). Both of these components of learning set obviously contribute to positive transfer. Thus, irrespective of the kind of learning involved (nonsense syllables, mazes, poetry, paired adjectives), practice on one task tends to facilitate the learning of another similar task providing that there is no conflictful overlapping of content between them.[155,170] Harlow's "Learning Set" phenomenon largely reflects the cumulative influence of "learning to learn" as a result of successive intra-and inter-task experience with a particular type of discrimination problem (see p. 87). Learning set is therefore a significant general condition of practice to bear in mind in ordering the distribution and sequencing of practice, as well as the optimal degree of inter-trial task homogeneity.

It is important on theoretical grounds not to confound the learning-to-learn and warm-up aspects of learning set. The former consists of relatively stable *cognitive* acquisitions concerned with the strategy of learning that are derived from past learning experience, and which influence the actual content and direction of ongoing learning activity; the latter consists of transitory *readiness* factors involved in the momentary focusing of attention, mobilization of

---

*Skills are generally differentiated from habits (a) in being executed more deliberately and less mechanically, and (b) in embodying a general capacity to perform a whole class of operations rather than mere facility in executing a particular exemplar of that class. When a person becomes highly proficient at a given skill, however, the psychological distinction between skill and habit tends to vanish: the entire class of operations then acquires nearly as much particularity as the former habit, and becomes almost as mechanical in its execution.

effort, and overcoming of initial inertia that are associated with "being appropriately set" to perform a given task. Warm-up effects, naturally, are rather rapidly dissipated,[50] accounting at most for part of the inter-task improvement in learning that occurs during the course of a single day's practice; longer-term improvement (e.g., from one day to another) must be accounted for solely in terms of learning-to-learn effects.[156] Irion[63] has shown that much rote forgetting is caused by the loss of set to recall that takes place during the retention interval. By using a "warming-up" (color-naming) task during the "rest" interval he was able greatly to facilitate the retention of paired associates.* In the case of meaningful retention, warm-up effects are also presumably operative, but probably less conspicuously so than in rote retention.

In programing meaningful material it is obviously important to preserve sufficient commonality between successive learning tasks to take advantage of both the learning-to-learn and the warm-up components of learning set. At the same time, however, enough heterogeneity of inter-task content should be introduced to prevent the mechanical perseveration of a given learning set, and to discourage rigidity of approach and the development of a rote learning attitude (see p. 202). The need for multiple warm-up periods is one of the chief disadvantages of distributed practice, and renders such distribution unfeasible in certain tasks requiring considerable sustained effort.

KNOWLEDGE OF RESULTS (FEEDBACK)

On theoretical grounds, knowledge of results or feedback would appear to be an extremely important practice variable. Nevertheless, because of serious gaps and inadequacies in the available research evidence, we possess very little unequivocal information either about its actual effects on learning or about its mechanism of action.

As previously indicated (see p. 181), some knowledge of results is apparently essential for learning in those perceptual-motor tasks where a variable or indeterminate response must be given to a constantly presented stimulus. If, for example, the learner is repeatedly asked to draw a three-inch line, he obviously cannot manifest any improvement unless he knows to what extent his efforts approximate the desired standard. In other instances, however, where *both* stimulus and response are provided (e.g., paired-associate learning), or where the learner must simply comprehend and internalize the material presented to him, feedback may conceivably facilitate learning and retention, but is certainly not indispensable for either outcome. Feedback, furthermore, is not even indispensable for all types of perceptual-motor learning. In tasks such as gunnery, where appropriate responses or stimulus-response connections are already well-established, enhancing knowledge of

---

*In the familiar retroactive inhibition paradigm, the net decrement in retention that results from the interpolation of a similar task, occurs *despite* the facilitating warm-up effect of the interpolated task. Evidently, the general retroactive facilitation attributable to warm-up is not great enough to overcome the specific interfering influence of similar content.

results (*e.g.*, by sounding a buzzer whenever the learner is exactly on target) improves current performance but does not result in any *transferable* gain in learning.[39]

An equally important issue, assuming that feedback is indispensable for some kinds of learning and has a facilitating influence on others, concerns the mechanism whereby this facilitation is effected. Behavioristically oriented theorists[54,62,99,140,141,153,160] tend to attribute the effects of feedback solely to reinforcement, thus equating knowledge of results with other kinds of reward for learning. Informing the learner that a given emitted or covert response[*] is correct, presumably reduces the cognitive and ego-enhancing drives motivating the response, and hence both increases the probability of its recurrence[**] ("law of effect"), as well as retroactively increases motivation for further learning. Awareness that the results of learning will be made available also constitutes an incentive condition, thereby enhancing the strength of the underlying drives. But the facilitating effects of feedback are hardly exhausted by these reinforcement and motivational mechanisms. Knowledge of results also has other purely *cognitive* effects on learning. It confirms appropriate meanings and associations, corrects errors, clarifies misconceptions, and indicates the relative adequacy with which different portions of the learning task have been mastered. Thus, as a result of the feedback he receives, the subject's confidence in the validity of his learning products is increased, and he is also better able selectively to focus his efforts and attention on those aspects of the task requiring further refinement.

On both motivational and cognitive grounds, feedback probably has less facilitating effect on meaningful than on rote learning. Since the achievement of understanding is a reward in its own right and requires less brute effort than rote learning, it is less necessary to invoke the energizing assistance of an incentive condition and of ego-enhancement drive. Selective reinforcement through drive reduction is similarly less necessary, even if it were possible, when logical considerations are applicable to the content of the learning task than when a purely arbitrary and verbatim connection must be established. The internal logic of the learning material also makes possible some implicit confirmation, correction, clarification, and evaluation of the learning product, even in the absence of any explicit provision of feedback.

Studies of feedback in automated instruction contexts have generally yielded equivocal findings because of failure to control other relevant variables. For example, the use of Pressey-type self-scoring tests providing "adjunct auto-instruction and immediate feedback (see studies by Pressey, Little, Stephens, and Jones, pp. 93 and 195), has been shown to enhance long-term academic achievement; but in all of these studies the Hawthorne effect was operative, and experimental and control groups were not equated with respect to frequency of exposure to relevant learning material. Similarly, although the value of Skinner-type auto-instruction programs is typically attributed to the

---

[*]For a discussion of the significance of the distinction between emitted and covert responses insofar as the reinforcing effect of feedback is concerned, see pages 90 and 193.

[**]As previously indicated (see footnote on p. 182) reinforcement probably occurs, if it all, only in rote learning.

reinforcement and motivational value of immediate feedback, it is obviously necessary to consider not only the *cognitive* effects of feedback in accounting for the presumed superiority of this instruction, but also the influence of such other concomitantly operative variables as size of the learning unit, step size, clarity of presentation, careful sequential organization of material, and consolidation of old material before new material is introduced. Automated instruction, moreover, has not been found to be uniformly superior to conventional teaching procedures (see pages 91 and 93); and in two studies of programed instruction where non-feedback variables *were* controlled, the provision of varying proportions of feedback (from zero to 100 per cent of the total frames used) was not significantly related to scores on an immediate[87,90] or delayed[90] criterion test of learning.

In all fairness, however, it should be pointed out that the dice are loaded against obtaining positive findings in the latter kinds of studies, both because meaningful learning is involved and because of the low error rate (see p. 194). Externally furnished feedback naturally cannot prove particularly helpful if implicit sources of feedback are available, and if the learner's responses are almost invariably correct in any case. One might therefore expect feedback to be more effective in the case of less able students and more difficult learning tasks.

Some research has also been conducted on the completeness, immediacy and relative frequency of feedback. Providing the entire correct answer facilitates concept learning more than does simply indicating "right" or "wrong,"[9,18] since it enables the learner who does not adequately know the answer to clarify and consolidate his knowledge. Trowbridge and Cason[160] also found that furnishing the subject with precise information about the magnitude and direction of his error is more effective than telling him "right" or "wrong" when he is learning to draw a line of specified length. Explanation of the logic of the correct answer is still another dimension of the completeness of feedback that influences learning. Subjects who are told why their answers are right or wrong learn more effectively than subjects who merely continue responding and receiving feedback until they obtain the correct answer.[11] Crowder's "intrinsic programming" (see p. 195) includes explanation of the nature of the error as an integral part of the branching procedure. In certain kinds of concept learning situations where many irrelevant cues are available, informing the subject when he is wrong facilitates learning more than does informing him when he is right;[25,105,106,107] "right" apparently gives less information than "wrong" under these circumstances because it also rewards irrelevant cues.

Research findings regarding the immediacy and frequency of feedback are more equivocal. Some investigators have reported that immediately given feedback has a significantly greater facilitating effect on learning than does delayed feedback;[2,104,130] but neither Evans, Glaser, and Homme[33] nor Sax[130] found a significant difference between the two kinds of feedback on learning and retention respectively. In any case, the evidence that errors made initially tend to persist despite repeated correction,[69] and that prompting is superior to confirmation (at least in the early stages of practice), suggests that, if at all possible, it is preferable to avoid errors in the first place rather than to correct them immediately. Except for one study[130] reporting no significant differences, continuously as opposed to intermittently administered feedback has been shown to be more effective in concept learning.[8,9,18] In more sequential types of programed instruction, however, the relative frequency of feedback does not appear to influence learning outcomes.[87,90]

To summarize, feedback is not generally indispensable for learning, but, on both motivational-reinforcement and cognitive grounds, should facilitate the learning process, more so in the case of rote than of meaningful learning. However the research evidence tends to be equivocal, particularly in relation to programed instruction, because of the failure to control other relevant variables. Further compounding the difficulty of interpreting the effect of feedback on meaningful programed learning, is the fact that both low error rate and the possibility of implicit feedback reduce the facilitating potential of explicitly provided feedback.

AMOUNT OF MATERIAL: TASK SIZE

The amount of material contained in a given learning task, *i.e.*, the relative size of the task, is an important consideration in programing subject matter and in arranging practice schedules. Task size influences the structure of the material and its difficulty, as well as the learner's motivation; and, as we shall see shortly, it is also a central issue in the field of automated instruction.

The relative efficacy of different task sizes is closely related to the previously considered part-whole problem in practice (see pp. 197–199), both because the total magnitude of the task confronting the learner is a significant factor determining his choice of approach, and because the part method obviously involves working with a smaller task size than does the whole method. Nevertheless the two issues are hardly coextensive. Task size is a much more inclusive issue than the choice of a whole or part strategy of practice. Only relatively rarely, in choosing between different task sizes in programing subject matter, is one faced with a decision that is comparable to the choice between memorizing a poem as a whole or memorizing it by stanzas. Although component task units of a subject-matter program are sequentially related to each other, they are related in a derivative or correlative sense rather than as successive links of a chain that would have to be welded together if first learned separately.

Rote versus Meaningful Learning

In the case of rote learning, the paramount consideration in deciding upon task size is the disproportionate increase in learning difficulty that occurs as length of task (*e.g.*, number of nonsense syllables) increases beyond immediate memory span.[97,98,124] This disproportionality manifests itself in progressively increasing learning time per unit of material;[*] it tends to be more marked at lower rather than at higher levels of practice,[99] when practice is massed rather

---

[*]When number of repetitions (trials) required for mastery is used as a criterion of learning difficulty, a spurious deceleration of difficulty level accompanies increasing task size.[29,59] This is because each repetition is counted as one trial *irrespective of* the length of time it takes.

than distributed,[59,98] and in slow as opposed to fast learners[17,121] For the most part the disproportionality seems to reflect the greater opportunity for intra-serial interference as the number of units in the task increases.[17,99] To some extent, also, it reflects the subject's initial discouragement as he contemplates the magnitude of the task confronting him, as well as unnecessary repetition of already learned items as yet unlearned items in the longer list are being acquired.[99] Length of rotely learned tasks, however, apparently has no effect on retention per se, *i.e.*, apart from its effect on learning. Thus, when lists of varying length are learned to the *same* criterion of mastery and are similarly reinforced, they are equally well retained.*[17]

In the case of meaningful learning, the same simple disproportionality between increase in difficulty level and increase in task size presumably does not prevail. The disproportionate increase in intra-serial interference accompanying increase in task size, which obviously has an important inhibitory effect on the formation of arbitrary, verbatim associations between discrete stimulus or stimulus-response components, has little relevance for the kind of learning involved in the substantive relational incorporation of potentially meaningful material within cognitive structure. Hence, although increasing the length of a meaningful learning task undoubtedly increases its difficulty, all other factors being equal, one might anticipate on theoretical grounds that the increase in difficulty would not be disproportionate to the increase in task size. Much more important for difficulty of meaningful learning and retention than length of task per se would be the logical structure, the lucidity, and the sequentiality of the material. The optimal size of task that the learner could conveniently manage in a given trial would also depend upon such considerations as age, cognitive maturity, subject-matter sophistication, intelligence, and motivation.

Research evidence on the length-difficulty relationship in meaningful learning is sparse and equivocal. Cofer's data clearly demonstrate that learning time increases much less rapidly with increasing length of task when prose passages are learned meaningfully than when they are learned rotely,[20] but the precise relationship between length and difficulty in the former instance is, unfortunately, less clearly indicated. Lyon[97,98] found a disproportionate increase in learning time with increase in the length of meaningful prose passages (except for lengths between ten and fifteen thousand words); it must be remembered, however, that verbatim learning was required in his study. Increasing the length of an instructional motion picture by adding more facts, while holding density (number of facts per minute) but not logical structure and continuity constant, did not result in a proportionate increase in the amount of information learned, but apparently had no detrimental effect on retention.[167] Hence much more definitive research studies are obviously needed before empirically warranted conclusions can be drawn regarding optimal task size in meaningful learning.

---

*Evidence indicating that longer lists are *better* retained than shorter lists under these circumstances[123,124] undoubtedly reflects the overlearning of some items in the more frequently repeated longer lists. Removal of paired-associate items from a list after three correct responses tends to eliminate this differenc in retention.[128]

Automated Instruction

Relatively small task size is one of the characteristic features of the currently flourishing automated instruction movement. In the "teaching machine" literature, task size is customarily subsumed under the term "step size," no distinction being made between degree of transition from one step or frame to another and the amount of material included in a single frame or presentation. It is true, of course, that if a given segment of material is simply divided into many small task units, on the one hand, or into a few larger task units, on the other, "task size" and "step size" are practically synonymous terms. Actually, however, it is quite possible to vary each dimension independently, once task size is determined as described above; this can be done either by adding or deleting steps or by otherwise modifying the task units so as to increase or decrease the amount of overlap between them. In the following discussion we shall consider each dimension as an independent variable.

Skinner[141] has presented a strong case for the prevailing practice of using small task units in programing subject matter. By making learning easy and painless and guaranteeing success, this approach enhances the learner's self-confidence and encourages him to persevere in his efforts. Furthermore, by insuring a low error rate, it avoids the initial occurrence and hence the recurrence of misconceptions and wrong responses, maximizes positive reinforcement, and minimizes negative reinforcement. Lastly, it makes possible immediate confirmation, clarification and correction, and practically guarantees that consolidation of prior material in the sequence occurs before new material is introduced (see p. 200). When larger task units are used, misconceptions cannot be corrected immediately after they arise, and there is no assurance that the learner will consolidate prior learnings before proceeding to later sections of the material.

Nevertheless, the small task-size approach in programing subject matter has many serious shortcomings. Although concerned with meaningful learning, it adopts a rote learning strategy in handling the task size variable; that is, it places major emphasis on the length-difficulty relationship, and ignores the logical structure of the material—both as a criterion of optimal task size and as a determinant of task difficulty in meaningful learning. In terms of both the logical requirements of meaningful learning material and the actual size of the task that can be conveniently accommodated by the learner, the frame length typically used by teaching machines* is artificially and unnecessarily abbreviated. It tends to fragment the ideas presented in the program so that their interrelationships are obscured and their logical structure is destroyed. As Pressey[117] observes:

"The student is shown this material one bit or frame at a time in the window of a mechanism or space of a programed textbook. He cannot readily look back at what he has been over or ahead to sense what is to come, or discover any outline or structure in the material. . . . For effective reading, for general

---

*In his "scrambled books," Crowder[24] departs somewhat from the small-frame approach. He believes in maintaining flexibility of task-unit size so as to make possible the communication of complex information. Hence he allows for task units of up to page-size length.

understanding of main ideas, and for adequate study and review, this procedure seems to be as clumsy as asking a person to apprehend a picture by letting him see, in a set order, only one square inch at a time . . .

"Study of a complex and structured subject seems better begun by an overview of reading matter to display the structure and order the complexity. A good book will show its structure in the table of contents and catalog its contents in the index; with such aids the learner can easily move about in its numbered pages with only the flick of a finger, using page headings and subheads in the text to guide him. He may turn back and forth from table or graph to related text, skip something already known, review selectively for major and difficult points. . . . Only after first contact with a complex structured topic should a student turn to auto-instruction for review and differentiation of major points in material. . . . The autoinstruction will then assure the student when he is right and identify and correct any misconceptions—as a good teacher or tutor might then do. Auto-instruction as an adjunct to the usual materials and methods of instruction would seem both more widely useful and more practicable than current efforts to replace textbooks and methods with radical initial programing" (pp. 31–33).

Just because task size is small and error rate is low, one cannot warrantedly assume that the learning of sequentially presented ideas is necessarily rendered easy and successful, and that consolidation of existing material is therefore assured before new material is presented. In fact the very fragmentation of content may serve to ensure mastery of the component task units at the expense of understanding the logic of the larger segments of subject matter of which they are a part. Beane,[7] for example, programed geometric proofs so that "most of the proofs involved less than 7 steps but still required the student to keep in mind a sizeable amount of information. . . . The steps of the program were small enough that the student could usually answer the next question regarding a particular step in a proof without difficulty. Evidence supporting this point of view is the relatively low error rate of approximately 8% for the low ability students on the linear program. However this does not mean that the student necessarily had a good grasp of the logical sequence or plan of the whole proof. This provides a real challenge to programers of material concerned with involved, logical arguments. Insuring that the student can take the next step successfully in a program, by sufficiently granulating the material and then arranging it systematically, is no guarantee that he will understand the logical development involved. Also the student will not remember very well the facts he does learn if he fails to comprehend the logical structure and relationships of the concepts presented" (p. 85).

The desirability of avoiding unnecessary errors and misconceptions also does not imply advocacy of an artificial simplification of ideas that spares the learner from making the necessary distinctions required for making meanings more precise and for testing the adequacy of existing understandings (see p. 195). Certain kinds of learning (e.g., problem-solving, acquiring perceptual-motor skills), moreover, demand first-hand experience in making and correcting errors (see p. 197). Melaragno[103] found that spaced negative reinforcement induced by deliberately inserting ambiguous, error-producing frames into a program, did not inhibit learning.

Finally, many of the advantages attributed to the small task-size format of teaching machines are not really inherent in small task size per se, but are reflective of small step size and careful sequential organization. Both of these latter procedures, of course, are perfectly compatible with the use of larger task units. When employing the larger task-unit format, one can also help insure consolidation of earlier presented material within the same task, by using appropriate organizers, by increasing the lucidity of presentation, and by maximizing sequential organization and reducing step size between component sections of the task unit.

STEP SIZE

Step size, *i.e.*, the relative magnitude of transition between task units, is also an important issue in programing meaningful subject matter. It can be reduced by increasing redundancy or overlapping of content, by making explicit reference to or comparisons with prior task content (integrative reconciliation), and by couching new material in terms of familiar concepts or experience. When large task units are used, it is also meaningful to speak of step size between successive components of the task unit.

The step-size variable is partly coextensive with the previously considered variable of task homogeneity or inter-task variability (see pp. 201–202). Unlike task homogeneity, however, it is more concerned with relative gradualness or abruptness of transition between the tasks of a sequentially organized program than with relative degree of homogeneity or heterogeneity of the exemplars used to develop a given concept or proposition. The relative effectiveness of different step sizes in a given learning program, therefore, is dependent in part upon achieving an appropriate balance between such considerations associated with both of these variables as conceptual generality, intratask mastery, learning to learn, warm-up effect, perseveration, rigidity, and boredom. Hence the choice of appropriate step size is likely to be quite specific to the particular learning task, the conditions of learning, and the characteristics of the learner. Research on step size within the context of automated instruction has been confined to the small task-unit format, and is generally inconclusive. Coulson and Silberman[22] found a small-step program more effective than a large-step program in terms of score on a criterial learning test, but less effective in terms of learning time; other investigators either found no significant differences between the two types of programs,[10,133,145] or reported their findings in terms of the more equivocal criterion of error rate.[35]

PACING

Pacing generally refers to the rate of introducing new subject matter material as determined by the length of the interval between component task units. Other subsidiary ways of influencing rate of coverage include (a) manipulation of step size (degree of overlap in content between successive task units; (b) increasing or decreasing the density (informational content) of task units;* and (c) regulating the number of initial repetitions and sub-

---

*An increase in the concentration of facts in an instructional film of specified length was not shown to result in a proportionate increase in informational learning.[167] However this finding may be partly explained by removal of the isolation effect (see p. 215).

sequent reviews given each task unit. All of these latter manipulations, of course, eventually affect the number of task units covered in a given interval of time, and hence the rate of covering new subject matter. Pacing, in other words, deals with the massing or distribution of *different* task units as opposed to the massing or distribution of trials of a particular task. Considering the potential importance of this variable for the programing of school material, it has been the subject of surprisingly little research.

Theoretically, it would seem plausible that an optimal average inter-task interval exists for every kind of subject matter, given learners of specified cognitive maturity and subject-matter sophistication. Thus it probably makes a difference, on the average, if 75 hours are to be spent in learning a particular segment of material, whether this learning time is distributed over two weeks, one month, two months, or a semester. First, sufficient time is necessary to recover from initial learning shock (see p. 58) before proceeding to new tasks. Second, the learner requires adequate time for contemplating the material in retrospect, for effecting integrative reconciliation, and for conducting adequately spaced reviews in conformity with Jost's laws (see p. 189). Presumably this latter amount of time is less extensive if he can concentrate on just one or two subjects rather than on a half-dozen. Third, it is important to avoid excessive cognitive strain and a feeling of harrassment, on the one hand, as well as unnecessary redundancy, lack of challenge, and boredom, on the other. Lastly, it is necessary to provide sufficient time for practice, particularly for slow learners, so that intra-task mastery or consolidation can be assured before new tasks are presented.

On logical grounds because of individual differences in cognitive maturity, intelligence, subject-matter sophistication, and motivation, it would be reasonable to expect that individualized pacing would be more effective for learning than the imposition of a uniform rate of coverage on all learners. Using the quality of past performance as a guide, such individualization could then be regulated by either teacher or pupils, the former having the advantage of greater objectivity and pedagogic sophistication, and the latter possessing more direct information about cognitive strain and degree of challenge, although this information is admittedly contaminated in part by such considerations as self-indulgence. Apart from the results of one study,[36] the limited experimental evidence available on the relative efficacy of self-regulated pacing,[109,135] does not indicate any superiority over teacher (or programer) regulated pacing.

DIFFICULTY OF THE MATERIAL

The difficulty of the learning task obviously affects learning time, rate of learning (slope of the learning curve), and the amount of material that is learned and retained.* These factors, in turn, influence the efficiency of learning effort. If the material is too difficult, the learner accomplishes disproportionately little for the degree of effort he expends; if it is too easy, his accomplishments are disappointingly meager in terms of what he could have

---

*For example, as the difficulty level of a nonsense-syllable task increases, the amount and rate of learning decreases; the rate of improvement also becomes more uniform or linear, rather than rapid at first and progressively slower.[84]

achieved, were greater effort demanded of him. As previously indicated, task difficulty is related to the size of the task unit (see p. 206), but can, nevertheless, be varied quite independently of task size.

Task difficulty also affects learning efficiency in other ways than by influencing amount and rate of learning relative to the effort expended. Excessively difficult material makes for an undesirably large number of initial errors and misconceptions that have to be unlearned; interferes with necessary intra-task mastery and consolidation in sequential learning programs; and depresses the learner's self-confidence, lowers his motivations, increases his anxiety, and promotes task avoidance. In meaningful problem-solving situations, it typically induces perseveration, rigidity, blind trial-and-error, and disorganization of behavior.[76] Inappropriately easy material, on the other hand, fails to stimulate and challenge the learner adequately, fostering boredom and disinterest.

Since the appropriate level of difficulty of a given task is always relative to the learner's age, cognitive maturity, subject matter sophistication, intelligence and motivation, it is best determined on an individual basis. When learning tasks are suitably adjusted to pupils' current achievement level, there are no significant differences between low, middle, and high IQ groups in learning, retention, and transfer (see footnote on p. 98). Previously cited generalizations suggesting that fast learners retain more than slow learners when degree of learning is held constant (see p. 183), fail to take into account the fact that the difficulty level of the material used in these experiments was more appropriate for the faster learning group.

Teaching machine programs that gear the difficulty of the material to the ability level of the lowest ability group, tend to reduce the relationship between general ability and ultimate learning outcomes. In addition to lowering difficulty level by such devices as prompting and the use of small task and step size,[143] such programs benefit the slow learner more than the fast learner by compensating for the former's relatively greater inability both to organize the material sequentially by himself and to keep pace with a rate of instruction aimed at the pupil of average ability. Stolurow (152, pp. 124, 126, 136-138) has summarized considerable research evidence showing increased homogeneity of performance following teaching machine training, as well as practically zero correlations between general ability scores and gain scores resulting from automated instruction.* When teaching machine programs are more demanding, however, low ability students make lower scores than high ability students on tests covering material completed by each group;[7,70,133,137,172] and if the abler students are also permitted to learn at their own pace and to complete as many programs as rapidly as they can, individual differences in achievement between the bright and the dull obviously tend to increase rather than decrease during the course of automated instruction.

INTERNAL LOGIC AND ORGANIZATION

Throughout this volume it has been repeatedly stressed that the conditions of learning primarily influence the meaningful acquisition and retention of

---

*See also evidence summarized on pp. 94–95.

ideas and information by modifying existing cognitive structure. Although the effect of such modification on learning and retention cannot be empirically demonstrated except by using the transfer paradigm (*i.e.*, by introducing related new tasks), the changes in cognitive structure wrought by practice or by exposure to successive aspects of the task obviously have an important impact on intra-task mastery itself. This is particularly true in the case of those kinds of learning in which each component task (as well as entire bodies of subject matter) tends to be compound in content and to manifest an internal organization of its own. Thus, in school learning, conditions influencing and altering cognitive structure are typically crucial both for the acquisition of a particular task as well as for transfer purposes (the learning of related new tasks); and of all the possible conditions of learning that affect cognitive structure, it is self-evident that none can be more significant than the internal logic and organization of the material. In previous chapters, we have already considered in great detail how learning material can be most effectively written and organized so as deliberately to induce those changes in cognitive structure that are most advantageous for the learning and retention of meaningful school material. Hence, in the present context, it will be necessary only to summarize briefly the more salient of these considerations.

Internal Logic

The internal logic of the task is obviously relevant for meaningful learning and retention outcomes since the existence of logical or potential meaning within the material (*i.e.*, its relatability to a hypothetical human cognitive structure with the necessary background knowledge) is a prerequisite for the emergence of psychological (phenomenological) meaning. Logical meaning, as previously pointed out (see p. 39), is a function of the plausibility, lucidity, and nonarbitrariness of the material, rather than of its logical or substantive validity. Hence "internal logic" is used somewhat idiosyncratically here to designate those properties of the material that enhance these latter criteria of logical meaning.

At least six aspects of the internal logic of material affect the extent to which it is endowed with potential meaning: (1) adequacy of definition and diction ('precise, consistent, and unambiguous definition and use of terms; definition of all new terms prior to use; and the use of the simplest and least technical language that is compatible with conveying precise meanings); (2) use of concrete-empirical illustrations and analogies when developmentally warranted or otherwise useful in the acquisition, clarification, or dramatization of meanings (see pp. 128 and 132); (3) the selection and organization of subject-matter content around principles that have the widest and most general explanatory and integrative power (see pp. 78–79); (4) systematic sequential organization of material with careful attention to gradation of difficulty level (see pp. 92 and 150); (5) encouragement of an active, precise, reflective, and analytic approach on the part of the learner by requiring him to reformulate the material in terms of his own vocabulary, experiential background and structure of ideas (see pp. 20, 197), and, under certain circumstances, to use autonomous discovery and problem-solving procedures (see pp. 132, 143); and (6) explicit delineation of the distinctive logic and philosophy of each subject matter discipline (its implicit epistemological assumptions; general problems of causality, categorization, inquiry, and measurement that are specific to the discipline; the distinctive strategy of learning how to learn the particular subject matter of the discipline).

Organizational Principles and Devices

The principles of progressive differentiation (see pp. 79-80) and integrative reconciliation (see pp. 80–81) have been represented throughout as being of central importance in the programing of meaningful subject matter. Optimal utilization of these principles presupposes not only their consistent use in the sequential presentation of subject matter material, but also the supplementary availability of a hierarchical series of advance "organizers." These latter organizers provide relevant ideational scaffolding, enhance the discriminability of the new learning material from previously learned related ideas, and otherwise effect integrative reconciliation at a level of abstraction, generality, and inclusiveness which is much higher than that of the learning material itself. To be maximally effective they must be formulated in terms of language, concepts, and propositions already familiar to the learner, and use appropriate illustrations and analogies.

True organizers, thus defined, should not be confused with ordinary introductory overviews. The latter are typically written at the same level of abstraction, generality, and inclusiveness as the learning material, and achieve their effect largely through repetition, condensation, selective emphasis on central concepts, and prefamiliarization of the learner with certain key words. Summaries are comparable to overviews in construction, but are probably less effective because their influence on cognitive structure is retroactive rather than proactive relative to the learning task. They are probably more useful, in place of the material itself, for purposes of rapid review than for original learning. However, insofar as they may imply to some learners that the material they do not include is relatively superfluous, they may promote neglect of and failure to study or review much significant subject matter. Lathrop and Norford[92] found that neither overviews nor summaries appreciably improved the learning of instructional films.

Organizers also have certain inherent advantages both over various kinds of intra-material organization (organizing aids within the body of the material), and over any existing subsumers within cognitive structure that could be used for organizational purposes. Unlike intra-material organization (executed in accordance with the principles of progressive differentiation and integrative reconciliation) that successively provides necessary anchorage for and differentiation of new ideas at a particularized level just before each new idea is encountered, organizers perform the same functions in advance at a much more global level before the learner is confronted with any of the new material. Hence, for example, a generalized model of class relationships is first provided as a general subsumer for all new classes, subclasses, and species before more limited subsumers (classes or subclasses) are provided for the particular subclasses or species they encompass; and the various kinds of forests are first distinguished from each other before the component subforests and trees and similarly differentiated. Spontaneously existing subsumers in cognitive structure lack both particularized relevance for the new material (since the learner cannot possibly anticipate its precise nature), as well as the benefit of the sophisticated knowledge of subject matter and pedagogy available to expert programers.

Perceptual organizers, in contrast to the integrative organizational devices just described, merely provide built-in mechanical aids that make the material perceptually more salient and apprehensible, or otherwise facilitate practice. These include rhythmic aids, vocal emphasis, the isolation* and familiarization effects of underlining, and the "fractionation" effect (breaking of wholes into parts) of providing headings and subheadings. Under certain circumstances, however, some perceptual organizers can be said to have true integrative effects (e.g., underlining that helps make ideational distinctions or emphasizes central concepts; headings that reveal the organizational structure of the material more clearly).

Perceptual or mechanical organizers generally facilitate meaningful learning—more so in the case of factual than of abstract material.** The learning of meaningful material, for example, is enhanced by appropriate vocal emphasis,[26] by underlining,[75] and by breaking instructional film content into parts by means of inserted questions.[88] The failure of informational learning to increase proportionately with increase in the density of facts in a film[167] (see footnote on p. 215) may be partly ascribed to the loss of the patterning or isolation effect as "filler" material is removed. Northrop[110] found that the use of headings facilitates the learning of factual films, but either has no significant effect on or inhibits the learning of more abstract films. The abstract material in this study was evidently more highly organized than the factual, simply because the abstract concepts themselves served an organizing function; hence the learners not only benefited less from the presence of extrinsic mechanical organizers, but also seemed in some instances to be distracted by them. Apparently, integrative organizers are required for material that is more abstract than informational in character. In none of the above studies, however, is it possible to distinguish clearly between the perceptual and the integrative effects of the organizers in question. Conflicting results have also been reported regarding the relative effects of such organizers on bright and dull students (see p. 94).

REFERENCES

1. Abel, L. B. The effects of shift in motivation upon the learning of a sensorimotor task. *Arch. Psychol.*, 1936, *29*, No. 205.

---

*In several adequately controlled laboratory studies, "isolation," effected by introducing patterned heterogeneity of content or color, has been shown to facilitate rote learning of segregated and immediately adjacent items.[129,134,144] Retention, however, was not facilitated.

**Christenson and Stordahl[19] obtained uniformly negative results in studying the effects on comprehension and retention of various combinations of such organizational aids as underlining, headings, outlines and summaries. However, the possibility of obtaining significant differences between experimental and control groups was seriously prejudiced by the leveling effects of using familiar learning material, using the same test as both a pretest and measure of retention, and testing the same subjects for both immediate and delayed retention.

2. Angell, G. W. The effect of immediate knowledge of quiz results on final examination scores in freshman chemistry. *J. educ. Res.*, 1949, *42*:391–94
3. Angell, D., and Lumsdaine, A. A. Prompted plus unprompted trials versus prompted trials alone in paired-associate learning. *Research Report* AIR-314–60-IR-129. Pittsburgh: American Institute for Research, October 1960.
4. Armistead, L. M. The effect of stimulus change on an exploratory drive in children. *Dissert. Abstr.*, 1961, *21*:2190.
5. Ash, P. The relative effectiveness of massed versus spaced film presentations. *J. educ. Psychol.*, 1950, *41*:19–30.
6. Auble, D., and Mech, E. V. Partial verbal reinforcement related to distributed practice in a classroom situation. *J. Psychol.*, 1953, *36*:165–86.
7. Beane, D. G. A comparison of linear and branching techniques of programmed instruction in plane geometry. *Technical Report* No. 1. Urbana, Ill: Training Research Laboratory, University of Illinois, July 1962.
8. Bourne, L. E., and Haygood, R. C. Effects of intermittent reinforcement of an irrelevant dimension and task complexity upon concept identification. *J. exp. Psychol.*, 1960, *60*:371-75.
9. Bourne, L. E., and Pendleton, R. Concept identification as a function of completeness and probability of information feedback. *J. exp. Psychol.*, 1958, *56*:413–20.
10. Briggs, L. J. Two Self-Instructional Devices. *Psychol. Rep.*, 1958, *4*:671–76.
11. Bryan, G. L., and Rigney, J. W. An evaluation of a method for shipboard training in operations knowledge. *Technical Report* No. 18. Los Angeles: Department of Psychology, University of Southern California, September 1956.
12. Bumstead, A. P. Distribution of effort in memorizing prose and poetry. *Amer. J. Psychol.*, 1940, *53*:423–27.
13. Bumstead, A. P. Finding the best method for memorizing. *J. educ. Psychol.*, 1943, *34*:110–14.
14. Buxton, E. W. An experiment to test the effects of writing frequency and guided practice upon students' skill in written expression. Unpublished Ph.D. Dissertation. Stanford, Calif.: Stanford University, 1958.
15. Cain, L. F., and Wiley, R. DeV. The effect of spaced learning on the curve of retention. *J. exp. Psychol.*, 1939, *25*:209–14.
16. Carr, H. A. Teaching and learning. *J. genet. Psychol.*, 1930, *37*:189–218.
17. Carter, L. J. Interrelationships among memory rate of acquisition and length of task. *Dissert. Abstr.*, 1959, *19*:1832.
18. Chansky, N. M. Learning: a function of schedule and type of feedback. *Psychol. Rep.*, 1960, *7*:362.
19. Christenson, C. M., and Stordahl, K. E. The effect of organizational aids on comprehension and retention. *J. educ. Psychol.*, 1955, *46*:65–74.
20. Cofer, C. N. A comparison of logical and verbatim learning of prose passages of different lengths. *Amer. J. Psychol.*, 1941, *54*:1–20.
21. Cook, J. O., and Spitzer, M. E. Supplementary Report: prompting versus confirmation in paired-associate learning. *J. exp. Psychol.*, 1960, *59*:275–76.
22. Coulson, J. E., and Silberman, H. F. Effects of three variables in a teaching machine. *J. educ. Psychol.*, 1960, *51*:135–43.
23. Coulson, J. E., *et al.* Effects of branching in a computer controlled auto-instructional device. TM-617. Santa Monica, Calif.: Systems Development Corporation, May 1961.

24. Crowder, N. A. Automatic tutoring by intrinsic programming. In *Teaching Machines and Programmed Learning* (A. A. Lumsdaine and R. Glaser, eds.) Washington, D. C.: National Education Association, 1960. pp. 286–98.

25. Curry, Carolyn. Supplementary report: the effects of verbal reinforcement combinations on learning in children. *J. exp. Psychol.*, 1960, 59:434.

26. Dearborn, W. F., Johnson, P. W., and Carmichael, L. Oral stress and meaning in printed material. *Science*, 1949, 110:404.

27. Dressel, P., Schmid, J., and Kincaid, G. The effect of writing frequency upon essay-type writing proficiency at the college level. *J. educ. Res.*, 1952, 46: 285–93.

28. Easley, H. The curve of forgetting and the distribution of practice. *J. educ. Psychol.*, 1937, 28:474–78.

29. Ebbinghaus, H. *Memory: A Contribution to Experimental Psychology.* New York: Teachers College, Columbia University, 1913.

30. Ellis, H. C. Distribution of practice and meaningfulness in verbal learning. *Psychol. Rep.*, 1960, 6:319–25.

31. Estes, W. K. Learning theory and the new "mental chemistry." *Psychol. Rev.*, 1960, 67:207–23.

32. Estes, W. K., Hopkins, B. L., and Crother, E. J. All-or-none and conservation effects in the learning and retention of paired associates. *J. exp. Psychol.*, 1960, 60:329–39.

33. Evans, J. L., Glaser, R., and Homme, L. E. An investigation of "teaching machine" variables using learning programs in symbolic logic. Pittsburgh: Department of Psychology, University of Pittsburgh, December 1960. ·

34. Evans, J. L., Glaser, R., and Homme, L. E. The development and use of a "standard program for investigating programmed verbal learning." Paper presented to American Psychological Association, Chicago, September 1960.

35. Evans, J. L., Glaser, R., and Homme, L. E. A preliminary investigation of variation in the properties of verbal learning sequences of the "teaching machine" type. In *Teaching Machines and Programmed Learning* (A. A. Lumsdaine and R. Glaser, eds.). Washington, D.C.: National Education Association, 1960. pp. 446–51.

36. Follettie, J. F. Effects of training response mode, test form, and measure on acquisition of semi-ordered factual materials. *Research Memorandum 24.* Fort Benning, Ga.: U.S. Army Infantry, Human Research Unit, April 1961.

37. Forlano, G. *School Learning with Various Methods of Practice and Rewards.* New York: Teachers College, Columbia University, 1936.

38. Fry, E. B. A study of teaching machine response modes. In *Teaching Machines and Programmed Learning* (A. A. Lumsdaine and R. Glaser (eds.). Washington, D.C.: National Education Association, 1960. pp. 469–74.

39. Gagné, R. M. Military training and principles of learning. *Amer. Psychologist*, 1962, 17:83–91.

40. Gagné, R. M., and Paradise, N. E. Abilities and learning sets in knowledge acquisition. *Psychol. Monogr.*, 1961, 75, No. 14.

41. Gates, A. I. Recitation as a factor in memorizing. *Arch. Psychol.*, 1917, 7 (Whole No. 40).

42. Gates, A. I., and Taylor, G. A. An experimental study of the nature of improvement resulting from practice in a motor function. *J. educ. Psychol.*, 1926, 17:226–36.

43. Gilbert, T. F. Overlearning and the retention of meaningful prose. *J. gen. Psychol.*, 1957, *56*:281–89.

44. Gillette, A. L. Learning and retention: a comparison of three experimental procedures. *Arch. Psychol.*, 1936, *28*, (Whole No. 198).

45. Goldbeck, R. A. The effect of response mode and learning material difficulty on automated instruction. Technical Report No. 1. Santa Barbara, Calif.: American Institute for Research, September, 1960.

46. Goldbeck, R. A., and Briggs, L. J. An analysis of response mode and feedback factors in automated instruction. *Technical Report* No. 2. Santa Barbara, Calif.: American Institute for Research, November 1960.

47. Goldbeck, R. A., Campbell, V. N., and Llewellyn, Joan E. Further experimental evidence on response modes in automated instruction. *Technical Report* No. 3. Santa Barbara, Calif.: American Institute for Research, December 1960.

48. Gordon, K. Class results with spaced and unspaced memorizing. *J. exp. Psychol.*, 1925, *8*:337–43.

49. Guthrie, E. R. *The Psychology of Learning.* New York: Harper, 1952.

50. Hamilton, C. E. The relationship between length of interval separating two learning tasks and performance on the second task. *J. exp. Psychol.*, 1950, *40*:613–21.

51. Harlow, H. F. Motivation as a factor in the acquisition of new responses. *In Current Theory and Research in Motivation.* Lincoln, Neb.: University of Nebraska Press, 1953. pp. 24–49.

52. Hillix, W. A., and Marx, M. H. Response strengthening by information and effect in human learning. *J. exp. Psychol.*, 1960, *60*:97–102.

53. Holaday, P. W., and Stoddard, G. D. Getting ideas from movies. In *Motion Pictures and Youth* (W. W. Charters, P. W. Holaday, and G. D. Stoddard, eds.). New York: Macmillan, 1933.

54. Holland, J. G. Teaching machines: an application of machines from the laboratory. In *Teaching Machines and Programmed Learning* (A. A. Lumsdaine and R. Glaser, eds.). Washington, D.C.: National Education Association, 1960. pp. 215–228.

55. Holland, J. G., and Porter, D. The influence of repetition of incorrectly answered items in a teaching-machine program. Paper presented to the American Psychological Association, Chicago, September 1960.

56. Hovland, C. I. Experimental studies in rote-learning theory: III. Distribution of practice with varying speeds of syllable presentation. *J. exp. Psychol.*, 1938, *23*:172–90.

57. Hovland, C. I. Experimental studies in rote-learning theory: V. Comparison of distribution of practice in serial and paired-associate learning. *J. exp. Psychol.*, 1939, *25*:622–33.

58. Hovland, C. I. Experimental studies in rote-learning theory: VI. Comparison of retention following learning to the same criterion by massed and distributed practice. *J. exp. Psychol.*, 1940, *26*:568–87.

59. Hovland, C. I. Experimental studies in rote-learning theory: VII. Distribution of practice with varying lengths of list. *J. exp. Psychol.*, 1940, *27*:271–84.

60. Hovland, C. I. Experimental studies in rote-learning theory: VIII. Distributed practice of paired associates with varying rates of presentation. *J. exp. Psychol.*, 1949, *39*:714–18.

61. Hovland, C. I., Lumsdaine, A. A., and Sheffield, F. D. *Experiments on Mass Communication.* Princeton, N. J.: Princeton University Press, 1949.

62. Hull, C. L. *Principles of Behavior.* New York: Appleton-Century, 1943.

63. Irion, A. L. Retention and warming-up effects on paired-associate learning. *J. exp. Psychol.,* 1949, *39:*669–75.

64. Irion, A. L., and Briggs, L. J. Learning task and mode of operation variables in use of subject matter trainer. AFPTRC-TR-57–8, October 1957.

65. Israel, M. L. Variably blurred prompting: I. Methodology and application to the analysis of paired associate learning. *J. Psychol.,* 1960, *50:*43–52.

66. Jenkins, J. G. Instruction as a factor in "incidental" learning. *Amer. J. Psychol.,* 1933, *45:*471–77.

67 Jones, R. S. Integration of instructional with self-scoring measuring procedures. Unpublished Ph. D. Dissertation. Columbus, Ohio: Ohio State University, 1950.

68. Jost, A. Die Assoziationfestigkeit in ihrer Abhängigkeit von der Verteilung der Wiederholungen. Z. *Psychol.* 1897, *14:*436–72.

69. Kaess, W., and Zeaman, D. Positive and negative knowledge of results on a Pressey-type punchboard. *J. exp. Psychol.,* 1960, *60:*12–17.

70. Keislar, E. R., and McNeil, J. D. Teaching scientific theory to first grade pupils by an auto-instructional device. *Harvard educ. Rev.,* 1961, *31:*73–83.

71. Keislar, E. R., and McNeil, J. D. A comparison of two response modes in an auto-instructional program with children in the primary grades. *J. educ. Psychol.,* in press.

72. Kimble, G. A. A further analysis of the variables in cyclical motor learning. *J. exp. Psychol.,* 1949, *39:*332–37.

73. Kimble, G. A. Performance and reminiscence in motor learning as a function of the degree of distribution of practice. *J. exp. Psychol.,* 1949, *39:*500–10.

74. Kimble, G. A., and Bilodeau, E. A. Work and rest as variables in cyclical motor learning. *J. exp. Psychol.,* 1949, *39:*150–57.

75. Klare, G. R., Mabry, J. E., and Gustafson, Lenore M. The relationship of patterning (underlining) to immediate retention and to acceptability of technical material. *J. appl. Psychol.,* 1955, *39:*40–42.

76. Klausmeier, H. J. Difficulty of the Task. Paper presented to the American Psychological Association, St. Louis, September 1962.

77. Koffka, K. *The Principles of Gestalt Psychology.* New York: Harcourt, 1935.

78. Köhler, W. *The Mentality of Apes.* New York: Harcourt, Brace, 1925.

79. Krechevsky, I. "Hypotheses" in rats. *Psychol. Rev.,* 1932, *39:*516–32.

80. Krechevsky, I. A study of the continuity of the problem-solving process. *Psychol. Rev.,* 1938, *45:*107–33.

81. Krueger, L. O. The relative effect of interspersing a recall at different stages of learning. *Arch. Psychol.,* 1930, *18,* (Whole No. 114), 15–25.

82. Krueger, W. C. F. The effect of overlearning on retention. *J. exp. Psychol.,* 1929, *12:*71–78.

83. Krueger, W. C. F. The optimal effect of recall during learning. *Arch. Psychol.,* 1930, *18,* (Whole No. 114), 26–34.

84. Krueger, W. C. F. Rate of progress as related to difficulty of assignment. *J. educ. Psychol.,* 1946, *37:*247–49.

85. Krumboltz, J. D. Meaningful learning and retention: practice and reinforcement variables. *Rev. educ. Res.,* 1961, *31:*535–46.

86. Krumboltz, J. D. and Weisman, R. G. The effect of overt vs. covert responding to programmed instruction on immediate and delayed retention. Paper presented to the American Educational Research Association, Atlantic City, N. J., February, 1962.

87. Krumboltz, J. D., and Weisman, R. G. The effect of intermittent confirmation in programmed instruction. Paper presented to the American Psychological Association, St. Louis, September 1962.

88. Kurtz, A. K., Walter, Jeanette S., and Brenner, H. The effects of inserted questions and statements on film learning. *Technical Report*-SDC. 269–7–16. Pennsylvania State College, Instructional Films Research Program, September 1950.

89. Kurtz, K. H., and Hovland, C. I. Concept learning with differing sequences of instances. *J. exp. Psychol.*, 1956, *4*:239–43.

90. Lambert, P. Schedules of reinforcement: effects on programmed learning. Paper presented to the American Psychological Association, St. Louis, September 1962.

91. Lashley, K. S. *Brain Mechanisms and Intelligence.* Chicago: University of Chicago Press, 1929.

92. Lathrop, C. W., and Norford, C. A. Contributions of film introductions and film summaries to learning from instructional films. *Technical Report*-SDC. 269–7–8, Pennsylvania State College, Instructional Films Research Program, November 1949.

93. Leuba, J. H., and Hyde, W. An experiment on learning to make hand movements. *Psychol. Rev.*, 1905, *12*:351–69.

94. Lockhead, G. R. A re-evaluation of evidence of one-trial associative learning. *Amer. J. Psychol.*, 1961, *74*:590–95.

95. Lorge, I. *The Influence of Regularly Interpolated Time Intervals upon Subsequent Learning.* New York: Teachers College, Columbia University, 1930.

96. Luh, C. W. The conditions of retention. *Psychol. Mongor.*, 1922, *31* (Whole No. 3).

97. Lyon, D. O. The relation of length of material to time taken for learning and optimum distribution of time. *J. educ. Psychol.*, 1914, *5*:1–9; 85–91; 155–63.

98. Lyon, D. O. *Memory and the Learning Process.* Baltimore: Warwick and York, 1917.

99. McGeoch, J. A., and Irion, A. L. *The Psychology of Human Learning.* New York: Longmans, Green, 1952.

100. McNeil, J. D., and Keislar, E. R. Individual differences and effectiveness of auto-instruction at the primary grade level. *Calif. J. educ. Res.*, 1961, *12*:160–64.

101. McTavish, C. L. Effect of repetitive film showings on learning. *Technical Report* SDC. 269–7–12, Instructional Film Research Program, Pennsylvania State College. Port Washington, N.Y.: Special Devices Center, November 1949.

102. Maier, N. R. F., and Hoffman, L. R. Quality of first and second solutions in group problem solving. *J. appl. Psychol.*, 1960, *44*:278–83.

103. Melaragno, R. J. Effect of negative reinforcement in an automated teaching setting. *Psychol., Rep.*, 1960, *7*:381–84.

104. Meyer, Susan R. A test of the principles of "activity," "immediate reinforcement," and "guidance" as instrumented by Skinner's teaching Machine. *Dissert. Abst.*, 1960, *20*:4729–30.

105. Meyer, W. J., and Offenbach, S. I. Effectiveness of paired verbal reinforcers as a function of task complexity. Paper presented to the Midwestern Psychological Association, May 1961.

106. Meyer, W. J., and Seidman, S. B. Age differences in the effectiveness of different reinforcement combinations on the acquisition and extinction of a simple concept learning problem. *Child Develpm.*, 1960, *31:*419–29.

107. Meyer, W. J., and Seidman, S. B. Relative effectiveness of different reinforcement levels. *Child Develpm.*, 1961, *32:*117–27.

108. Michael, D. N., and Maccoby, N. Factors influencing verbal learning from films under varying conditions of audience participation. *J. exp. Psychol.*, 1953, *46:*411–18.

109. Mitzel, H. Comparison of the effectiveness of individualized with traditional instruction in ninth-year mathmatics. Paper presented to the American Educational Research Association, Atlantic City, N. J., February 1962.

110. Northrop, D. S. Effects on learning of the prominence of organizational outlines in instructional films. *Human Engineering Report-SDC.* 269–7–33. Pennsylvania State College, Instructional Films Research Program, October, 1952.

111. Page, E. B. Teacher comments and student performance: a seventy-four classroom experiment in school motivation. *J. educ. Psychol.*, 1958, *49:*173–81.

112. Patten, E. F. The influence of distribution of repetitions on certain rote learning phenomena. *J. Psychol.*, 1938, *5:*359–74.

113. Peterson, H. A. Recitation or recall as a factor in the learning of long prose selections. *J. educ. Psychol.*, 1944, *35:*220–28.

114. Peterson, H. A., Ellis, M., Toohill, N., and Kloess, P. Some measurements of the effect of reviews. *J. educ. Psychol.*, 1935, *26:*65–72.

115. Popp, Helen, and Porter, D. Programming verbal skills for primary grades. *A V Communication Rev.*, 1960, *8:*165–75.

116. Postman, L. Repetition and paired-associate learning. *Amer. J. Psychol.*, 1962, *75:*372–89.

117. Pressey, S. L. Basic unresolved teaching-machine problems. *Theory into Practice*, 1962, *1:*30–37.

118. Pressey, S. L. New theory, no "programing," new future. Paper presented to the American Psychological Association, St. Louis, September 1962.

119. Pyle, W. H. Economical learning. *J. educ. Psychol.*, 1913, *4:*148–58.

120. Pyle, W. H. *The Psychology of Learning*, rev. ed. Baltimore: Warwick and York, 1928.

121. Reed, H. B. Distributed practice in addition. *J. educ. Psychol.*, 1924, *15:*248–9.

122. Robinson, E. S. Some factors determining the degree of retroactive inhibition. *Psychol. Monogr.*, 1920, *28* (Whole No. 128).

123. Robinson, E. S., and Darrow, C. W. Effect of length of lists upon memory for numbers. *Amer. J. Psychol.*, 1924, *35:*235–43.

124. Robinson, E. S., and Heron, W. T. Result of variations in length of memorized material. *J. exp. Psychol.*, 1922, *5:*428–48.

125. Rock, I. The role of repetition in associative learning. *Amer. J. Psychol.*, 1957, *70:*186–93.

126. Roe, A., *et al.* Automated teaching methods using linear programs. *Report* No. 60–105. Los Angeles: University of California Department of Engineering, December 1960.

127. Rubin-Rabson, G. Studies in the psychology of memorizing piano music: VII. A comparison of three degrees of overlearning. *J. educ. Psychol.,* 1941, *32*:688–96.

128. Sand, M. C. The effect of length of list upon retroactive inhibition when degree of learning is controlled. *Arch. Psychol.,* 1939, *33,* (Whole No. 238).

129. Saul, E. V., and Osgood, C. E. Perceptual organization of material as a factor influencing ease of learning and degree of retention. *J. exp. Psychol.,* 1950, *40*:372–79.

130. Sax, G. Concept acquisition as a function of differing schedules and delays of reinforcement. *J. educ. Psychol., 1960, 51*:32–36.

131. Schoer, L. Effect of list length and interpolated learning on the learning and recall of fast and slow learners. Doctor's thesis. Iowa City: State University of Iowa, 1961.

132. Schrom, N. Missouri high school English offerings reported by University of Missouri freshman in relation to their freshman English placement scores. Unpublished Ph.D. dissertation. Columbia, Mo.: University of Missouri, 1953

133. Shay, C. B. Relationship of intelligence to step size on a teaching machine program. *J. educ. Psychol.,* 1961, *52*:98–103.

134. Siegel, P. S. Structure effects within a memory series *.J. exp. Psychol.,* 1943, *33*:311–16.

135. Silberman, H. F. Self-instructional devices and programmed materials. *Rev. edus. Res.,* 1962, *32*:179–93.

136. Silberman, H. F., Melaragno, R. J., and Coulson, J. E. Confirmation and prompting with connected discourse material. *Psychol. Rep.,* 1961, *8*:401–406.

137. Silberman, H. F., *et al.* Fixed sequence versus branching autoinstructional methods. *J. educ. Psychol.,* 1961, *52*:166–72.

138. Silverman, R. E., and Alter, Millicent. Note on the response in teaching machine programs. *Psychol., Rep.,* 1960, *7*:496.

139. Skaggs, E. B., Grossman, S., Krueger, L. O., and Krueger, W. C. F. Further studies of the reading-recitation process in learning. *Arch. Psychol.,* 1930, *18* (Whole No. 114).

140. Skinner, B. F. *The Behavior of Organisms:* New York: Appleton-Century, 1938.

141. Skinner, B. F. Teaching machines. *Science,* 1958, *128*:969–77.

142. Slamecka, N. J. Studies of retention of connected discourse. *Amer. J. Psychol.,* 1959; *72*:409–16.

143. Smith, Leone M. Programed learning in elementary school: an experimental study of relationships between mental abilities and performance. *Technical Report* No. 2. Urbana, Ill.: Training Research Laboratory, University of Illinois, August 1962.

144. Smith, M. H., and Stearns, Ellen. The influence of isolation on the learning of the surrounding material. *Amer. J. Psychol.,* 1949, *62*:369–81.

145. Smith, W., and Moore, J. W. Size of step and achievement in programed spelling. Lewisburg, Pennsylvania: Bucknell University, September 1961.

146. Sones, A. M., and Stroud, J. B. Review with special reference to temporal position. *J. educ. Psychol.,* 1940, *31*:665–76.

147. Spight, J. B. Day and night intervals and the distribution of practice. *J. exp. Psychol.,* 1928, *11*:397–98.

148. Spitzer, H. F. Studies in retention. *J. educ. Psychol.*, 1939, *30*:641–56.
149. Starch, D. *Educational Psychology*. New York: Macmillan, 1927.
150. Stevenson, H. W. Latent learning in children. *J. exp. Psychol.*, 1954, *47*:17–21.
151. Stolurow, L. M. A comparative study of methods of programing materials for efficient learning in self-instructional devices. Cooperative Research Project No. HEW 661, SAE 8370. Urbana, Ill.,: Training Research Laboratory, University of Illinois, June 1961.
152. Stolurow, L. M. *Teaching by Machine*. Washington, D.C.: U.S. Office of Education, 1961.
153. Thorndike, E. L. *Human Learning*. New York: Century, 1931.
154. Thorndike, E. L. *The Fundamentals of Learning*. New York: Teachers College, Columbia University, 1932.
155. Thune, L. E. The effect of different types of preliminary activities on subsequent learning of paired-associate material. *J. exp. Psychol.*, 1950, *40*: 423–38.
156. Thune, L. E. Warm-up effect as a function of level of practice in verbal learning. *Amer. Psychologist*, 1950, *5*:251.
157. Tiedeman, H. R. A study of retention in classroom learning. *J. educ. Res.*, 1948, *41*:516–31.
158. Tolman, E. C. *Purposive Behavior in Animals and Men*. New York: Century, 1932.
159. Tolman, E. C., Hall, C. S., and Bretnall, E. P. A disproof the law of effect and a substitution of the laws of emphasis, motivation, and disruption. *J. exp. Psychol.*, 1932, *15*:601–614.
160. Trowbridge, M. H., and Cason, H. An experimental study of Thorndike's theory of learning. *J. gen. Psychol.*, 1932, *7*:245–48.
161. Tsai, L-S. The relation of retention to the distribution of relearning. *J. exp. Psychol.*, 1927, *10*:30–39.
162. Underwood, B. J. Verbal behavior in the educative process. *Harvard educ. Rev.*, 1959, *29*:107–17.
163. Underwood, B. J., and Keppel, G. One-trial learning. *J. verb. Learn. verb. Behav.*, 1962, *1*:1–13.
164. Underwood, B. J., Rehula, R., and Keppel, G. Item selection and paired-associate learning. *Amer. J. Psychol.*, 1962, *75*:353–71.
165. Underwood, B. J., and Richardson, J. Studies of distributed practice: XIII. Interlist interference and the retention of serial nonsense lists. *J. exp. Psychol.*, 1955, *50*:39–46.
166. Underwood, B. J., and Schulz, R. W. *Meaningfulness and Verbal Learning*. Chicago: Lippincott, 1960.
167. Vincent, W. S., Ash, P., and Greenhill, L. P. Relationship of length and fact frequency to effectiveness of instructional motion pictures. *Technical Report* SDC. 269-7-7, Pennsylvania State College, Instructional Film Research Program, November 1949.
168. Walker, C. C. and Stolurow, L. M. A comparison of overt and covert response in programed learning. *J. educ. Res.*, 1962, in press.
169. Ward, A. H., and Davis, R. A. Acquisition and retention of factual information in seventh grade general science during a semester of eighteen weeks. *J. educ. Psychol.*, 1939, *30*:116–25.

170. Ward, L. B. Reminiscence and rote learning. *Psychol. Monogr.*, 1937, *49*, (Whole No. 220).

171. Wittrock, M. C. Mediation theory applied to discovery learning: cueing and prompting mediated responses. Los Angeles: Department of Education, University of California, 1962.

172. Wittrock, M. C. Response mode in the teaching of kinetic molecular theory verbal mediators to primary school students. Los Angeles: Department of Education, University of California, 1962.

173. Wollen, K. A. One-trial versus incremental-paired associate learning. *J. verb. Learn. verb. Behav.*, 1962, *1*:14–21.

174. Woodworth, R. S. *Experimental Psychology*. New York: Holt, 1938.

175. Youtz, Adella C. An experimental evaluation of Jost's laws. *Psychol. Monogr.*, 1941, *53*, (Whole No. 238).

CHAPTER 9.

Motivational Variables in Meaningful Reception Learning

THE PURPOSE OF THIS CHAPTER is not to examine in broad perspective the role of motivational factors in human behavior, or even their effects on learning generally. Its scope is limited to a consideration in general terms of how motivational variables influence meaningful reception learning and retention, *i.e.*, of how they impinge on and interact with the cognitive processes whereby such learning and retention take place, and at what temporal points in these processes their influence is manifested. Hence no systematic attention will be given to different theories of motivation; to the effects of drives, motives, incentives, rewards, and reinforcement on learning; or to the relative impact of various kinds of motivational, affective, attitudinal, personality, and interpersonal variables in different types of learning situations.

Even with respect to meaningful reception learning, the intention is not to consider systematically the effects of motivational variables on short-or long-term learning outcomes, but to *contrast* the underlying mechanisms of these motivational variables with those of the cognitive variables with which we have been primarily concerned in this volume. Thus, for example, there will be no discussion of the effects of anxiety on intensity of motivation for meaningful reception learning, on aspirations for academic achievement, on motivational orientation to learning, or on quantitative or qualitative aspects of the learning process. As pointed out previously (see p. 2), such topics can be examined more relevantly and economically within the framework of another body of learning theory devoted to subjective or noncognitive facets of learning, or within the framework of a more general treatise on school learning or educational psychology. By way of illustration, however, without making any attempt to cover these or related areas exhaustively, two specific problems of particular relevance for school learning will be considered in some detail, namely, the effects of intention and attitudinal bias, respectively, on meaningful learning and retention.

ROLE AND KINDS OF MOTIVATION IN MEANINGFUL RECEPTION LEARNING

Motivation is probably less indispensable for meaningful reception learning than it is for any other kind of learning. Because such learning requires relatively little effort, and, when successful, furnishes its own reward, less reliance need be placed on existing drives and motives within the learner, on incentive conditions, and on extrinsic rewards than is the case, for example, in rote learning or problem-solving. But to assert that meaningful reception learning (particularly of a fragmentary and short-term nature) can occur in

the absence of motivation, does not, of course, imply denial of the fact that motivation can significantly facilitate learning whenever it is present and operative.

The causal relationship between motivation and learning is also typically reciprocal in nature. Both for this reason, and because motivation is not an indispensable condition of learning, it is unnecessary to postpone learning activities until appropriate interests and motivations have been developed. Frequently the best way of teaching an unmotivated student is to ignore his motivational state for the time being, and to concentrate on teaching him as effectively as possible. Much to his surprise and his teacher's, he will learn despite his lack of motivation; and from the satisfaction of learning he will hopefully develop the motivation to learn more. Paradoxically, therefore, we may discover that the most effective method of developing intrinsic motivation to learn is to focus on the cognitive rather than on the motivational aspects of learning, and to rely on the motivation that is developed retroactively from successful educational achievement.

Also because meaningful learning provides its own reward, cognitive drive (the desire for knowledge as an end in itself) is more important than in rote or instrumental learning, and is potentially the most important kind of motivation in meaningful reception learning. Cognitive drive is probably derived in a very general way from curiosity tendencies and from related predispositions to explore, manipulate, understand, and cope with the environment.[50] These latter predispositions, however, originally manifest potential rather than actual motivating properties, and are obviously nonspecific in content and direction. Their potential motivating power is actualized in expression and particularized in direction by the developing individual, both as a result of successful exercise and the anticipation of future satisfying consequences from further exercise, and as a result of internalization of the values of those significant persons in the familial and cultural environments with whom he identifies. Far from being largely endogenous in origin, therefore, specific cognitive drives or interests are primarily acquired and dependent upon particular experience. Hence we observe again that the relationship between cognitive drive and learning, like the relationship between motivation and learning generally, is reciprocal from a cause-effect standpoint.

Despite the potential centrality of cognitive drive for the motivation of meaningful reception learning, it is nevertheless true that in our utilitarian, competitive, and achievement-oriented culture, such extrinsic considerations as career advancement, ego enhancement, and anxiety reduction become, with increasing age, progressively more significant sources of motivation for school learning.* Even material rewards tend to become less ends in themselves than symbols of academic status, achievement, and competitive advantage, and hence subsidiary sources of self-esteem. Eventually, of course, the viability of the cognitive drive as an intrinsic, task-oriented type of motivation is impaired as a consequence of the almost exclusive prior association of intellectual interests and activities with ego-enhancement and anxiety-reduction

---

* Beginning with the first four years of school life, for example, ratings of achievement and recognition-seeking behavior remain quite stable, and are predictive of similar behavior during adolescence and early adult life.[32]

motives. If the desire to learn and understand is almost invariably exercised in the context of competing for grades, obtaining degrees, preparing for a vocation, striving for advancement, and reducing the fear of academic and occupational failure, there is little reason for believing that much of it survives as a goal in its own right.° This trend is reflected in the progressive decline in school interests and intellectual enthusiasm as children move up the academic ladder.[22]

Hence, if we wish to develop the cognitive drive so that it remains viable during the school years and in adult life, it is necessary to move still further away from the educational doctrine of gearing the curriculum to the spontaneously expressed interests, current concerns, and life-adjustment problems of pupils. Although it is undoubtedly unrealistic and even undesirable in our culture to eschew entirely the utilitarian, ego-enhancement, and anxiety-reduction motivations for learning, we must place increasingly greater emphasis upon the value of knowing and understanding as goals in their own right, quite apart from any practical benefits they may confer. Instead of denigrating subject matter knowledge, as so many allegedly progressive educators have done over the past fifty years, we must discover more efficient methods of fostering the long-term acquisition of meaningful and usable bodies of knowledge, and of developing appropriate intrinsic motivations for such learning.

Even though *particular* instances of learning may be largely unmotivated, for significant, *long-term* meaningful learning of subject matter to occur, it is undoubtedly true that the subject matter in question must be related to felt needs. Inability to see any need for a subject is the reason students mention most frequently for losing interest in high-school studies.[51] Doing, without being interested in what one is doing, results in relatively little permanent learning,[11] since it is reasonable to suppose that only that material can be meaningfully incorporated and integrated into cognitive structure on a long-term basis, which is relevant to areas of concern in the psychological field of the individual. Learners who have little need to know and understand, quite naturally expend relatively little learning effort; manifest an insufficiently meaningful learning set; fail to develop precise meanings, to reconcile new material with existing concepts, and to reformulate new propositions in their own terms; and do not devote enough time and effort to practice and review. Material is therefore never sufficiently consolidated to form an adequate foundation for sequential learning. Hence it is unrealistic to expect that school subjects can be effectively learned and retained until pupils develop a felt need to acquire knowledge as an end in itself—since much school knowledge can never be rationalized as necessary for meeting the demands of daily living. Once such a need is developed, learning naturally becomes more meaningful; but it is difficult to stimulate the development of such needs until subject matter can be presented meaningfully in the first place.

°It is true, of course, that some intrinsic motivation or cognitive drive may be developed retroactively as a consequence of successful learning, even though the intellectual activity in question is *originally* motivated by extrinsic considerations. Nevertheless, if major emphasis *continues* to be placed on extrinsic motives, the cognitive drive developed in this fashion fails to become a significant motivating factor.

MOTIVATIONAL MECHANISMS IN MEANINGFUL RECEPTION LEARNING AND RETENTION

Cognitive variables are *directly* implicated in the cognitive interactional process during meaningful reception learning and retention, and are therefore directly involved in the determination of dissociability strength. *Their effects are also mediated through the same mechanisms in both learning and retention.* Typically, however, *motivational and attitudinal* variables are *not directly* involved in the cognitive interactional process. They energize and expedite this process during learning by enhancing effort, attention, and immediate readiness for learning, and thereby facilitate dissociability strength catalytically and nonspecifically (rather than through direct involvement in the parameters of the interactional process). Furthermore, the effects of motivational variables on learning and retention, respectively, unlike their cognitive counterparts, are *not* mediated through the *same* mechanisms. After learning is completed, these variables cannot independently affect dissociability strength (that is, apart from their effects on learning itself), and can only influence retention during the reproductive phase of memory by elevating thresholds of availability and by shaping the qualitative aspects of imaginative reconstruction (see pp. 50, 230).

Thus, motivational and attitudinal factors affect meaningful reception learning and retention in ways that are qualitatively different from the comparable effects of relevant cognitive variables. These latter variables (*e.g.*, the availability of relevant subsumers and their relative stability and clarity) directly and specifically influence the parameters of the cognitive interactional process underlying meaningful reception learning and retention, and are thus organically involved in the determination of dissociability strength. Motivational and attitudinal variables, on the other hand, are not organically involved in the cognitive interactional process or in the determination of dissociability strength. For the most part they merely impinge on it in nonspecific facilitating fashion. The one exception to this generalization involves the effects of meaningful learning set, integrative drive, and self-critical attitudes, which influence the emergence, precision, and integratedness of meanings (see pp. 20, 22), but not their retention.

It is also reasonable to assume that the effects of cognitive variables on meaningful reception learning continue along similar lines during retention and are mediated by the same mechanisms (see p. 51). Whatever these effects on the interactional process are, they are simply extended temporally from learning to retention. Thus the rate at which dissociability strength declines during retention is always proportional to the initial dissociability strength influenced by these same variables during the course of learning. However the mechanism whereby motivational variables affect learning cannot persist into retention because a necessary point of contact is lacking. Hence, whenever motivational factors appear to affect retention independently of learning, a new mechanism is required to mediate this influence, a mechanism that is operative not during the retention interval per se, but during the reproductive stage of memory.

Learning

During meaningful reception learning, motivational and attitudinal variables may energize all or selected aspects of the learning field. They impinge catalytically on the cognitive interactional process without affecting any of its basic parameters (e.g., the availability of relevant appropriate sub-sumers; the latter's stability, clarity, and discriminability from the learning task). Hence they neither determine any of its qualitative attributes, nor differentially influence dissociability strength apart from a nonspecific facilitating effect on learning. Through such mechanisms as mobilization of effort and concentration of attention, more repetitions of the material are completed within the stipulated learning time, and each repetition is conducted more efficiently. The net result is an over-all increase in dissociability strength for the learning process so energized. Illustrative of the energizing effect of motivation on learning is the fact that subjects who have high needs for achievement tend to reach solutions in problem-solving tasks more often than do subjects with low achievement needs.[16] On a long-term basis, high achievement motivation also tends to be associated with greater academic achievement,[26,46] and used in conjunction with measures of academic aptitude, is an excellent predictor of college performance.[49]

In addition to its energizing effects on meaningful reception learning, motivation also mobilizes nonspecifically the individual's immediate readiness for such learning by lowering the thresholds of those general kinds of perceptions and responses that are customarily implicated in this learning. Exemplifying this latter mechanism is the lowering of reaction times that occurs in response to instructions to "work faster"[34] (as opposed to task-oriented instructions or instructions to relax). It is important, however, not to confuse this nonspecific motivational facilitation with the more direct and specific influence on dissociability strength exerted by such other motivational and attitudinal variables as meaningful learning set, integrative drive, and self-critical attitudes (see p. 228). As a result of the operation all of these facilitating motivational mechanisms during learning, clearer and more stable meanings are acquired and retained, which, in turn, facilitate the sequential type of learning involved in the mastery of subject matter.

An optimal level of motivation or ego-involvement (neither too high nor too low) apparently exists for complex kinds of learning.[21] According to Bruner,[10] impelling drive states may conceivably disrupt meaningful generic learning by overemphasizing the particularity of newly learned concepts, and by limiting the learner's ability to apply previously learned principles to newly learned tasks, and hence "to go appropriately beyond the information given" (p. 55). In support of this proposition he cites an experiment conducted by Postman and himself, in which subjects under stress made less improvement than a nonstress group in lowering their perceptual thresholds while learning to recognize tachistoscopically-presented three-word sentences.

Motivational and attitudinal variables (e.g., ego-involvement, ego threat, attitudinal bias) also influence learning outcomes during the perceptual phase of learning (see p. 51) before the cognitive interactional process per se is inaugurated. Information and ideas obviously have to be perceived first before they can be incorporated into cognitive structure. During the perceptual stage, motivational variables may raise or lower perceptual thresholds,[10,38] as well as influence perceptual content through such mechanisms as selective emphasis, omission, and distortion (see p. 65).

Retention

Once the learning sessions have been completed and the cognitive interactional products have been formed, a channel of communication no longer remains open for the energizing and expediting aspects of motivation to influence dissociability strength, even in a catalytic or nonspecific sense.° At this point, therefore, it is more parsimonious to postulate that motivational and attitudinal variables continue to affect retention outcomes, independently of their prior effects on learning, only insofar as they impinge on the repro- -ductive aspects of memory.

Both theoretical considerations and the weight of the available evidence suggest that motivational factors influence meaningful retention selectively by inhibiting rather than facilitating particular thresholds of recognition and recall. Positive ego-involvement and favorable attitudinal bias, in other words, do not increase retention by lowering thresholds of memorial elicitation, but, rather, strong motivation to forget and certain kinds of attitudinal bias (i.e., in ego-threatening or anxiety-producing situations) may selectively promote forgetting by raising thresholds of availability (repression). Thus, unlike the situation in learning, not only is the selective influence of motivational variables on retention inhibitory rather than facilitating (catalytic), but the influence of these variables is also mediated solely through a change in thresholds of memorial elicitation, without any change whatsoever in dissociability strength itself. Although the latter remains constant, recall or recognition is nevertheless rendered momentarily more difficult because of the selective elevation of particular thresholds of availability.°°

Unlike the situation in meaningful learning, the availability thresholds of *rotely* learned items can probably be *both lowered and raised* by motivational and attitudinal variables (see below, p. 231, for examples). In this respect, thresholds of availability for rotely learned materials are comparable to the operation of those drive states that generally account for fluctuations in the organism's relative disposition to respond behaviorally or perceptually to particular environmental stimuli.[4] But whereas it is not difficult at all to understand how and why availability thresholds of discrete and isolated traces of images, responses, and associations can be readily lowered by motivational variables, the threshold of availability of a component meaningful idea, embedded within a larger conceptual system, is quite another matter. In the latter situation, the threshold of availability is not a neural property of a discrete trace unit representative of prior behavioral or conscious experience, but is determined by the complex interaction of many attentional, ideational, and motivational factors, that *invariably tend to increase resistance to memo-*

°As will be pointed out below, in the discussion of selective retention of those controversial materials toward which learners have a positive as opposed to a negative attitudinal bias (see p. 238), positive ego-involvement (in this instance, positive attitudinal bias) *can* facilitate retention by increasing dissociability strength. However, this is not a genuine motivational effect on retention, but is attributable to *cognitive* or nonaffective components of attitude structure which, in the case of positive attitudinal bias, tend to provide a highly clear and stable set of subsuming concepts for the learning and retention of the controversial material.

°°As previously indicated (see pp. 66–67), motivational and attitudinal factors not only help determine, by raising thresholds of availability, whether or not material of near-threshold dissociability strength is available in the reproductive phase, but also influence qualitatively the content of what is reconstructed.

rial elicitation of available meanings at or near threshold strength. Thus the *primary* effect of all of these factors, including the motivational, is to elevate thresholds of availability or to make the memories in question less available in relation to their intrinsic dissociability strength. Lowering of thresholds of availability for meaningfully learned material can only occur indirectly, as a result of counteracting or disinhibiting the inhibitory factors that temporarily raise them.

It still has to be empirically determined whether a motivational factor, such as the existence of a strong incentive to recall during the reproductive phase, can *indirectly* lower thresholds of availability for meaningfully learned material by disinhibiting existing threshold-raising or memory-inhibiting factors (*e.g.*, distraction, inattention, inertia, disinclination toward effort). However it is known that such inhibitory conditions as initial learning shock and the competition of alternative memories tend to dissipate spontaneously (see p. 58). Moreover, hypnosis,[41] through selective focusing of attention and increased "suggestibility", can reduce the inhibitory effect of both competing memories, and of motives and attitudes promoting repression as, for example, in the case of anxiety-producing material. The disinhibiting effects of hypnosis are greater for meaningful than for rote memory,[41] probably because of the short retention span that characterizes rotely learned material. The associative or dissociability strength of learned material must obviously be near threshold level before disinhibition can effectively increase availability.

Some illustrations will now be given of how positive ego-involvement can conceivably facilitate *rote* (as opposed to meaningful) *retention* by lowering thresholds of availability. These examples only include instances in which the differentially greater retention attributed to positive ego-involvement cannot be easily accounted for in terms of greater initial learning. In task-oriented learning situations, subjects tend to remember interrupted tasks better than completed tasks when they are really interested in and intend to complete the tasks in question[9,30,42,52] (the Zeigarnik effect). However, in ego-oriented situations where noncompletion constitutes an ego threat and completion is ego enhancing, more completed tasks are remembered.[29,42] Ego-oriented subjects retain significantly more nonsense syllables after one week than do task-oriented subjects, despite the lack of significant differences between the two groups in original learning;[19] and elementary-school children tend to recall high test grades best and low test grades least well.[25] Alper[2] found that *delayed* recall of nonsense syllables and three-place digits is inferior, as expected, to *immediate* recall in task-oriented groups, but not in ego-oriented groups. Subjects show better recall of actually bogus (but purportedly genuine) ratings of *themselves* when they agree rather than disagree with the ratings made, and when the ratings are favorable rather than unfavorable.[47] The direction of the error of recall under these circumstances is such as to make the bogus ratings more compatible with self-ratings.[47] These differential findings, however, are not obtained when subjects are asked to learn bogus ratings of *other* students.[43]

Methodological Considerations. Any attempt to investigate the effects of motivational and attitudinal variables on retention, or to define the mechanisms whereby such effects are produced is self-evidently fraught with numerous methodological difficulties and hazards. In the first place, it is obviously essential to isolate the influence of motivation on memory processes *per se*, from the mere residual influence on retention outcomes that necessarily follows from the prior effects of motivational factors on learning itself. (Individuals who learn more originally, also have more to remember later than do individuals who originally learn less.) Thus, unless this methodological requirement is satisfied, it is impossible to claim that motivation independently influences retention.

One way of separating the learning and retention effects of motivation from each other is to match experimental and control groups in terms of learning outcomes, either by allowing one of the groups additional learning trials, or by differentially assigning subjects to each group so as to render the two groups equivalent in mean learning score. If such a procedure is not practicable, it is necessary, at the very least, to have separate measures of learning and retention, and to show that the retention difference between the two groups is reliably greater than the learning difference between them. This methodological criterion is particularly essential in studying qualitative changes in recall that are presumably attributable to motivational factors. Differential mnemonic omission, selection, or distortion of content can only be demonstrated with confidence by comparing successive delayed reproductions with an immediate test of recall rather than with the original stimulus material. Still another method of handling this problem in certain instances is to refrain from introducing the motivational variable until *after* the learning sessions and tests are completed. But whereas this latter method is very feasible, for example, in experiments testing the effects of deliberate intention to remember, it cannot possibly be used in studies where the motivational variable necessarily inheres in the very conditions or content of the learning task.

Unfortunately, the derivation of separate learning and retention measures in these experiments creates an additional opportunity for confounding the effects of motivation on learning and retention respectively. An immediate test of recall tends to enhance or reinforce the motivationally induced changes effected during the perceptual and learning phases of the learning-retention process. Hence delayed recall is probably influenced more by accentuation of the learning effects of motivation (as a result of the very occurrence of immediate recall) than by the later, presumably mnemonic influence of motivation on the learned material. Furthermore, an immediate test of recall provides a review of the learning material, and thus, by serving as a leveling factor, tends to reduce potential differences between experimental and control groups. For both reasons, therefore, it is advisable to use separate subgroups of these groups for measuring learning and retention.

Another related hazard stems from the possibility of differential rehearsal during the retention interval. Ego orientation or positive ego-involvement is more likely to induce such rehearsal (or even attempts at surreptitious review) than is task orientation or negative ego-involvement. This variable cannot be completely controlled, but its effects can be limited somewhat by using esoteric learning materials, and, where feasible, by restricting the intensity of ego-involvement. The extent to which this variable contaminates the experimental findings can also be ascertained in part by obtaining introspective reports from subjects.

A third methodological problem in this type of research is the difficulty of controlling and independently measuring the kind and degree of ego-involvement operative in the experimental situation. Mere manipulation of learning conditions and materials cannot guarantee that individual subjects will manifest the type and intensity of ego-involvement which the experimenter judges appropriate for the circumstances. It is also extremely difficult to obtain a valid independent measure of ego-involvement. The subject's own self-ratings may not correspond to his actual attitudes or motives. This is especially true in the case of learning tasks and conditions that presumably instigate severe anxiety and hence promote repression. By definition, this latter affect (and process) would be operative, at least in part, below the level of conscious availability, and thus would resist direct, denotative measurement.

Lastly, there is the difficult methodological problem of distinguishing between the effects on retention of the respective cognitive and affective components of attitude structure. A set of ideas of particular stability, clarity, discriminability, and relevance for the learning task, as well as a complex of feelings of specifiable direction and intensity, characterize any attitude;* and, except when anxiety-producing learning materials are used (as will be pointed out below), it is probably the cognitive rather than the affective aspects of attitude structure that account for the differential retention of controversial materials that are either in accord or conflict with existing attitudes. In any case, before differences in retention outcomes can be attributed to the influence of purely attitudinal variables (*i.e.*, to the affective component of attitudes) on retention, it is first necessary to hold constant or eliminate the effect of the latter cognitive variables on criterial retention scores.

Drive Reduction and Reinforcement

Motives and drives not only have a nonspecific energizing influence on meaningful reception learning, but their satisfaction (*i.e.*, reward, drive reduction) also provides, retroactively, another source of facilitation in relation to further learning trials and related new learning tasks. Successful learning (satisfaction of cognitive and ego-enhancing drives for acquiring new knowledge) energizes subsequent learning efforts by enhancing the learner's self-confidence, by encouraging him to persevere, and by increasing the subjective attractiveness of the learning task. At the same time it tends to maintain in a state of immediate readiness the general kinds of perceptions and responses involved in meaningful reception learning (see p. 229); motivates the individual to make further use of, that is, to practice, rehearse, and perform what he has already learned; and encourages him to continue developing and exercising the motives that were satisfied or rewarded, namely, the desire for knowledge both as an end in itself and as a means of enhancing status and self-esteem.

Whether drive reduction has a *direct* and selective reinforcing effect on the

---

*This formulation of attitude structure is consistent with Peak's concept of an attitude as consisting of an interrelated group of ideas organized around a perceptual or conceptual nucleus and manifesting affective properties.[35]

drive-reducing response *itself* (thereby increasing the probability of its recurrence), and how this effect is mediated, are exceedingly complex and controversial topics, full discussion of which is obviously beyond the scope of this book. It will suffice to take the position here that drive reduction selectively reinforces responses only in the *rote* learning of discrete, arbitrary, and verbatim stimulus or stimulus-response connections. Within this context, it is more parsimonious to believe that the underlying mechanism of response facilitation in rote learning is not a retroactive increase in habit or associative strength (as a consequence of the satisfying effects induced by the response), but is reflective of two changes in the threshold of elicitation or availability.

First, satisfying and habitual instrumental association of particular responses with the motives or needs that instigate them, gradually tends to give these responses a pre-emptive drive-reducing status (canalization). That is, when specific needs or motives are operative, they *selectively* lower the thresholds of *only* those responses whose drive-reducing properties have been previously established. In fact, this selective lowering of response thresholds is coextensive with the concept of *drive state*,[4] in contradistinction to the concept of *drive determinant* (needs, motives, incentives, intense and persistent stimuli of physiological or environmental origin); this latter concept refers only to the factors instigating a particular drive state. Second, it is possible that the memory of positive hedonic or affective tone associated with a particular rewarding or drive-reducing response provides further opportunity for the lowering of thresholds of response availability.

In meaningful reception learning, on the other hand, no mechanisms exist through which the satisfying effects of drive reduction can lead directly to reinforcement of successful (drive-reducing) meanings. Unlike the informational consequences of drive reduction, these effects cannot increase the dissociability strength of previously learned meanings; they can only energize meaningful learning catalytically on succeeding trials or related tasks. And, as previously pointed out, thresholds of availability for meaningfully learned ideas presumably cannot be directly lowered by any kind of variable, motivational or otherwise (see p. 230).

Drive reduction, whether of cognitive or extrinsic drives, also has all of the cognitive or informational effects of feedback. These latter effects are probably more important for meaningful reception learning and retention than are the motivational and reinforcement consequences of drive reduction. By indicating areas of confusion, by correcting errors, by clarifying ambiguities and misconceptions, and by confirming appropriately understood meanings, the cognitive aspects of drive reduction consolidate the stability and clarity of learned material (increase its dissociability strength), enhance the subject's confidence in the correctness of his understandings, and enable him to focus his learning efforts selectively on inadequately learned portions .of the material. They not only have informational value for subsequent trials of the same learning task, but also have transfer value for related new tasks.[24]

THE EFFECTS OF INTENTION ON MEANINGFUL
LEARNING AND RETENTION

Deliberate intention to learn (*i.e.*, in response to explicit instructions) is not essential for learning as long as belongingness is present (see pp. 180–181).

Such belongingness prevails, even in the absence of explicit instructions, either when the learning material is potentially meaningful, or when habitual expectancies are applicable to rote learning tasks. In the latter instances, of course, a certain amount of implicit or self-instruction may be operative. Nevertheless, many experiments show that deliberate learning in response to explicit instructions is both more effective,[8,20,33,40] and more precise and specific,[37] than is unintentional or implicitly instructed learning. To explain these findings it is only necessary to invoke the typical energizing and expediting effects of motivation on learning. We have already considered why incidental practice, in the sense of being unstructured and uncontrived, rather than unintentional, does not lead to efficient learning outcomes (see p. 200).

Somewhat more important for long-term school learning is the widespread belief that intention to *remember* facilitates the retention of learned verbal materials. Actually, however, the experimental evidence bearing on this issue is quite equivocal for one or both of two reasons: the experimental arrangements have been such as (a) to induce intentions to learn rather than to remember, or (b) to make impossible the isolation of the effects of intention on learning from its effects on retention.

Numerous studies, for example, have shown that intention to remember enhances the longevity of retention. When subjects learn material with the expectation of recalling it for a designated period of time, recall is superior for the expected as against either a longer or shorter interval.[1,6,17,45] Lester[27] demonstrated that retention is facilitated by expectation of recall and by foreknowledge of the occurrence and possible effect of interpolated materials. Unfortunately, however, since differential intentions to remember were introduced at the time of original learning, these experiments did not isolate the effects of the intention on what was learned in the first place from its effects on retention per se. Under the circumstances, therefore, all of the superior retention could be plausibly attributed to the energizing effects of the intention on learning, without assuming that it had any independent influence on retention.

To test this latter interpretation, Ausubel, Schpoont, and Cukier[5] conducted an experiment in which undergraduate students learned an extended historical passage, and were then tested on it immediately afterwards. *After* this test, an explicit intention to remember was induced by announcing that an equivalent form of the test would be given two weeks later. The same procedure was followed with a control group except that an *unannounced* retest was administered. The two groups were not significantly different in mean learning scores or in the percentage of material retained from test to retest. It was concluded, therefore, that intention to remember in the previously reported studies primarily facilitated retention by enhancing learning rather than by virtue of any effect on the retention process itself. The reason why positive ego-involvements, such as intention to remember, presumably do not facilitate retention is because motivational variables, as postulated above, can neither influence dissociability strength *after* the material is already learned, nor lower thresholds of availability for meaningfully learned material.

In another group of studies, it was shown that retention is superior[31,36,39] and retroactive inhibition less marked[39] when practice is accomplished by "intent to learn" than when learning takes place incidentally. That this difference is largely attributable to superior original learning, however, is demonstrated by the fact that it no longer prevails when experimental and control subjects are equated for original mastery of the learning task.[6] In any event, the evidence yielded by such studies is at best indirect, because in each instance an explicit experimental set was induced to *learn* material for immediate reproduction rather than to *retain* it for an extended period of time.

Intention to remember in situations characterized by positive ego-involvement, facilitates *rote* retention, probably by selectively lowering relevant thresholds of memorial availability. This mechanism, which, of course, does not apply to meaningful learning, presumably accounts for the greater recall of interrupted than of completed tasks (see p. 231). It also helps explain such common real-life illustrations of selective retention as the waiter's greater memory of his customers' bills immediately before rather than immediately after payment, and the greater tendency for husbands, upon seeing a mailbox, to think of "letters," before rather than after mailing the letters they promised to mail. Both of these latter phenomena, however, can also be partly explained in terms of the meaningfulness or belongingness of the learning task. The association between a particular customer and his bill or between letter and mailbox is no longer as meaningful after the intention in question is completed as before; that is, the items to be associated are less relevantly related, or manifest less belongingness in relation to each other.

THE EFFECTS OF ATTITUDINAL VARIABLES ON MEANINGFUL LEARNING AND RETENTION

Learning. Little doubt exists that the learner's prevailing attitude structure differentially enhances and inhibits the learning of controversial materials that are congruous and incongruous, respectively, with it. Both motivational and cognitive variables are probably involved in such differential learning outcomes. When their attitudes toward the controversial material are favorable, subjects are highly motivated to learn; they expend more intense and concentrated effort, and relevant perceptual, cognitive, and response thresholds are generally lowered. Under these circumstances there is also less need for selective perceptual emphasis, omission, or distortion of material. Furthermore, since the cognitive component of the attitudes in question is well-established, the subjects possess clear, stable and relevant subsumers for incorporating the new ideas. When, however, their attitudes toward the controversial material are unfavorable, all of these mechanisms operate in precisely the opposite direction.

Several studies[13,28,53] have demonstrated that controversial materials are learned most readily when they are consistent rather than inconsistent with the subject's evaluative framework. But in none of the aforementioned studies, despite the fact that selective learning was attributed solely to affective mechanisms, was any attempt made to differentiate between the respective effects on learning of the cognitive and affective components of attitude structure. Fitzgerald,[14,15] however, conducted a classroom experiment, involving the ability of central Illinois high-school students to learn the Southern point of view about the Civil War, in which the cognitive factor (knowledge about the Civil War period) was held constant. The learning difference attributable to affective factors, or to attitudinal bias *per se* under these conditions, was in the predicted direction (*i.e.*, in favor of the relatively pro-Southern or positively biased group), but was not statistically significant. In this same study, two additional findings pointed to the influence of cognitive variables on learning outcomes. Not only did cognitive organizers facilitate the learning of the controversial material, but the more knowledgeable subjects, irrespective of attitudinal bias, were also better able to learn the material, presumably because they found it more discriminable from previously learned related ideas than did the less knowledgeable subjects.

Further evidence concerning the role of cognitive factors in the effects of attitude structure on learning, comes from Jones and Kohler's study of the interaction between attitudinal bias and plausibility in their effects on learning. These investigators found that prosegregation subjects learned plausible prosegregation and implausible antisegregation statements better than they learned implausible prosegregation and plausible antisegregation statements. The reverse was true of the antisegregation subjects. Evidently, plausibility enhanced the learning of the position favored by a particular subject and inhibited the learning of the position he opposed. This suggests that controversial material is learned least well when it is least relatable to the prevailing ideational component of attitude structure, *i.e.*, when favorable material is implausible and unfavorable material is plausible.

Gustafson[17] found that members of three different American ethnic groups selectively learned best those facts about American history and culture that pertained to their own ethnic group. This finding held up even when *general* knowledge of American history and culture was held constant. But since the effects of *specific* knowledge of *own*-group culture (in relation to which the differential learning was manifested) were not controlled, the influence of ideational factors on learning outcomes was not eliminated. The results of this study are therefore consistent with the hypothesis that both cognitive and motivational mechanisms account for the effects of positive ego-involvement on learning.

Retention. In many studies[3,12,48] of the effects of attitude structure on retention, no measure of initial learning was obtained. Hence there was no certain way of ruling out the possibility that selective differences in retention (in favor of the group positively biased toward the material) were wholly attributable to attitudinal effects on learning. In some studies,[13,28,44] however, where retention was measured both immediately after learning and at subsequent intervals thereafter, original differences in learning between positively and negatively biased groups were found to widen progressively during the course of the retention interval. These latter findings suggest that attitude structure exerts an *additional* facilitating influence on retention that is independent of its cognitive and motivational effect on learning.

But although attitudinal variables undoubtedly facilitate the *learning* of controversial material through both cognitive and motivational mechanisms, it is likely that cognitive factors alone mediate most of the effects of attitude structure on *retention*. In the first place, as pointed out earlier, motivational variables cannot independently affect the cognitive interactional process or dissociability strength during the retention period (*i.e.*, once the learning phase of the process is completed). Second, even though it is theoretically possible for negative attitudinal bias directly to raise (if not to lower) thresholds of availability for controversial material, this mechanism applies only in those relatively rare instances where anxiety-producing material is repressed. Yet despite the fact that the "repression" explanation is almost universally invoked to explain selective forgetting of controversial materials, it hardly seems likely that such materials are capable of instigating significant amounts of anxiety. In none of these studies, furthermore, was the influence of cognitive factors controlled.

The cognitive mechanism that purportedly mediates the effects of attitude on retention is the complex of ideas that, together with various affective components (*i.e.*, attitudinal bias *per se*), characterizes the structure of all attitudes. Controversial materials that instigate positive affect or attitudinal bias are relatable to a set of subsuming ideas that are clearer, more stable, more relevant, and more discriminable from the learning task than are the general run of subsumers in the learner's cognitive structure; and the reverse holds true for controversial materials instigating negative affect or attitudinal bias. Although these ideational factors are part of attitude structure, they influence retention in the same manner as cognitive variables generally, resulting in the progressive divergence of retention scores for subjects whose attitudinal bias toward the controversial material is positive and negative respectively.

Fitzgerald's previously described experiment (14, 15) was primarily designed to test this latter hypothesis by measuring and controlling the effects of cognitive factors (knowledge of the Civil War period) on retention. As in the Edwards,[13] Taft,[44] and Levine and Murphy[28] studies, he also found a suggestive tendency toward differential forgetting on the basis of the degree of congruence of the Civil War passage with the subject's attitudinal framework. However, when the influence of the cognitive dimension of attitude structure was eliminated, the residual affective dimension of attitude structure (*i.e.*, attitudinal bias) had no differential effect on retention.° Thus it appears that in nonanxiety-producing situations, selective retention can be more parsimoniously attributed to the cognitive rather than to the affective dimension of attitudes.

"In learning 'other-side' arguments, the conceptual schema constituting the cognitive dimension of attitudes is usually devoid of relevant subsuming ideas to which the new material can be functionally related. The material, therefore, cannot be readily anchored to cognitive structure, competes with existing meanings, and is consequently ambiguous and subject to rapid forgetting. In the case of positive attitudinal bias, it seems reasonable to suppose that the cognitive dimension of attitude structure contains more relevant and appropriate subsuming concepts than in the case of negative bias. Hence the material

---

°In Gustafson's experiment,[18] selective retention of own-ethnic group material occurred even after general knowledge of American culture was held constant. But, as already explained, since the effects of specific knowledgeability were not eliminated, the influence of cognitive factors was not completely controlled. The "repression" hypothesis is also particularly inapplicable here, inasmuch as all of the material was favorable to the ethnic group under discussion.

can be readily anchored to cognitive structure, need not compete with existing meanings, and is therefore less ambiguous and subject to forgetting."[15]

Further substantiating the cognitive interpretation is the fact that organizers facilitated the retention of the controversial material.

REFERENCES

1. Aall, A. Ein neues Gedächtnisgesetz? Experimentelle Untersuchung über die Bedeutung der Reproduktions-perspektive. Z. Psychol., 1913, 66:1–50.

2. Alper, Thelma G. Task orientation versus ego orientation in learning and retention. Amer. J. Psychol., 1946, 59:236–48.

3. Alper, Thelma G., and Korchin, S. J. Memory for socially relevant material. J. abnorm. soc. Psychol., 1952, 47:25–37.

4. Ausubel, D. P. Introduction to a threshold concept of primary drives. J. gen. Psychol., 1956, 56:209–29.

5. Ausubel, D. P., Schpoont, S. H., and Cukier, Lillian. The influence of intention on the retention of school materials. J. educ. Psychol., 1957, 48:87–92.

6. Biel, W. C., and Force, R. C. Retention of nonsense syllables in intentional and incidental learning. J. exp. Psychol., 1943, 32:52–63.

7. Boswell, F. D., and Foster, W. S. On memorizing with the intention permanently to retain. Amer. J. Psychol., 1916, 27:420–26.

8. Bromer, J. A. A comparison of incidental and purposeful memory for meaningful and nonsense material. Amer. J. Psychol., 1942, 55:106–108.

9. Brown, J. F. Über die dynamischen Eigenschaften der Realitäts-und Irrealitätsschichten. Untersuchungen zur Handlungs-und Affektpsychologie XIV. Psychol. Forsch., 1933, 18:2–26.

10. Bruner, J. S. Going beyond the information given. In Contemporary Approaches to Cognition. Cambridge, Mass.: Harvard University Press, 1957. pp. 41–70.

11. Cantor, N. The Teaching-Learning Process: A Study in Interpersonal Relations. New York: Dryden, 1953.

12. Clark, K. B. Some factors influencing the remembering of prose material. Arch. Psychol., 1940, 36, (Whole No. 253).

13. Edwards, A. L. Political frames of reference as a factor influencing recognition. J. abnorm. soc. Psychol., 1941, 36:34–50.

14. Fitzgerald, D. Cognitive versus affective factors in the learning and retention of controversial materials. Unpublished Ph.D. dissertation. Urbana, Ill.: University of Illinois, 1962.

15. Fitzgerald, D., and Ausubel, D. P. Cognitive versus affective factors in the learning and retention of controversial material. J. educ. Psychol., 1963, in press.

16. French, Elizabeth, and Thomas, F. H. The relation of achievement motivatoin to problem-solving effectiveness. J. abnorm. soc. Psychol., 1958, 56:45–48.

17. Geyer, M. T. Influence of changing the expected time of recall. J. exp. Psychol., 1930, 13:290–92.

18. Gustafson, Lucille. Relationship between ethnic group membership and the retention of selected facts pertaining to American history and culture. J. educ. Sociol., 1957, 31:49–56.

19. Heyer, A. W., and O'Kelly, L. I. Studies in motivation and retention: II. Retention of nonsense syllables learned under different degrees of motivation. J. Psychol., 1949, 27:143–52.

20. Huang, I. Experimental studies on the role of repetition, organization, and the intention to learn in rote memory. *J. gen. Psychol.*, 1944, *31*:213–17.
21. Iverson, M. A., and Reuter, Mary E. Ego-involvement as an experimental variable. *Psychol. Rep.*, 1956, *2*:147–81.
22. Jersild, A. T., and Tasch, Ruth J. *Children's Interests*. New York: Teachers College, Columbia University, 1949.
23. Jones, E. E., and Kohler, R. The effects of plausibility on the learning of controversial statements. *J. abnorm. soc. Psychol.*, 1958, *57*:315–320.
24. Keislar, E. R. A descriptive approach to classroom motivation. *J. Teacher Educ.*, 1960, *11*:310–15.
25. Koch, Helen L. The influence of some affective factors upon recall. *J. gen. Psychol.*, 1930, *4*:171–90.
26. Krug, R. E. Over- and under-achievement and the Edwards Personal Preference Schedule. *J. appl. Psychol.*, 1959, *43*:133–37.
27. Lester, Olive P. Mental set in relation to retroactive inhibition. *J. exp. Psychol.*, 1932, *15*:681–99.
28. Levine, J., and Murphy, G. The learning and forgetting of controversial material. *J. abnorm. soc. Psychol.*, 1943, *38*:507–17.
29. Lewis, Helen B., and Franklin, M. An experimental study of the role of the ego in work: II. The significance of task-orientation in work. *J. exp. Psychol.*, 1944, *34*:195–215.
30. Marrow, A. J. Goal tensions and recall: I; II. *J. gen. Psychol.*, 1938, *19*:3–35; 37–64.
31. Maso, N. La valeur de l'activité de l'esprit dans la fixation des idées: contribution expérimentale à la théorie de l' "école active." *Arch. Psychol. Genève*, 1929, *21*:275–92.
32. Moss, H. A., and Kagan, J. Stability of achievement and recognition seeking behaviors from early childhood through adulthood. *J. abnorm. soc. Psychol.*, 1961, *62*:504–13.
33. Myers, G. C. A study in incidental memory. *Arch. Psychol.*, 1913, *5*, (whole No. 26).
34. Owen, W. A. Effects of motivating instructions on reaction time in grade school children. *Child Develpm.*, 1959, *30*:261–68.
35. Peak, Helen. Attitude and motivation. In *Nebraska Symposium on Motivation*. Lincoln, Neb.: University of Nebraska Press, 1955.
36. Peterson, J. The effect of attitude on immediate and delayed recall: a class experiment. *J. educ. Psychol.*, 1916, *7*:523–32.
37. Postman, L., and Senders, Virginia L. Incidental learning and generality of set. *J. exp. Psychol.*, 1946, *36*:153–65.
38. Postman, L., Bronson, Wanda C., and Gropper, G. L. Is there a mechanism of perceptual defense? *J. abnorm. soc. Psychol.*, 1953, *48*:215–24.
39. Prentice, W. C. H. Retroactive inhibition and the motivation of learning. *Amer. J. Psychol.*, 1943, *56*:283–92.
40. Reed, H. B. Factors influencing the learning and retention of concepts. I. The influence of set. *J. exp. Psychol.*, 1946, *36*:71–87.
41. Rosenthal, B. G. Hypnotic recall of material learned under anxiety and non-anxiety producing conditions. *J. exp. Psychol.*, 1944, *34*:369–89.
42. Rosenzweig, S. An experimental study of 'repression' with special reference to need-persistive and ego-defensive reactions to frustration. *J. exp. Psychol.*, 1943, *32*:64–74.

43. Shaw, F. J., and Spooner, A. Selective forgetting when the subject is not ego-involved. *J. exp. Psychol.*, 1945, 35:242–47.
44. Taft, R. Selective recall and memory distortion of favorable and unfavorable material. *J. abnorm. soc. Psychol.*, 1954, 49:23–28.
45. Thisted, M. N., and Remmers, H. H. The effect of temporal set on learning. *J. appl. Psychol.*, 1932, 16:257–68.
46. Uhlinger, Carolyn A., and Stephens, M. W. Relation of achievement motivation to academic achievement in students of superior ability. *J. educ. Psychol.*, 1960, 51:259–66.
47. Wallen, R. Ego-involvement as a determinant of selective forgetting. *J. abnorm. soc. Psychol.*, 1942, 37:20–39.
48. Watson, W. S., and Hartmann, G. W. The rigidity of a basic attitudinal frame. *J. abnorm. soc. Psychol.*, 1939, 34:314–35.
49. Weiss, P., Wertheimer, M., and Groesbeck, B. Achievement motivation, academic aptitude, and college grades. *Educ. psychol. Measmt.*, 1959, 19:663–66.
50. White, R. W. Motivation reconsidered: The concept of competence. *Psychol. Rev.*, 1959, 66:297–333.
51. Young, F. M. Causes for loss of interest in high-school subjects as reported by 631 college students. *J. educ. Res.*, 1932, 25:110–115.
52. Zeigarnik, B. Über das Behalten von erledigten und unerledigten Handlungen. *Psychol. Forsch.*, 1927, 9:1–85.
53. Zillig, M. Einstellung und Aussage. *Z. Psychol.*, 1928, 106:58–106.

Index of Names

Aall, A., 239
Abel, L. B., 215
Abercrombie, M. L. J., 91, 103
Adams, J. A., 87, 103
Allen, D. C., 103
Allport, G. W., 62n, 72, 73
Alper, T. G., 231, 239
Alter, M., 222
Anderson, G. L., 47, 167, 172
Anderson, H. H., 103, 123, 135
Angell, D., 216
Angell, G. W., 216
Annett, M., 136
Archimedes, 162
Armistead, L. M., 216
Aschner, M. J. Mc, 92, 103
Ash, P., 216, 223
Atkin, J. M., 128n, 136, 172
Atwater, S. K., 103
Auble, D., 216
Austin, G. A., 104
Ausubel, D. P., 14, 33, 47, 73, 104, 136, 172, 235, 239

Bach, J. S., 99
Baer, C. J., 136
Ballard, P. B., 73
Bartlett, F. C., 64–66, 73, 88, 96
Battig, W. F., 104
Beane, D. G., 209, 216
Beberman, M., 104
Bensberg, G. J., 104
Berkowitz, L., 96, 104
Biel, W. C., 239
Bilodeau, E. A., 219
Blake, E., 33, 73, 104, 219
Bond, R. D., 104
Boswell, F. D., 239
Bousfield, W. A., 104
Braine, M. D. S., 136
Brand, H., 73

Braun, H. W., 46n, 47
Brenner, H., 220
Bretnall, E. P., 223
Briggs, L. J., 216, 218, 219
Bromer, J. A., 239
Bronson, W. C., 240
Brooks, L. O., 174
Broverman, D. M., 97, 104
Brown, J., 73
Brown, J. F., 239
Brown, L. T., 162, 171, 173
Brown, R. W., 117n, 136
Brown, W., 62n, 73
Brownell, W. A., 33, 47, 104, 172
Bruce, R. W., 104
Bruner, J. S., 33, 53, 73, 77, 86, 101, 104, 131, 136, 145, 153, 157, 158, 159, 161, 162, 163, 164, 172, 229, 239
Bryan, G. L., 216
Bumstead, A. P., 216
Burt, C., 136
Burtt, H. E., 73
Buxton, E. W., 216

Cain, L. F., 216
Callantine, M. F., 104
Campbell, V. N., 218
Cantor, N., 239
Carey, J. E., 88, 104
Carmichael, L., 73, 217
Carr, H. A., 216
Carter, L. J., 216
Cason, H., 223
Chansky, N. M., 216
Check, J. F., 107
Christensen, P. R., 106, 107, 110
Christenson, C. M., 215n, 216
Cieutat, V. J., 47
Clark, K. B., 239
Cofer, C. N., 47, 207, 216

242

Index of Subjects